CW01370960

BIBLIOGRAPHY OF
WESTERN LANGUAGE PUBLICATIONS ON KOREA
1588-1950

Published by Myongji University Press, 2008

http://home.mju.ac.kr/~press

Copyright © 2008 by The Myongji - LG Korean Studies Library
Printed in Seoul, Korea

All rights reserved.
No part of this book may be reproduced in any form or by any electronic
or mechanical means, including information storage and retrieval systems,
without permission in writing from the publisher.
For information address The Myongji - LG Korean Studies Library,
50-3 Namgajwadong, Seodaemungu, Seoul, Korea

First Printing : March 2, 2008

ISBN 978-89-7335-353-8 93010

To Young Koo You and Bon-Moo Koo

BIBLIOGRAPHY OF
WESTERN LANGUAGE PUBLICATIONS ON KOREA 1588-1950
THE MYONG JI - LG KOREAN STUDIES LIBRARY

compiled by Sung-hwa Cheong and Alexander Ganse

Seoul 2008

INTRODUCTION

Myongji University has been actively collecting western publications on Korea with the aid of the LG Group since 1995. Since then, the university and its scholars have been creating a library of more than 12,000 books and 2,500 microfilms. Myongji-LG Korean Studies Library has become the leading institute in researching Korea-related western rare books and documents. It is not an exaggeration to say that Myongji-LG Korean Studies Library was the first one to focus on Western impression on Korean civilization. These books and documents will be important resources and great contributions to researches on Korean studies.

The goal of this bibliography is to provide scholars in Korea with access to resources that portrayed how modern westerners delivered Korea in their original languages. This bibliography may serve as a catalogue of western language publications on Korea, and as a complementary publications to works of M. Courant 1894 (0001), H. H. Underwood 1931 (0006), G. StG. M. Gompertz 1963 (0010a) and R.A. Domschke / R. Goossmann 1982 (0010b).

This bibliography specifically lists only the titles stored at Myongji-LG Korean Studies Library. It is important to note, however, that some of the books which were acquired under the assumption that they referenced Korea, in fact were not relevant sources or the reference on Korea turned out to be of superficial nature that was not justifiable under any of the aforementioned bibliographies. Such cases are denoted with comments such as "Not on Korea", under the respective bibliography entry.

A few numbers have been deleted in the process of eliminating double listings. Following the model of Gompertz 1963, the bibliography lists titles by subjects. As some titles qualify to be listed under several categories, looking into more general or related subject categories might yield better search results as opposed to merely looking under subject categories that are of interest. An index of persons and a chronological list of titles published until 1850 are added to make it easier to find a specific title.

Sung-hwa Cheong, Alexander Ganse

TABLE OF CONTENTS

I.)	BIBLIOGRAPHIES	0001-0010b
II.)	NEWSPAPERS, MAGAZINES	
II.a)	GENERAL	0011-0022
II.b)	ON ASIA	0023-0036
II.c)	ON KOREA	0037-0040
III.)	ENCYCLOPEDIC LITERATURE	
III.a)	ENCYCLOPEDIAS, GENERAL	0041-0046
III.b)	ENCYCLOPEDIAS, ON THE FAR EAST	0047-0053
IV.)	GEOGRAPHY & TRAVEL	
IV.a)	ATLASES	0054-0063
IV.b)	GAZETTEERS, GEOGRAPHICAL DICTIONARIES	0064-0080
IV.c)	SAILING DIRECTORIES	0081-0090
IV.d)	WORLD GEOGRAPHY	0091-0118
IV.e)	EAST ASIAN GEOGRAPHY	0119-0150
IV.f)	AREA HANDBOOKS	
	IV.f.1) CHINA	0151-0180
	IV.f.2) MANCHURIA	0181-0189
	IV.f.3) RUSSIAN FAR EAST / SIBERIA	0190-0194
	IV.f.4) JAPAN	0195-0236
	IV.f.5) KOREA	0237-0266

IV.g) TRAVEL GUIDES		
IV.g.1) GENERAL	0267-0269	
IV.g.2) FAR EAST	0270-0287	
IV.g.3) CHINA	0288-0297	
IV.g.4) MANCHURIA	0298-0300	
IV.g.5) JAPAN	0301-0314	
IV.g.6) KOREA	0315-0327	
IV.h) TRAVELOGUES		
IV.h.1) TRAVELOGUE COLLECTIONS	0328-0342	
IV.h.2) WORLDWIDE	0343-0403	
IV.h.3) FAR EAST	0404-0532	
IV.h.4) CHINA	0533-0572	
IV.h.5) MANCHURIA, MONGOLIA, TURKESTAN	0573-0594	
IV.h.6) RUSSIAN FAR EAST, SIBERIA	0595-0604	
IV.h.7) JAPAN	0605-0637	
IV.h.8) KOREA	0638-0700	
IV.i) ETHNOGRAPHY	0701-0744	
IV.j) GEOLOGY & METEOROLOGY	0745-0751	
IV.k) ASTRONOMY	0752-0754	
V.) HISTORY		
V.a) WORLD HISTORY	0755-0779	
V.a.1) EAST ASIA	0780-0816	
V.a.2) CHINA	0817-0856	
V.a.3) MANCHURIA, TURKESTAN	0857-0860	
V.a.4) RUSSIAN FAR EAST	0861-0865	
V.a.5) JAPAN	0866-0904	
V.a.6) KOREA	0905-0927	
V.b) CONTEMPORARY HISTORY & POLITICS		
V.b.1) WORLDWIDE	0928-0952	
V.b.2) FAR EAST	0953-1093	
V.b.3) CHINA	1094-1171	
V.b.4) MANCHURIA, MONGOLIA, TURKESTAN	1172-1198	

V.b.5) RUSSIAN FAR EAST	1199-1207
V.b.6) JAPAN	1208-1330
V.b.7) KOREA	1331-1376
V.c) ON ASIAN EMIGRANTS	1377-1379
V.d) MILITARY HISTORY	
V.d.1) SECOND OPIUM WAR, 1859-1860	1380
V.d.2) FRENCH EXPEDITION OF 1866	1381
V.d.3) U.S. EXPEDITION OF 1871	1382-1384
V.d.4) SINO-JAPANESE WAR 1894-1895	1385-1393
V.d.5) BOXER REBELLION 1897-1901	1394
V.d.6) RUSSO-JAPANESE WAR 1904-1905	1395-1495
V.d.7) WORLD WAR I, 1914-1918	1496-1497
V.d.8) SINO-JAPANESE WAR 1937-1945 AND WORLD WAR II 1941-1945	1498-1502
V.d.9) THE KOREAN WAR 1950-1953	1503-1507
V.d.10) OTHER MILITARY HISTORY	1508-1520
VI.) BIOGRAPHY	
VI.a) BIOGRAPHICAL DICTIONARIES	1521-1523
VI.b) COMPILATIONS OF BIOGRAPHIES BY TOPIC	1524-1525
VI.c) BIOGRAPHIES OF HISTORICAL FIGURES	1526-1529
VI.d) BIOGRAPHIES OF POLITICAL FIGURES	1530-1546
VI.e) BIOGRAPHIES OF MILITARY FIGURES	1548-1551
VI.f) BIOGRAPHIES OF MISSIONARIES	1552-1583
VI.g) BIOGRAPHIES OF OTHERS	1584-1593
VI.h) DIARIES, MEMOIRS OF WESTERN RESIDENTS OF THE FAR EAST	1594-1639
VII.) CULTURE	
VII.a) CULTURE : IN GENERAL	1640-1650
VII.a.1) CHINESE CULTURE	1651-1653
VII.a.2) JAPANESE CULTURE	1654-1657

VII.a.3) KOREAN CULTURE	1658
VII.b) CULTURE : LANGUAGE	
VII.b.1) LANGUAGES OTHER THAN KOREAN	1659-1665
VII.b.2) KOREAN LANGUAGE	1666-1690
VII.c) CULTURE : NAMES	1691-1693
VII.d) CULTURE : LITERATURE	
VII.d.1) MYTHS, LEGENDS, FAIRY TALES	1694-1713
VII.d.2) NOVELS ETC.	
VII.d.2.1) NOVELS ETC. ON THE FAR EAST	1714-1733
VII.d.2.2) NOVELS ETC. ON KOREA	1734-1774
VII.d.3) POLITICS DISGUISED AS FICTION	1775-1776
VII.d.4) FICTION, NOT RELATED TO KOREA	1777-1779
VII.e) CULTURE : ARTS	
VII.e.1) ART HISTORY	
VII.e.1.1) ART HISTORY : FAR EAST	1780-1801
VII.e.1.2) ART HISTORY : CHINA	1802-1808
VII.e.1.3) ART HISTORY : JAPAN	1809
VII.e.1.4) ART HISTORY : KOREA	1810-1812
VII.e.2) PICTORIAL ARTS	1813-1817
VII.e.3) CERAMICS, POTTERY	1818-1830a
VII.e.4) ARTS AND CRAFTS - OTHERS	1831-1845
VII.f) CULTURE : SPORTS	1846
VII.g) CULTURE : PHILOSOPHY	1847-1854
VII.h) CULTURE : EASTERN SCIENCE & KNOWLEDGE	1855
VII.i) CULTURE : RELIGION	
VII.i.1) EASTERN RELIGION IN GENERAL	1856-1864
VII.i.2) BUDDHISM	1865-1871
VII.i.3) OTHER EASTERN RELIGIONS	1872-1880
VIII.) CHRISTIANITY AND MISSIONS	
VIII.a) GENERAL WORKS	1881-1883
VIII.b) CATHOLIC CHURCH	
VIII.b.1) GENERAL	1884-1894

VIII.b.2) IN ASIA	1895-1914
VIII.b.3) IN KOREA	1915-1926
VIII.c) PROTESTANT CHURCHES	
VIII.c.1) IN GENERAL	1927-1941
VIII.c.2) IN ASIA	1942-1950
VIII.c.3) IN KOREA	1951-1973
IX.) SCIENCE	
IX.a) IN GENERAL	1974
IX.b) MEDICINE, HEALTH	1975-1981
IX.c) BIOLOGY	1982-1998
IX.d) SOCIOLOGY	1999-2011
X.) ADMINISTRATION	2012-2022
XI.) ECONOMICS	
XI.a) ECONOMIC STATISTICS	2023-2039
XI.b) ECONOMICS : ADDRESSBOOKS	2040
XI.c) ECONOMICS : COUNTRY & AREA STUDIES	
XI.c.1) THE WORLD	2041
XI.c.2) THE FAR EAST	2042-2043
XI.c.3) JAPAN	2044-2050
XI.c.4) KOREA	2051-2054
XI.d) ECONOMIC HISTORY	2055-2058
XI.e) AGRICULTURE, FORESTRY & FISHERY	2059-2068
XI.f) MINING, INDUSTRIES & TECHNOLOGY	2069-2080
XI.g) RAILWAY & TRANSPORTATION	2081-2084
XI.h) TRADE	2085-2100
XI.i) EXPOSITIONS	2101-2110
XI.j) ECONOMY - OTHERS	2111-2113

XII.) RECREATION
   XII.a) SPORTS   2114-2118
   XII.b) PHILATELY   2119
   XII.c) CUISINE   2120

XIII.) OTHERS   2121-2123
   Chronological List of Titles Published 1588-1850
   Index of Persons
   Index of Periodicals

I.) BIBLIOGRAPHIES

0001   1894   FRE 199 (3 ex.)
Courant, Maurice. Bibliographie Coreenne [Korean Bibliography]
Paris: Ernest Leroux (vols.1-3), Imprimerie Nationale (vol.4), small 4to, 4vols., vol.1: 1894, 502pp., vol.2: 1895, 538pp., vol.3: 1896, 446pp., clxxvii pp., plates, index, vol.4: supplement ... jusqu'en 1899, 1901, 122pp.

0002   1904   FRE 198e2
Cordier, Henri. Bibliotheca Sinica. Dictionnaire Bibliographique des Ouvrages Relatifs a L'Empire Chinois [Chinese Library. Bibliographic Dictionary of Works related to the Chinese Empire]
Paris: Librairie Orientaliste & Americaine, 1904-1924, 4to, 5vols., xvi +4439 pages in total; Gompertz 2231

0003   1912   FRE 201
Cordier, Henri. Bibliotheca Japonica. Dictionnaire Bibliographique des Ouvrages Relatifs a L'Empire Japonais Ranges par ordre Chronologique jusqu'a 1870 Suivi d'un appendice renfermant la liste alphabetique des principaux ouvrages parus de 1870 a 1912 [Japanese Library. Bibliographic Dictionary of Works related to the Japanese Empire. Listed in chronological order until 1870 with an appendix containing an alphabetical list of major works published between 1870 and 1912]
Paris: Imprimerie Nationale, 1912, large 8vo, xii, 762pp.; Gompertz 2238

0004   1927   ENG 1305e3
Rye, Reginald Arthur. The Students Guide to the Libraries of London
London: University of London Press, 1927, 3rd edition, large 8vo, xxv, 580pp.

0005 **1928   ENG 1092**
Nachod, Oskar. Bibliography of the Japanese Empire. 1906-1926
Leipzig: Karl W. Hiersemann, 1928, 2 vols, 8vo, vol.I x, 384pp., vol.II pp.385-832; Gompertz 2246

0006 **1931   ENG 794 vol.20**
Underwood, Horace H. Partial Bibliography of Occidental Works on Korea with a Paper on Occidental Literature on Korea
Seoul : Royal Asiatic Society, Korea Branch, Transactions of the Korea Branch of the Royal Asiatic Society, vol.XX, 1931, 8vo, 183 + xvi pp.

0006a **1936   ENG 762**
Kokusai Bunka Shinkokai. Catalogue of Periodicals written in European Languages and Published in Japan
n.pl.: Kokusai Bunka Shinkokai (The Society for International Cultural Relations), 1936, small 8vo, 51pp.

0007 **1939   ENG 635**
Kerner, Robert J. Northeast Asia, a Selected Bibliography
Berkeley, California: University of California Press, 1939, large 8vo, 2 vols., 714, 652pp.; Gompertz 2266

0008 **1940   GER 89e2**
Bibliographischer Alt-Japan Katalog 1542-1853 [Bibliographic Catalogue Old Japan, 1542-1853]
Kyoto: Deutsches Forschungsinstitut 1940, Reprint 1977, small 4to, xxxviii, 415pp.; Gompertz 2267

0009 **1944   SPA 8**
Amezua y Mayo, Agustin G. de. Bibliografia de D. Francisco Rodriguez Marin [Bibliography on Francisco Rodriguez Marin]
Madrid: Aldus, S.A. de Artes Graficas, 1944, 8vo, 73pp.

0010 **1950   ENG 653**
Parry, Albert (comp.). Korea, An annotated Bibliography of Publications in the Russian Language
Washington D.C.: The Library of Congress, Reference Dept. 1950. 4to, 84pp.; Co-compilers John T. Dorosh, Elizabeth Gardner Dorosh

Bibliographies published after 1950

0010a   1963   ENG 794 v. 40
Gompertz, Geoffrey St. George Montague. The First Sectors of a Revised and Annotated Bibliography of Western Literature on Korea from the Earliest Times until 1950, based on Horace G. Underwood's Partial Bibliography of Occidental Literature on Korea
Seoul: Royal Asiatic Society, Korea Branch, Transactions of the Korea Branch of the Royal Asiatic Society 1963

0010b   1982   GER 10011-1
Domschke, R. Andreas, Goosmann, Rudolf. Korea-Bibliographie I. Verzeichnis der deutschprachigen Literatur 1655-1949 [Korea Bibliography I. Register of German Language Publications 1855-1949]
München: Weltforum 1982, 12mo, xxii, 233pp.

II.) NEWSPAPERS, MAGAZINES

II.a) GENERAL

Note : Only magazines of which the Myong Ji - LG Korean Studies Library has a significant number of volumes are listed here. If the collection has only one or two volumes, the respective articles of interest are listed under the specific subject; if the collection has a significant number of issues and the magazine covers a specific topic, the magazine is listed under that topic.

0011   ENG 796
The Graphic
London: Office Strand, folio, vols.49-50 (Jan.-Dec. 1894), vols.69-70 (Jan.-Dec. 1904)

0012   ENG 795
Illustrated London News
London: George C. Leighton, folio, vols.2-4 (Jan. 1843 -June 1844), vols.8-21 (Jan. 1846-Dec. 1852), vols.24-39 (Jan. 1854-Dec. 1861), vols.42-46 (July 1862-June. 1865), vols.48-65 (Jan. 1866-June 1874); vol.67 (July-Dec. 1875), Vols.69-72 (July 1876-June 1878), vols.74-78 (Jan. 1879-June 1881), vols.80-107 (Jan. 1882-Dec. 1895), vol.112 (Jan.-June 1898), vol.115 (July-Dec. 1899), vol.118 (Jan.-June 1901), vol.137 (July-Dec. 1910), vols.154-155 (Jan.-Dec. 1919), exhibition supplement no.XVIII-XIX 1851

0013   FRE 288
L'Illustration. Journal Hebdomaire Universel
Paris : L'Illustration, 4to, vols.XLIX-L (Jan.-Dec. 1867), CIII-CVI (Jan. 1894-Dec. 1905), CXXIII-CXXIV (Jan.-Dec. 1904), CXXIX-CXXX (Jan.-Dec. 1907), CLXIX-CLXX (Jan.-Dec. 1927); we have two copies of vols. 105, 106, 130

Bibliography of Western Language Publications on Korea

0014   1905   ENG 468

Palmer, Samuel. Palmer's Index to the Times Newspaper

London: Samuel Palmer, Richmond House, 1905, 8vo, various paging

0015   ENG 159

Chambers Journal of Popular Literature, Science and the Arts

London & Edinburgh: W. & R. Chambers, large 8vo, in stock vols. 1880, 1888, 1893, 1895

0016   ENG 179

The People's Magazine. An Illustrated Miscellany for Family Reading

London: Society for Promoting Christian Knowledge, large 8vo, in stock vols.11 (Jan.-June 1873), 12 (July-Dec. 1873)

0017   ENG 1094

The Weekly

London: The Weekly, 4to, in stock vols.5 and 6 (1905), no index

0018   ENG 1290

The Cornhill Magazine

London: Cornhill, 8vo, in stock New Series vol. xvii, July-Dec. 1904

0019   FRE 56

Le Correspondent [The Correspondent]

Paris: Bureau du Correspondent, folio; in stock vol. 214 (1904)

0020   ENG 1097 v.3 (2 ex.)

The History of the Times. Vol.3 : The Twentieth Century Test, 1884-1912

London: The Office of the Times, 1947, large 8vo, 861pp., index; 2 Korea entries

0021   ENG 965

Fortune

NY: Time Inc., monthly, folio; in stock vol.29 no.4, April 1923; Japan and the Japanese

0022   ENG 1386

Over Sea and Land: A Monthly Magazine for Boys and Girls

New York: The Woman's home and Foreign Missionary Organizations of the Presbyterian Church, 1910, 8vo, in stock : August 1910 issue, Japan-Korea, 65pp.; religious magazine, addressing children

II.b) ON ASIA

0023   ENG 106
Asia. The American Magazine on the Orient
NY: The American Asiatic Association, 4to; in stock vol.19, 1919, vol.20, 1920 (only issue no.9), vol.21, pts. 1 and 2, 1921, vol.24, 1924 (only issue no.4), vol.30 pt.1, Jan.-June 1930

0024   ENG 1458
The Asiatic Journal and Monthly Register for British and Foreign India, China and Australasia
London: Kingsbury, Parbury and Allen. New Series. 8vo, vols. 11 (1833), 12 (1833), 13 (1834), 14 (1834), 15 (1834), 23 (1837), 24 (1837), 25 (1838) 26 (1838), 27 (1839), 29 (1841)

0025   ENG 126
Chinese Repository
Canton, China: printed for the proprietors, 8vo, vols.1-20, May 1832-Dec. 1851

0026   ENG 900
The Far East
Official Organ of the Maynooth Mission to China, St. Columban's, Navan, Ireland, large 8vo, vols. 1918-1993, 1995-1996

0027   ENG 324
The Hansei Zasshi
Tokyo: The Hansei Zasshi Office, 8vo; in stock vols.12 no.2, nos.4-12, vol.13 nos.1-12, 1897-1898

0028   ENG 693
Asiatic Society of Japan. Transactions of the Asiatic Society of Japan
Tokyo: Asiatic Society of Japan, 8vo, vols. 1929 and 1937

0029   FRE 205
Japon et Extreme Orient [Japan and the Far East]
Paris: Edmond Bernard, small 8vo; in stock vols.1-12, bound in 5, 1923-1924 (complete)

0030   FRE 189
Journal Asiatique [Asiatic Journal]
Paris: Imprimerie Nationale, 8vo; in stock vols. 6 pp.160-242, Aug.-Oct. 1885, vol.7 pp.223-332, Febr.-Apr. 1886

0031 GER 45
Ost-Asien. Monatsschrift für Handel, Industrie, Politik, Wissenschaft, Kunst etc. Die erste Monatsschrift eines Japaners in Europa [Monthly for Trade, Industry, Politics, Science, Arts etc. The First Monthly in Europe edited by a Japanese]
Berlin: Otto Eisner, edited by Tamai Kisak, large 8vo, vols.1-3, 5-7, 1898-1900, 1902-1904

0032 ENG 704
Journal of the North China Branch of the Royal Asiatic Society
Shanghai: Kelly & Walsh, 8vo; in stock vol.64, 1933

0033 GER 152
Geist des Ostens [Spirit of the East], Monatsschrift für volkstümliche Asienkunde [Monthly for Popular Knowledge on Asia]
München: Verlag des Ostens, edited by Hermann von Staden, 8vo; in stock nos.5-8 pp.324-315 (1914), nos.9-12 pp.330-476 (1915)

0034 GER 149
Asien [Asia] Organ der Deutsch-Asiatischen Gesellschaft [Magazine of the German-Asiatic Society]
Berlin: H. Pätel, edited by Max Vosberg-Rekow; folio, in stock vols. 1902-1905, bound in 2

0035 ENG 1399
The Chinese Social and Political Science Review
Peiping: Chinese Social and Political Science Association, ed. by Minch'ien Tuk Zung Tyan; in stock 1930-1932, 8vo, bound in one volume, ill., maps, no index; pp.1-152, 281-388; 35 pp. supplement, pp.337-474, pp.194-542

0036 ENG 11677
Harvard Journal of Asiatic Studies
Cambridge MA: Harvard Yenching Institute, 8vo; in stock vol.1 no.1 1936, no index

II.c) ON KOREA

0037   ENG 792
Korean Repository
Seoul: Trilingual Press, 8vo, vols.1-5 1892-1898, complete; not published in 1893, 1894

0038   ENG 793
Korean Review
Seoul: Methodist Publishing House, edited by Homer B. Hulbert, vols. 1-6, 1901-1905, complete; 8vo, in 1905 two volumes were published

0039   ENG 794
Transactions of the Korean Branch of the Royal Asiatic Society
Seoul: Royal Asiatic Society, 8vo, vols.1-31 (1900-1948/1949), complete for the period until 1950

0040   ENG 1327
Voice of Korea
Washington D.C.: Political Affairs Institute, 4to; in stock issues 1944-1962 (1 box)

III.) ENCYCLOPEDIC LITERATURE

III.a) ENCYCLOPEDIAS, GENERAL

0041   1901   ENG 1302
Wood, James. (ed.). The Nuttall Encyclopedia of Universal Information
London: Frederik Warne 1901. 8vo, viii, 700pp.; contents: on Corea p.164, Chemulpo p.138

0042   1905   ENG 1324
The Modern Cyclopedia of Universal Information
London: Greshen, 8 vols., 8vo, vol.1 1905. 512pp., vol.2 1905. 512p., vol.3 1905. 512pp., vol.4 1905. 512pp., vol.5 n.d. 512pp., vol.6 1905. 512pp., vol.7 n.d. 512pp., vol.8 n.d. 512pp.; contents: on Corea vol.3 pp.34-35, on Chemulpo vol.2 p.378, on Fu-San vol.4 p.96, on Söul vol.4 p.96

0043   c.1906   ENG 1321
The Harmsworth Encyclopedia
London: Amalgamated Press / Th. Nelson & Son, n.d.; Vol.V, c.1906. large 8vo, Hosanna-Marjoram, pp.3205-4000; contents: on Korea pp.3631-3633

0044   1920   ENG 1307
The New Age Encyclopedia
London: Th. Nelson 1920. 12mo, 10 vols., vols.1-6 1920, 480pp. each, vols.7-10 1921, 480pp. each; contents: on Korea vol.6 pp.278-279; on Chemulpo vol.3 p.17, on Fusan vol.5 p.44, on Seoul vol.9 p.218

0045   1925   ENG 1031
Monroe, Paul (ed.). A Cyclopedia of Education
NY: MacMillan (1911) 2nd edition 1925. 4to, 5 vols. in 3, 654, 726, 682, 739, 892 pp.; contents: Korea vol.3 pp.526-528

0046 1932 GER 206
Knaurs Konversationslexikon A-Z [Knaur's Conversational Lexicon]
Berlin: Th. Knaur 1932. 12mo, 1874 columns, ill.; contents: on Korea col.792

0047 n.d. (1932 to 1937) ENG 1325
Mee, Arthur. The Children's Encyclopedia
London: Educational Book Co. n.d., 10 vol.; vol.1 missing, large 8vo, vol.2 pp.765-1504, vol.3 pp.1505-2244, vol.4 pp.2245-2988, vol.5 pp.2989-3724, vol.6 pp.3725-4468, vol.7 pp.4469-5796, vol.8 pp.5197-5934, vol.9 pp.5935-6672, vol.10 pp.6673-7382; contents : on Korea pp.7094, 7096

III.b) ENCYCLOPEDIAS, ON THE FAR EAST

0048 1776 FRE 283
Missionaires de Pekin. Memoires Concernant l'Histoire, les Sciences, les Arts, les Moeurs, les Usages &c des Chinois [Memories Relating to the History, the Sciences, the Arts, the Customs, the Habits etc. of the Chinese]
Paris: Nyon 1776-1786. 11 vols. (of a total of 15), small 4to. vol.1 : 1776, 485pp., plates, vol.2 : 1777, 650pp., vol.3 : 1778, 504pp., vol.4 : 1779, 510pp., vol.5 : 1780, 518 pp., vol.6 : 1780, 380pp., vol.7 : 1782, 396pp., plates, index, vol.8 : 1782, 376pp., plates, vol.9 : 1783, 470pp., plates, vol.10 : 1784, 510pp., vol.11 : 1786, 609pp.

0049 1842 ENG 1224
Langdon, William B. Ten Thousand Things Relating to China and the Chinese
London: Chinese Collection 1842. 8vo, 273pp., ill., no index

0050 1891 ENG 55e2
Chamberlain, Basil Hall. Things Japanese : being notes on the various subjects connected with Japan for the use of travellers and others
London: Keegan, Paul, Trench, Trubner and Co. Ltd. 1891. revised and enlarged edition. 8vo. ii, 503pp. + 63pp. book ads, maps

0050a 1908 ENG 830 (2 ex.)
Allen, Horace N. Things Korean. A Collection of Sketches and Anecdotes, Missionary and Diplomatic
NY: Fleming H. Revell 1908. 8vo, 256pp., ill.; Gompertz 433

0051   1912   GER 37

Chamberlain, Basil Hall. Allerlei Japanisches (Things Japanese) Notizen über verschiedene Japanische Gegenstände für Reisende und Andere [Things Japanese. Notices on various Japanese subjects, for travellers and others]

Berlin: Hans Bondy, 1912. 8vo, 596pp., index. German edition of ENG 55e2, translated by Bernhard Kellermann.

0052   1925   ENG 100e5

Ball, J. Dyer. Things Chinese, or, notices connected with China.

Shanghai, Hong Kong and Singapore: Kelly & Walsh, 1925, 5th ed., 8vo, iv, 766pp., index

0053   1941   GER 173

Ramming, M. Japan-Handbuch. Nachschlagewerk der Japankunde [Japan Handbook Reference for Japanology]

Berlin: Steiniger 1941, 740pp., ill., map, plates

IV.) GEOGRAPHY & TRAVEL

IV.a) ATLASES

0054   1656   GER 130

Martini, Martino, O.S.J. Novus Atlas Absolutissimus. Das ist generale Welt-Beschreibung. Das Eilfte Theil, beschreibet China [New Absolute Atlas. Which is the Exact Description of the World. Part 11, describing China]

Amsterdam: J. Blaeu, 1656. large folio, various paging; 177, 40, xiii pp., ill., maps; content: on Korea pp.173-175

0055   1737   FRE 287

D'Anville, Jean Baptiste. Nouvel atlas de la Chine, de la Tartarie Chinoise et du Thibet, Contenant les Cartes Generales & Particulieres de ces Pays, ainsi que la Carte du Royaume de Coree; la plupart Levees sur les Lieux par Ordre de l'Empereur Cang-Hi avec toute l'Exactitude Imaginable, Soit par les PP. Jesuites Missionaires a la Chine, Soit par des Tartares du Tribunal des Mathematiques, & toutes Revues par les memes Peres

[New Atlas of China, Chinese Tartary and Tibet, containing General and Detail Maps of these Countries, as well as a Map of the Kingdom of Korea, mostly drawn at the Location on the Order of Emperor Cang-Hi with all exactness imaginable, partly by the Jesuit missionaries in China, partly by the Tartars of the Mathematics Tribunal, and all reviewed by the aforementioned fathers]

La Hayes (= Den Haag): H. Scheurleer, 1737. very large folio, 12 pp. of text and 42 maps

0056   n.d. (1823)   FRE 298

Sage, A. le. Atlas Historique, Genealogique, Chronologique et Geographique

[Historical, Genealogical, Chronological and Geographical Atlas]
(Paris: Charles Antoine Teste 1823) folio 136pp.

0057   1884 ENG 1012
Yamatoya, M. New Map of Tokyo
folded map

0058   1896 FRE 208
Cordier, Henri. Description d'un Atlas Sino-Coreen [Description of a Sino-Korean Atlas]
folio, 14pp., plates; Gompertz 269

0059   1898 ENG 141
Edward Stanford. Eastern China, Japan and Korea
folded map

0060   1903 ENG 111
Beach, Harlan P. A Geography and Atlas of Protestant Missions : their environment, forces, distribution, methods, problems, results and prospects at the opening of the twentieth century.
New York: Student Volunteer Movement for Foreign Missions, 1903, vol.1, 8vo, 571pp., bibliography, index; vol.2 : folio, 54pp., maps; content : numerous Korea entries in vol.1

0061   1904 ENG 571e2
Russo-Japanese War Map
Edinburgh: W. Johnston, 2nd edition, 885x565 cm.

0062   1913 GER 133
Sprigade, P. and Moisel, M. Deutscher Kolonialatlas mit illustriertem Jahrbuch [German Colonial Atlas, with illustrated yearbook]
Berlin: Dietrich Reimer, 17th edition, edited by Deutsche Kolonialgesellschaft, 1913. small 4to, 43pp., 8 double-page maps, 18pp.; comment: Maps don't show Korea, but ferry lines connecting Tsingtau (Qingdao) with Korea

0063   1931 ENG 802
Branom, Frederick K. (ed.) New Census Atlas of the World : Complete 1930 Census
Chicago: The Reilly & Lee Co., 1931. 4to, 256p., ill., map

IV.b) GAZETTEERS, GEOGRAPHICAL DICTIONARIES

0064 1795 ENG 864e2
A Compendious Geographical Dictionary, Containing a Concise Description of the Most Remarkable Places, Ancient and Modern, in Europe, Asia, Africa and America
London: W. Peacock, 2nd edition, 1795. 16mo, not paginated

0065 1811 SWE 9
Djurberg, Daniel. Geografiskt Lexicon [Geographical Lexicon]
Örebro: Nils Magnus Lindh, 2 vols., 1811-1813. 12mo, 404, 586pp.

0066 1823 FRE 263
Vosgien. Dictionnaire Geographique [Geographical Dictionary]
Paris: Menard et Desenne 1823, small 8vo, 672 pp.; content : at front a chapter on geography by J.D. Goigoux; contents: on Korea (Coree) pp.170-171

0067 1827 ENG 483e3
Virtue, G. The New London Universal Gazetteer, or Alphabetical Geography, containing a Description of the various Countries, Kingdoms, States, Cities, Towns, Mountains, Seas, Rivers, Harbours &c of the World ; an Account of the Population, Government, Customs & Religion of the Inhabitants; the Boundaries & Natural Productions of each Country, &c. physical, political, statistical & commercial, compiled from the best English & Foreign modern authorities. Accompanies by Maps & views.
London: G. Virtue, 1827, 8vo, xx, 994pp., ill., maps; contents: on Corea p.258

0068 1827 ENG 1090e18
Brookes, R. The General Gazetteer, or Compendious Geographical Dictionary
London: A. Piquot 1827, 8vo, unpaginated; contents: Corea entry (1 page)

0069 1834 ENG 1025
Brookes, R. The London General Gazetteer or Compendious Geographical Dictionary, containing a description of the nations, empires, kingdoms, states, provinces, cities, towns, forts, seas, harbours, rivers, lakes, canals, mountains, capes etc. of the known world; with the extent, boundaries and national

productions of each country; the government, customs, manners, and religion of the inhabitants; the trade manufactures, and curiosities of the cities and towns, with their longitude and latitude, bearing and distance in English Miles, from Remarkable Places; and the various historical events, by which they have been distinguished.

updated by John Marshall, London: T. Tegg & son, 1834, 8vo, 800pp.; contents: on Korea pp.222-223

0070   1839   FRE 334
Ennery & Hirth. Dictionnaire General de Geographie Universelle Ancienne et Moderne, Historique, Politique, Litteraire et Commerciale [General Dictionary of Universal Ancient and Modern, Historical, Political, Literary and Commercial geography]

Strasbourg: no publisher, 4 vols., 1839-1841. large 8vo, vol.1 1839, 778pp., vol.2 1840, 847pp., vol.3 1840, 848pp., vol.4 1841, 1126pp.; contents: on Coree vol.2 pp.131-132

0071   1863   FRE 332e2
Bouillet, M.N. Dictionnaire Universel d'Histoire et de Geographie [Universal dictionary of history and geography]

Paris: Hachette 1863. large 8vo, 1922, 147pp., contents: on Corea p.423

0072   1870   ENG 1301
Smith, F. Porter. A Vocabulary of Proper Names in Chinese and English of Places, Persons, Tribes and Sects in China, Japan, Corea, Annam, Siam, Burmah, the Straits and adjacent Countries, co-compiled by M.B. Lond.

Shanghai: Presbyterian Mission Press 1870. large 8vo, 72, ix pp.

0073   1873   ENG 579
Blackie, W.G. The Imperial Gazetteer : a general directory of geography, physical, political,
statistical, and descriptive.

London: Blackie & Son, 1873. 2 vols., small 4to, vol.1 : 1308 + 216pp., vol.2 : 1287 + 284pp., ill.

0074   1883   DUT 4e2
Jurrius, J. Kramers' Geographisch Woordenboek der Geheele Aarde. Tweede Druk, geheel Herzien en naar de Beste Bronnen Bewerkt. [Kramers

Geographic Dictionary Covering the Entire Earth, entirely Reviewed using the Best Sources]

Gouda: G.B. van Goor Zonen, 1883. 8vo, vol.1 : 582pp., vol.2 : xxxviii, 1196pp.

0075　　　　　　　　　　　　　　1889　　　ENG 884e19
Vincent, Benjamin. Haydn's Dictionary of Dates and Universal Information, relating to All Ages and Nations.

London: Word, Lock & Co., 1889. 8vo, 1052pp.

0076　　　　　　　　　　　　　　1903　　　ENG 1093
Kato, B., Kanazawa, S. A Catalogue of the Romanized Geographical Names of Korea

Tokyo: University of Tokyo Press 1903. 12mo, vi, 90, 88pp.

0077　　　　　　　　　　　　　　1914　　　ENG 879eR
Patrick, David. Chambers's Concise Gazetteer of the World, pronouncing topographical, statistical, historical.

London: W.R. Chambers 1914. assisted by William Geddie, 8vo, 768pp.

0078　　　　　　　　　　　　　　(c.1932)　　ENG 888
Hammerton, Sir J.A. The World Pictorial Gazetteer and Atlas, An Encyclopedia of all Countries, their Natural Features and Resources, their Cities, Towns, Villages and Historic Places, and the Native Races of the World, embodying about 20,000 Separate Articles.

London: the Fleetway House, n.d. (c.1932). 8vo, 1024pp., contents: on Korea p.632

0079　　　　　　　　　　　　　　1943　　ENG 609 (2 ex.)
Place Name Index for Korea (Chosen), November 1943

Washington D.C.: Army Map Service 1943. large 8vo, xi, 63pp.

0080　　　　　　　　　　　　　　1909　　　ENG 780
Papinot, E. Historical and Geographical Dictionary of Japan

Yokohama etc.: Kelly & Walsh, n.d., 8vo, 841pp., maps, appendices

IV.c) SAILING DIRECTORIES

0081   1801   ENG 908e2
Laurie, Robert and Whittle, James (ed.). The Oriental Navigator, or New Directories for Sailing to and from the East Indies, China, New Holland etc., also for the use of the country ships, trading in the India and China Seas, Pacific Ocean etc., collected from the manuscripts, journals, memoirs & observations of the most experienced officers in the honourable East India Company service, or commanders of ships in the country trade, from those of foreign navigators acquainted with the Indian and Eastern Seas, and from the last Edition of the French Neptune Oriental, by Mons. d'Apres de Manevillette, being a necessary Companion to the Complete East India Pilot.
London: R. Laurie and J. Whittle (1794) revised edition 1801. 4to, 655pp., ill.

0082   1861   ENG 6e3
King, John W. The China Pilot : The coasts of China, Korea and Manchuria; the sea of Japan, gulfs of Tartary and Amur, and sea of Okhotsk ; also the Babuyan, Bashi, Formosa, Meiaca-Sima, Lu-Chu, Mariana, Bonin, Japan, Saghalin, and Kuril Islands.
London: The Hydrographic Office. Admiralty, 1861. 8vo, ix, 469pp., index, published by order of the Lords Commissioners of the Admiralty; Gompertz 1919

0083   1873   ENG 867 Vol.4
Jarrad, Frederick W. The China Sea Directory, vol.IV, comprising the coasts of Korea, Russian Tartary, the Japan Islands, Gulfs of Tartary and Amur, and the Sea of Okhotsk; also the Meiaco, Liu-Kiu, Linschoten, Mariana, Bonin, Saghalin, and Kuril Islands.
London: Hydrographic Office, Admiralty 1873. 8vo, 386pp., index; Gompertz 1921

0084   1886   ENG 183e3
Findlay, Alexander George. A Directory for the Navigation of the North Pacific Ocean with Descriptions of its Coasts, Islands, etc., from Panama to Behring Strait, and Japan; its Winds, Currents and Passages.
London: Richard Holmes Laurie, 1886. large 8vo, xxxiv+1, 315pp. + 9pp. ads, ill., maps, index, Spine

27

title: North Pacific Ocean and Japan Directory.

0085 **1904** **ENG 19**

Sailing Directions for Japan, Korea, and Adjacent Seas from Yalu River, the Boundary between Korea and China, to the Komandorski Islands, also the Ogasawara (Bonin) Islands etc., southward of Japan, and the Kuril Islands. Formerly published as China Sea Directory, Vol. IV.

London: The Hydrographic Office. The Lords Commissioners of the Admiralty, 1904. Notices to Mariners issued during 1907 relating Directions for Japan, Korea, and Adjacent Seas. Gompertz 1929

0086 **1909** **ENG 915**

Asiatic Pilot. Published by the Hydrographic Office, under the Admiralty of the Secretary of the Navy.

Vol.1 : East Coast of Siberia, Sakhalin Island and Korea,
Washington: GPO 1909, 1st ed. 8vo, 318pp., maps, index

Vol.2 : The Japan Islands,
Washington: GPO 1910, 1st ed. 8vo, 627pp., maps, index

Vol.3 : Coast of China, Yalu River to Hongkong, with Formosa,
Washington: GPO 1910, 1st ed. 8vo, 691pp., maps, index

Vol.4 : The Shores of the China Sea from Singapore Strait to and including Hongkong,
Washington: GPO 1915, 1st ed. 8vo, 571pp., maps, index

Vol.5 : Sunda Strait and the Southern Approaches to the China Sea with west and north coasts of Borneo and off-lying dangers,
Washington: GPO 1915, 1st ed. 8vo, 519pp., maps, index

Vol.6 : The Coasts of Sumatra and the adjacent straits and islands
Washington: GPO 1917, 1st ed. 8vo, 610pp., maps, index

0087 **1918** **ENG 915e2**

Asiatic Pilot

Washington D.C.: Hydrographic Office, 2nd edition, 3 vols. out of 6, 1918-1920. 8vo

0088 **1932** **ENG 1428e3**

U.S. Navy Department, Hydrographic Office. Sailing Directories for Siberia & Chosen

Washington: GPO 3rd ed., 1932. 8vo, 582pp.

0089   1937   ENG 1264
China Sea Pilot
London: Hydrographic Department of the Admiralty, 1937. vol. 3, 8vo, 652pp., maps

0090   1948   ENG 1340e2
Hurd, Archibald. Ports of the World
London: The Shipping World, 2nd edition, 1948. 8vo, 1138pp., 24pp. ads; contents: on Korea (Chosen) pp.866-868

IV.d) WORLD GEOGRAPHY

0091   FRE 256
Bulletin de la Societe de Geographie Commerciale de Paris
[Bulletin of the Society of Commercial Geography of Paris]
vol.1 1879, vol.4-40 1882-1918, 8vo

0092   FRE 257
Compte Rendu des Seances de la Societe de Geographie
[Report on the Sessions of the Geographical Society]
Paris : Societe de Geographie, 7th series, vols. 1882-1887, 1889-1899, 8vo

0093   ENG 625
National Geographic
Washington D.C.: National Geographic Society
Vols. 21.11 (1910), 36.1-3 (1919), 46.4 (1924), 46-47.2 (1924-1925), 64 (1933), 66 (1934), 88.4 (1945), 91.1-6 (1947), 95.3 (1949)

0094   ENG 865
The Geographic Journal
London: Royal Geographical Society, 8vo, vol.7 Jan-June 1896, vol.10 July-Dec. 1897, vol. 13 Jan-June 1899, vol.16 July-Dec. 1900, vol.18 July-Dec. 1901, vol.41 Jan.-June 1913, vol.42 July-Dec. 1913, vol.76 July-Dec. 1930

0095   GER 186
Mitteilungen der Geographischen Gesellschaft in Wien [Transactions of the Geographical Society of Vienna]

Wien: Verlag der Geographischen Gesellschaft. 8vo, in stock vol.71, 1928, nos.1-10, bound in 4, edited by Hermann Leiter

0096   GER 24
Petermanns Geographische Mitteilungen [Petermann's Geographical Information]
Gotha: Justus Perthes; 4to, in stock : vols.29 (1883), 43 (1897), 75 (1929)

0097   ENG 506
Proceedings of the Royal Geographic Society and Monthly Record of Geography
London: Royal Geographic Society; large 8vo, in stock : vol.8 no.5, pp.289-312, 1886; vol.9 no.9 pp.531-538, 1887, vol.14 no.3, pp.146-161, 1892

0098   ENG 1118 v.4
Royal Geographic Society : Supplementary Papers
London: John Murray, 8vo, in stock : vol.1 pt.4 1886, pp.443-650, index. contents: not on Korea

0099   FRE 276
Memento Geographique. Evenements et Faits Importantes. [Geographical Souvenirs. Events and Important Facts]
Weekly; successor of "Bibliotheque illustre des voyages autour du monde"; editor M.P. Lemosof, 8vo, spine title : Voyages autour du monde [Travels around the World]; in stock : vol.1 nos.1-26, Oct.1897-Apr.1898; vol.2 nos.27-51, May-Oct.1898

0100   1707   DEN 10
Plug, Hendrich Ovesen. Den Danske Pillegrim, eller en almindelig Geographisk, og der hos kort Historisk Beskrivelse over den heele Bekiende Werden [The Danish Pilgrim, or a General Geographical, and with it a Short Historical Description of the Entire Known World]
Kiøbenhavn: no publisher 1707. 12mo, 1201pp., index. contents: on Kongeriket Corea eller Korea (Kingdom Corea or Korea) pp,537-539

0101   1740   FRE 345
Buffier, P., O.S.J. Nouveaux Elemens d'Histoire et de Geografie, a l'Usage des Pensionaires du Colege de Louis le Grand [New Elements of History and Geography for the Usage of the Pensionaries of the College of Louis the Great]

Paris: Pierre-François Giffort nouvelle edition, 1740. 12mo, 169 pp., ads., 235 pp., ads.; contents: not on Korea

0102   1788   FRE 270

Tableau de l'Univers ou Geographie Universelle
[Chart of the Universe, or Universal Geography]

Paris: Leclerc 1788, 4 vols., 12mo, total 1675pp.; contents: on Korea vol.4 p.120

0103   1806   ENG 967

Pinkerton, John. Modern Geography. A description of the empires, kingdoms, states, and colonies; with the oceans, seas, and Isles; in all parts of the world; including the most recent discoveries and political alternatives, digested on a new plan

London: T. Cadell 1806, 8vo, 676pp., maps, index; contents: on Korea in chapter on Chinese Tartary

0104   1824   GER 136

Stein, Christian Gottfried Daniel. Handbuch der Geographie und Statistik nach den neuesten Ansichten für die gebildeten Stände, Gymnasien und Schulen [Handbook of geography and statistics, for the educated, for high schools and schools, compiled according to the newest reports]

Leipzig: J.C. Hinrichs 1824, 3 vols., 12mo, 656pp., index, 954pp., index, 863pp., index; contents: on Korea : III pp.399-405

0105   1826 SWE 2 : 2.1, 2.2, 4

Palmblad, Vilhelm Fredrik. Handbok I Physiska och Politiska, Aeldre och Nyare Geographien [Handbook of Physical and Political, Older and Newer Geography]

Upsala: Palmblad & Co., 1826-1834, small 8vo, we have vol.1 pt.1 1826, vol.1 pt.2 1827, vol.4 1834

0106   1846   FRE 279e3

Balbi, Adrien. Abrege de Geographie : redige sur un nouveau plan, d'apres les derniers traites de paix et les decouvertes les plus recentes [Summary of Geography : drawn up following a new plan, considering the newest peace treaties and the latest discoveries]

Bruxelles: Meline, Cans et Cie., 1846. small 4to, 2 vols., bound in 1, lxxvi, 804, 513pp., index. contents: on Korea pp.763-764

0107   1848   FRE 173e2
Gaultier, l'Abbe. Elemens de Geographie [Elements of Geography]
Paris: Renouard 1848, 16mo, 12pp.; contents: Asia pp.43-54

0108   n.d. (c.1860/1866)   ENG 1313
Stewart. Modern Geography
frontispiece torn out; 12mo, 472pp., ill., maps, index; contents: Corea dealt with under Chinese Tartary, pp.224-226. comment: perhaps : Alexander Stewart, A Compendium of Modern Geography, 1864

0109   1882   FRE 40 : 7 (3 ex.)
Reclus, Elisee. Geographie Universelle. La Terre et les Hommes. Vol.7. L'Asie Orientale. [Universal Geography. The Land and the People. Vol.7 : East Asia]
Paris: Hachette 1882. 4to, 884pp., ill., maps, index; contents: on Korea pp.649-683

0110   1891   ENG 1103
Kirby, Mary & Elizabeth. The World at Home; or, Pictures and scenes from far off lands
London: T. Nelson & sons 1891. 8vo, 296pp., ill., no index; contents: mainly on Asia

0111   1905   ENG 1288 Vol.2
Hope Moncrieff, A.R. The World of Today
London: Gresham 1905, only vol.2 : Asia (not Far East), large 8vo, 266pp., 8pp.ads, ill., maps

0112   1906   ENG 873e35
Meiklejohn, J.M.D. A New Geography on the Comparative Method
London: Meiklejohn & Holden 1906. 35th revised edition, 12mo, 578pp., ill., map, index

0113   1912   ENG 1303
Hugh, Robert. The International Geography
NY: Appleton 1912. 8vo, 1088pp., contents: on Korea pp.542-544

0114   1914   FRE 61
Bres, H.S. Mon Premier Tour du Monde [My First Tour of the World]
Paris: Hachette 1914. large 8vo, 64pp., ill., maps. children's book on geography

0115   1918   ENG 1286
Williams, Graeme. The World We Live in

London: Waverley 1918. small 4to, vol.4 : pp.697-984, contents: on Korea pp.973-974

0116   1918   ENG 1187
Fawcett, C.B. Frontiers. A Study in Political Geography
Oxford: Clarendon 1918. 16mo, 107pp., maps, index; contents: 2 Korea entries

0117   1923   ENG 12
Cornish, Vaughan. The Great Capitals. An Historical Geography
London: Methuen & Co. Ltd., 1923. 8vo, xii, 296pp., maps, index

0118   n.d.   ENG 883
Fleure, H.J. et al. Geography. The world and its peoples. A survey of the physical, climatic and vegetational characteristics of the earth as the environment of mankind, together with a description of the main regions of the world and of the peoples who inhabit them, and a brief account of the probable development of man's struggle with his physical environment from earliest times
London: Odhams Press, n.d.. 8vo, 378pp., ill., index. contributions by many professors

IV.e) EAST ASIAN GEOGRAPHY

0119   1672   GER 83
Arnold, Christoph. Wahrhaftige Beschreibungen Dreyer Mächtigen Königreiche : Japan, Siam und Corea
[True description of three mighty kingdoms : Japan, Siam and Korea]
Nürnberg: Michael und Johann Friedrich Endters, 1672. 12mo, 1148pp., ill., index. contents: on Korea pp.884-900 (Hamel) Gompertz 39; Domschke/Goossmann 22

0120   1792   GER 69
Borheck, A.C. Erdbeschreibung von Asien nach Bankes, Blakes, Cooks und Lloyds grossem Englischen Werke, mit Zuziehung der besten neuesten Reisebeschreibungen für Deutsche bearbeitet von Dr. August Christian Borheck [Geographical description of Asia, based on the English work by Banke, Blake, Cook and Lloyd, the best newest travelogues also consulted,

prepared for German readers by Dr. August Christian Borheck]
Düsseldorf: Johann Christian Danzer, 1792-1794. 3 vols., 8vo, total 2332pp., index

0121   1800   ENG 569
Pennant, Thomas. The View of India extra Gangem, China and Japan. Vol.3 in the series : The Outlines of the Globe.
London: Luke Hansard, 1800. 4to, xi, 284 [13] pp.; contents: map. Korea (listed as part of China) pp.165-171

0122   1812   GER 110 Vol.12
Lindner, Friedrich Ludwig. Neueste Kunde von Asien [Newest Knowledge of Asia]. Vol.3 : Süd und Ostasien [South and East Asia]. Vol.12 in the Series : Neueste Länder und Völkerkunde. Ein geographisches Lesebuch [Newest Geography and Ethnography. A Geographic Reader]
Prag, no publisher 1812. small 8vo, 585pp., ill., maps, index; contents: on Korea : pp.368-381

0123   1822   GER 26
Hassel, G. Das Sinesische Reich, Japan und den östlichen Archipel. [The Chinese Empire, Japan and the Eastern Archipelago]. in the series : Vollständiges Handbuch der neuesten Erdbeschreibung [Complete handbook of the newest geography]. 4th series, 4th volume
Weimar: Geographisches Institut 1822. small 8vo, 920pp., index; contents: on Korea pp.370-387

0124   1822   SWE 7:11
Zimmermann, E.A.W. Korea, Japan, Tunkin och Cochinchina [Korea, Japan, Tongking and Cochinchina] in the series : Jorden och dess Invånare. Historisk Tafla af det Adertonde Århundradets Upptäckter om fremmande Folkslag och Länder [The Earth and its Inhabitants. Historic Table of the 18th Century's Records on Foreign People and Lands]. Part 11.
Stockholm: Zacharias Häggström, 1822. 16mo, 330pp., translated from the German; contents: on Korea pp.11-43

0125   1832   FRE 330
San Kokf Tsou Ran To Sets, ou Aperçu General de trois Royaumes 三國通監 圖說[Novel of the Three Kingdoms], translated from Japanese-Chinese by J. Klaproth

Paris: Oriental Translation Fund of Great Britain and Ireland, MDCCCXXXII (1832), 4to, 288pp.; contents: pp.11-168 : Description de la Coree, Gompertz 91

0126   1860   DUT 11
Weitzel, A.W.T. Batavia in 1858 of schetsen en beelden uit de hoofdstad van Neerlandsch Indie [Batavia in 1858, or Sketches and Images of the Capital of the Netherlands Indies]
Gorinchem: J. Noordduin 1860. 8vo, 208pp.; contents: not on Korea

0127   n.d. (before 1876)   ENG 800
Hughes, William. Philips' Geographical Manuals : The Geography of Asia
London & Liverpool: George Philip & Son, n.d., vi, 12mo, pp.331-451, map; comment : William Hughes lived from 1818 to 1876

0128   1882   FRE 21
Postel, Raoul. L'Extreme Orient. Cochinchine, Annam, Tong-kin [The Far East. Cochinchina, Annam and Tongking]
Paris: Degorce-Cadot 1882. 16mo, 307pp.; contents: not on Korea

0129   1887   FRE 299
Bonnetain, Paul. L'Extreme Orient [The Far East]
Paris: Maison Quantin 1887. 4to, 613pp., ill., index; contents: on Corea pp.341-342

0130   1888   FRE 267:7
Niox, Lieutenant Colonel. Geographie Militaire. Vol.VII : L'Expansion Europeenne. Empire Britannique et Asie [Military Geography : Vol.VII : European Expansion. The British Empire in Asia]
Paris: L. Baudoin 1888. 12mo, 295pp., map; contents: on Korea pp.279-280

0131   1891   ENG 1433
Reclus, Elisee. The Earth and its Inhabitants. Asia.
NY: Appleton (1884) 1891. large 8vo, 4 vols., vol.1 504 pp., vol.2 492 pp., vol.3 512 pp., vol.4 504 pp.; contents : Korea in vol.2 pp.334-354

0132   1892   FRE 17
Lanier, L. L'Asie. Choix de Lectures de Geographie [Asia. A selection of lessons on geography]

Paris: Bellin Freres 1892. 12mo, 887pp.; contents: pp.663-676 on Korea

| 0133 | 1896 | ENG 552 |

Keane, A.H. Stanford's Compendium of Geography and Travel. Asia.

London: Edward Stanford, 1896. 2 vols., 8vo, Vol.1 : Northern and Eastern Asia, xxiv, 514pp., Vol.2 : Southern and Western Asia, xxiv, 526pp., ill., maps, index

| 0134 | 1897 | ENG 1155 |

Carpenter, Frank G. Carpenter's Geographical Reader : Asia

NY: American Book Co. 1897. 12mo, 307pp., ill., maps, index; contents: on Korea pp.76-92; Gompertz 277

| 0135 | n.d. (c.1900) | FRE 18 |

Fallex, M. and Hentgen, A. L'Asie au debut de XXe siecle [Asia at the start of the 20th century]

Paris: Ch. Delagrave, no date. 12mo, 343pp.; contents: pp.281-297 on Manchuria and Korea

| 0136 | 1904 | GER 46e2 |

Sievers, Wilhelm. Asien [Asia]

Leipzig etc.: Bibliographisches Institut 1904. large 8vo, 712pp., ill., maps, index, ads; contents: on Korea pp.315-339

| 0137 | 1904 | ENG 254 (4 ex.) |

Whigham, H.J. Manchuria and Korea

New York: Charles Scribner's Sons, 1904. 8vo, 245pp., ill., map

| 0138 | 1908 | ENG 208 |

Zwemer, Samuel M. and Brown, Arthur Judson. The Nearer and Farther East : Outlines of Moslem Lands and of Siam, Burma and Korea

New York: MacMillan 1908. 12mo, xvi, 326pp., 5pp. ads. Textbook issued by the Central Committee of the United Study of Mission

| 0139 | 1910 | ENG 1422 |

Clough, Ethlyn T. (ed.). Oriental Life

Detroit: Bay View Reading Club 1910. small 8vo; contents: chapters xv (Heber Jones : The Hermit Nation and her People, pp.183-194), xvi (Samuel McClintock, A Vanishing Empire, pp.195-209) on Korea

0140 1916 ENG 207
Allen, Nellie B. Asia
Boston etc.: Ginn and Company, 1916. 12mo, xx, 450pp., ill., maps, index. Geographical and Industrial Studies. Textbook meant for the upper level of grammar school education, with a chapter on Formosa and Korea

0141 1919 ENG 85
Gibbons, Herbert Adams. The New Map of Asia
New York: Century, 1919. 8vo, xiv, 571pp., maps, index. contents: on Korea pp.346-369

0142 1928 ENG 770
Bunker, Frank F. Lands and Peoples : China and Japan
Philadelphia: Lippincott 1928. 12mo, 253pp.

0143 1928 FRE 64 : 4.1
Sion, Jules. Geographie Universelle. Asie des Moussons, Pt.1 : Generalites - Chine - Japon [Universal Geography. Asia of the Monsoons. Generalities, China, Japan]
Paris: Armand Colin 1928. small 4to, 272pp.; contents: on Korea pp.245-251

0144 1933 ENG 1194
Lyde, Lionel W. The Continent of Asia
London: MacMillan 1933. 8vo, 777pp., ill., maps, index; contents: on Chosen pp.724-728

0145 1937 ENG 921
Nippon Yusen Kaisho. Glimpses of the East. Nippon Yusen Kaisho's Official Guide. The Principal Ports of the World
Vol.20, 1937-1938, Tokyo 1937. 4to, not continually paged, ill., maps

0146 1939 (1929) ENG 1228e4
Stamp, L. Dudley. Asia. A Regional and Economic Geography
London: Methuen (1929) 1939. 4th edition 1939, 8vo, 704pp., ill., map, index

0147 1942 ENG 1136
Brodrick, Alan Houghton. Little China. The Annamese Lands
Oxford: UP 1942. 8vo, 332pp., ill., index; contents: several Korea entries

0148   1946 (1929)   ENG 1228e6
Stamp, L. Dudley. Asia. A Regional and Economic Geography
London: Methuen (1929) 6th edition 1946. 704pp., ill., map, index

0149   1946   FRE 90
Lasker, Bruno. Bibliotheque Geographique. Les peuples d'Asie en mouvement [Geographic Library. The peoples of Asia on the move]
Paris: Payot 1946. small 8vo, 200pp.

0150   1946   ENG 1435e2
Quinn, Vernon. Picture Map Geography of Asia
Philadelphia: Lippincott (1946) 1955. large 8vo, 122pp.; contents: on Korea pp.111-117

IV.f) AREA HANDBOOKS

IV.f.1) CHINA

0151   1639   LAT 2
Ricci, Matteo O.S.J. De Regno Chinae [On the Kingdom of China]
Leiden: Elzevir 1639. small 16mo, 365pp., ill., index, edited by P. Nicolai Trigautii

0152   1787   FRE 28e2
Grosier, M. l'Abbe. Description generale de la Chine [General Description of China]
Paris: Moutard 1787. 2 vols., small 8vo, 647, 512pp.; ill., map; contents: on Coree vol.1 pp.264-279

0153   1818   FRE 28e3 (2 ex.)
Grosier, M. l'Abbe. De la Chine, ou Description Generale de cet Empire. Redigee d'apres les Memoires de la Mission de Pe-kin. Ouvrage qui contient la description topographique des quinze provinces de la Chine, celle de la Tartarie, des iles et des divers etats tributaires qui en dependent; le nombre de ses villes; le tableau de sa population; les trois regnes de son histoire naturelle, rassembles et donnes pour la premiere fois avec quelque etendue; et l'expose de toutes les connoissances acquises et parvenues jusqu'ici en Europe sur le gouvernement, la religion, les lois, les moeurs, les usages, les sciences et les

arts des Chinois [About China, or general description of tht empire. Drawn up on the memories of the mission at Peking. A work which contains a topographical description of the 15 provinces of China, those of Tartary, the islands and diverse tributary states which are dependent on it, the names of its cities, the table of its population, the three kingdoms of its natural history, collected and given for the first time in this extent, and showing all the acquired knowledge and achievements which were transferred from Europe, in the fields of government, religion, laws, customs, habits, sciences and the arts of the Chinese]

Paris, no publisher 1818-1820. small 8vo, 7 vols. Vol.1 : lxxx, 400pp., ill., maps, 1818; vol.2 : 552pp., 1818; vol.3 : 464pp., 1819; vol.4 : 512pp., 1819; vol.5 : 468pp., 1819; vol.6 : 475pp., 1819; vol.7 : 420pp., 1820; contents: on Korea : vol.4 pp.340-353

0154　　　　　　　　　　　　　　　1838　　ENG 1270

Medhurst, W.H. China. It's State and Prospects, with especial reference to the spread of the gospel

Boston: Crocker & Brewster 1838. large 12mo, 472pp., map, no index; contents: not on Korea

0155　　　　　　　　　　　　　　　1841　　DUT 5

Davis, J.F. China en de Chinezen

translated by C.J. Zweerts, 3 vols., Amsterdam: Beijerinck 1841, 8vo, 378+325+327 pp., ill.

0156　　　　　　　　　　　　　　　1847　　ENG 812

Martin, R. Montgomery. China : Political, Commercial and Social; in an Official Report to Her Majesty's Government

London: Madden 1847. 8vo, 2 vols., vol.1 432pp., vol.2 502pp., maps

0159　　　　　　　　　　　　　　　1865　　FRE 356

Escayrac de Lauture, Comte d'. Memoires sur la Chine [Memoires of China]

Paris: Librairie du Magasin Pittoresque 1865. 4to, 100+129+127+79+93pp., maps, ill., no index

0160　　　　　　　　　　　　　　　1886　　ENG 1134 V.1

Davis, John Francis. The Chinese. A General Description of the Empire of China and its Inhabitants

London: Charles Knight 1886. 8vo, 420pp., only vol.1, ill., no index

0161　　　　　　　　　　　　　　　1893　　ENG 409 (2 ex.)

Gundry, R.S. China and her Neighbours : France in Indo-China, Russia and China, India and Thibet

London: Chapman and Hall, 1893. 8vo, xxi, 408, 40pp., maps; contents: pp.217-294 on Korea, written in 1884

0162   1894   ENG 127 (2 ex.)

Clark, James Hyde. Story of China and Japan embracing their geographical positions, enormous resources, wealth, emperors and courts, governments and people, manners and customs, how the people of these great nations live and die and maintain in oriental splendor the China and Japan of to-day. Together with a sketch of Corea and the Coreans, and the causes leading to the conflict of 1894.

Philadelphia: Oriental Publishing Company, 1894. large 8vo, 416pp., ill., map., from choiciest Chinese, Japanese and Corean literature extant, assisted by Chang Wong of China and K. Tatoni of Japan;
contents : Corea pp.207-229. Gompertz 223

0164   1899   ENG 1140

Gorst, Harold E. Imperial Interest Library : China

London: Sands 1899, 8vo, 300pp., ill., maps, index; contents: on Korea pp.4, 234

0165   1900   ENG 60e3

Martin, W.A.P. A Cycle of Cathay : or China, South and North. With personal reminiscences

New York: Fleming H. Revell Company (1896) 1900. 8vo, 464pp., ill., map

0166   1901 ENG 235eR (2 ex.)

Williams, S. Wells. The Middle Kingdom, a survey of the geography, government, literature, social life, arts, and history of the Chinese Empire and its inhabitants.

New York: Charles Scribner's Sons 1901. Revised edition, 2 vols., 8vo, vol.1 xxxv, 836pp., vol.2 xii, 775pp., ill., maps,index;   Gompertz 138

0167   1902   FRE 331

Reclus, Elisee et Onesime. L'Empire du Milieu. Le Climat, le Sol, les Races, la Richesse de la Chine [The Setting of the Empire, the Climate, Soil, Races, the ealth of China]

Paris: Hachette 1902, large 8vo, 667pp., maps, bibliography

0168   1908   ENG 776 (2 ex.)
L. Richard's Comprehensive Geography of the Chinese Empire and Dependencies
Shanghai, T'usewei Press 1908. 8vo, 713pp., translated from the Chinese into English, revised and enlarged by M. Kennelly, O.S.J.

0169   1909   ENG 622
Thomson, John Stuart. The Chinese
Indianapolis: Bobbs-Merritt Co. 1909. 8vo, 441pp., ill., index

0170   1914   ENG 1065
Moule, Arthur Evans. The Chinese People
London: Society for Promoting Christian Knowledge, 1914. 8vo, 469pp., maps, index

0171   1917   ENG 683e2
Parker, E.H. China : her history, diplomacy, and commerce, from the earliest times to the present day
London: John Murray, second edition 1917. 8vo, xxx, 419pp., ill., maps, index

0172   1922   ENG 492
Lew, T.T. et al. China today : through Chinese eyes
London: Student Christian Movement, 1922. 12mo, 144pp., Contributions by T.T. Lew, Dean, Theological Faculty, Peking Univ., Hu Shih, Prof., "Renaissance Leader", Y.Y. Tsu, Prof., St. John's College, Shanghai, Cheng Ching Yi, Chairman, National Conference of Christian Workers

0173   1923   ENG 493
Hodgkin, Henry T. China in the Family of Nations
New York: George H. Doran Company, 1923. 12mo, 267pp., bibliography, index, Selly Oak Colleges Publications No.4,

0174   1925   FRE 246:1
Maspero, George. La Chine [China]. in the series : Bibliotheque d'Histoire et de Politique [Historical and Political Library].
Paris, Librairie Delagrave 1925. 12mo, 310pp.

0175   1929   ENG 11 (2 ex.)
Buxton, L.H. Dudley. China : the Land and the People. A Human Geography.

With a chapter on the climate by W.G. Kendrew
Oxford: Clarendon Press 1929. 8vo, 333pp., ill., maps, index

0176   1934   ENG 714
Cressey, George B. China's Geographic Foundations : a Survey of the Land and its People
New York: McGraw 1934. 8vo, 436pp., ill., maps, bibliography, index

0177   1934   ENG 1087
Lyall, L.A. The modern World. China
London: Ernest Benn 1934. 8vo, 383pp., map, index; contents: not on Korea

0178   1945   ENG 877
Rattenbury, Harold B. Face to Face with China
London: George C. Harrap & Co., 1945. 8vo, 144pp., ill., index, large map

0179   1945   ENG 1255 2/3
Naval Intelligence Division. China proper.
Vol.II : Modern History and Administration
Vol.III : Economic Geography, Ports and Communications
H.M. Intelligence Division 1945. 8vo, 2 vols., Geographical Handbook Series, vol.2 : 370pp., ill., maps, index; vol.3 : 653pp., ill., map, index; contents: a number of Korea entries. Of Vol.3 the Collection has 2 copies

0180   1947   ENG 1064
Spencer, Cornelia. The Land of the Chinese People
London: Museum Press 1947. 8vo, 136pp., ill., index

IV.f.2) MANCHURIA

0181   1910   ENG 673
Hosie, Alexander. Ito Edition. Manchuria and its People, Resources and Recent History. Oriental Series, Vol.14:
Boston: Millet 1910. 8vo, 320pp., ill., index

0182　　　　　　　　　　　　　1922　　　　ENG 320
South Manchuria Railway Company. Manchuria : Land of Opportunities
New York: S.M.R. 1922. 8vo, ix, 113 pp., ill., map, index

0183　　　　　　　　　　　　　1925　　　　ENG 308

Adachi, Kinnosuke. Manchuria : A Survey
New York: Robert McBride, 1925. 8vo, xvii, 401pp., ill., map, index

0184　　　　　　　　　　　　　1928　　　　ENG 256
Kinney, Henry W. Modern Manchuria and the South Manchuria Railway Company
Dairen: Japan Advertiser, 1928. 8vo, 91pp., ill., map

0185　　　　　　　　　　　　　1932　　　　FRE 91
Balet, J.C. Le drame de l'extreme-orient. La Mandchourie historique-politique-economique son avenir [The drama of the Far East. Manchuria historical, political, economic, its future]. in the series: Bibliotheque Politique et Economique [Political and Economic Library].
Paris: Payot 1932. small 8vo, 222pp., map. Foreword by François de Tessan, Vice President Commission des Affaires Etrangeres

0186　　　　　　　　　　　　　1933　　　　ENG 742
Scherer, James A.B. Manchukuo. A Bird's Eye View
Tokyo: Hokuseido 1933. 12mo, 145pp., ill., index

0187　　　　　　　　　　　　　1936　　　　ENG 469
Collier, D.M.B. and Malone, Lt. Colonel L'Estrange. Manchoukuo : Jewel of Asia
London: George Allen & Unwin, 1936. 8vo, 267pp., ill., index

0188　　　　　　　　　　　　　1938　　　　FRE 81
Collier, D.M.B. and Malone, Lt. Colonel l'Estrange. Le Mandchoukouo. Joyau de l'Asie. Naissance d'un pays. Population, moeurs, coutumes, religions, ressources agricoles, minieres, economiques. L'Industrialisation du Mandchoukouo [Manchuria, Jewel of Asia. The birth of a country. The population, customs, habits, religions, the agricultural, mineral and economic

resources, the industrialization of Manchukuo]. in the series: Bibliotheque Geographique [Geographical Library].

Paris: Payon 1938. 8vo, 234pp., translated from the English by Robert Waldteufel

0189　　　　　　　　　　　　　　　1941　　　　　　GER 3
Fochler-Hauke, Gustav. Die Mandschurei. Eine geographisch-politische Landeskunde auf Grund eigener Reisen und des Schrifttums [Manchuria. A geographic-geopolitic area study based on personally conducted expeditions and on the literature]. in the series: Schriften zur Weltpolitik Nr.3 [Publications on world politics no.3]

Heidelberg: no publisher 1941. small 4to, xv, 448pp., ill., maps, bibliography, index

IV.f.3) RUSSIAN FAR EAST / SIBERIA

0190　　　　　　　　　　　　　1899　　ENG 115 (2 ex.)
Vladimir. Russia on the Pacific and the Siberian Railway

London: Sampson, Low, Marston and Company, 1899. 8vo, xii, 373pp., ill., maps, index. comment: Vladimir is a pseudonym.

0191　　　　　　　　　　　　　1902　　ENG 478 (3 ex.)
Fraser, John Foster. The Real Siberia : together with an account of a dash through Manchuria

London etc.: Cassell 1902 (MCMII). 8vo, xvi, 279, 16pp., ill.

0192　　　　　　　　　　　　　　　1902　　　　　ENG 1176
Norman, Henry. All the Russias. Travels and Studies in European Russia, Finland, Siberia

London: William Heinemann 1902. large 8vo, 476pp., ill., index; contents: on Korea p.41

0193　　　　　　　　　　　　　　　1925　　　　　ENG 1123
Makeev, Nicholas, and O'Hara, Valentina. Russia

London: Ernest Benn 1925, 8vo, 345pp., index; contents: on Korea p.64

0194　　　　　　　　　　　　　　　1944　　　　　ENG 1193
Mandel, William. The Soviet Far East and Central Asia

International Secretariat, Institute of Pacific Relations 1944. 8vo, 158pp., contents: on Korea pp.26, 44, 45

IV.f.4) JAPAN

0195   1832   DUT 18
Siebold, Philipp Franz von. Nippon. Archief voor de beschrijving van Japan [Nippon. Archive for the description of Japan]
Leiden : Siebold, Amsterdam : J. Muller, Leiden : C.C. van der Hoek 1832, folio, map, vi, 15, 8pp.

0196   1877   ENG 152e2
Griffis, William Elliot. The Mikado's Empire
N.Y.: Harper & Brothers (1876) 1877. 8vo, 635pp., ill., index

0197   1877   ENG 1278
Eden, Charles H. Japan Historical and Descriptive
London: Marcus Ward 1877. 12mo, 328pp., 32pp. ads, index, ill.; contents : not on Korea

0198   1881   GER 131
Rein, J.J. Japan nach Reisen und Studien im Auftrage der Königlich Preussischen Regierung dargestellt [Japan, described on behalf of the Royal Prussian Government, based on travels and studies], 2 volumes

Volume 1 : Natur und Volk des Mikadoreiches [Nature and People of the Mikado's Empire]
Leipzig: Wilhelm Engelmann 1881. 8vo, 630pp., ill., map, index

Volume 2 : Land- und Forstwirthschaft, Industrie und Handel [Agriculture and Forestry, Industry and Trade]
Leipzig: Wilhelm Engelmann 1886, 8vo, 678pp., ill., map, index

0199   1888   ENG 427e2
Rein, J.J. Japan : Travels and Researches Undertaken at the Cost of the Prussian Government
NY: A.C. Armstrong 1888. large 8vo, x (2), 543pp., ill., maps, index; translated from German

0200   1894   ENG 238 (3 ex.)
Northrop, Henry Davenport. The Flowery Kingdom, Land of the Mikado. Or China, Japan and Corea. Containing their complete history down to the present

time, manners, customs and peculiarities of the people, superstitions; idol worship; industries; natural scenery, etc. etc.
Chicago: Bell & Co., 1894. 8vo, 608pp., ill. With an introduction by Hon. John Russell Young; contents: on Korea pp.513-548

0201   **1895**   **ENG 138**
Saunby, John W. (Rev.). Japan : the land of the Morning
Toronto: Methodist Mission Rooms, 1895. 12mo, 302pp., ill.

0202   **1895**   **SPA 2**
Lome, Enrique Dupuy de. Estudios sobre el Japon [Studies on Japan]
Madrid: Sucesores de Rivadaneyra 1895. 16mo, 409pp.

0203   **1897**   **GER 58e2**
Siebold, Philipp Franz von. Nippon. Archiv zur Beschreibung von Japan und dessen Neben und Schutzländern Jezo mit den südlichen Kurilen, Sachalin, Korea und den Liukiu Inseln
[Nippon. Archive for the description of Japan and its adjacent and tributary countries, Hokkaido with the Southern Kuriles, Sachalin, Korea and the Ryukyu Islands]
Würzburg: Wörl 1897. large 8vo, 2 vols., vol.1 : 421pp., vol.2 : 342pp., map, ill., Gompertz 92; Domschke/Goossmann 958

0204   **1897**   **ENG 1006**
Brinkley, F. Japan. Described and illustrated by the Japanese.
Boston: J.B. Millet 1897. 10 vols., large 4to, in total 383pp.

0205   **1898**   **FRE 23 (2 ex.)**
Martin, Felix. Le Japon Vrai [The true Japan]
Paris: Charpentier 1898. 12mo, 294pp., contents: on Korea pp.145-214

0206   **1900**   **GER 177**
Königsmarck, Graf Hans von. Japan und die Japaner [Japan and the Japanese]
Berlin: Allgemeiner Verein für Deutsche Literatur 1900. 8vo, vii, 313pp.

0207   **1902**   **ENG 340**
Hartshorne, Anna C. Japan, and her people

Philadelphia: Henry T. Coates & Co., 1902. 8vo, 2 vols., vol.1 : x, 378pp., vol.2 : vi, 374pp., map

0208   1902   ENG 1271
Stead, Alfred. Japan, our new ally
London: T. Fisher Unwin 1902. 12mo, 250pp., ill., index; contents: several Korea entries

0209   1904   ENG 771e3
Clement, Ernest Wilson. A Handbook of Modern Japan
Chicago: A.C. McClurg & Co. 1904. 12mo, 395pp., ill., maps, index, ads

0210   1904   ENG 289 (2 ex.)
Stead, Alfred (ed.). Japan by the Japanese : a survey by its highest authorities
London: William Heinemann / NY: Dodd, Mead & Co., 1904. 8vo, xxvii, 697pp., index

0211   1904   GER 98 (2 ex.)
Stead, Alfred (ed.). Unser Vaterland Japan. Ein Quellenbuch geschrieben von Japanern [Our Fatherland Japan. A Sourcebook written by Japanese]
Leipzig: E.H. Seeman, 1904. large 8vo. xxvi, 736pp., with numerous contributions by numerous Japanese authors & institutions, including Baron Suyematsu. translation of the aforelisted title

0212   1905   ENG 25
Knox, George William. Imperial Japan. The Country & its People
London: George Newnes Ltd., 1905. 8vo, xi, 294pp., ill., index

0213   1905   ENG 1181
Hearn, Lafcadio. Japan. An Attempt at Interpretation
NY: MacMillan 1905, 8vo, 549pp., contents: on Korea pp.204, 303

0214   1905   ENG 984
Wollant, Gregoire de. The Land of the Rising Sun
NY: Neale 1905. 8vo, 401pp., translated from the Russian by the author

0215   1906   ENG 193eR
Knapp, Arthur May. Feudal and Modern Japan
Yokohama: The Advertiser Publishing Co., 1906. 12mo, 372pp., xxiv pp., bibliography

0216   1906   ENG 280eR
Griffis, William Elliot. Japan in History, Folklore and Art

Myongji-LG Korean Studies Library

Boston and New York: Houghton, Mifflin and Co., 1906. 12mo, x, 246pp., 4pp. ads, index. Riverside Library for Young People

0217   **1906**   **ENG 763e2**

Stead, Alfred. Great Japan. A Study in National Efficiency

London etc.: The Bodley Head, 1906 (MDCCCCVI). 8vo, xxii, 481pp., index, ads, foreword by the Earl of Rosebery

0218   **1906**   **GER 157e3**

Munzinger, Carl. Japan und die Japaner [Japan and the Japanese]

Stuttgart: D. Gundert, 3rd edition, 1906. 8vo, 172pp.

0219   **1907**   **ENG 62**

Davidson, Augusta M. Campbell. Present-Day Japan

London: T. Fisher-Unwin, 1907 (MCMVII). 8vo, 366pp., ill., index

0220   **1908**   **ENG 253**

Montgomery, H.B. The Empire of the East

London: Methuen 1908. 8vo, xii, 307pp., ill., index, ads

0221   **1912**   **ENG 67**

Longford, Joseph H. Japan of the Japanese

London: Sir Isaac Pitman & Sons Ltd., 1912. 8vo, x, 314pp., 24pp. ads + 29 plates, index

0222   **1913**   **ENG 59**

Mitford, E. Bruce. Japan's Inheritance. The Country, its People and their Destiny.

London: T. Fisher Unwin, 1913. 8vo, 383pp., ill., maps; contents: reference on Korea

0223   **1918**   **FRE 11 (2 ex.)**

Bellessort, Andre. Le Nouveau Japon [The New Japan]

Paris: Librairie Academique, 1918. 16mo, 312pp.; contents: on Korea pp.223-266

0224   **1918**   **FRE 12**

Gerard, A. Nos Allies d'Extreme Orient [Our Allies in the Far East]. in the series: Bibliotheque Politique et Economique [Political and Economic Library].

Paris: Payot 1918. 16mo, 249pp.

0225   1919   ENG 175 (3 ex.)
Morton-Cameron, W.H. (ed.). Present Day Impressions of Japan. The History, People, Commerce, Industries and Resources of Japan and Japan's Colonial Empire : Kwantung, Chosen, Taiwan, Karafuto
Yokohama etc.: The Globe Encyclopedia Company, 1919. large 4to, 931pp., ill.

0226   1919   ENG 964
Methodist Episcopal Church. The Land that Lacks Only Christ - Japan
NY: Methodist Episcopal Church, Board of Foreign Missions, 1919. 4to, not paginated, ill.

0227   1922   ENG 116
Scott, J.W. Robertson. The Foundations of Japan. Notes made during journeys of 6,000 miles in the rural districts as a basis for a sounder knowledge of the Japanese people
London: John Murray, 1922. 8vo, xxv, 446p., ill., index; contents: few Korea-entries in index

0228   1929   FRE 240
Tessan, François de. Le Japon mort et vif [Japan dead and alive]
Paris: Baudiniere 1929. 12mo, 253pp., foreword by Paul Claudel

0229   1931   GER 129
Trautz, Dr. M. (ed.). Philipp Franz von Siebold / Nippon / Archiv zur Beschreibung von Japan / vollständiger Neudruck der Urausgabe, vol.3 [Philpp Franz von Siebold, Nippon, Archive for the description of Japan, complete reprint of the original edition, vol.3]
Berlin: Verlag Ernst Wasmuth 1931. large 4to, pp.1445-1875, supplement and index volume

0230   1937   GER 64
Okubo, Toshitake. Nippon, ein Überblick. Anhang : Mandschukuo [Japan, a survey. Appendix : Manchukuo]
Tokyo: Nippon Dempo Tsushinsha (1937), 8vo, 594pp., ill., map

0231   1942   FRE 141
Ray, Jean. Le Japon. Grande Puissance Moderne [Japan. A Modern Great Power]
Paris: Plon 1942. 12mo, 235pp.

0232　　　　　　　　　　　　　　　　　1943　　　ENG 656
Smith, Guy Harold and Good, Dorothy. Japan. A Geographical View
NY: American Geological Society 1943. large 8vo, (iv) 14pp., map, with collaboration of Shannon McCune

0233　　　　　　　　　　　　　　　　　1944　　　ENG 1020
Price, Willard. Japan's Islands of Mystery
NY: John Day, 6th impression 1944. 8vo, 264pp., map, index

0234　　　　　　　　　　　　　　　　　1944　　　GER 171e2
Scharschmidt, Clemens. Japan
Berlin: Junker und Dünnhaupt (1942) 2nd edition 1944. 8vo, 160pp.

0235　　　　　　　　　　　　　　　　　1946　　　ENG 1096
Price, Willard. Key to Japan
London: W. Heinemann 1946. 12mo, 283pp.; contents: numerous Korea entries

0236　　　　　　　　　　　　　　　　　1947　　　FRE 154
Duboscq, Andre. Les Japonais [The Japanese]
Paris: S.E.F.I., 1947. 12mo, 202pp.

IV.f.5) KOREA

0237　　　　　　　　　　　　　　　　　1868　　　FRE 302
Rosny, Leon de. Sur la Geographie et l'Histoire de la Coree [Geography and History of Korea]
Nancy: Imprimerie Orientale de V. Raybois 1868. 8vo, 22pp.

0238　　　　　　　　　　　　　　　　　1882　　　ENG 153 (3 ex.)
Griffis, William Elliot. Corea, the Hermit Nation
NY: Charles Scribner's Sons, 1882. 8vo, xxviii, 462pp., ill., map, index; Gompertz 132

0239　　　　　　　　　　　　　　　　　1886　　　ENG 229 (5 ex.)
Lowell, Percival. Choson : The Land of the Morning Calm. A Sketch of Korea
Boston: Ticknor & Co. 1886. 8vo, x, 412pp., plates, maps; Gompertz 159

0240　　　　　　　　　　　　　　　　　1888　　　ENG 159 Vol.5

Carles, W.R. The Hermit Land

in : Chambers Journal of Popular Literature, Science and Arts, 1888, large 8vo, pp.209-212; Gompertz 188

0241   1894   ENG 490

Nelson, T. (publisher). Corea of To-day

London: T. Nelson & Sons, 1894. 16mo, 128pp., ill. Much of this book has been extracted from "Corea from its capital" by G.W. Gilmore, M.A. New matter has been added with reference to the present crisis.

0242   1894   FRE 253e2

Tournafond, Paul. La Coree [Korea]

Paris: Tequi, new edition 1894, 16mo, 170pp., map; Gompertz 168

0243   1894   FRE 68 : 1894

Aunis, R. d' La Coree et les Coreens [Korea and the Koreans]

in : Journal des voyages et des aventures de terre et de la mer 1894, front pp.493-497, 518-524; compare No. 0245

0244   1894   FRE 68 : 1894

Demays, V. La Coree et les Coreens [Korea and the Koreans]

in : Journal des voyages et des aventures de terre et de la mer 1894, end pp.145-148, 167-170, 176, 180-181, 192

0245   1894   FRE 70 : 1894

Aunis, R. d' La Coree et les Coreens [Korea and the Koreans]

in : Revue Encyclopedique, 4th year, No.95, 1894, pp.493-497; compare No.0243; Gompertz 241

0246   1895   GER 122

Pogio, M.A. Korea

Wien und Leipzig: Wilhelm Braumüller 1895. 8vo, 248pp., map, translation from Russian by St. Ritter von Ursyn-Pruszynski; Gompertz 264; Domschke/Goossmann 821

0247   1895   ENG 745

Gardner, Christopher Thomas et al. Corea

Brisbane: Australasian Association for the Advance of Science, 1895. 8vo, 50, lxxxv pp., ill., maps. With contributions by J.S. Gale, J.H. Hunt, G.H. Jones, M.N. Trollope, Harry H. Fox, L.O. Warner

0248   1895   ENG 74 (2 ex.)
Miln, Louise Jordan. Quaint Korea
NY: Scribner's 1895. 8vo, 306pp.; Gompertz 253

0249   1896   ENG 500 (3 ex.)
Savage-Landor, A. Henry. Corea or Chosen. The Land of the Morning Calm
London: W. Heinemann, 1896. 8vo, xiii, 304pp., ill., index, ads; Gompertz 252

0250   1902   ITA 3
Rossetti, Carlo. L'Impero di Corea [The Empire of Korea]
in : L'Italia Coloniale 1902. 4to, 30pp., maps; Gompertz 343

0251   1904 FRE 195e2 (2 ex.)
Laguerie, Villetard de. La Coree Independante, Russe, or Japonaise [Korea independent, Russian or Japanese]
Paris: Librairie Hachette et C., 1904. 12mo, viii, 304pp., ill.

0252   1904   DUT 30
Miln, L.J. Het Gesloten Rijk
translated by S. Kalfe, Amsterdam: Scheltens & Giltay, 1904. 12mo, 200pp., ill.; Gompertz 393

0253   1906   ENG 120 (3 ex.)
Hulbert, Homer B. The Passing of Korea
NY: Doubleday, Page & Co., 1906 / London : W. Heinemann 1906. 8vo, xii, 473pp., ill., index; Gompertz 415

0254   1907   ENG 1356 (2 ex.)
Jones, George Heber. Korea, the Land, People and Customs
Cincinnati: Jennings and Graham 1907. 16mo, 110 pp.

0255   1910   ENG 221
Hamilton, Angus et al. Korea : its History, its People and its Commerce
Boston: Millet 1910. 8vo, 326pp., ill., index. Oriental Series vol.8 Co-authors Herbert Austin, Viscount Masatake Terauchi, Japanese Resident General; Gompertz 445

0256   1920   DUT 1 (3 ex.)
Hamel, Hendrik. Verhaal van het Vergaan van het Jacht de Sperwer : en van het Wedervaren der Schipbreukelingen op het Eiland Quelpaert en het

vasteland van Korea (1653-1666) met eene beschrijving van dat rijk door Hendrik Hamel [Narrative of the Shipwreck of the Yacht "De Sperwer" and what happened to the Shipwrecked on the island of Quelpaert and on the Korean Mainland (1653-1666) with a Description of that Kingdom by Hendrik Hamel]
s'Gravenhage: Martinus Nijhoff 1920. 8vo, 165pp., ill., map, bibliography, index. edited by B. Hoetinck; Gompertz 51

0257 1921 FRE 350
La Coree Contemporaine [Contemporary Korea]
Paris: J. Demoulin, 1921, 12mo, 94 pp., F.H. Smith, Mullett Merrick et al.; Gompertz 513

0258 1930 ENG 113 (5 ex.)
Drake, Henry Burgess. Korea of the Japanese
London: Bodley Head 1930. 8vo, 225pp., ill.; Gompertz 577

0259 1931 ENG 518
Buskirk, James Dale van. Korea. Land of the Dawn
NY: Missionary Education Movement of the United States and Canada 1931, 12mo, xii, 212pp., bibliography, map

0260 1939 ENG 726
Matsuzawa, Tatsuo. New Tyosen
n.pl., Government-General of Tyosen, 1939. 8vo, 18pp.

0261 1945 ENG 842 (2 ex.)
Military Intelligence Division. Terrain Handbook Korea
Washington: War Department, September 1945, Confidential, 12mo, 162pp., ill., maps

0262 1945 GER 81
Lautensach, Hermann. Korea. Eine Landeskunde auf Grund eigener Reisen und der Literatur [Korea. An area study based on personally conducted travels and on literature]
Leipzig: K.F. Köhler 1945. 8vo, 542pp., ill., maps, bibliography, index; Gompertz 676; Domschke/Goossmann 672

0263 1946 ENG 1304
David, F.D. Our Neighbors, the Koreans

World Horizon Series, NY: Field Afar Press 1946. 12mo, 90pp.

0264   1946   ENG 715 (2 ex.)
Nelson, M. Frederick. Korea and the Old Orders in Eastterb Asia
Baton Rouge: Louisiana State Univ., 1946. 8vo, 326pp., appendices, bibliography, index

0265   1950   GER 12 (2 ex.)
Lautensach, Hermann. Korea : Land - Volk - Schicksal [Korea : Land - People - Fate]
Stuttgart: Köhler 1950. large 8vo, 136pp., ill., maps

0266   1950   ENG 384 (4 ex.)
McCune, George M. Korea Today
Cambridge MA: Harvard Univ. Press 1950. 8vo, xxi, 372pp., maps, bibliography, index

IV.g) TRAVEL GUIDES

IV.g.1) GENERAL

Note : Landscape & Sight Illustration Publications are listed here, too

0267   1920   ENG 918 s.1
Ruddick, Lilian S. Travel Tips on Travel Tips. Containing seventeen hundred interesting, classified questions on travel, answered in the Burton Holmes travelogues
Chicago: the Burton Holmes Travelogue Bureau, 1920. 8vo, 108+61 pp.; contents: on Japan and Korea pp.74-84

0268   c. 1933   ENG 887
Gibbs, Sir Philip. Wonders of the World. A popular and authentic account of the marvels of nature and of men as they exist to-day
n.pl. : Hutchinson & Co., n.d. (c. 1933). 8vo, 744pp., ill., index; contents: p.439 on Korea

0269   1936   ENG 546e7
Lorenz, D.E. The Round the World Traveller : a Complete Summary of

Practical Information
NY: Fleming H. Revell, 7th revised edition 1936. 12mo, 490pp., ill., maps, index,

IV.g.2) FAR EAST

0270   1882   ENG 789e2
Meyer, L.C. Far Off. Asia described with anecdotes and illustrations
London: Hatchards, new revised edition 1882. 16mo, 552pp., ill,, map; contents: not on Korea

0271   1890   ENG 787e2
Meyer, L.C. Far Off. Asia described with anecdotes and illustrations
London: Hatchards, new revised edition 1890. 16mo, 562pp., ill,, map; contents: not on Korea

0272   1900   ENG 788e2
Meyer, L.C. Far Off. Asia described with anecdotes and illustrations
London : Hatchards, new revised edition 1900. 16mo, 563pp., ill,, map; contents: on Korea pp.562-563

0273   1900   FRE 214
Scidmore, Eliza Ruhamah. Par L'Occident a L'Extreme Orient. Guide des principales villes de la Chine et du Japon avec une notice sur la Coree [From the West to the Far East. A guide to the major cities of China and Japan, with a note on Korea]
n.pl., La Compagnie du Chemin de Fer Pacifique Canadien, 1900. 8vo, 74pp., maps

0274   1911   ENG 46 (2 ex.)
Elias, Frank. Peeps at many lands : The Far East : China, Korea & Japan
London: Adam and Charles Black 1911. 8vo, viii, 213pp., ill.; contents: map, on Korea pp.85-140; Gompertz 456

0275   1912   ENG 89
Madrolle's Guide Books. Northern China, the Valley of the Blue River, Korea
Paris: Hachette, 1912. 16mo, 471pp., ill., maps, index

0276   1913   FRE 26e2
Guides Madrolle. Chine du Nord et Vallee du Fleuve Bleu, Coree [Madrolle Guidebooks : North China, Blue River Valley, Korea]

Paris: Hachette 1913. 12mo, 12, xxvii, 454pp., ads, ill., maps; Gompertz 743 (on 1904)

0277   1913   ENG 92:1/3 (4 ex.)
The Imperial Japanese Government Railways. An official guide to Eastern Asia : Trans-continental connections between Europe and Asia

Tokyo: The Imperial Japanese Government Railways, 1913-1914, 16mo, 3 vols., vol.1 : Manchuria & Chosen, xii, lxxxvi, 350pp., ill., maps, index. vol.2 : South western Japan, xii, cciv, 370pp., ill., maps, index; vol.3 : North-Eastern Japan, x, 488 pp., ill., maps, index; Gompertz 750

0278   1916   FRE 27e2
Guides Madrolle. Chine du Sud, Java, Japon : Presqu'ile Malaise, Siam, Indochine, Philippines, Ports Americaines [Madrolle Guidebooks : South China, Java, Japan, the Malayan Peninsula, Siam, Indochina, the Philippines, the American ports]

Paris: Hachette 1916. 12mo, 12, xxvii, cxxxvi, 520pp., ads, bibliography, ill., maps

0279   1920   ENG 197e4
Cook, Thomas (publisher). Peking, North China, South Manchuria and Korea

London: Thomas Cook and Son, 1920. 12mo, 161pp., xxiv pp., ads, ill., maps, index

0280   1924   ENG 197e5
Cook, Thomas (publisher). Cook's Guide to Peking, North China, South Manchuria and Korea

London: Thomas Cook and Son, 1924. 12mo, 143pp., ads, maps, ill., index

0281   1928   ENG 757
Takimoto, J. Guide Book to Japan, Manchuria, Korea & China

Tokyo: Interntional Tourist Bureau, 1928. 16mo, 298pp., ill., map. The author was an official with the South Manchurian Railway Co.

0282   1930   GER 43 (2 ex.)
Trautz, F.M. Orbis Terrarum. Japan, Korea und Formosa. Landschaft, Baukunst, Volksleben [Orbis Terrarum. Japan, Korea, Formosa, landscape, architecture, life of the people]

Berlin: Atlantis 1930. 4to, 256pp., ill.; Gompertz 585; Domschke/Goossmann 1022

0283   c.1930   ENG 345 (2 ex.)
Trautz, F.M. Orbis Terrarum. Japan, Korea and Formosa. The Landscape,

Architecture, Life of the People.
NY: Westermann n.d. (c.1930). 4to, xxx, 256pp., ill., translated from the German; Gompertz 610, has 1933

0284　　　　　　　　　　　　　　1931　　　GER 126
Hürlimann, Martin. Die Wunder Asiens. ein Bilderwerk vom Grossen Erdteil [The Wonders of Asia, a Pictorial Book on the Great Continent]
Berlin: Axel Juncker 1931. folio, 240pp., ill.; contents: on Korea pp.226-232

0285　　　　　　　　　　　　　　1935　　　ENG 1427
Nyberg, Ragnar, Zacke, Alvar. On the Dragon Seas. A sailor's adventure in the Far East
London: Hurst & Blackett 1935, 16mo, 287pp., translated from the Swedish by Edith M. Nielsen

0286　　　　　　　　　　　　　　n.d.　　　FRE 179
Neziere, Joseph de la. L'Extreme Orient en Images. Siberie, Chine, Coree, Japon [The Far East in Images. Siberia, China, Korea, Japan]
Paris: Felix Juven, no date. 4to, 56pp., ill. (no page numbering)

0287　　　　　　　　　　　　　　n.d.　　　ENG 868
Bishop, Isabella L. Views in the Far East
Tokyo: S. Kajima, n.d., oblong 8vo, 60pp., (only ill.)

IV.g.3) CHINA

0288　　　　　　　　　　　　　　1667　　　LAT 11
Kircheri, Athanasii O.S.J. China monumentis qua sacris qua profanis, nec non variis, naturae & artis spectaculis, aliarumque rerum memorabilium argumentis illustrata, auspiciis Leopoldi Primi. [Sacred and Profane Monuments of China, as well as various spectacular things both natural and artistic, and other memorabilia illustrated by words (the publication being) sponsored by (Holy Roman Emperor) Leopold I.]
Amstelodami (Amsterdam): Joannem Janssonius, 1667 (MDCLXVII). folio, 237, [11] pp., ill., index

0289　　　　　　　　　　　　　　1669　　　ENG 1439t
Nieuhof, Jan. An Embassy of the East India Company of the United Provinces

to the Grand Tartar Cham, Emperor of China, trsl. by John Ogilby.
Reprint: Menston: Scolar Press, (1669) n.d., folio, 327, 106pp., ill.

0290　　　　　　　　　　　　　　1843　　　　FRE 282
Allom, Thomas (illustrator). L'Empire Chinois (= China illustrated) [The Chinese Empire]
London and Paris: Fisher 1843-1845, 4to, 4 vols. bound in 2, vols.1-2 68, 76pp., ill., vol.3-4 74, 73pp., ill., maps, index; text by Clement Pelle

0291　　　　　　　　　　　　　　1858　　　　ENG 180
Allom, Thomas, The Chinese Empire Illustrated / China Illustrated : Habits & C. of that ancient and exclusive nation.
London / NY: The London Printing and Publishing Co.,[1858-1859]. 4to, 2 vols., Spine Title : The Chinese Empire. vol.1: xii, 184pp., plates, map, vol.2 : 140pp., plates.

0292　　　　　　　　　　　　　　1877　　ENG 205 (3 ex.)
Eden, Charles H. China : historical and descriptive. With an appendix on Corea.
London: Marcus Ward 1877. 12mo, 334, 24pp., ill., map, index; contents: Corea : its institutions and social conditions, pp.281-332, Gompertz 121

0293　　　　　　　　　　　　　　1880　　　　ENG 205e2
Eden, Charles H. China : historical and descriptive. With an appendix on Corea.
London: Marcus Ward 1880. 12mo, 334pp., ill., map, index; contents: Corea : its institutions and social conditions, pp.281-332, Gompertz 121

0294　　　　　　　　　　　　　　1901　　　　ENG 414
Browne, George Waldo. China : the Country and its People, with an introduction by the Hon. John D. Long
Boston: Dana Estes 1901. large 8vo, xiii, 477pp.

0295　　　　　　　　　　n.d. (after 1912)　　ENG 1247e2
Crow, Carl. The Travelers' Handbook for China
Shanghai: Kelly & Walsh, n.d. (after 1912). 12mo, maps, ill., 241pp., ads; contents: on Korea pp.35, 44-45

0296　　　　　　　　　　　　　　1920　　　　ENG 1252e2
Darwent, C.E. Shanghai : A Handbook for Travellers and Residents of the

Chief Objects of Interest in and around the Foreign Settlements and Native City
Shanghai: Kelly & Walsh, 1920. 8vo, xvi, 191, xiii pp., index; contents: not on Korea

0297   1922   ENG 782e2

Bredon, Juliet. Peking : a historical and intimate description of its chief places of interest
Shanghai etc.: Kelly & Walsh, second revised and enlarged edition 1922. 8vo, x, 524pp., ill., maps, plans, index

IV.g.4) MANCHURIA

0298   1919   ENG 807

Bank of Chosen. Pictorial Chosen and Manchuria
Seoul: Bank of Chosen, 1919. 4to, 316pp., ill., map

0299   1923   ENG 670

Konishio, Y. Port of Dairen
Dairen: South Manchurian Railway Co., 1923. large 8vo, 48pp., plates

0300   n.d. (c.1936)   ENG 1160

Ryojun (Port Arthur)
n.pl.: South Manchuria Railway Co., n.d. (c.1936). 12mo, 21pp., ill.

IV.g.5) JAPAN

0301   1899   ENG 547e5

Chamberlain, Basil Hall. A Handbook for Travellers in Japan
London: John Murray, 5th edition, 1899. 12mo, ix, 577, 54pp., ill., maps

0302   1907   ENG 547e8

Chamberlain, Basil Hall & Mason, W.B. A Handbook for Travellers in Japan, including the whole Empire from Saghalien to Formosa
London: John Murray 1907. 12mo, ix, 570pp., ads, ill., maps, Spine Title : Murray's Hand-book Japan.

0303　　　　　　　　　　　　　　　1914　　　ENG 93
Terry, T. Philip. Terry's Japanese Empire, including Korea and Formosa, with chapters on Manchuria, the Trans-Siberian Railway, and the chief ocean routes to Japan
London: Constable and Co., 1914. 16mo, cclxxii, 799pp., ads, ill., maps, index; contents: on Korea pp.693-773; Gompertz 1914

0304　　　　　　　　　　　　　　　1915　　　FRE 34 (2 ex.)
Challaye, Felicien. Le Japon illustre [Japan illustrated]
Paris: Larousse 1915. 4to, 304pp., ill.

0305　　　　　　　　　　　　　　　1915　　　ENG 954
Japan Hotel Association. Hotels in Japan
Tokyo: Japan Hotel Association, 1915. 12mo, 30pp., ill.

0306　　　　　　　　　　　　　　　1919　　　ENG 515
Japan Hotel Association. Japan. Tourist's Hand Book
Tokyo: Japan Hotel Asociation c/o Traffic Department, Imperial Government Railways, 1919. 12mo, 118pp., ill., map

0307　　　　　　　　　　　　　　　1922　　　ENG 329
Japanese Government Railways. The Hot Springs of Japan (and the Principal Cold Springs) including Chosen, Taiwan, South Manchuria
Tokyo : Japanese Government Railways 1922. 12mo, xviii, 486, 2pp., ill., map; Gompertz 754

0308　　　　　　　　　　　　　　　1923　　　FRE 248
Chemins de Fer de l'Etat Japonais. Livret-Guide du Japon 1923 [Guide book to Japan 1923]
Tokyo: Chemins de Fer de l'Etat Japonais, 1923. 12mo,, 106pp., ill., map

0309　　　　　　　　　　　　　n.d. (1926)　　ENG 960
Japan Government Railways. Japan and South Manchuria
Tokyo: Tappan n.d. (1926). oblong 8vo, 72 columns, ads, ill.

0310　　　　　　　　　　　　　　　1930　　　ENG 330e2
Terry, T. Philip. Terry's Guide to the Japanese Empire, including Korea and Formosa, with chapters on Manchuria, the Trans-Siberian Railway, and the

chief Ocean Routes to Japan
Boston: Houghton 1930. 12mo, 1080pp., ill., maps, ads

0311 n.d. (1933) ENG 554 (2 ex.)
Japanese Government Railways. Japan
Tokyo: Japanese Government Railways, n.d. (1933). large 8vo (52pp.), ill., map

0312 1934 ENG 380
Akimoto, Shunkichi. The Lure of Japan
Tokyo: Hokuseido 1934. 8vo, 371pp., ill., index

0313 1935 ENG 698
Japanese Government Railways. Pocket Guide to Japan : with Special Reference to Japanese Customs, History, Industry, Education, Art, Accomplishments, Amusements etc.
Tokyo: Board of Tourist Industry, 1935. 12mo, xv, 182pp., ill., maps, index

0314 1936 FRE 133
Direction Generale du Tourisme, Chemins de Fer du Gouvernement Japonais, Tokyo. Petit Guide du Japon. Comprenent une Description Speciale des Coutumes, de l'Histoire, de l'Industrie, de l'Instruction .. 1936 [Pocket Guide to Japan, containing a special description of the customs, history, industry, education .. 1936]
Tokyo: Direction Generale du Tourisme, 1936. 12mo, 199pp., ill., map

IV.g.6) KOREA

0315 1913 FRE 241
Courant, Maurice. Coree [Madrolle Guidebooks : Korea]
Paris: Hachette 1913. 12mo, pp.397-442, ads, ill., map (= FRE 26e2 pp.397-442); Gompertz 744 (on 1904)

0316 1914 ENG 827
Imagawa, Ryoho Uichiro. Complete Work of the Kongo-san (The diamond mountains), Korea

Seoul, no publisher 1914. oblong small folio, 3, 36pp., ill., text in English and Japanese

0317 — 1917 — ENG 1429
Japan Tourist Bureau. Guide to Keijyo (Seoul), Chosen

n.pl.: Japan Tourist Bureau, 1917. 12mo, illustrated, folded, unpaginated

0318 — 1920 — ENG 1411
South Manchuria Railway Co. Chosen

Keijo (Seoul): Keijo Office, South Manchurian Railway Co., 1920. small 8vo, folded, 10pp.

0319 — 1920 — ENG 1480
Government General of Chosen. Illustrated Chosen

Seoul: Government-General of Chosen 1920. large 8vo, 40 plates

0320 — n.d. [1920] — ENG 668
Government General of Chosen. Chosen in Picture

Seoul: Government-General of Chosen, [1920]. large 8vo, 68pp., 58 plates

0321 — 1920 — ENG 937 (2 ex.)
Newman, E.M. Korea and its People

In The Mentor, vol.8 no.5, April 15 1920. Dept. of History and Travel, 1920. 8vo, ill., 12pp. + 6 full page loose leaf commented photos

0322 — 1927 — ENG 823
Administrative Office of Chosen. Trip in Chosen

Wakayama City: Department of Railways, 1927. oblong small 4to album, not paginated, ill., text in Japanese and English

0323 — 1937 — ENG 1409
Japan Tourist Bureau. Touring Chosen & Manchoukuo

n.pl.: Japan Tourist Bureau 1937. 12mo, 40pp., ill.

0324 — 1945 — ENG 1352
Allied Geographical Section. Kyongsong - Keijo - Seoul

n.pl.: Allied Geographical Section 1945. 43pp., ill., maps

0325 — 1948 — ENG 701
Troop Information & Education Section, Headquarters XXIV Corps. Korea

Seoul: Headquarters XXIV Corps, 1948. 8vo, xii., 219pp., ill. With an introduction by Lt. General John L. Hodge

0326   1950   ENG 1335
Armed Forces Information & Education Division. A Pocket Guide to Korea
n.pl.: Armed Forces Information & Education Division 1950. 16mo, ill., 48pp.

0327   n.d.   ENG 1157
Chosen Hotel. Guide to Hotel, Keijo, Korea
Keijo (Seoul): Chosen Hotel, n.d., illustrated, 60pp., oblong 8vo

IV.h) TRAVELOGUES

IV.h.1) TRAVELOGUE COLLECTIONS

0328   GER 132
Illustriertes Jahrbuch der Weltreisen [Illustrated Yearbook on World Travels]
edited by Wilh. Berdrow, Leipzig & Wien: Karl Prochaska; 4to, in stock vols.1904, 1905, 1907, 1908

0329   1715   FRE 260:1/3, 4.2
Bernard, Jean Frederic. Recueil de Voyages au Nord contenant divers Memoires tres utiles au Commerce & a la Navigation [Collection of Voyages to the North containing a number of very useful Reports on Commerce and Navigation]
Amsterdam: J.F. Bernard, MDCCXV-MDCCXVIII (1715-1718), 4 vols. out of 9, 12mo, vol.1 : 1715, 200pp., ill., map; vol.2 : 1715, 298pp., plates, map, vol.3 : 1745, 342pp., ill., map, vol.4 pt.2, 1718, 248pp., ill., map; contents: on Korea : vol.4 pt.2 pp.1-82 (Hamel, translated from the Dutch), pp.83-96 Lettre sur le Ginseng, by Pere Jartoux, O.S.J., Procureur Generale des Missions des Indes & de la Chine, pp.301-340 (Voyage de l'Empereur de la Chine dans la Tartarie Orientale & Occidentale par P. Verbiest O.S.J.), vol.3 pp.32-43 (Monsr. de l'ile sur le Japon), pp.44-56 (Relation de la Decouverte de Jesso, trad. du Hollandois), pp.57-141 (Relation concernant le Japon par François Caron trad. du Hollandois), pp.142-179 (Relation de la Tartarie Orientale par le P. Martini), pp.180-256 Additions & Memoires touchant le Japon; Gompertz 42

0330   1744   ENG 1285
Churchill's Voyages
London: Henry Lintot and John Osborn, 3rd edition, folio, 6 volumes; vol.1 MDCCXLIV (1744), 668pp., vol.2 MDCCXLIV (1744), 743pp., vol.3 MDCCXLV (1745), 793pp., vol.4 MDCCXLV (1745), 780pp., vol.5 MDCCXLVI (1746), 708pp., vol.6 MDCCCLVI (1746), 824pp. + index to all 6 volumes + publisher's preface; contents: on Korea vol.4 pp.719-742 (Hamel); Gompertz 41

0331   1745   ENG 570

Astley, Thomas (compiler). A New General Collection of Voyages and Travels : Consisting of the most Esteemed Relations, which have been hitherto published in any language;

London: Thomas Astley, MDCCXLV (1745). 4 vols., small 4to, Brief Title : Astley's Collection of Voyages, vol.1 : xi, 680pp., ill., maps, vol.2 : viii, 732pp., ill., maps, vol.3 : vi, 605pp., ill., maps, vol.4 : vii, 751pp., ill., maps, index; contents: on Korea : article p.319-347. "Geographical Observations and History of Korea, by Jean-Baptiste Regis, Jesuit"; Gompertz 22

0332   1749   FRE 261

Exiles, Antoine François Prevost d' Histoire Generale des Voyages [General History of Travels]

Paris: Didot 1748-1749. 4to, vol.5, 1748, viii, 564pp., maps, ill., vol.6, 1748 (2 ex.), x, 608pp., maps, ill.; 24 (1749); Gompertz 23

0333   1750   GER 117 : 6, 7. 11

Schwabe, J.J. et al. Allgemeine Historie der Reisen zu Wasser und Lande : oder Sammlung aller Reisebeschreibungen. Durch eine Gesellschaft Gelehrter Männer im Englischen zusammengetragen, ins Deutsche übersetzt [General History of Voyages on Water and on Land, or Collection of All Voyage Descriptions compiled by a Society of Learned Men in the English, translated into German]

Leipzig: Arkstee und Merkus, 1750-1753. 4to vol.6 : 608pp., ill., 1750, vol.7 : 728pp., ill., 1750, vol.11 : 712pp., ill., 1753; contents: on Korea : pp.555-608; Gompertz 24; Domschke/Goossmann 937

0334   1754   DEN 2:9

Anonymous. Samling af alle Reisebeskrivelser [collection of all travelogues]

Kiøbenhavn (Copenhague): no publisher 1754. 8vo, 508pp., translated from the French; contents: on Korea pp.340-404, contains an edition of Hamel pp.363-404

0335   1796   ENG 803 : 2, 5, 9, 11-13, 15

Mavor, William. Historical Account of the Most Celebrated Voyages, Travels, and Discoveries, from the Time of Columbus to the Present Period

London: E. Newbery, 1796-1797. 16mo, vol.II : 1796, 290pp., vol.V : 1796, 284pp., vol.IX : 1797, 311pp., vol.XI : 1797, 267pp., vol.XII : 1797, 285pp., vol.XIII : 1797, 302pp., vol.XV : 1797, 284pp.; contents: on Korea : vol.12 pp.157-242, Journey of John Bell Esq. from St. Petersburgh to Pekin with an Embassy from his Imperial Majesty, Peter the Great, to Kambi, Emperor of China; vol.15 pp.181-284, Travels in Japan and other countries, by Charles Peter Thunberg, vol.9 pp.229-311 Historical

Narrative on Lord MacArtney's Embassy to China, vol.11 pp.221-267, Travels in China, by the Jesuits le Compte and du Halde

0336 1805 GER 125

Sprengel, M.G. and Ehrmann, Theophil Friedrich (ed.). Kapt. Will. Rob. Broughton's Entdeckungsreise in das Nördliche Stille Meer in den Jahren 1795, 1796, 1797 und 1798 [Captain Will. Rob. Broughton's Expedition to the Northern Pacific in the Years 1795, 1796, 1797 and 1798]. in the series: Bibliothek der Neuesten und Wichtigten Reisebeschreibungen zur Erweiterung der Erdkunde. [Library of the Newest and Most Important Voyages to Expand the Knowledge of Geography]

Weimar: F(ürstlich) S(ächsisches) Landes-Industrie-Comptoir, 1805. small 8vo, xx, 352, 92, 64pp., map, translated from the English by Theophil Friedrich von Ehrmann, also contains S. Papon's Reise in das Departement der Seealpen [S. Papon's travel into the Departement Alpes Maritimes] (1805) and J.R., Reise nach der Insel Martinique [J.R., Journey to the Island of Martinique]

0337 1826 FRE 187

Dufay, Jules. Histoire des Voyages dans cette Partie du Monde. Guerres - Moeurs - Produits - Anecdotes. [History of Travels to those Parts of the World. Wars - Customs - Products - Anecdotes] : l'Asie [Asia]. in the series: Bibliotheque Universelle des Voyages [Universal Library of Travels].

Paris: de Courval, 3 vols., 1826. 12mo, ill.

0338 1829 FRE 250 : 5, 6, 8, 9

Briand, P.C. Les Jeunes Voyageurs en Asie [The Young Voyagers in Asia]

Paris: Hivert 1829. 16mo, vol.5 213pp., vol.6 246pp., vol.8 243pp., vol.9 246pp.; contents: on Korea vol.9 pp.119-137

0339 1839 FRE 181

Eyries, J.B. Voyage Pittoresque en Asie et en Afrique. Resume Generale des Voyages Anciens et Modernes [Voyage in Asia and Africa. General Summary of Ancient and Modern Voyages]

Paris: Fume et Cie., 1839 (MDCCCXXXIX). small 4to, 426, 160pp., ill., maps, indices; contents: on Korea pp.131-146

0340 1868 DEN 3

Illustreret Tidskift før de Nyeste Reisebeskrivelser [Illustrated Magazine

Featuring the Newest Travelogues]
Kiøbenhavn : Philipsens 1868. 4to, 208pp.

0341　　　　　　　　　　　　　　　　　　　1905　　　ENG 1021
Purchas, Samuel. Hakluytus Posthumus, or Purchas His Pilgrimes. Contayning a History of the World and Sea Voyages and Lande Travells by Englishmen and others

Vol.I : Glasgow: James MacLelose 1905, 8vo, 504pp., ill., maps (first edition 1625), Vol.II : 1905, 8vo, 548pp., Vol.III : 1905, 8vo, 570pp., Vol.IV : 1905, 8vo, 572pp., Vol.V : 1905, 8vo, 529pp., Vol.VI : 1905, 8vo, 542pp., Vol.VII : 1905, 8vo, 570pp., Vol.VIII : 1905, 8vo, 593pp., Vol.IX : 1905, 8vo, 570pp., Vol.X : 1905, 8vo, 525pp., Vol.XI : 1905, 8vo, 649pp., Vol.XII : 1905, 8vo, 631pp., Vol.XIII : 1905, 8vo, 558pp., Vol.XIV : 1905, 8vo, 592pp., Vol.XV : 1905, 8vo, 568pp., Vol.XVI : 1905, 8vo, 579pp., Vol.XVII : 1905, 8vo, 550pp., Vol.XVIII : 1905, 8vo, 540pp., Vol.XIX : 1905, 8vo, 549pp., Vol.XX : 1905, 8vo, 414pp., index; contents: on Korea : Vol.III p.554 (Richard Cocks 1614), Vol.XII pp.260, 263, 308 (L. Frois); Gompertz 15 note

0342　　　　　　　　　　　　　　　　　　　1920　　　ENG 918
Burton Holmes' Travelogues

Chicago etc.: The Travelogue Bureau, 1920. 8vo, 14 vols., ill. Vol.1 Morocco, 1920, vol.2 Algeria, Southern Spain, 1920, vol.3 Greece, 1920, vol.4 Egypt, Southern Italy, Switzerland, 1920, vol.5 Paris, Oberammergau, Corsica, 1920, vol.6 London, Paris, Berlin, 1920, vol.7 Norway, Sweden, Denmark, 1920, vol.8 St. Petersburg, Moscow, Transiberian Railroad, 1920, vol.9 Down the Amur, Peking, 1920, vol.10 Seoul, the Capital of Korea (pp.1-112), Japan, 1920, vol.11 Hawaii, Edge of China 1920, vol.12 Yellowstone, Grand Canyon, 1920, vol.13 Rio de Janeiro & Brazil, Buenos Aires, Iguassu, 1920, vol.14 England, Scotland, Ireland, 1920, Supplment : Travel Tips on Travel Trips 1920

IV.h.2) WORLDWIDE

0343　　　　　　　　　　　　　　　　　　　1701　　　ITA 6
Carletti, Francesco. Ragionamento di Francesco Carletti Fiorentino sopra le Cose de la Vedute ne suoi Viaggi si dell' Inde Occidentali, e Orientali come d'altri Paesi [Report of the Florentine Francesco Carletti about Maters related to his Vessel and his Travels to the West and East Indies as well as to Other Countries]

Firenze: Giuseppe Manni, 1701. 16mo, 2 parts in 1, 166, 395pp., index at front; contents: on Korea pp.36-411 Gompertz 33

0344   1834   ENG 1267

Efendi, Evliya (= Evilya Çelebi). Narrative of Travels in Europe, Asia and Africa in the 17th Century, translated from the Turkish by Joseph von Hammer

London: Johnson, reprint of the 1834 edition, 1968. 4to, 196, 251, 244pp, contents: not on Korea

0345   1859   ENG 143

Anonymous. Voyages round the World.

NY: Harper & Brothers 1859. 16mo, ill., 401pp., index; contents: ch.v pp.231-307 : Krusenstern, Kotzebue and Lütke; ch.vi pp.308-362 : Hall, Ruschenberger and Fitzroy; one Corea entry in index

0346   1871   ENG 885e5

Pumpelly, Raphael. Across America and Asia. Notes of a Five Years' Journey around the World, and of Residence in Arizona, Japan and China.

N.Y.: Leypoldt & Holt, 5th revised edition, 1871. 8vo, xvi, 454pp., maps; contents : on Korea (Korean embassy to Peking) pp.303-304 (2 ill.)

0347   1879   ENG 922

Young, John Russell. Around the World with General Grant. A narrative of the visit of General U.S. Grant, Ex-President of the United States, to various countries in Europe, Asia and Africa in 1872, 1878 and 1879 to which are added certain conversations with General Grant on questions connected with American politics and history.

NY: The American News Co., 1879. Vol.I 4to, 631pp., ill., maps, Vol.II 4to, 631pp.; contents: not on Korea, although the map in the book indicates otherwise (Chefoo mistakenly placed in Korea)

0348   1891   ENG 151

Arnold, Sir Edwin. Seas and Lands. Reprinted by permission of the proprietors of the Daily Telegraph from letters published under the title "By Sea and Land"

NY: Longman, Green 1891. 8vo, x, 530pp., ill., index; contents: mostly on Japan, Korea not listed in index

0349   1897   GER 191

Schanz, Moritz. Ein Zug nach Osten [An Eastward Journey]

Vol.1 : Reisebilder aus Indien, Birma, Ceylon, Straits Settlements, Java, Siam [Travel Images from India, Burma, Ceylon, Straits Settlements, Java, Siam]

Vol.2 : Reisebilder aus China, Korea, Ostsibirien, Japan, Alaska und Canada [Travel Images from China, Korea, Eastern Siberia, Japan, Alaska and Canada]
Hamburg: W. Manke & Söhne 1897. 2 vols., 8vo, 423, 424pp.; Gompertz 283; Domschke/Goossmann 899

0350   1903   ENG 415
Mar, Walter del. Around the World through Japan
London: Adam & Charles Black 1903. 8vo, xvii, 435pp., ill., index; Gompertz 347

0351   1904   ENG 415e2
Mar, Walter del. Around the World through Japan
London: Adam & Charles Black (1903) 2nd edition 1904. 8vo, xvii, 435pp., ill., index; Gompertz 347

0352   1907   ENG 1394
Bryan, William Jennings. The Old World and Its Ways. Describing a tour around the world and journey through Europe
St. Louis: Thompson 1907; contents: ch.VIII pp.90-100 on Korea

0353   c.1909   FRE 7
Lannelongue, O.M. Un Tour du Monde (Octobre 1908-Juillet 1909) [A World Tour, October 1908-July 1909]
Paris: Larousse n.d. (c.1909). 8vo, 350pp., ill.; contents: pp.257-262 : eight hours in Korea

0354   1911   ENG 978e3
Abraham, J. Johnston. The Surgeon's Log. Being impressions of the Far East
London: Chapman & Hull, 3rd ed., 1911. 8vo, ix, 337pp., ill.

0355   1911   ENG 1368
Morgan, R.C. Glimpses of Four Continents, being an Account of the Travels of Richard Cope Morgan
London: Morgan & Scott 1911. 8vo, xi, 388pp., ill.

0356   1911   ENG 275
Hart, Albert Bushnell. The Obvious Orient
12mo, 369pp., index; contents : numerous Korea entries

0357   c.1911   ENG 440
Fremantle, Francis. A Traveller's Study of Health and Empire
London: John Cuseley, n.d. (c.1911). 8vo, xii, 369pp., ill.

0358 (1912) ENG 472 (2 ex.)
Hedin, Sven. From Pole to Pole. A Book for Young People
London: MacMillan (1912), 1st ex. 1914, 2nd ex. 1928. 8vo, xv, 407pp., ill., maps, translated from the Swedish, abridged; contents: on Korea pp.197-199

0359 1913 ENG 904
Wheeler, W.W. The Other Side of the Earth
no place, no publisher, 1913. 8vo, 208pp., ill.; contents: on Korea pp.98-111

0360 1914 ENG 312 (2 ex.)
Ridger, A. Loton. A Wanderer's Trail : being a Faithful Record of Travel in many Lands
NY: Henry Holt Co. 1914. 8vo, 403pp., ill., index; contents: on Korea pp.152-169

0361 n.d. (bef.1914) ENG 1095
Mitton, G.E. Round the Wonderful World
London: T.C. & E.C. Jack, n.d. (before 1914). 8vo, ill., 398pp., index; contents: not on Korea

0362 1946 FRE 142
Farrere, Claude, et O.D. de S. La Garde aux Portes de l'Asie. Journal de Bord [The Guard of the Ports of Asia. A Board Diary]
Lyon: Gutenberg 1946. 12mo, 137pp.; contents: on naval actions in the Eastern Mediterranean 1915, not on Korea

0363 1920 GER 101e2
Berger, A. Aus einem verschlossenen Paradies [From a Paradise closed up]
Berlin: Paul Parey (1906) 1920. large 8vo, xi, 353pp., ill., map; contents: on Korea pp.62-75

0364 1921 ENG 528
Ortman, Blanche Sellers. New York to Peking
San Francisco: privately printed, 1921. 12mo, 146pp., ill.; contents: on Korea pp.82-97; Gompertz 510

0365 1921 ENG 536
Stidger, William L. Flash-Lights from the Seven Seas
NY: Doran [1921]. 12mo, 214pp., ill., introduction by Bishop Francis J. McDonnell

0366 1921 ENG 314
Fletcher, Alfred C.B. From Job to Job around the World

NY: Dodd, Mead & Co. (1916) 1921. 8vo, vi, 307 pp., ill.; contents: on Korea pp.67ff

0367 1921 ENG 1367
Davidson, Norman J. Modern Travel. A Record of Exploration, Travel, Adventure & Sport in all Parts of the World during the Last Forty Years, Derived from Personal Accounts of the Travellers
London: Seeley, Service & Co. 1921. 8vo, 320pp., ill., index; contents: not on Korea

0368 1922 ENG 1131 (2 ex.)
MacKenzie, F.A. Russia before Dawn
London: T. Fisher Unwin, 1922. 8vo, 288pp., ill., contents: on Korea p.195

0369 1923 GER 48
Büchler, E. Rund um die Erde. Erlebtes aus Amerika, Japan, Korea, China, Indien und Arabien [Around the World. Adventures from America, Japan Korea, China, India and Arabia]
Bern: E. Büchler & Co., 1923. small 8vo, 303pp., ill.; contents: on Korea pp.173-180; Gompertz 545 (on 1925); Domschke/Goossmann 145

0370 1923 ENG 1017
Northcliffe, Alfred Viscount. My Journey round the World (16. 7. 1921-26. 2. 1922), edited by Cecil & St. John Harmsworth
Philadelphia: Lippincott 1923. 8vo, 326pp., ill., map, index; contents: on Korea chapter xvi, pp.121-131

0371 1924 ENG 1007
Savage-Landor, A. Henry. Everywhere. The Memoirs of an Explorer.
London: T. Fisher Unwin 1924. 8vo, 526pp., ill., map, index; contents: on Korea pp.96-106; (memories from 1890)

0372 1924 ENG 1461
Dix, Dorothy. My Trip around the World
Philadelphia: Penn Publishing 1924. 8vo, 311pp., ill.; contents: chapter VIII : Quaint Little Korea pp.104-116

0373 1924 SPA 7
Ibanez, Vicente Blasco. La vuelta al mundo de un novelista [Trip around the World by a Novelist]

Valencia: Prometeo 1924. 12mo, 3 vols., 345, 345, 374pp.; contents: on Corea vol.1 pp.321-335

0374　　　　　　　　　　　　　　1925　　　ENG 1109
Benson, Stella. The Little World
London: MacMillan 1925. 12mo, 293pp., no index

0375　　　　　　　　　　　　　　1925　　　ENG 875e2
Butler, Frank Hedges. Round the World
London: T. Fisher Unwin (1924), 2nd ed. 1925. 8vo, 269pp., ill., index; contents: on Korea pp.62-67

0376　　　　　　　　　　　　　　1925　　　ENG 1117
Keyserling, Count Hermann. The Travel Diary of a Philosopher
London: Jonathan Cape, 2 vols., 1925. 8vo, ill., 336, 405pp., philosophical subject index in vol.2. Translated from the German by J. Holroyd Reese; contents: not on Korea

0377　　　　　　　　　　　　　　1926　　　ENG 325
Wells, Linton. Around the World in Twenty-Eight Days
Boston & New York: Houghton Mifflin (Riverside), 1926. 8vo, xxiv, 276pp., ill., with an introduction by Vilhjalmur Stefansson

0378　　　　　　　　　　　　　　1927　　　ENG 146
Parlette, Ralph. A Globegadder's Diary
Chicago: Parlotte-Padget 1927. 8vo, xx, 466pp., ill.; contents: on Korea pp.370ff

0379　　　　　　　　　　　　　　1927　　　GER 128
Bamberger, Gustav. Circum Mundum. Reiseschilderungen einer Autofahrt rund um die Erde [Around the World. Description of a Voyage around the World by Car]
Leipzig: Gressner & Schramm, n.d. (1927). 8vo, 217pp., ill.

0380　　　　　　　　　　　　　　1928　　　FRE 140 : 1/3
Ibanez, V. Blasco. Le Voyage d'un Romancier autour du Monde [The Voyage of a Novelist around the World]
Paris: Flammarion 1928. 12mo, 3 vols., vol.1 : 390pp., vol.2 : 392pp., vol.3 : 415pp., translated from the Spanish by Renee Lafont; contents: Korea in vol.1

0381　　　　　　　　　　　　　　1929　　　ENG 323
Benson, Stella. Worlds within Worlds.

Myongji-LG Korean Studies Library

NY and London: Harper & Brothers 1929. 8vo, 308pp., ill.; contents: on Korea pp.238ff

0382　　　　　　　　　　　　　　　　1929　ENG 321　(2 ex.)

Andrews, Roy Chapman. Ends of the Earth

NY: National Travel Club 1929. 8vo, 365pp., ill., contents: on Korea pp.147-190

0383　　　　　　　　　　　　　　　　1930　　　FRE 102

Chable, Jacques-Edouard. Jazz, Boomerang et Kimonos, Voyage autour du monde [Jazz, boomerang and kimono. A Voyage around the world]

Geneva: Librarie Alexandre Julien, 1930. 8vo, 191pp., ill.

0384　　　　　　　　　　　　　　　　1931　　　GER 20

Katz, Richard. Schnaps, Kokain und Lamas. Kreuz und quer durch wirres Südamerika [Brandy, cocaine and lamas. Crisscrossing a chaotic South America]

Berlin: Ullstein 1931. 8vo, 253pp.; contents: not on Korea

0385　　　　　　　　　　　　　　　　1931　　　ENG 1311

Toynbee, Arnold J. A Journey to China (World Tour)

London: Constable 1931. 8vo, 345pp., maps; contents: author visited Korea briefly

0386　　　　　　　　　　　　　　　　1932　　　GER 21

Katz, Richard. Ernte. Des Bummels um die Welt 2. Folge. [Harvest. Part 2 of a Stroll around the World]

Berlin: Ullstein 1932. 8vo, 275pp., ill., map

0387　　　　　　　　　　　　　　　　1932　　　ENG 674

Murchie, Guy Jr. Men on the Horizon. Vagabond Encounters with the Orient and the Occident

Boston, MA: Houghton Mifflin Co., 1932. 8vo, 309pp., ill., map; contents: on Korea pp.218-228

0388　　　　　　　　　　　　　　n.d. (1933)　　　GER 94

Katz, Richard. Ein Bummel um die Welt. Zwei Jahre Weltreise auf Kamel und Schiene, Schiff und Auto [A Stroll around the World. Two Years of a World Trip on Camel and Rail, Ship and Car]

Leipzig: Eugen Rentsch, n.d. (c.1933). 8vo, 279pp., ill.

0389   1934   FRE 158e14
Larrouy, Maurice. Eaux Glacees. Mandchourie - Japon - Canada - Etats Unis [Frozen Waters. Manchuria - Japan - Canada - United States]
Paris: A. Fayard 1934. 12mo, 446pp.; contents: on Korea pp.131-147

0390   1935   GER 39
Katz, Richard. Heitere Tage mit braunen Menschen [Merry Days with Brown People]
Leipzig: Eugen Rentsch, 1935. 8vo, 239pp., ill., map

0391   1935   FRE 147
Chadourne, Marc. Tour de la Terre [A Tour of the World]
Paris: Plon 1935. 12mo, 2 vols., vol.1 : Extreme Orient, 248pp., vol.2 : Extreme Occident, 249pp.

0392   1935   ENG 1114e2
Katz, Richard. Loafing round the Globe. A Two Years' Tour through Africa, Asia, Australia, N.Z., Polynesia and America
London: Hutchinson 1935. translated from the German by Gerald Griffin. 8vo, 288pp., ill.

0393   1938   FRE 96
Moncharville, M. Pages Africaines et Asiatiques [African and Asiatic Pages]
Paris: A. Pedone 1938. 8vo, 303pp.

0394   1939   ENG 896
Keyes, Sir Roger. Adventures Ashore and Afloat
London: Harrap 1939. 8vo, 373pp., index, ill. Author British Admiral, took part in the Boxer Expedition. contents : on Fusan ch.xvii (pp.174ff), on Sino-Japanese War ch. xiv, pp.148ff

0395   1940   ENG 711
Forman, Harrison. Horizon Hunter : The Adventures of a Modern Marco Polo
NY: National Travel Club, 1940. 8vo, 314pp., ill., map, index

0396   1941   ITA 7
Carletti, Francesco. Giro del Mondo del buon Negriero (1594-1606) di Francesco Carletti [The World Tour of the Good Negriero* (1594-1606) by Francesco Carletti]

Myongji-LG Korean Studies Library

Milano: Valentino Bomplani, 1941. 12mo, Reprint of "Raggionamenti sopra le cose vedute ne Viaggi dell' Indie Occidentali e d'altri Paesi, 383pp., index; comments: on Korea pp.121-123; see No.0343
* name of his vessel

| 0397 | 1942 | ENG 1373 |

Beaton, Maude Hill. From Cairo to Khyber to Celebes
NY: Liveright 1942, 8vo, 261pp.. contents: ch.xviii on Korea, pp.209-218

| 0398 | 1943 | ENG 599 |

Andrews, Roy Chapman. Under a Lucky Star : a Lifetime Adventure.
NY: Blue Ribbon [1943]. small 8vo, 300pp.

| 0399 | 1946 | ENG 902 |

Atwell, William Hawley. Wandering and Wondering
Dallas:, no publisher, 1946. 8vo, 338, xiii pp., ill., index; contents: on Korea pp.31, 33, 73

| 0400 | 1946 | ENG 1115e4 |

Sherwood, Martyn. The Voyage of the Tai-Mo-Shin
London: Geoffrey Bles (1935) 4th edition 1946. 12mo, ill., 269pp., maps, no index; contents: not on Korea

| 0401 | 1947 | ENG 754 |

Bodley, R.V.C. The Quest
NY: Doubleday & Co., 1947. 8vo, 368pp.

| 0402 | 1949 | ENG 1113 |

Carrington, Dorothy (ed.). The Travellers' Eye. Compilation of historical travellers' reports
(Boston): Pilot Press 1949. 8vo, 388pp., ill., index; contents: on Korea p.199

| 0403 | n.d. | ENG 755 |

Hall, Mary Daniels. Snap Shots around the World : Vistas of many Lands
Sterling, IL: G.E. Bishop n.d. (1923 or later). 12mo, 120pp., ill.; contents: on Korea pp.53-67

IV.h.3) FAR EAST

| 0404 | 1668 | GER 123 |

Olearius, A. (ed.). Morgenländische Reisebeschreibung. Worinnen der Zustand der Ost-Indianischen Länder, Städte und der Einwohner Leben, Sitten, Handthierung und Glauben, wie auch die gefährliche Schiffahrt über das Oceanische Meer berichtet wird. ed. by A. Olearius [Oriental Travelogue. In which the condition of the East Indian lands, cities and the life of the inhabitants, their customs and religion as well as the dangerous sea travel across the ocean is reported]

Schleswig: no publisher 1668. large 8vo, 226pp., ill.; the map is missing; contents: mostly the travelogue of Johann Albrecht Mandelslo, who visited India. Part III of the account is a geography of Asia, country by country, based on written sources. On Japan pp.216-226, partly an extract of François Caron

0405   1692   ENG 813e3

The Voyages and Adventures of Ferdinand Mendez Pinto, a Portugal; during his travels for the space of one and twenty years in the Kingdoms of Ethiopia, China, Tartaria, Cauchinchina, Calaminham, Siam, Pegu, Japan, and a great part of the East Indies

London: R. Bently, J. Tonson, F. Saunders & T. Bennet, 1692. small 4to, 326pp., ill., translated into English by F.C. Gent

0406   1790   FRE 338

Lesseps, Jean Baptiste Barthelemy, Baron de. Journal Historique du Voyage de M. de Lesseps, Consul de France, employe dans l'Expedition de M. le Comte de la Perouse, en qualite d'interprete du Roi, depuis l'instant ou il a quitte les Fregates. Françoises au Port Saint Pierre & Saint Paul du Kamtschatka, jusqu'a son arrivee en France, le 17 Octobre 1788. (La Perouse expedition to Kamchatka)

Paris: Imprimerie Royale 1790. small 8vo, 2 vols., 375, 280 pp.

0407   1797   FRE 278

Milet-Mureau, M.L.A. Voyage de La Perouse autour de Monde [Expedition of la Perouse around the world]

Paris: Imprimerie de la Republique, An V (1797). 4to, 4 vols. + vol.5, folio, vol.1 : 346pp., vol.2 : 398pp., vol.3 : 422pp., vol.4 : 309pp., ill., maps, index, vol.5 : Atlas de Voyage de la Perouse, unpaged; Gompertz 52

0408   1798   FRE 33

Milet-Mureau, M.L.A. Voyage de La Perouse autour de Monde [Expedition

of la Perouse around the world]
Paris: Plassan, An VI (1798). small 8vo, 3 vols., vol.1 : lxviii, 368pp., vol.2 : 414pp., vol.3 : 316pp., appendix; Gompertz 52

0409　　　　　　　　　　　　　　　　　　1799　　　　　SWE 12
Resa omkring Jorden af Herr de la Perouse Åren 1785 och följande [The Journey around the World by Mr. de la Perouse in the year 1785 and following]
Stockholm: Johan Pfeiffer 1799. 12mo, 342pp.

0410　　　　　　　　　　　　　　　　　　1799　　　　　GER 118
Perouse, Jean-François Galoup de la. Entdeckungsreise in den Jahren 1785, 1786, 1787 und 1788 [Journey of Discovery in the Years 1785-1788]
Berlin: Voss 1799. vols.16 and 17, vi, 256, 254pp., ill.; Gompertz 54

0411　　　　　　　　　　　　　　　　　　1804　　　　　ENG 775
Broughton, William Robert. A Voyage of Discovery of the North Pacific Ocean: in which the Coast of Asia, from the Lat. of 35' North to the Lat. of 52' North, the island of Insu (commonly known under the name of the land Jesso), the North, South, and East Coast of Japan, the Lieuchieux and the Adjacent Isles, as well as the Coast of Corea, have been examined and surveyed, performed in his Majesty's Sloop Providence, and her Tender, in the Years 1795, 1796, 1797, 1798
London : T. Cadell and W. Davies in the Strand, 1804. small 4to, x, 393pp., ill., map; contents: on Korea pp.311, 322-359; Gompertz 56

0412　　　　　　　　　　　　　　　　　　1807　　　　　FRE 265
Broughton, William Robert. Voyage de Decouvertes dans la Partie Septentrionale de l'Ocean Pacifique, fait par le Capitaine W.R. Broughton, Commandant la Corvette de S.M.B. la Providence et sa conserve, pendant les annees 1795, 1796, 1797 et 1798; dans lequel il a parcouru et visite la cote d'Asie, depuis le 35' degre nord, jusqu'an 52 ; l'ile d'Insu, ordinairement appelee Jesso; les cotes Nord, Est et Sud du Japon, les iles de Likeujo et autres iles voisines, ainsi que la Cote de Coree [Voyages and Discoveries in the Northern Part of the Pacific Ocean, made by Captain W.R. Broughton, Commander of His Majesty's Corvette Providence in the Years 1795, 1796, 1797 and 1798,

during which he travelled and visited the Coasts of Asia between the latitude of 35 and 52 degrees north; the islands of Insu, usually called Jesso, the North, East and South Coast of Japan, the Islands of Ryukyu and other adjacent Islands as well as the Coast of Korea]

Paris: Dentu 1807 (MDCCCVII). 2 vols., small 8vo, vol.1 243pp., vol.2 338pp., ill., map; translated by J.B.B.E.; Gompertz 57

0413   1817   ENG 169 (2 ex.)
M'Leod, John. Narrative of a Voyage, in His Majesty's Late Ship Alceste, to the Yellow Sea along the coast of Corea, and through its numerous hitherto undiscovered islands, to the islands of Lewchew; with an account of her shipwreck in the straits of Gaspar.

London: John Murray 1817. the first edition, 8vo, 288pp., ill., Gompertz 61

0414   1818   ENG 169e2
M'Leod, John. Voyage of his Majesty's Ship Alceste along the Coast of Corea, to the islands of Lewchew, with an account of her subsequent shipwreck

London: John Murray, 1818. 8vo, 323pp., ill.

0415   1818   ENG 567 (4 ex.)
Hall, Basil. Account of a Voyage of Discovery to the West Coast of Corea and the Great Leo-choo Island

London: John Murray, 1818. small 4to, xi, 222pp., plated, appendices of cxxx + (70) pp., ill., map. contents: includes a vocabulary of the Loo-Choo language by H.J. Clifford Esq.; on Korea pp.1-57; Gompertz 66

0416   1818   FRE 271
MacLeod, John. Voyage du Capitaine Maxwell, Commandant l'Alceste, Vaisseau de S.M.B., sur la mer Jaune. Le Long des Cotes de la Coree, et dans les iles de Liou-tchiou, avec la relation de son naufrage dans le detroit de Gaspar, ayant a bord l'ambassade angloise, a son retour de la Chine [Voyage of Captain Maxwell, Commander of the Alceste, a ship of Her Majesty, on the Yellow Sea along the Coast of Korea and to the Islands of Ryukyu, with an Account of its Shipwreck at the Strait of Gaspar, with the British Envoy on Board, on his Way back from China]

Paris: Chez Gide Fils, Librairie, 1818. 8vo. 359pp., ill., map, translated from the English by Charles-Auguste Def; Gompertz 63

0417   1819   ENG 169e3

M'Leod. Voyage of his Majesty's Ship Alceste. Along the Coast of Corea, to the Island of Lewchew, with an account of her subsequent shipwreck

London: John Murray 1819. 8vo, 339pp., ill.; Gompertz 62

0418   1820   SWE 3

McLeod, John. Capitaine Maxwells Resa på Gula Hafvet, Längs Kusterne af Corea Och Öarne Liu-Tchiu; Jemte berättelse om dess Skeppsbrott uti Gasparsund, då Engelska Ambassaden på återresan ifrån Sina var om bord på skeppet Alcest [Captain Maxwell's Journey on the Yellow Sea, along the Coasts of Korea and the Ryukyu Islands, with a Report of its Shipwreck in Gaspar Sound, when the British Envoy was on Board returning from China]

Upsala: Palmblad & Co., 1820. small 8vo, 168pp., anonymously translated from the French edition; Gompertz 65

0419   1820   ITA 2

Hall, Basilio. Relazione d'un viaggio di scoperte alla costa orientale della Corea ed alla Grand'Isola Lu-Tsciu del Capitano Basilio Hall [Narrative of a journey of discovery along the west coast of Korea and to the Grand Island of Ryukyu by Captain Basil Hall]

Milan: Giambattista Sonzogno 1820. 12mo, 312pp.; Gompertz 69

0420   1827   FRE 268

Timkovski, G. Voyage a Peking, a travers la Mongolie, en 1820 et 1821 [Voyage to Peking, across Mongolia, in 1820 and 1821]

Paris: Librairie Orientale de Dondey-Dupre Pere et Fils, 1827. 3 vols., Vol.1 : 8vo, xii, 480pp., Vol.2 : 8vo, 459pp., Vol.3 : 4to, 32pp., 12 plates, maps; translated from the Russian, corrected and commented by J. Klaproth; contents: on Korea vol.2 pp.94-99

0421   1827   ENG 811

Timkovski, George. Travels of the Russian Mission through Mongolia to China, and residence in Peking, in the years 1820-1821

London: Longman 1827. 8vo, 2 vols., vol.1 : 468pp., ill., map, vol.2 : 496pp., ill., map, index, with corrections and notes by Julius von Klaproth : Gompertz 90

0422   1827   ENG 1417
Constable's Miscellany of Original and Selected Publications in the Various Departments of Literature, Science and the Arts. Hall's Voyages
Edinburgh: no publisher, 1827. 3 vols., 16mo, vol.1 1826, 322pp., vol.2 1827, 313pp., vol.3 1827, 311pp., no index; contents : Vol.I : Voyage to Loo-Choo and other Places in the Eastern Sea 1816; Vol.II : Extracts from a journal, written on the coasts of Chili, Peru, and Mexico, in the years 1820, 1821, 1822, by Captain Basil Hall, R.N. F.R.S. in two volumes.

0423   1840   ENG 1359
Hall, Basil. Narrative of a Voyage to Java, China, and the Great Loo-Choo Island
London: no publisher 1840. 8vo, MDCCCXL, 80pp., attached two more travelogues to Chili, Peru and Mexico, of 80 pages each

0424   1848   ENG 750
Belcher, Edward. Narrative of a Voyage of H.M.S. Samarang, During the Years 1843-1846. Employed Surveying the Islands of the Eastern Archipelago : Accompanied by a Brief Vocabulary of the Principal Languages.. with Notes on the Natural History of the Islands by Arthur Adams
London: Reeve, Benham, and Reeve 1848. 2 vols., 8vo, xxxix, 358, 574pp.; contents: on Korea pp.225ff., 439ff.

0425   1857   ENG 167
Habersham, A.W. The North Pacific Surveying and Exploring Expedition ; or My Last Cruise. Where Went and What We Saw : Being an account of visits to the Malay and Loo Choo Islands, the coasts of China, Formosa, Japan, Kamschatka, Siberia and the mouth of the Amoor River
Philadelphia: J.B. Lippincott & Co. 1857. large 8vo, 507pp., ill., ads

0426   1859   ENG 148
Tronson, J.M. Personal Narrative of a Voyage to Japan, Kamtschatka, Siberia, Tartary, and Various Parts of Coast of China, in H.M.S. Barracouta
London: Smith 1859. 8vo, xiii, 414pp., ill., map, ads; contents: on Korea pp.384ff

0427   1861   ENG 479
Johnston, James D. China and Japan : being a Narrative of the Cruise of the

U.S. Steam-Frigate Powhattan, in the years 1857, '58, '59 and '60
Philadelphia etc.: Charles Desilver, 1861. 8vo, 448pp., ill., maps, ads.

0428   1867   ENG 11776
Morga, Antonio de. The Philippine Islands, Moluccas, Siam, Cambodia, Japan, and China, at the Close of the Sixteenth Century (1609)
NY : reprint of the English translation by Henry A. Stanley published in 1867, Burt Franklin, no date, 8vo, 431pp.

0429   1870   ENG 378
Lawrence, James B. China and Japan, and a Voyage thither, an Account of a Cruise in the Waters of the East Indies, China and Japan
Hartford: Case 1870. 8vo, 444pp., ill., appendix

0430   1870   ENG 831
Adams, Arthur. Travels of a Naturalist in Japan and Manchuria
London: Hurst & Blackett, 1870. 8vo, 334pp., ill.; contents: on Korea pp.125-166; Gompertz 82

0431   1883   FRE 25e17
Valentin, F. Voyages et Aventures de Laperouse [Voyages and Aventures of La Perouse]
Tours: Alfred Mame et Fils., 1883. 16mo, 288p., ill.

0432   1886   ENG 1362
Young, Frederick. The Cruise of the 'Trenton' in European and Asian Waters from 1883-1886
NY : John Medole & Son, 2nd print 1886, 12mo, 103pp.. contents: on Korea pp.59-60

0433   1889   ENG 1300
Cradock, Lt. C. Sporting Notes in the Far East
London: Griffith, former Okeda & Welsh 1889. 8vo, 213pp., ill., no index

0434   1890   GER 59:2
Spillmann, Joseph O.S.J. Durch Asien : ein Buch mit vielen Bildern für die Jugend. Japan, China und Indien (Ost- und Südasien) [Through Asia : a book with many images for the youth. Japan, China and India East and South Asia]
Freiburg im Breisgau: Herdersche Verlagsbuchhandlung 1890. only vol.2, 4to, x, 538pp., ill.; contents:

on Korea pp.75-106

0435 1893 ENG 718e4
Scidmore, Eliza Ruhamah. Westward to the Far East. Japan, Korea, China, Siam, Java, Burma, India
n.pl., Canadian Pacific Railroad Co., 4th edition, 1893. 8vo, 74pp., ill.

0436 1896 ENG 236 (4 ex.)
Veitch, James Herbert. A Travellers Notes or Notes of a Tour through India, Malaysia, Japan, Corea, the Australian Colonies and New Zealand during the years 1891-1893
London: James Veitch 1896. 4to, 217pp., ill., map, index; contents: on Korea pp.139-154

0437 1896 FRE 224
Vigneron, Lucien. Portraits Jaunes. (Coreens, Japonais, Chinois). Scenes de la vie Chinoise [Yellow Portraits (Koreans, Japanese, Chinese). Scenes of Chinese Life]
Tours: Alfred Mame & Fils, 1896. large 8vo, 158pp., ill.; author travelling priest; Gompertz 271

0438 1896 GER 139
Ehlers, Otto Ehrenfried. Im Osten Asiens [In Asia's East]
Berlin: Allgemeiner Verein für Deutsche Literatur 1896. viii, 391pp.; Gompertz 310; Domschke/ Goossmann 244

0439 1898 ENG 338
Ford, John D. An American Cruiser in the East. Travels and Studies in the Far East : The Aleutian Islands, Behring's Sea, Eastern Siberia, Japan, Korea, China, Formosa, Hong Kong and the Philippine Islands
NY etc.: Barnes 1898. 8vo, 468pp., ill., maps, index; contents: on Korea pp.237-292; Gompertz 287

0440 1900 ENG 453 (3 ex.)
Leroy-Beaulieu, Pierre. The Awakening of the East. Siberia-Japan-China
London: Heinemann 1900 / NY : McClure 1900. 8vo, xxvii, 300pp., ads

0441 1900 FRE 52
Pimodan, Commandant de. Promenades en Extreme Orient (1895-1898). De

Marseilles a Yokohama, Japon, Formosa, Iles Pescadores, Tonkin, Yezo, Siberie, Coree, Chine [Strolls in the Far East (1895-1898). From Marseille to Yokohama, Japan, Formosa, the Pescadores Islands, Tongking, Hokkaido, Siberia, Korea, China]

Paris: Honore Champion, 1900. 8vo, 377pp., pp.326-333; contents: on Korea; Gompertz 308

0442   1900   FRE 354

Monnier, Marcel. Itineraires a travers l'Asie leves au cours du voyage accompli durant les annees 1895, 1896, 1897, 1898, sur l'initiative et pour le compte du journal Le Temps, publie sous le patronage de la Societe de Geographie avec le concours du Ministere de l'Instruction Publique et des Beaux Arts [Itineraries across Asia, raised during a voyage conducted in the years 1895-1898, on the initiative ad the account of the magazine Le Temps, published under the patronage of the Geographic Society and the Ministry for Public Instruction and the Fine Arts]

Paris : Plon 1900. 4to, unpaginated, map

0443   1901   ENG 1395

Holmes, Burton. Down the Amur / Peking / the Forbidden City

Battle Creek, Michigan: Little Prester MCMI (1901). large 8vo, 336pp., ill., no index

0444   1902   ENG 833

Blakeney, William. On the Coasts of Cathay and Cipango Forty Years ago. A Record of Surveying Service in the China, Yellow and Japan Seas on the Seaboard of Korea and Manchuria

London: Elliot Stock, 1902. 8vo, 344pp., ill., maps; Gompertz 323; contents: on a visit of 1859, mainly Fusan

0445   1902   ENG 718e10

Scidmore, Eliza Ruhamah. Westward to the Far East. Japan, Korea, China, Siam, Java, Burma, India

n.pl., Canadian Pacific Railroad Co., 10th edition, 1902. 12mo, 61pp., ill., map; Gompertz 742

0446   1903   ENG 970

Shoemaker, Michael Myers. The Great Siberian Railway, From St. Petersburg to Pekin.

NY: Putnam's 1903. 8vo, 243pp., ill., index

0447   1903   FRE 46
Halkin, Joseph. En Extreme Orient 1900-1901 : Recit et notes de voyage. Ceylon, Java, Siam, Indo-Chine, Ile de Hai-nan, Chine, Japon, Coree, Siberie [In the Far East 1900-1901 : Voyage Narrative and Notes : Ceylon, Java, Siam, Indochina, Hainan Island, China, Japan, Korea, Siberia]
Bruxelles etc.: O. Schepens & Cie. 1903. small 4to, 446pp., ill.

0448   1903   FRE 134 (2 ex.)
Matignon, J.J. L'Orient Lointain [The Furthest East]
Paris: A. Storck & Co., 1903. 12mo, 306pp., ill.; Gompertz 340

0449   1904   FRE 174
Marsay, Comte de. Une Croisiere en Extreme-Orient [A Cruise in the Far East]
Paris: Librairie Ch. Delagrave 1904. 12mo, 271pp.

0450   1904   ENG 457 (3 ex.)
Hatch, Ernest F.G. Far Eastern Impressions. Japan-Korea-China
London: Hutchinson 1904. 8vo, xiii, 257pp., ill., map, index; contents: on Korea pp.41-122

0451   1904   ENG 691
Pasfield Oliver, S. The Dryden House Memoirs. Memoirs and Travels : of Mauritius Augustus Count de Benyowsky
London: Kegan Paul Trench Trubner & Co., 1904. 8vo, xxxvi, 636pp., ill., bibliography, index

0452   1905   FRE 290e2
Nettancourt-Vaubecourt, Jean de. En Zig-Zag de Singapour a Moscou [Zigzagging from Singapore to Moscow]
Paris : Plon 1905. 12mo, 327pp., no index; contents: on Coree pp.234-279 (Sept cent kilometres en Coree)

0453   1905   ENG 338e3
Ford, John D. An American Cruiser in the East. Travels and Studies in the Far East : The Aleutian Islands, Behring's Sea, Eastern Siberia, Japan, Korea,

China, Formosa, Hong Kong and the Philippine Islands
NY etc.: Barnes 1898. 8vo, xiii, 537pp., ill., maps, index; contents: on Korea pp.237-292

0454   1906   GER 56 (2 ex.)
Huber, Max. Tagebuchblätter aus Sibirien, Japan, Hinter-Indien, Australien, China, Korea [Diary Pages from Siberia, Japan, Southeast Asia, Australia, China and Korea]
Zürich: Schultheiss 1906. 8vo, xix, 504pp., map; Gompertz 428; Domschke/Goossmann 474

0455   1906   ENG 349 (3 ex.)
Vaya, Count Vay de, et de Luskod. Empires and Emperors of Russia, China, Korea and Japan; Notes and Recollections
NY: Dutton / London: John Murray 1906, 8vo, xxxii, 399pp., ill., index, translated; contents: on Korea pp.189-274; Gompertz 417

0456   1907   ENG 261
Penfield, Frederic Courtland. East of Suez. Ceylon, India and Japan
NY: Century, 1907. 8vo, xvii, 349pp., ill.

0457   1907   ENG 484
Jerningham, Hubert. From West to East. Notes by the Way
London: John Murray 1907. 8vo, xiii, 351pp., ill., map, index; contents: on Korea pp.240-258

0458   1907   ENG 465
Story, Douglas. To-Morrow in the Far East
London: Chapman & Hall 1907. 8vo, 267pp., index, contents: pp.88-154 on Korea

0459   1908   FRE 115
Vaya, Comte Vay de, et de Luskod, P.A. Empires et Empereurs [Empires and Emperors]
Paris: Emile-Paul, 1908. small 8vo, 370pp., translated from English by le Marquis d'Avaray; contents: on Korea pp.169-240; Gompertz 436

0460   1908   ENG 264
Ronaldshay, M.P. A Wandering Student in the Far East
Edinburgh and London: William Blackwood and Sons, 1908. 2 vols., vol.1 : xviii, 317pp., ill., map, vol.2 : viii, 360pp., ill., index

0461   1909   ENG 70 (2 ex.)
Austin, Major Herbert H. A Scamper through the Far East. Including a visit to Manchurian Battlefields
London: Edward Arnold, 1909. 8vo, xvi, 352pp., ill., maps, index; Gompertz 438

0462   1909   GER 204
Bockenheimer, Ph. Rund um Asien [Around Asia]
Leipzig: Klinkhardt & Biermann 1909. 8vo, 479pp., ill., index; contents: one Korea entry

0463   1909   ENG 692
Peck, Ellen M.H. Travels in the Far East
NY: Crowell 1909. 8vo, xxii, 349pp.

0464   1909   GER 183
Krieglstein, Eugen. Aus dem Lande der Verdammnis (Der Ferne Osten) [From the Land of Damnation; The Far East]
Berlin: Deutsches Verlagshaus 1909. 12mo, 347pp.

0465   1910   FRE 223e2
Leclercq, Julien. Chez les Jaunes : Japon-Chine-Mandchourie [With the Yellow People : Japan-China-Manchuria]
Paris: Plon-Nourrit 1910. 2nd edition, 12mo, 299pp., ill.

0466   1910   ENG 1432
Grew, J.C. Sport and Travel in the Far East
Boston: Houghton Mifflin 1910. 8vo, 264pp., ill., index; contents: not on Korea

0467   1911   ENG 444
Ronaldshay, Earl of. An Eastern Miscellany
Edinburgh and London: William Blackwood and Sons 1911. 8vo, xiv, 422pp.; contents: on Korea pp.349-368

0468   1911   GER 16
Martin, L. Meine letzte Ostasienfahrt. Ein Vademecum für die beneidenswerten Reisenden zum "Fernen Osten" mit Schiff und Bahn [My last journey to the Far East. A vademecum for the enviable traveller to the Far East, by ship and rail]

Berlin: Dietrich Reimer 1911. large 8vo, viii, 281pp.; contents: on Korea pp.248-262, Domschke/Goossmann 722

0469   1912   DUT 2:1

Muller, Hendrik P.N. Azie gespiegeld. Reisverhaal en Studien. De Phillipijnen, Siam, Fransch Indo-China, Korea, Mantsjoerije, de Siberische Weg [Asia in the Mirror. Travel narrative and studies. The Philippines, Siam, French Indochina, Korea, Manchuria, the Siberian Railroad]

Utrecht: H. Honig 1912. large 8vo, viii, 476pp., ill., index, the first volume of several; contents: on Korea pp.341-400; Gompertz 496, on 1918

0470   1912   ENG 295 (2 ex.)

Gardner, George Peabody. Chiefly the Orient. An undigested journal

Privately printed, Massachusetts 1912. 8vo, x, 375pp., ill., bibliography; contents: An account of a journey through the Orient in 1910-1911

0471   1913   FRE 252

Maufroid, A. De Java au Japon : par l'Indo-Chine, la Chine et la Coree [From Java to Japan : via Indochina, China and Korea]

Paris: Plon 1913. 12mo, iii, 407pp.

0472   1914   FRE 139 (3 ex.)

Brieux. Au Japon; par Java, la Chine, la Coree [To Japan, via Java, China, Korea]

Paris: Ch. Delagrave 1914. 12mo, 304pp.

0473   1914   ENG 764

Jeffries, W. Carey. Two Undergraduates in the East

London: Sports and Sportsmen 1914. 12mo, xvi, 167pp., ill.

0474   1914   ENG 1338

Brown, Frank L. A Sunday School Tour of the Orient

NY: Doubleday 1914. 12mo, 374pp., ill., no index; contents: on Korea pp.xiii-xvi

0475   1914   ENG 1266

Hackmann, H. A German Scholar in the East. Travel Scenes and Reflections

translated by Daisie Rommel, London : Kegan Paul, Trench, Tribner & Co. 1914. 8vo, 223pp., ill., no index

0476   1915   ENG 753
Allen, William C. A Quaker Diary in the Orient
San Jose, CA : Wright-Eley Co., 1915. 8vo, 101pp., ill.; contents: on Korea pp.47-53

0477   1917   ENG 752
Walcott, Frederica A. Letters from the Far East : Notes of a visit to China, Korea and Japan, 1915-1916
Woodstock Vermont : The Elm Tree Press 1917. small 8vo, 151pp., ill.; contents: on Korea pp.35-46

0478   1918   FRE 227 (2 ex.)
Bellessort, Andre. Un Français en Extreme Orient au Debut de la Guerre [A Frenchman in the Far East at the Start of the War]
Paris: Perrin 1918. 12mo, 160pp.

0479   1919   ENG 443 (2 ex.)
Walsh, James A. Observations in the Orient by a Maryknoller. Observations in the Orient : the Account of a Journey to Catholic Mission Fields in Japan, Korea, Manchuria, China, Indo-China and the Philippines
Ossining NY: Catholic Foreign Mission Soc. of America [1919]. 8vo, 323pp., ill., map, index; contents: on Korea pp.82-97

0480   1921   GER 65 (2 ex.)
Jessen, Peter. Japan, Korea, China. Reisestudien eines Kunstfreundes. [Japan, Korea, China. Studies of a travelling friend of the arts]
Leipzig: E.A. Seemann, 1921. 12mo, 165pp., ill.; contents: on Korea pp.79-104; Gompertz 515; Domschke/Goossmann 487

0481   1921   FRE 159e5
Loti, Pierre, and Viaud, Samuel, his son. Supremes Visions d'Orient. Fragments de Journal Intime [Supreme Visions of the Orient. Fragments of an intimous journal]
Paris: Calmann Levy 1921. 5th edition, 12mo, 316pp.; contents: 1910 travel diary

0482   1922   DUT 10
Rutgers, H.C. Door Amerika, Japan en Korea naar China [Via America, Japan and Korea to China]

Zeist: J. Ploegsma 1922. 8vo, 233p., ill.; contents: the author spent 2 days in Seoul; "Twee dagen in Seoul" pp.74-89, one photo

0483 1922 ENG 194
Erdman, Charles R. Within the Gateways of the Far East : A Record of Recent Travel
NY etc.: Revell 1922. 12mo, 128pp., ill.; contents: on Korea pp.70-93

0484 1924 ENG 619
Collins, Gilbert. Far Eastern Jaunts
London: Methuen, 1924. 8vo, viii, 282pp., map, ill.; contents: travelogue, author travelled Japan and China, passed through Korea, nothing on Korea; Gompertz 531

0485 1924 ENG 417
Buxton, L.H. Dudley. The Eastern Road
London etc.: Kegan, Paul, Trench, Truebner & Co. 1924. 8vo, xii, 258 pp., ill.

0486 1924 FRE 6
Farrere, Claude. Mes Voyages. La Promenade d'Extreme Orient. De Marseille a Saigon. En Indo-Chine. En Chine. Les Chinois peints par eux-memes. Au Japon. Le vieux Japon. Le Japon nouveau [My Voyages. The Tour of the Far East. From Marseille to Saigon. In Indochina. In China. The Chinese painted by themselves. To Japan. The Old Japan. The New Japan]
Paris: Flammarion 1924. small 8vo, 277pp., ill.

0487 1924 ENG 973
Hendley, Charles M. Trifles of Travel
N.Y.: Rider Press, 1924. 8vo, 300pp.; contents: not on Korea; Gompertz 535

0488 1925 ENG 42
Huntington, Ellsworth. West of the Pacific
NY: Scribner's 1925. 8vo, 453pp., ill., index

0489 1925 ENG 1361
Dixon, G.C. From Melbourne to Moscow
Boston: Little, Brown & Co. 1925, 8vo, 319pp., on Korea : pp.149-165

0490 1925 GER 188
Gontscharow, Iwan A. Die Fregatte Pallas [The Frigate Pallas]
Frankfurt/Main: Fischer (1925) reprint, n.d., 8vo, 399pp.

0491 1926 ENG 328
Kirtland, Lucian Swift. Finding the Worth While in the Orient
London etc.: George G. Harrap, n.d. (-1926). 12mo, xxiv, 462pp., ill., index; contents: on Korea pp.93-112; Gompertz 546

0492 1926 FRE 122
Bellessort, Andre. La Perouse
Paris: Plon 1926. 12mo, 126pp., map

0493 1926 ENG 1482
Atwell, William Hawley. Japan, China, Korea and the Philippines
Dallas: W.H. Atwell, 1926. 8vo, 22pp., ill.

0494 1927 FRE 129
Longrais, F. Joüon des Voyages de Jadis et d'Aujourd'hui. Extreme Asie. De Yokohama a Singapore [Voyages of long ago and of today. The Far East. From Yokohama to Singapore]
Paris: Berger-Levrault, 1928. 8vo, 227 pp., ill.

0495 1927 ENG 974
Humphrey, Seth K. Loafing through the Pacific
NY: Doubleday 1927. 8vo, 306pp., ill.; contents: on Korea pp.273-283; Gompertz 554

0496 n.d. (1927) GER 185
Krieglstein, Eugen. Aus dem Lande der Verdammnis (Der Ferne Osten) [From the Land of Damnation; The Far East]
Berlin: Thomas Knaur n.d. (1927). 8vo, 315pp.

0497 1928 FRE 78 (2 ex.)
Chauvelot, Robert. Visions d'Extreme Orient. Coree - Chine - Indochine - Siam - Birmanie [Visions of the Far East. Korea, China, Indochina, Siam, Burma]
Paris: Berger-Levrault 1928. 8vo, 227pp., ill.

0498 1928 ENG 367
Grenfell, Sir Wilfred Thomason. Labrador Looks at the Orient : Notes of Travel in the Near and the Far East
Boston and NY: Houghton Mifflin 1928. 8vo, 207pp., ill.; contents: on Korea pp.262-273; Gompertz 560

0499 1930 ENG 326 (3 ex.)
Palmer, Frederick. Look to the East
NY: Dodd, Mead 1930. 8vo, 332pp.; contents: American traveller returns to Japan, China and Korea after an absence of 25 years. In this book he describes the situation in the countries as he now sees it

0500 1930 ENG 401
Childers, James Saxon. Through Oriental Gates : the Adventures of an Unwise Man in the East
NY: Appleton 1930. 8vo, 333pp., ill., maps; contents: on Korea pp.140-170; Gompertz 579

0501 1930 FRE 137
Katz, Richard. Une Annee en Extreme Orient [A Year in the Far East]
Paris: Editions Montaigne 1930. 12mo, 281pp., translated from the German by H. Zylberberg

0502 1930 FRE 148
Farrere, Claude. Voyage de la Perouse 1785-1788 [Voyage of La Perouse 1785-1788]
Paris: La renaissance du Livre 1930. 12mo, 273pp., map

0503 1930 ENG 1404
Hamilton, Alexander. A New Account of the East Indies (1727)
Repr. by Sir William Foster, Hakluyt 1930. 2 vols., small 4to, vol.1 vii, 259pp., vol.2, 225pp., index; contents: not on Korea

0504 1930 FRE 222
Anonymous. Voyage de la Perouse autour du monde, publie d'apres tous les manuscrits de l'auteur et illustre de dessins et de cartes executes par les artistes qui prirent part aux voyages d'exploration du Comte Jean-François de la Perouse [Voyage of la Perouse around the World, based on all manuscripts of the author and illustrated after the maps and sketches drawn by the artists who participated in the Expeditions of Jean-François de la Perouse] in the series

Voyages et Decouvertes [Voyages and discoveries].
Paris: Editions du Carrefour 1930. large 8vo, xvi, 293pp., ill., map

0505　　　　　　　　　　　　　1931　　GER 38 (2 ex.)
Katz, Richard. Funkelnder Ferner Osten. Erlebtes in China, Korea, Japan [Sparkling Far East. Adventures in China, Korea, Japan]
Berlin: Ullstein 1931 / Leipzig: Eugen Rentsch, 1935. 8vo, 299pp., ill., map; Gompertz 595; Domschke/Goossmann 504

0506　　　　　　　　　　　　　1931　　　　GER 95
Landenberger, E. Ostasien im Zick-Zack [Zigzagging East Asia]
Stuttgart: E. Landenberger 1931. 8vo, 156pp., ill.; contents: on Korea pp.136-142

0507　　　　　　　　　　　　　1932　　　　FRE 292e4
Les Voyages adventureux de Fernand Mendez-Pinto [The Adventurous Voyages of Fernand Mendez-Pinto]
Translated by Jacques Boulanger, Paris: Plon 1932. 8vo, 287pp., no index

0508　　　　　　　　　　　　　1933　　　　FRE 221
Une visite : aux Eveques et Pretres de la Societe des Missions Etrangeres de Paris, par Mgr. de Guebriant, Archeveque de Marcianopolis, Superieur General : Nos missionaires d'Extrem-Orient [A visit : with our bishops and priests of the Society for Foreign ission of Paris, by Mr. de Guebriant, Archbishop of Marcianopolis, Superior General. Our missionaries in the Far East]
Paris: Missions Etrangeres 1933. large 8vo, 214pp., ill., maps

0509　　　　　　　　　　　　　1933　　　　ENG 880
Lyttelton, Edith. Travelling Days
London: Geoffrey Blas 1933. 8vo, 240pp.; contents: pp.87-106 on Korea

0510　　　　　　　　　　　　　1933　ENG 1030 (2 ex.)
Borland, Beatrice. Passports for Asia
NY: Ray Long & Richard Smith, 1933. 8vo, 318pp., ill., maps; contents: on Korea pp.35-37

0511　　　　　　　　　　　　　1934　　　　ENG 601
Harris, Walter B. East Again : The Narrative of a Journey in the Near, Middle

and Far East
NY: Dutton 1934. 8vo, 342pp., ill., index, Foreword by Sir James M. Macleod

0512   1934   GER 77e2
Bunsen, Marie von. Im Fernen Osten. Eindrücke und Bilder aus Japan, Korea, China, Ceylon, Java, Siam, Kambodscha, Birma und Indien [In the Far East. Impressions and Illustrations from Japan, Korea, China, Java, Siam, Cambodia, Burma and India]
Leipzig: Köhler & Amelang 1934. 8vo, 160pp., ill.; contents: on Korea pp.60-63; diary from 1911; Gompertz 626; Domschke/Goossmann 148

0513   n.d. (c.1935)   ENG 1085
Ponder, Capt. S.E.G. In Asia's Arms
London: Stanley Paul, n.d. (c.1935). 8vo, ill., 255pp., index; contents: on Korea pp.169-170

0514   1936   ENG 411
Katz, Richard. Rays from the Far East
London: Hutchinson 1936. 8vo, 287, 24pp., ill., maps, index, translated from the German by Gerald Griffin; contents: on Korea pp.163-188; Gompertz 642

0515   1936   ENG 1029
Lum, Bertha. Gangplanks to the East
NY: Henkle-Yeardale 1936. 8vo, 315pp., bibliography; contents: on Korea pp.103-142; Gompertz 643

0516   1936   ENG 916
Beckmann, Frank Harrison. West of the Golden Gate
Boston: Stratford 1936. 8vo, 257pp., ill.; contents: pp.93-96 on Korea

0517   1937   ENG 1027
Thomas, Lowell. Wings over Asia. A Geographic Journey by Airplane, by L.Th. and Rexford W. Barton
Chicago etc.: John C. Winston 1937. 8vo, 399pp., map, ill., index; contents: on Korea pp.126-142; Gompertz 657

0518   1937   ENG 1431
Körber, Lili. Adventures in the East
London: John Lane the Bodley Head 1937. 8vo, 347pp., no index

0519   1937   ENG 1466
Comfort, Mildred Houghton. Peter and Nancy in Asia
Chicago: Beckley-Cordy 1937. 12mo, 283pp., map, ill.; contents: pp.244-255; The Land of the Morning Calm, From Manchuria to Chosen

0520   1939   ENG 398 (3 ex.)
Harris, Audrey. Eastern Visas
London: Collins 1939. 8vo, 392pp., ill., map; contents: pp.39-54 on Korea; Gompertz 668

0521   1940   ENG 1265
Wells, Carveth. North of Singapore
Camden N.J.: Haddon 1940. large 8vo, 271pp., ill.; no index; contents : not on Korea

0522   1941   ENG 696
Clune, Frank. Sky High to Shanghai. An Account of my Oriental Travels in the Spring of 1938, with Side Glances at the History, Geography and Politics of the Asiatic Littoral. Written with charity to all and malice to none
Sydney and London: Angus and Robertson 1941. 2nd impression, 8vo, xiv, 379pp., ill., maps, bibliography

0523   1944   FRE 146
Ross, Colin. La Nouvelle Asie [The New Asia]
Paris: Sorlot 1944. 12mo, 259pp., translated from the German by J. Lambert

0524   1945   ENG 1438
Beaton, Cecil. Far East
London: Batsford 1945. ill., 8vo, 120pp.

0525   1945   ENG 905e2
Patric, John. A Yankee Hobo in the Orient
Oregon: Frying Pan Creek 1945. 8vo, 512pp.

0526   1948   ENG 1294
Neill, Stephen. The Cross over Asia
Canterbury: Canterbury Press 1948. 8vo, 159pp., ill.; contents: travelogue by Archbishop of Canterbury Stephen Neill who travelled Asia (the Philippines, Formosa, Korea etc.) on behalf of the World Council of Church Studies Dept.

0527　　　　　　　　　　　　　1949　　　　ENG 874
Sitwell, Osbert. Escape with me. An Oriental Sketch-Book
London: MacMillan 1949. 8vo, 340pp., ill., index; contents: index not on Korea; p.174 Korean labourers in Peking

0528　　　　　　　　　　　　　1950　　　　NOR 1
Nielsen, Aage Krarup. Fra Korea til Bali [From Korea to Bali]
Oslo: Nasjonalførlaget 1950. 8vo, 204pp.

0529　　　　　　　　　　　　　n.d.　　　　FRE 244
Dubosq, Andre. Inspirations de l'Asie [Inspirations from Asia]
Paris: Sorlot, n.d., 12mo, 93pp.

0530　　　　　　　　　　　　n.d. (c.1952)　　　FRE 131
Rey, Maria del. Zigzags dans le Pacifique [Zigzagging the Pacific]
Paris: Correa, n.d., 12mo, 248pp., translated from American English by Desiree Manfred; contents: on Korea pp.199-220,

0531　　　　　　　　　　　　n.d. (c.1888)　　　FRE 258
Anonymous. Voyage de la Perouse autour du Monde 1785-1788 [Voyage of La Perouse around the World, 1785-1788]
Limoges: Marc Barbou et Cie., no date. 8vo, 365pp., ill., illustrations following pp.14, 30, 60, 258 have been cut out

0532　　　　　　　　　　　　n.d. (c.1936)　　　FRE 233
Gonnel, Suzanne. Nous partons pour l'Extreme Orient [We leave for the Far East]
Paris: Chanth, n.d., 12mo, 180pp., ill.

IV.h.4) CHINA

0533　　　　　　　　　　　　　1665　　　　DUT 17
Nieuhof, Joan. Het Gezantschap der Neerlandtsche Oost-Indische Compagnie, ann den grooten Tartarischen Cham, den tegenwoordigen Keizer van China: waar in de gedenkwaerdighste Geschiedenissen, die onder het reizen door de Sineesche Landtschappen, Quangtung, Kiangsi, Nanking, Xantung en Peking,

en aan het Keizerlijke Hof te Peking, sedert den jare 1655. tot 1657. zijn voorgevallen, op het bondigste verhandelt worden, beneffens een Naukeurige Beschryving der Sineesche Steden, Dorpen, Regeering, Wetenschappen, Hantwerken, Zeden, Godsdiensten, Gebouwen, Drachten, Schepen, Bergen, Gewassen, Dieren, etc. en Oorlogen tegen de Tarters [The Embassy of the Netherlands' East India Company to the Great Tartarian Khan, the Voyage across Chinese Landscapes to the Imperial Court at Peking in the Years 1655 to 1657 are narrated, also including a detailed and exact Description of the Chinese Cities, Villages, Government, Sciences, Artisans, Customs, Religions, Architecture, Clothing, Ships, Mountains, Rivers, Animals etc. and of their Wars against the Tartars]
Amsterdam: J. van Meurs 1665. 4to, 2 pts. in 1, 259pp., ill., index

0534   1666   FRE 317
Nieuhof, Joan. Ambassade des Hollandois a la Chine, ou voyage des ambassadeurs de la Compagnie Hollandoise des Indes Orientales vers le Grand Chan de Tartarie, maintenant Empereur de la Chine [Embassy of the Dutch to China, or Journey of the Ambassadors of the Dutch Company of the East Indies to the Great Khan of Tartary, presently Emperor of China]
Paris: Sebastien Mabre-Cramoisy 1666. edited by Thevenot Melchisedec, 4to, 216pp.

0535   1669   ENG 1439t
Nieuhof, Jan. An Embassy of the East India Company of the United Provinces to the Grand Tartar Cham, Emperor of China, trsl. by John Ogilby
Reprint : Menston, Scolar Press, n.d., 4to, 31pp.
attached : A Narrative on the Success of an Embassage sent by John Maatzuyker de Badem, General of Batavia, unto the Emperor of China and Tartary 1655, written by a Jesuit in these Parts, 4to, 106pp., ill.

0536   [1693]   DUT 17e2
Nieuhof, Joan. Het Gezantschap der Neerlandtsche Oost-Indische Compagnie, ann den grooten Tartarischen Cham, den tegenwoordigen Keizer van China: waar in de gedenkwaerdighste Geschiedenissen, die onder het reizen door de Sineesche Landtschappen, Quangtung, Kiangsi, Nanking, Xantung en Peking, en aan het Keizerlijke Hof te Peking, sedert den jare 1655. tot 1657. zijn voorgevallen, op het bondigste verhandelt worden, beneffens een Naukeurige

Beschryving der Sineesche Steden, Dorpen, Regeering, Wetenschappen, Hantwerken, Zeden, Godsdiensten, Gebouwen, Drachten, Schepen, Bergen, Gewassen, Dieren, etc. en Oorlogen tegen de Tarters [The Embassy of the Netherlands' East India Company to the Great Tartarian Khan, the Voyage across Chinese Landscapes to the Imperial Court at Peking in the Years 1655 to 1657 are narrated, also including a detailed and exact Description of the Chinese Cities, Villages, Government, Sciences, Artisans, Customs, Religions, Architecture, Clothing, Ships, Mountains, Rivers, Animals etc. and of their Wars against the Tartars]

Amsterdam: 1693. 4to, 2 pts. in 1, 258pp., ill., map, index; title page missing

0537   1698   ENG 1473e2

Le Comte, Louis, O.S.J. Memoirs and Observations Topographical, Physical, Mathematical, Mechanical, Natural, Civil and Ecclesiastical, Made in a Late Journey through the Empire of China

London: G. Huddleston and the Black-moor's head 1698. translated from the French, 12mo, 517pp. + index, ill.; contents: not on Korea

0538   1771   FRE 339

Voyage de Mons. Olof Toree Aumonier de la Compagnie Suedoise des Indes Orientales fait a Suede a la Chine etc., depuis le premier Avril 1750 jusqu'au 26 Juin 1752 [The Voyage of Mr. Olof Toree, vicar in the service of the Swedish East India Company, made from Sweden to China etc., between April 1st 1750 and June 26th 1752]

Swed. East India Company, to India, China, 12mo, 92pp.

0539   1796   FRE 275

Anderson, Aenaeas. Relation de l'Ambassade du Lord MacArtney a la Chine, dans les Annees 1792, 1793 et 1794 contenant les diverses particularites de cette Ambassade, avec la description des moeurs des Chinois, et celle de l'interieur du pays, des villes etc. etc. [Report of the Embassy of Lord MacArtney to China in the Years 1792, 1793 and 1794, containing various particularities of this Embassy, with a Description of the Customs of the Chinese, and one of the interior of the Country, its Cities etc. etc.]

Paris: Bocquillon etc., L'An IV (= 1796). 2 vols., 8vo, vol.1 : 255pp., vol.2 : 227pp., ill., translated from the English

0540   1798   ENG 125e2

Staunton, George. An Authentic Account of an Embassy from the King of Great Britain to the Emperor of China including cursory observations made, and information obtained, in travelling through that ancient Empire, and a small part of Chinese Tartary. Together with a relation of the Voyage undertaken on the Occasion by his Majesty's Ship the Lion, and the Ship Hindostan, in the East India Company's service, to the Yellow Sea, and Gulf of Pekin, as well as of their return to Europe; with notices of the several places where they stopped in their way out and home, being the islands of Madeira, Teneriffe, and St. Jago, the port of Rio de Janeiro in South America, the Islands of St. Helena, Tristan d'Acunha, and Amsterdam; the Coasts of Java, and Sumatra, the Nanka Isles, Pulo-Condore, and Cochin-China. Taken chiefly from the Papers of his Excellency the Earl of MacArtney, Knight of the Bath, his Majesty's Embassador Extraordinary and Plenipotentiary to the Emperor of China; Sir Erasmus Gower, Commander of the Expedition, and of other Gentlemen in the several departments of the Embassy.

Spine title : Macartney, Embassy to China 1796

London: G. Nicol MDCCXCVIII (1798). 12mo, 4 vols., vol.1 : xvi, 429pp., vol.2 : xv, 383pp., vol.3 : map, xvii, 490pp., vol.4 folio, maps and ill., unpaged; Atlas volume, mentioned in the seller's description, not found

0541   1798   FRE 274

Staunton, George. Voyage dans l'interieur de la Chine et en Tartarie, fait dans les Annees 1792, 1793 et 1794, par Lord MacArtney, Ambassadeur du Roi d'Angleterre aupres l'Empereur de la Chine, avec la relation le cette Ambassade, celle du Voyage entrepris a cette occasion par les Vaisseaux de Lion et l'Indostan, et des details tres-curieux sur les Colonies Espagnoles, Portugaises et Hollandaises, ou ces Vaisseaux ont relache [Voyage into the Interior of China, and to Tartary, made in the Years 1792, 1793 and 1794 by Lord MacArtney, Ambassador of the King of England to the Emperor of China, with a Report on that Embassy, its Voyage made on that occasion thereby the ships Lion and Hindostan, and curious details about the Spanish, Portuguese and Dutch Colonies and their ships]

Paris: Buisson 1798. 4 vol., small 8vo, vol.1 : 512pp., ill., vol.2 : 412pp., vol.3 : 399pp., vol.4 : 325pp.,

Myongji-LG Korean Studies Library

ill., maps, index; Staunton used the notes of Sir Erasmus Gower, expedition commander, and of other expedition participants. British minister plenipotentiary at the court of the Emperor of China. Translated by J. Castera

0542   1817   ENG 814

Ellis, Henry. Journal of the Proceedings of the late Embassy to China; comprising a correct narrative of the public transactions of the Embassy, of the Voyage to and from China, and of the Journey from the mouth of the Pei-Ho to the return to Canton. Interspersed with Observations upon the face of the country, the polity, moral character, and manners of the Chinese Nation
Spine Title : Macartney's Embassy to China

London: John Murray 1817. 4to, 526pp., ill., map. Ellis was the 3rd Commissioner of the Embassy; Gompertz 58

0543   1822   ENG 431

Anonymous. Diary of a Journey Overland, through the Maritime Provinces of China, from Manchao, on the South Cost of Hainan, to Canton, in the Year 1819 and 1820.
in the series: Voyages and Travels. Vol.VI

London: La Richard Phillips & Co., 1822. 8vo, 116pp., Spine title : Manchao to Canton; contents: includes a number of further short articles on East Asia

0544   1833   ENG 156

Gutzlaff, Charles. Journal of Two Voyages along the Coast of China, in 1831, and 1832, the first in a Chinese junk, the second in the British ship Lord Amherst, with Notices of Siam, Corea, and the Loo-Choo Islands and Remarks to the Policy, Religion etc. of China.

NY: John P. Haven, MDCCCXXXIII (1833). 12mo, xii, 332pp.; Gompertz 76

0545   1833   ENG 943

Anonymous. Papers Relating to the Voyage undertaken by the Ship "Amherst"

1833, 4to, 149pp.; contents: pp.102-149 Remarks on a Voyage to the North-Eastern part of China, Corea and Loo-Choo, by Rev. Charles Gutzlaff

0546   1834   ENG 156.2

Gutzlaff, Charles. Journal of Three Voyages along the Coast of China in 1831, 1832 and 1833, with notices of Siam, Corea and thje Loo-Choo Islands

London: Frederick Westley and A.H. Davis 1834. 8vo, xcvi, map, 450pp.; To which is prefixed an introductory essay on the policy, religion etc. of China by Rev. W. Ellis; contents : Corea on pp.316-357; Gompertz 77

0547   1834   ENG 156.2e3
Gutzlaff, Charles. Journal of Three Voyages along the Coast of China in 1831, 1832 and 1833, with notices of Siam, Corea and the Loo-Choo Islands
London: Thomas Ward, n.d. (1834). 12mo, 312pp., map; To which is prefixed an introductory essay on the policy, religion etc. of China by Rev. W. Ellis; contents: Corea on pp.227-249

0548   1834   ENG 496e2
Lindsay, H.H. Report of Proceedings on a voyage to the Northern Ports of China in the Ship Lord Amherst, Extracted from papers, printed by order of the House of Commons, relating to the trade in China
London: B. Fellowes, (1833) 1834. 8vo, 296pp., contains two separate reports by H.H. Lindsay and Charles Gutzlaff; contents: on Korea pp.214-259, 293-296

0549   1855   ENG 144
Gutzlaff, Charles. Visit to the Chinese Coast, and Other Books for the Young
American Tract Society, n.d. (c.1855). 16mo; A collection of seven 16pp. tracts on various subjects - the first is on Gutzlaff's China trip; stories individually paginated

0550   1859   ENG 124
Oliphant, Laurence. Narrative of the Earl of Elgin's Mission to China and Japan in the Years 1857, '58, '59
Edinburgh & London: W. Blackwood MDCCCLIX (1859). 2 vols., 8vo, vol.1 : xiv, 492pp., ill., maps, vol.2 : xi, 496pp., ill., maps. Oliphant was Lord Elgin's private secretary.

0551   1860   ENG 140
Huc, M. The Chinese Empire : a Sequel to Recollections of a Journey through Tartary and Thibet
London: Longman, Green, Longman and Roberts (1854) 1860. 12mo, new edition, xxviii, 566 pp., ill., index. Translated from the French

0552   1870   ENG 155e2
Loch, Henry Brougham. Personal Narrative of Occurrences during Lord Elgin's Second Embassy to China 1860
London: Murray 1870. 12mo, xii, 298pp., ill., maps; Loch was Lord Elgin's private secretary on this mission.

0553   1870   ENG 451 (2 ex.)
Williamson, Alexander. Journeys in North China, Manchuria, and Eastern Mongolia : with some account of Corea
London: Smith, Elder 1870. 8vo, 2 vols., vol.1 : xx, 444pp., vol.2 : viii, 442pp., ill., maps, appendices; contents: on Korea vol.2 pp.295-312; Gompertz 105

0554   1876   FRE 67 Vol.1876.1 (2 ex.)
Choutze, T. Pekin et le Nord de la Chine [Peking and the North of China]
in: Le Tour du Monde 1876, pp.337-352

0555   1882   ENG 231e4
Lindley, Augustus F. A Cruise in Chinese Waters. Being the Log of "The Fortuna". Containing tales of adventures in foreign climes by land and sea
London: Cassell 1882. 8vo, 256pp., ill., ads

0556   1883   ENG 149
Colquhoun, Archibald Ross. Across Chryse. Being the Narrative of a Journey of Exploration through the South China Border Lands from Canton to Mandalay
London: Sampson Low etc., 1883. 8vo, 2 vols., vol.1 : xxx, 420pp., ill., map, vol.2 : xvi, 408pp., ill., maps, index, 34pp. ads; contents: not on Korea

0557   1888   ENG 499e2
Cumming, C.F. Gordon. Wanderings in China
Edinburgh and London: William Blackwood, MDCCCLXXXVIII (1888). 8vo, vi, 528, 22pp., ill., map, index; contents: on Korea pp.513-515

0558   1899   ENG 575
Bishop, Isabella Bird. The Yangtze Valley and Beyond : an Account of Journeys in China, chiefly in the Province of Sze Chuan and among the Man-Tse of the Somo Territory
London: John Murray 1899. 8vo, xv, 557pp., ill., maps, index; contents: not on Korea

0559   1899   ENG 1091
Foster, Mrs. Arnold. In the Valley of the Yangtse
London Missionary Society 1899. 8vo, 216pp., ill., no index, frontispiece, table of contents missing

0560				1900		ENG 297
Rockhill, William W. The Journey of William of Rubruck to the Eastern Parts of the World, 1253-55, as narrated by himself, with two accounts of the earlier journey of John of Plan de Carpine
London: Printed for the Hakluyt Society 1900. 8vo, lvi, 304, 20pp., index; translated from the Latin by William W. Rockhill

0561				1900		ENG 1089
Campbell, P.D. Captain Royal Navy. Logbook H.M.S. "Barfleur", China, 1898-1900
manuscript, 4to, unpaginated; May 28th 1898-Nov. 1st 1900

0562				1901		GER 180 v.1
Wolf, Eugen. Meine Wanderungen. Vol.1 : Im Innern Chinas [My Wanderings. I : In China's Interior]
Stuttgart etc.: DVA 1901. large vo, 298pp.

0563				1902		ENG 482
Birch, John Grant. Travels in North and Central China
London: Hurst and Blackett 1902. 8vo, xvi, 379pp., ill.

0564				1907		GER 51
Richthofen, Ferdinand Freiherr von. Tagebücher aus China [China Diaries]
Berlin: Reimer 1907. 2 vols., large 8vo, vol.1 : 588pp., vol.2 : 375pp., ill., map. Ferdinand von Richthofen (1833-1905), German explorer and geologist, extensively travelled through 13 Chinese provinces from 1868-1872. His journals, regarding southern parts of Manchuria and Korea, were posthumously edited by E. Tiessen on behalf of von Richthofen's wife.

0565				1917		ENG 1033
Bell, Archie. The Spell of China
Boston: Page 1917. 8vo, 404pp., ill., index; contents: numerous Korea entries; Gompertz 487

0566				1923		ENG 354 (2 ex.)
Franck, Harry A. Wandering in North China
NY : Century [1923]. 8vo, xx, 592pp., ill., map; contents: on Korea pp.3-70; Gompertz 522

0567				1924		ENG 416
Holm, F. My Nestorian Adventure in China : a popular Account of the Holm-

Nestorian Expedition to Sian-Fu and its Results

London: Hutchinson & Co. 1924. 8vo, 335pp., bibliography, index; Introduction by Rev. Abraham Yohannan, Prof. of Columbia Univ.

0568 1928 ENG 421

Carpenter, Frank G. Carpenter's World Travels. Familiar Talks about Countries and Peoples. China

Garden City, NY: Doubleday, Doran, 1928. 8vo, xiv, 306pp., ill., map

0569 1933 ENG 217

Hedin, Sven. Jehol City of Emperors

NY: Dutton 1933. 8vo, 278pp., ill., index; translated from the Swedish by E.G. Nash

0570 1933 ENG 1317

Sewell, William G. The Land and Life of China

London: Edinburgh House 1933. 12mo, 144pp., ill., index; contents: not on Korea

0571 1940 ENG 1275

Wingate, Col. A.W.S. A Cavalier in China

London: Grayson & Grayson 1940. 8vo, 327pp., ill., index; contents: numerous Korea entries

0572 n.d. FRE 73e5

Allou. En Chine [In China]

Paris: Ch. Delagrave, n.d., large 8vo, 296pp.

IV.h.5) MANCHURIA, MONGOLIA, TURKESTAN

0573 1832 GER 121

Hyakinth, Archimandrite (i.e. Bitchurin, Nikita Yakovlevich). Denkwürdigkeiten über die Mongolei : Von dem Mönch Hyakinth [Things Noteworthy on Mongolia. By Hyakinth the Monk]

Berlin: G. Reimer 1832, 8vo, xiv, 426pp., ill., map; translated from the Russian by Karl Friedrich von der Borg

0573a 1854 FRE 203

Huc, M. L'Empire Chinois : faisant suite a l'ouvrage in tifule [The Chinese Empire]

Paris: L'Imprimerie Imperiale 1854. 8vo, 2 vols., vol.1 : 426pp., vol.2 : 440pp.

0573b   n.d. (1855)   ENG 1204

Huc, E. Travels in Tartary, Thibet, and China

London: Office of the National Illustrated Library, n.d., 2 vols., trsl. by W. Hazlitt, 12mo, 293, 304pp., ill., no index

0574   1863   ENG 581

Fleming, George. Travels on Horseback in Manchu Tartary : Being a Summer's ride beyond the Great Wall of China

London: Hurst and Blackett 1863. large 8vo, xvi, 579pp., ill., map, index

0575   1887   ENG 506 : 1887

James, H.E.M. A Journey in Manchuria

in: Proceedings of the Royal Geographic Society and Monthly Record of Geography Vol.9 No.9, 1887, 8vo, pp.531-538, map

0576   1888   ENG 441 (2 ex.)

James, H.E.M. The Long White Mountain : or a Journey in Manchuria : with some Account of the History, People, Administration and Religion of that Country

London: Longmans, Green 1888. 8vo, 502pp., index, ill., map, appendix; Gompertz 187

0577   1899   ENG 506 : 1899

Turley, Robert T. Through the Hunkiang Gorges, or Notes of a Tour in "No-Mans-Land", Manchuria

in: Proceedings of the Royal Geographic Society and Monthly Record of Geography Vol.1899, 8vo, pp.292-302; Gompertz 843

0578   1904   ENG 506 : 1904

Turley, Robert T. Southern Manchuria and Korea : I., A Visit to the Yalu Region and Central Manchuria

in: Proceedings of the Royal Geographic Society and Monthly Record of Geography Vol.1904, 8vo, pp.473-492; Gompertz 353

0579   1910   ENG 239 (5 ex.)

Kemp, E.G. The Face of Manchuria, Korea and Russian Turkestan.

London: Chatto & Windus MDCCCCX (1910). 8vo, xiii, 248pp., ill., map, index; Miss Kemp and a lady companion travelled across Asia in 1910; Gompertz 446

0580 1914 FRE 68

Broussenard, Louis. Sans-le sou chez les diables jaunes [Without a Penny among the Yellow Devils]

in: Journal des voyages et des aventures de terre et de mer [Journal of Voyages and Adventures on Land and Sea] 1914, pp.41-43, 70-72, 79-81, 96-97, 113-116, 134-136, 156-158, 170-171, 189-191, 214-216; contents: on Manchuria

0581 1917 ENG 336

Tisdale, Alice. Pioneering Where the World is Old. Leaves from a Manchurian Note-Book

NY: Holt 1917. 8vo, 227pp.

0582 1921 ENG 593

Sowerby, Arthur de C. The Exploration of Manchuria

in: Annual Report for 1919, Smithsonian Institution, Washington : GPO 1921. pp.455-470

0583 1922 FRE 212e3

Lemoine, Laurent. De France en Extreme-Orient : Au Pays des Pagodes [From France to the Far East ; to the Land of the Pagodas]

Paris: Librairie Catholique Emmanuel Vitte 1922. 8vo, xiii, 222pp.

0584 1926 FRE 230e2

Huc, Evariste-Regis. Souvenirs d'un Voyage dans la Tartarie. Volume title : I : Dans la Tartarie, II : Dans le Thibet [Souvenirs from a Voyage in Tartary. Vol.I : in Tartary, Vol.2 : in Tibet]

Paris: Plon 1926-1927. new edition published and preface by H. d'Ardenne de Tizac, 12mo, vol.1 : xiv, 301pp., vol.2 : xiv, 318pp., map

0585 1929 ENG 358

Lattimore, Owen. The Desert Road to Turkestan

Boston: Little 1929. 8vo, 373pp., index, appendix, maps

0586 1930 ENG 9

Lattimore, Owen. High Tartary

Boston: Little, Brown & Co. 1930. 8vo, 370pp., ill., maps; contents: covers the Manchu, Mongols, T'ung-kan, Quazaqs, Dirghiz, Turki & other peoples of Central & Eastern Asia. The author did not travel east of central Manchuria.

0587 1932 ENG 400
Lattimore, Owen. Manchuria. Cradle of Conflict
NY: MacMillan 1932. 8vo, 311pp., maps, index

0588 1932 ENG 250
Woodhead, H.G.W. A Visit to Manchukuo
Shanghai: Mercury Press (1932). 8vo, 112pp., ill., maps; Author, editor of The China Year Book, was instrumental in the removal of Japanese forces from some of those troubled areas, but suffered the brutal murder of his wife by the police force in Manchuria

0589 1933 GER 63
Schnee, Heinrich. Völker und Mächte im Fernen Osten. Eindrücke von der Reise mit der Mandschurei-Kommission [Peoples and Powers in the Far East. Impressions from the Trip with the Manchuria Commission]
Berlin: Deutsche Buch Gemeinschaft 1933. 12mo, 366pp., ill.; contents: on Korea pp.135-145

0590 1934 ENG 730
Johnson, Cliford. Pirate Junk : Five Months Captivity with Manchurian Bandits
NY: Scribner 1934. 8vo, 238pp., ill., map

0591 1934 GER 40
Lindt, A.R. Im Sattel durch Mandschukuo. Als Sonderberichterstatter bei Generälen und Räubern [In the Saddle through Manchukuo. As Special Correspondent with Generals and Bandits]
Leipzig: Brockhaus 1934. 8vo, 272pp., ill., map

0592 1937 ENG 1192
Huc, Abbe. Travels in Tartary and Thibet (1844-1846)
London: Herbert Joseph 1937. 12mo, 352pp., no index

0593 1938 GER 114
Sorge, Wolfgang. Erlebtes Mandschukuo. Die Jugend eines altneuen Kaiserreiches [Manchuria as I saw it. The Youth of an Oldnew Empire]
Berlin: Kommodore 1938. 8vo, 308pp., ill., map, index

0594 1938 FRE 116
Fleming, Peter. Au Coeur de la Tartarie (News from Tartary) [To the Heart of Tartary]
Paris: Gallimard, 6th edition 1938. small 8vo, 294pp., map, translated from the English by S. and P. Bourgeois

IV.h.6) RUSSIAN FAR EAST, SIBERIA

0595 1864 ENG 157
Collins, Major Perry. Overland Explorations in Siberia, Northern Asia, and the great Amoor river country; incidental notices of Manchooria, Mongolia, Kamschatka, and Japan, with Map and Plan of an Overland Telegraph around the World, via Behring's Strait and Asiatic Russia to Europe
Spine title : Voyage down the Amoor
NY: D. Appleton and Co. (1860) 1864. 12mo, map, iv, 468pp., ill., ads. Author was commercial agent of the U.S. for the Amoor River, travelled there in 1856.

0596 1890 ENG 447
Gowing, Lionel F. Five Thousand Miles in a Sledge : a Mid-Winter Journey across Siberia
NY: D. Appleton and Co., 1890. small 8vo, xix, 257pp., ill., map, ads

0597 1903 ENG 80 (3 ex.)
Hawes, Charles H. In the Uttermost East, being an Account of Investigations among the Natives and Russian Convicts of the Island of Sakhalin, with Notes on Travel in Korea, Siberia and Manchuria
London & N.Y.: Harper & Brothers 1903 / NY: Charles Scribner & Sons, 1904. 8vo, xxx, 478pp., ill., maps, index, glossary; contents: on Korea pp.1-23; Gompertz 346

0598 1903 ENG 1127e2
Deutsch, Leo. Sixteen Years in Siberia. Some Experiences of a Russian Revolutionist, translated by Helen Chisholm
London: John Murray 1903. 8vo, 310pp., ill., map, index; contents: on Korea p.351

0599   1904   ENG 1126
Gerrare, Wirt. Greater Russia. The Continental Empire of the Old World.
London: William Heinemann 1904. 8vo, 317pp., ill., map, index; contents: several Korea entries

0600   1904   ENG 80e2 (2 ex.)
Hawes, Charles H. In the Uttermost East, being an Account of Investigations among the Natives and Russian Convicts of the Island of Sakhalin, with Notes on Travel in Korea, Siberia and Manchuria
London & N.Y.: Harper & Brothers 1904. 8vo, xxx, 478pp., ill., maps, index, glossary; contents: on Korea pp.1-23

0601   1904   FRE 72 : 1904
Labbe, Paul. Une Soiree a Vladivostok [An Evening Reception in Vladivostok]
in : A Travers le Monde, 1904, pp.345-348

0602   1905   GER 75
Hawes, Charles H. Im äussersten Osten : Von Korea über Wladiwostok nach der Insel Sachalin [In the Uttermost East. From Korea via Vladivostok to Sakhalin Island]
Berlin: Karl Siegismund 1905. 8vo, 575pp., ill., map, translated from the English; contents: on Korea pp.34-20; Gompertz 410

0603   1914   ENG 121
Nansen, Fridtjof. Through Siberia. The Land of the Future.
NY: Frederick A. Stokes Co. 1914. large 8vo, xvi, 478pp., ill., map, index; contents: this includes some mentioning of Russian influence at the Korean frontier and Koreans in Vladivostok.

0604   1924   GER 57 : 2
Arsenjew, Wladimir K. In der Wildnis Ostsibiriens. Forschungsreisen im Ussurigebiet [In the Wilderness of Eastern Siberia. Expeditions in the Ussuri Region]
Berlin: August Scherl (1924). vol.2, 8vo, 364pp., ill., map. Translated from the Russian by Franz Daniel; contents: on Korea pp.173-181

IV.h.7) JAPAN

0605   1792-1794   GER 190

Karl Peter Thunbergs Reise durch einen Theil von Europa, Afrika und Asien, hauptsächlich in Japan, in den Jahren 1770 bis 1779 [K.P. Thunberg's Journey through a part of Europe, Africa and Asia, mainly in Japan, in the Years 1770 to 1779]

Berlin: Haude u. Spener 1792-1794. translated by Christian Heinrich Grootcurd; Swedish original 1784, 2 vols., 8vo, 292, 266pp., ill.

0606   1792   GER 140.7

Forster, Johann Reinhold (ed.). Karl Peter Thunbergs Reisen in Afrika und Asien, vorzüglich in Japan, während der Jahre 1772 bis 1779, auszugsweise übersetzt von Kurt Sprengel [Karl Peter Thunberg's Travels in Africa and Asia, mainly in Japan, during the Years 1772 to 1779, translated in excerpts by Kurt Sprengel]

in: Magazin von merkwurdigen der Neuesten Reisebeschreibungen, vol.7, 12mo, 293pp.

0607   1809   ENG 576

Thunberg, Karl Peter. Thunberg's Voyages. Voyages to the Indian Seas and Japan: between the years 1770 and 1779

London: Philips 1809. 16mo, pp.254-372; extracted from Philips Voyages' major edition, published without title page.

0608   1856   ENG 178

Hawks, Francis L. Narrative of the Expedition of an American Squadron to China Seas and Japan, performed in the Years 1852, 1853 and 1854, under the Command of Commodore M.C. Perry, United States Navy

Washington: A.O.P. Nicholson 1856. volumes 1 and 2 out of 3 volumes, published by the order of the Congress of the United States, 4to, vol.1 : xvii, 537pp., vol.2 : 414pp., facsimile of treaty, index, charts.

0609   1872   ENG 1043

Taylor, Bayard (compiler). Series title : Illustrated Library of Travel, Exploration and Adventure. Title : Japan in Our Day

NY: Scribner 1872. 8vo, 280pp., ill.

0610　　　　　　　　　　　　　1878　　　　　FRE 1
Guimet, Emile. Promenades Japonaises [Strolls in Japan]
Paris: G. Charpentier 1878. 4to, 212pp., ill., by Felix Regamey

0611　　　　　　　　　　　　　1880　　　　　ENG 605
St. John, H.C. Notes and Sketches from the Wild Coasts of Nipon : with Chapters on Cruising after Pirates in Chinese Waters
Edinburgh: David Douglas 1880. 8vo, xxiii, 392, 20pp., ill., map

0612　　　　　　　　　　　　　1884　　　　　ENG 765
Greey, Edward. The Bear Worshippers of Yezo and the Island of Karafuto (Saghalin) or the Adventures of the Jewett Family and their friend Oto Nambo
Boston etc.: Lee and Shepard 1884. large 8vo, 304pp., ill.; contents: not on Korea

0613　　　　　　　　　　　n.d. (c.1898)　　　ENG 386
Bird, Isabella L. Unbeaten Tracks in Japan : an Account of Travels on Horseback in the Interior, including Visits to the Aborigines of Yezo and the Shrine of Nikko and Ise
New York: G.P. Putnam's Sons, n.d. (after 1880). 2 vols. in 1, 8vo, xxiv, 407pp., xii, 383pp., ill., map, appendix

0614　　　　　　　　　　　　　1904　　　　　FRE 19e4
Guerville, A.B. de. Au Japon [To Japan]
Paris: Alphonse Lamerre 1904. 12mo, 276pp.; contents: on Korea pp.171-185

0615　　　　　　　　　　　　　1905　　　　　SWE 5
Hesse-Wartegg, Ernst von. Öst-Asien I vara dagar. Japan och Korea [East Asia in Our Days. Japan and Korea]
Stockholm: Fahlcrantz & Co. 1905. small 4to, 315pp., ill.; translated from the German by Ernst Lundquist; Gompertz 414

0616　　　　　　　　　　　　　1906　　　　　ENG 1049
Redesdale, Lord. The Garter Mission to Japan
London: MacMillan 1906. 8vo, 280pp., index

0617　　　　　　　　　　　　　1907　　　　　ENG 781
Schiff, Jacob H. Our Journey to Japan
manuscript 1907, 4to, 164pp., ill., unpaginated

0618　　　　　　　　　　　　　　　　1911　　　　　ENG 994
Seitz, Don C.　Surface Japan. Short Notes of a Swift Survey
NY: Harper & Brothers 1911. 4to, 158pp., ill.

0619　　　　　　　　　　　　　　n.d. (c. 1912)　　　ENG 1263
Exner, A.H.　Japan as I Saw it
London: Jarrold & Son, n.d. (c. 1912). 8vo, 259pp., ill., no index

0621　　　　　　　　　　　　　　1917　ENG 966 : 1/2　(2 ex.)
Morse, Edward S.　Japan Day by Day. 1877, 1878-79, 1882-83
Boston: Houghton & Mifflin 1917. 2 vols., 8vo, 441, 436pp., index in vol.2, ill.

0622　　　　　　　　　　　　　　　　1917　　　　　ENG 989
Bell, Archie.　A Trip to Lotus Land
NY: John Lane 1917. 8vo, 287pp., ill., index; comment: author spent 3 days in Seoul

0623　　　　　　　　　　　　　　　　1920　　　ENG 918 : 10
Burton Holmes' Travelogues, volume 10 (Seoul, Korea, Japan)
Chicago: The Travelogue Bureau (1908) 1920. 8vo, 343pp., ill., index; contents: on Seoul pp.1-112; see No.0342

0624　　　　　　　　　　　　　　　　1921　　　　　ENG 1032
Street, Julian.　Mysterious Japan
NY: Doubledasy, Page & Co. 1921. 8vo, 349pp., ill., index; contents: 2 Korea entries

0625　　　　　　　　　　　　　　　　1923　　　　　ENG 399
Bigelow, Poultney.　Japan and Her Colonies. Being Extracts from a Diary Made Whilst Visiting Formosa, Manchuria, Shantung, Korea and Saghalin in the Year 1921.
London: Edward Arnold & Co. 1923. 8vo, 276pp., index, ads

0626　　　　　　　　　　　　　　　1924　　ENG 273　(3 ex.)
Tietjens, Eunice.　Japan, Korea and Formosa. in the series: Burton Holmes Travel Stories, a Series of International Silent Readers.
Chicago: Wheeler Pub., 1924. 12mo, 404pp., ill.; Series edited by William H. Wheeler and Burton Holmes

0627   1925   GER 11 (2 ex.)
Schalek, Alice. Japan, das Land des Nebeneinander : Eine Winterreise durch Japan, Korea und die Mandschurei [Japan, the Land of Juxtaposition : A Winter Journey through Japan, Korea and Manchuria]
Breslau: Ferdinand Hirt, 1925. 8vo, 403pp., ill., map; Domschke/Goossmann 898

0628   1925   ENG 79
Carpenter, Frank G. Carpenter's World Travels : Japan and Korea
NY: Doubleday 1925. 8vo, 310pp., ill., map, index; contents: Korea pp.241-296

0629   1926   ENG 79e2
Carpenter, Frank G. Carpenter's World Travels : Japan and Korea
NY: Doubleday 1926. 8vo, 310pp., ill., map, index; contents: Korea pp.241-296

0630   1927   GER 80
Goldschmidt, Richard. Neu-Japan. Reisebilder aus Formosa, den Ryukyuinseln, Bonininseln, Korea und dem südmandschurischen Pachtgebiet [New Japan. Travel Illustrations from Formosa, the Ryukyu Islands, the Bonin Islands, Korea and the Leased Territory in South Manchuria]
Berlin: Julius Springer 1927. 8vo, vi, 303pp., ill., maps; contents: on Korea pp.238-290; Domschke/Goossmann 360

0631   1929   ENG 1002
Haring, Douglas Gilbert. The Land of Gods and Earthquakes
NY: Columbia University Press 1929. 8vo, 203pp., ill.

0632   1933   ENG 337
Bodley, R.V.C. A Japanese Omelette. A British Writer's Impressions of the Japanese Empire
Tokyo: Hokuseido 1933. 8vo, 242pp., ill., index; contents: on Korea pp.109-119

0633   1938   ENG 313
Price, Willard. Children of the Rising Sun
NY: National Travel Club 1938. 8vo, 316pp., ill., index; contents: pp.143-166 on Korea

0634   1939   GER 60
Sieburg, Friedrich. Die Stählerne Blume. Eine Reise nach Japan [The Steelen

Flower. A Journey to Japan]
Frankfurt (Main): Societäts-Verlag 1939. small 8vo, 188pp., ill.

0635   1941   ENG 379e2
Franck, Harry A. The Japanese Empire. A Geographical Reader. in the series: Travels in Many Lands.
Dansville: Owen (1927) 1941. 12mo, 258pp., ill., maps, glossary

0636   1942   ENG 917
James, Neill. Petticoat Vagabond in Ainu Land and up and down Eastern Asia.
NY: Charles Scribner's Sons 1942. 317pp., ill., index; contents: pp.246-264 on Korea

IV.h.8) KOREA

0638   1880   ENG 213 (3 ex.)
Oppert, Ernest. A Forbidden Land : Voyages to the Corea. With an Account of its Geography, History, Productions and Commercial Capabilities &c. &c.
NY: Putnam 1880. 8vo, 349pp., ill., maps, appendix; comment: Oppert was a German merchant adventurer; the book was published decades after he "visited" Korea; Gompertz 83

0639   1880   ENG 159 : 1880
Oppert, Ernest. A Visit to Corea
in: Chambers Journal of Popular Literature, Science and the Arts, Vol.1, 1880, pp.598-600

0640   1886   ENG 506 : 1886
Carles, W.R. Recent Journeys in Korea
in: Proceedings of the Royal Geographic Society and Monthly Record of Geography 1886, No.5, 8vo, pp.289-312; Gompertz 173

0641   n.d. (c.1890)   FRE 5
Vautier, Claire and Frandin, Hippolyte. En Coree [In Korea]
Paris: Ch. Delagrave, n.d. (c.1890). 8vo, 188pp., ill.; Gompertz 404 (dated 1905)

0642   1890   FRE 285 Vol.56
Varat, M. Charles. Une Mission en Coree [A Mission in Korea]
in: Le Monde Illustre, vol.56, 1890, pp. 103-106

0643　　　　　　　　　　　　　　　1891　　　ENG 1440
Campbell, Charles W. Report by Mr. C.W. Campbell of a Journey in North Corea in September and October 1889
London: Harrison & Sons 1891. 39pp., Diplomatic Blue Books; Gompertz 196

0644　　　　　　　　　　　　　　　1892　　　FRE 184
Varat, Charles. Voyage en Coree, explorateur charge de missions ethnographiques par le ministre de l'instruction publique 1888-1889 [Voyage in Korea, on an Ethnographic Mission for the Minister of Public Instruction, 1888-1889]
Paris: La Tour du Monde 1892, pp.289-368

0645　　　　　　　　　　　　　　　1892　　ENG 506 : 1892
Campbell, Charles W. A Journey through North Korea to the Ch'ang-Pai Shan
in: Proceedings of the Royal Geographic Society and Monthly Record of Geography Vol.14, 1892, No.3, 8vo, pp.142-161; Gompertz 204

0646　　　　　　　　　　　　1892ENG 462Vol.8, no.11
Campbell, Charles W. A Recent Journey in Northern Korea
in: Scottish Geographic Magazine Vol.VIII, 1892, pp.579-590; Gompertz 203

0647　　　　　　　　　　　　　　　1892　　FRE 67 Vol.43
Varat, Charles. Voyage en Coree [Voyage in Korea]
in: Le Tour du Monde, Vol.43, 1892, pp.289-263; Gompertz 214

0648　　　　　　　　　　　　　　　1894　　　ENG 1028
Cavendish, A.E.J. Korea and the Sacred White Mountain, being a Brief Account of a Journey in Korea in 1891. Together with an Account of an Ascent of the White Mountain, by Captain H.E. Goold-Adams
London: Philip & Son 1894. 8vo, 224pp., ill., index; Gompertz 222

0649　　　　　　　　　　　　　1894　　ENG 462 Vol.X
Cavendish, A.E.J. Two Months in Korea
in: Scottish Geographic Magazine Vol.X, 1894, pp.561-573, map; Gompertz 229

0650　　　　　　　　　　　　　　　1894　　FRE 288 Vol.CIV
Chaille-Long. En Coree [In Korea]
in: L'Illustration, vol.CIV, 1894, 4to, pp.178-179

0651	1895	GER 82

Hesse-Wartegg, Ernst von. Korea : Eine Sommerreise nach dem Land der Morgenruhe 1894 [Korea : A Summer Journey to the Land of the Morning Calm 1894]

Dresden etc.: Carl Reissner 1895. large 8vo, 220pp., ill., map; Gompertz 263; Domschke/Goossmann 448

0656	1897	GER 24 Vol.43

Mauer, J.P. Freiherr von Grünau's Tour durch Korea [Baron von Grünau's Tour through Korea]

in: Petermann's Geographische Mitteilungen Vol.43, 1897, p.295

0657	1898	ENG 168 (5 ex.)

Bishop, Isabella S. Bird. Korea and her Neighbours : A Narrative of Travel, with an Account of the Recent Vicissitudes and Present Position of the Country

London: John Murray 1898. 2 vols., vol.1 : xvii, 261pp., ill., map, vol.2 : x, 321pp., ill., map, index, ads; Preface by Sir Walter Hillier, British Consul-General for Korea; Gompertz 284

0658	1898	ENG 168eAm

Bishop, Isabella S. Bird. Korea and her Neighbours : A Narrative of Travel, with an Account of the Recent Vicissitudes and Present Position of the Country

NY: Fleming H. Revell MDCCCXCVIII (1898). 8vo, 488pp., ill., map, index (both volumes of the original English edition here edited in one single volume); Gompertz 284

0659	1904	FRE 200

Bourdaret, Emile. En Coree [In Korea]

Paris: Plon-Nouritt et Cie. 1904. 12mo, ii, 361pp., ill.; Gompertz 351

0660	1904	FRE 232

Ducrocq, Georges. Pauvre et Douce Coree [Poor and Gentle Korea]

Paris: H. Champion 1904. 12mo, 87pp., ill.; Gompertz 337

0661	1904	FRE 232e2

Ducrocq, Georges. Pauvre et Douce Coree [Poor and Gentle Korea]

Paris: H. Champion 1904. 12mo, 87pp., ill.; Gompertz 337

0662	1904	ENG 467 (4 ex.)

Hamilton, Angus. Korea

NY: Charles Scribner's Sons 1904. 8vo, xliii, 313pp., ill., maps, index; Gompertz 348

0663 1904 ENG 467e2
Hamilton, Angus. Korea
London: William Heinemann 1904. 8vo, xliii, 309pp., ill., map, index; Gompertz 348

0664 1904 GER 79 (2 ex.)
Hamilton, Angus. Korea. Das Land des Morgenrots nach seinen Reisen geschildert [Korea : The Land of the Sunrise described based on his Travels]
Leipzig: Otto Sparner 1904. translated from the English, 8vo, 295pp., ill., map, index; Gompertz 349; Domschke/Goossmann 411

0665 1904 FRE 62
Pange, Jean de. En Coree [In Korea]
Paris: Hachette 1904. 8vo, 63pp., ill., map; Gompertz 383

0666 1904 FRE 72 : 1904
Pange, Jean de. A Travers la Coree [Across Korea]
in: A Travers le Monde 1904, pp.65-68, 73-76, 81-84; Gompertz 381

0667 1904 FRE 178 (2 ex.)
Hagen, A. Une Voyage en Coree [A Voyage in Korea]
in: Le Tour du Monde 1904 pp.133-156; Gompertz 373

0668 1905 GER 67 (2 ex.)
Genthe, Siegfried. Korea
Berlin: Allgemeiner Verlag für Deutsche Literatur 1905. 8vo, 343pp., edited by Dr. G. Wegener, after the author having being murdered in Morocco; Gompertz 408

0669 1905 ENG 168e2 : 2
Bishop, Isabella S. Bird Korea and her Neighbours : a Narrative of Travel, with an Account of the Vicissitudes and Position of the Country
London: John Murray 1905. 8vo, v, 321pp., ill., map, index; only volume 2; Gompertz 284

0670 1905 GER 132
Hamilton, Angus. Quer durch Korea [Across Korea]
in: Jahrbuch der Weltreisen, Vol.4, 1905, pp.200-215; excerpt from A.H., Durch das Land der Morgenfrische, Leipzig, 1904

0671	n.d. (c.1905)	FRE 4 (2 ex.)
Hamilton, Angus. En Coree. Esquisse historique - la cour imperiale - les factions du palais - agriculture et commerce, ports a traites - l'action etrangere - interets russes et japonais - la femme en Coree - la vie monacale bouddhique [In Korea. Historical Sketch - the Imperial Court - Palace Factions - Agriculture and Commerce, Ports and Treaties - Foreign Actions - Russian and Japanese Interests - the Women in Korea - the Life of Buddhist Monks]

Paris: Felix Juven n.d. (c.1905). large 8vo, 374pp., ill., map; translated from the English by L. Bazalgette; Gompertz 431

0672	n.d. (c.1905)	GER 74 (2 ex.)
Sieroszewski, Waclaw. Korea : Land und Volk nach eigener Anschauung gemeinverständlich geschildert [Korea : Land and People Described, Based on Personal Observation]

Berlin: Continent, n.d. (c.1905). 8vo, 296pp., ill., map, index, translated by Stefania Goldenring; Gompertz 409; Domschke/Goossmann 961

0673	1906	GER 73
Zabel, Rudolf. Meine Hochzeitsreise durch Korea während des Russisch-Japanischen Krieges [My Honeymoon in Korea during the Russo-Japanese War]

Altenburg, Sachsen-Altenburg: Stephan Geibel 1906. large 8vo, xvi, 462pp., ill., map, index; Gompertz 427; Domschke/Goossmann 1125

0674	1908	ENG 154 (3 ex.)
Ladd, George Trumbull. In Korea with Marquis Ito

NY: Charles Scribner's; London : Longman, Green 1908. 477pp.

0675	1909	GER 13
Kroebel, Emma. Wie ich an den Koreanischen Kaiserhof kam; Reise-Eindrücke und Erinnerungen [How I Came to the Korean Imperial Court. Voyage Memories and Impressions]

Berlin-Schöneberg: Jacobsthal 1909. large 8vo, 184pp., ill.; Gompertz 443; Domschke/Goossmann 621

0676	1910	ENG 201 (2 ex.)
Coulson, Constance C.D. Peeps at Many Lands : Korea

London: Adam and Charles Black 1910. 12mo, v, 85pp., ill.; Gompertz 447

0677 1912 SWE 4
Grebst, W. A:son. I Korea. Minnen och Studier fran "Morgonstillhetens Land" [In Korea. Thoughts and Studies of the Land of the Morning Calm]
Göteborg: Forlagsaktiebolaget Västra Sverige 1912. 8vo, 368pp., ill.; Gompertz 466

0678 1915 GER 2 (2 ex.)
Weber, Norbert O.S.B. Im Lande der Morgenstille. Reise-Erinnerungen an Korea [In the Land of the Morning Calm. Memories of a Journey in Korea]
München: Karl Seidel 1915 / Freiburg im Breisgau: Herdersche Verlagsbuchhandlung 1915, 4to, 457pp., ill., map, index; comment: Author Benedictine archabbot of St. Ottilien Abbey; he travelled Korea for 6 months in 1911; Gompertz 480; Domschke/Goossmann 1072

0679 1916 ENG 244
Gordon, Mrs. E.A. Symbols of 'The Way' Far East, and West
Tokyo: Maruzen 1916. 8vo, 172pp., addenda, ill., index; contents: travelogue mainly on Korea, focussed on religion; Gompertz 1172

0680 1920 ENG 106 Vol.20
Tisdale, Alice. The Feet of the Mighty. A Korean Highroad
in: Asia. The American Magazine on the Orient Vol.20 No.9, 8vo, pp.789-794; Gompertz 506

0681 1921 GER 195
Hanstein, Otfrid von. Bei den Tigerjägern. Reise-Erzählung aus dem Innern von Korea, "dem Lande der Morgenfrische" [With the Tiger Hunters. Travelogue from the Interior of Korea, the "Land of Morning Calm"]
Leipzig: Gustav Fock 1921. 12mo, 312pp., ill.; Domschke/Goossmann 423

0682 1921 ENG 106 Vol.21
Coatsworth, Elizabeth J. Through the Diamond Mountains of Korea with the Ancients
in: Asia. The American Magazine on the Orient Vol.21 No.1 8vo pp.16-23

0683 1923 ENG 277 (2 ex.)
Urquhart, E.J. Glimpses on Korea
Mountain View, California: Pacific Press 1923. 12mo, 103pp., ill.

0684 1923 GER 2e2 (2 ex.)
Weber, Norbert O.S.B. Im Lande der Morgenstille. Reise-Erinnerungen an

Korea [In the Land of the Morning Calm. Memories of a Journey in Korea]
München: St. Ottilien, Oberbayern : Missionsverlag 1923. 4to, 457pp., ill., map, index; comment: Author Benedictine archabbot of St. Ottilien Abbey; he travelled Korea for 6 months in 1911; Gompertz 480; Domschke/Goossmann 1072a

0685   1924   ENG 746
Herbert, Agnes. Peeps at Many Lands : Korea
London: A. & C. Black, 1924. 12mo, 88pp., ill.; Gompertz 538

0686   1924   ENG 625 Vol.4
Kedleston, Marquess Curzon of. In the Diamond Mountains of Korea
in: National Geographic Magazine 1924, Vol.46, No.4, pp.325-473; Gompertz 707

0687   1926   GER 161
Klautke, Paul. Keum Gang San, die Diamantberge Koreas [Korea's Diamond Mountains]
Tokyo: Deutsche Gesellschaft für Natur- und Völkerkunde, Mitteilungen vol.21, 1926. 8vo, 60pp., ill.; Gompertz 708; Domschke/Goossmann 525

0688   1927   GER 102
Weber, Norbert O.S.B. In den Diamantbergen Koreas [In Korea's Diamond Mountains]
Oberbayern: Missionsverlag St. Ottilien 1927. 8vo, ix, 27, 108pp., ill.; comment: Author archabbot of St. Ottilien, travelled to Korea Kumgangsan area in 1925; Gompertz 709; Domschke/Goossmann 1068

0689   1936 ENG 511 Vol.3 (2 ex.)
Hett, G.V. A Korean Journey
in: The Geographic Magazine Vol.3 1936, pp.274-292; Gompertz 644

0690   1937   SWE 13
Bergman, Sten. I Morgonstillhetens Land [In the Land of the Morning Calm]
Stockholm: Albert Bonnier 1937. 230pp.; Gompertz 660

0691   1937   FRE 167 (2 ex.)
Kang, Younghill. Au pays du matin calme [In the Land of the Morning Calm]
Paris: Plon 1937. 12mo, 285pp.

0693   1938   ENG 900 Vol.21
A Missionary Priest. Pen Sketches of Korea: Korea, the Land of Mystery - Korean Salutations, Reminiscent of the Gospels - Korean Crowds - Korean Character - Education in Korea
in: The Far East, Vol.21, 8vo, pp.126-128

0694   1939   ENG 900 Vol.22
Quinlan, Thomas. In the Mountain Mission of Kogendo. An Account of Our New Mission Field in Korea, and of its Inhabitants
in: The Far East, Vol.22, 8vo pp.54-56

0695   1939   ENG 900 Vol.22
O'Connor, Rev. Patrick. In the Morning Calm. Waking up to a Land of 21,000,000 Lovable People
in: The Far East, Vol.22, 8vo, pp.270-273

0696   1944   GER 50 (2 ex.)
Bergman, Sten. Durch Korea : Streifzüge im Lande der Morgenstille [Through Korea. Expeditions in the Land of Morning Calm]
Zürich: Albert Müller Verlag 1944. 8vo, 178pp., ill., map, translated from the Swedish by Dr. Ernst Alker; Domschke/Goossmann 96

0697   1947   ENG 625 Vol.91
Hodge, John R. With the U.S. Army in Korea
in: National Geographic Vol.91 No.6 pp.829-840; Gompertz 687

0698   1948   GER 96
Towitsch, A.G. and Burow, G. 2 x Korea [Two Times Korea]
Berlin (East): Volk und Welt 1948, 16mo, 167pp., ill., translated from the Russian, comment: pro-North Korea

0699   n.d.   FRE 5e2
Vautier, Claire and Frandin, Hippolyte. En Coree [In Korea]
Paris: Ch. Delagrave n.d., 8vo, 188pp., ill.

0700   n.d.   FRE 5e4
Vautier, Claire and Frandin, Hippolyte. En Coree [In Korea]
Paris: Ch. Delagrave n.d., 8vo, 188pp., ill.

IV.i) ETHNOGRAPHY

0701   1830   ITA 1
Ferrario, Giulio. I Costume Antico e Moderno o Storia del Governo, della Milizia, della Religione, della Arti, Scienze ed Usanze di Tutti I Popoli Antichi e Moderni. Asia [Antique and Modern Costumes and the History of Government, Military, Religion, Arts, Sciences and Traditions of All Peoples, Antique and Modern. Asia]
Firenze : Celli E Ricci, 2nd edition, vol.2 : della Cina, della Corea (pp.331-354), della Giappone, della Terra di Jesso, delle Isole di Lieu-Kieu; 16mo, 451pp.; Gompertz 89

0702   1841   ENG 694
Siebold, Philipp Franz von. Manners and Customs of the Japanese
Series/Spine Title : The Family Library No.132
NY: Harper & Brothers 1841. 12mo, 298pp., ill.

0703   1846   SPA 1
El Globo. Costumbres, Usos y Trajes de Todas las Naciones : Asia [The Globe. Costumes, Habits and Suits of All Nations - Asia]
Barcelona: Imprente Hispana 1846. large 8vo, ill., 538pp.; contents: pp.527-538 on Korea and Tibet

0704   n.d. (c.1860)   ITA 11 (2 ex.)
Gubernatis, A. de. I popoli del mondo usi e costume [Habits and Costumes of the People of the World]
Milano: Francesco Vallardi n.d., 8vo, 2 vols., 591, 583pp., ill.

0705   1882   ENG 498
Keane, Augustus H. Stanford's Compendium of Geography and Travel, for General Reading; Asia : with Ethnological Appendix
London: Edward Stanford 1882. 8vo, xxxi, 723pp., ill., map, index. Based on von Hellwald's "Die Erde und ihre Völker", translated from the German by A.H. Keane

0706   1886   FRE 182 : 1886
Coste, Eugene. Und Fete en Coree [A Feast in Korea]
in: Les Missions Catholiques, 1886, pp.399-400, 449-452, 461-464, 474-477, map in appendix; Gompertz 763

0707   1894   ENG 1102e4
Smith, Arthur H. Chinese Characteristics
NY: Fleming H. Revell, 4th edition 1894. small 8vo, 342pp., ill., index; contents: not on Korea

0708   1899   ENG 471
Keane, A.H. Man, Past and Present
Series title : Cambridge Geographical Series
Cambridge: UP 1899. 8vo, xii, 584pp., ill., index

0709   n.d. (c.1900)   ENG 1323
Anonymous. The Living Races of Mankind
London: Hutchinson n.d. (c.1900). 2 vols., 4to, vol.1 384pp., maps, ill., vol.2 pp.385-776, ill., index; contents: on Korea vol.1 pp.154-160

0710   1900   ENG 1334
Shaw, Edward R. Big People and Little People of Other Lands
N.Y.: American Book Co. 1900. 12mo, 128pp., ill.; contents: chapters on China, Japan; not on Korea

0711   1902   FRE 320
Chantre, E., Bourdaret, E. Les Coreens. Esquisse Anthropologique [The Koreans. An Anthropological Outline]
Lyon: Societe d'Anthropologie de Lyon, A. Rey 1902, large 8vo, 19pp.. Gompertz 867

0712   1904   FRE 72 : 1904
Bourdaret, E. Le culte des morts en Coree [The Cult of Death in Korea]
in: A Travers le Monde 1904, pp.177-180, 190-191; Gompertz 896

0713   1904   FRE 72 : 1904
Bourdaret, M. Les sepultures en Coree [Burial Places in Korea]
in: A Travers le Monde 1904, pp.221-222; Gompertz 897

0714   1904   ENG 1370
Menpes, Mortimer. World's Children

London: Adam & Charles Black (1903) repr. 1904. 8vo, 246pp., ill., no index; contents: no Korea-chapter

0715 1905 FRE 68 : 1905
Balet, J.C. Aiko ! Aikio ! Aiko ! Funerailles Coreennes [Aigoo ! Aigoo ! Aigoo ! Korean Funerals]
in: Journal des voyages et aventures de terre et de la mer 1905, pp.193-195

0716 1905 FRE 68 : 1905
Balet, J.C. La Vie a Seoul. Marchands Coreens [Life in Seoul. Korean Merchants]
in: Journal des voyages et aventures de terre et de la mer 1905, p.268

0717 n.d. (c. 1905) ENG 505
Hammerton, J.A. (ed.). Peoples of All Nations
London: Fleetway House, 7 volumes, n.d. (c. 1905). 8vo, ill., maps, plates; vol.1 pp.1-784 Abyssinia to British Empire, vol.2 pp.785-1568 British Empire to Dahomey, vol.3 pp.1569-2352 Danzig to France, vol.4 pp.2353-3120 Georgia to Italy, vol.5 pp.3121-3888 Japan to Norway, vol.6 pp.3889-4672 Palestine to Sin-Kiang, vol.7 pp.4673-5436 South Africa to Wales; on Korea vol.5 pp/3237-3265, by F.A. McKenzie

0718 1907 FRE 297
Thalasso, Adolphe. Anthologie de l'Amour Asiatique [Anthology of Asian Love]
Paris: Societe de Mercure de France MCMVII (1907). 12mo, 377pp.; contents: on Coree pp.185-189

0719 1908 ENG 494
Keane, A.H. The World's Peoples : a Popular Account of Their Bodily & Mental Characters, Beliefs, Traditions, Political and Social Institutions
London: Hutchinson 1908. small 8vo, xi, 434pp., ill., index; contents: on Korea pp.163-165

0720 1910 ENG 1001
Markino, Yoshio. A Japanese Artist in London
Philadelphia: George W. Jacobs 1910. 8vo, 204pp., ill.

0721 1911 FRE 68 : 1911
Perigny, Maurice de. Les Chapeaux Coreens [Korean Hats]
in: Journal des voyages et aventures de terre et de mer 1911 p.66

0722　　　　　　　　　　n.d. (c.1912)　　　　　GER 52
Ritter, Gustav A. Die Völker der Erde. Asien. Populäre Schilderungen der Länder und der Lebensweise, Sitten und Gebräuche der eingeborenen Bevölkerung unter besonderer Berücksichtigung der Entdeckungs- und Forschungsreisen von Al. v. Humboldt, M.A. Castren, A.R. v. Middendorf, Karsten Niebuhr, Gebr. Schlagintweit, I. Kreitner, M. Garnier, E. Bonvalot, W. Junghuhn, Graf v. Szechenyi, A.D. Carey, C.R. Littledale, F.E. Youshusband, Fetschenko, A. Prschewalskij, Koslow, A.E. Nordenskjöld, G. Radde, F.v. Richthofen, Sven Hedin u.v.a. sowie der Niederlassungen und Besitzergreifungen der Europäer von der Entdeckung des Seeweges nach Ostindien im Mittelalter bis zur Gegenwart [Peoples of the Earth. Asia. Description of the Countries and of the Way of Life, Customs and Traditions of the Indigenous Population, with Special Consideration of the Expeditions and Travels of .... as well as of the Settlements and Acquisitions of the Europeans from the Discovery of the Sea Route to India in the Middle Ages until our Present Time]

Berlin: Merkur, n.d. (c.1912). 8vo, xii, 680pp., ill., maps; contents: on Korea pp.563-574

0723　　　　　　　　　　　　　　　1913 FRE 68 : 1913 (end)
Formin, Victor. Epouvantails Coreens [Korean Scarecrows]
in: Journal des voyages et aventures de terre et de mer 1913 p.328

0724　　　　　　　　　　　　　　　　1915　　　ENG 1129
Barnard, H. Clive. Asia in Pictures. Pictures of Many Lands
London: A.C. Black 1915. large 8vo, 64pp., ill., no index; contents: pp.57, 61 on Korea

0725　　　　　　　　　　　　　　　1919　　ENG 106 Vol.19
Goan, Elizabeth. Asiatic Hats
in: Asia. The American Magazine on the Orient Vol.19, 1919, pp.1155-1160

0726　　　　　　　　　　　　　　1922　ENG 505 : 5　(2 ex.)
Hammerton, J.A. Peoples of all Nations : their Life Today and the Story of their Past. Volume 5, Title : Japan to Oman.
London: The Fleetway House, n.d. (1922). 8vo, pp.3121-3888, ill.; contents: on Korea pp.3237-3286, by F.A. McKenzie

0727 1922 GER 148
Buschan, Georg. Illustrierte Völkerkunde [Illustrated Ethnography]
Stuttgart: Strecker und Schröder, 3rd edition, 8vo, 3 vols., 1922-1926. 704, 1106, 686pp., ill.

0728 1924 ENG 969
Huckel, Oliver. The Secret of the East. Observations and Interpretations
N.Y.: Crowell 1924. 8vo, 368pp., ill.

0729 1925 ENG 1200
Buxton, L.H. Dudley. The Peoples of Asia
London: Kegan, Paul, Trench & Trübner 1925. 8vo, 271pp., ill., index; contents: several Korea entries; Gompertz 1012

0730 1925 GER 137
Doegen, Wilhelm. Unter fremden Völkern. Eine neue Völkerkunde. [Among Alien Peoples. A New Ethnography]
Berlin: Otto Stolberg 1925. 8vo, 383pp., contents: pp.96-115; Die Koreaner, by F.W.K. Müller; Domschke/Goossmann 193

0731 1929 ENG 927
Phillips, Grace Darling. Far Peoples
Chicago: UP 1929. 8vo, 274pp., songs index; contents: on Korea pp.67-99

0732 n.d. ENG 1430
Paton, Frank H.L. Glimpses of Korea, as seen through Australian Eyes ... and an Australian Camera.
Melbourne : Brown, Prior &. Co., small 8vo, 84pp., ill., (missionary)

0733 n.d. ENG 1310
Hammerton, J.A. Manners & Customs of Mankind
London: Amalgamated Press n.d., 3 vols., 4to, vol.1 460pp., vol.2 pp.461-908, vol.3 pp.909-1336, ill., index; contents: several Korea entries

0734 1932 ENG 240e3 v.4(2ex.)
Clewell, Gladys D. Lands and Peoples. The World in Color
NY: Grolier Society 1932. 393pp., ill.

0735 1932 ENG 240e16
Grolier Society. Lands and Peoples. The World in Color. Vol.IV : Southern Asia & the Far East.
NY: Grolier Society 1932. 8vo, 384pp., ill., maps

0736 1935 GER 78
Buschan, Georg (ed.). Die Völker Asiens, Australiens und der Südseeinseln : llustrierte Völkerkunde [The Peoples of Asia, Australia and the Pacific Islands. Illustrated Ethnography]
Berlin: Globus 1935. 8vo, xxii, 1078pp., ill., maps, bibliography, index; contents: on Korea pp.649-659

0737 1936 ENG 511 Vol.3
Hett, G.V. Some Ceremonies in Seoul
in: The Geographical Magazine Vol.3, 1936, pp.179-184

0738 1938 ENG 900 Vol.21
Quinlan, Thomas. The Feat of Excited Insects. Zenra Nan Do, Korea
in: The Far East, Vol.21, 1938, 8vo, pp.176-177

0739 1939 ENG 900 Vol.22
Monaghan, Patrick. A Cycle in Cathay. Golden Jubilee Celebrations in Moppo.
in: The Far East, Vol.22, 1939, 8vo, p.129

0740 1944 GER 92
Eickstedt, Egon Freiherr von. Rassendynamik von Ostasien. China und Japan, Tai und Kmer von der Urzeit bis heute [Race Dynamics of East Asia. China and Japan, Thai and Khmer from Prehistoric Times until Today]
Berlin: de Gruyter 1944, large 8vo, xii, 648pp., ill.; contents: on Korea pp.476-480; comment: author Prof. of Anthropology and Ethnology, Univ. Breslau. This book applies the Nazi 'Race Science' on the peoples of East Asia; Domschke/Goossmann 247

0741 1946 GER 44 : 1946
Chang, K. Koreanische Volkssitten [Korean Folk Customs]
in: Du. Schweizerische Monatsschrift, 1946, no.4, pp.21-25

0742   n.d.   ENG 505e2

Hammerton, J.A. (ed.). Peoples of All Nations : A Colourful Pageant of the Races of the Modern World

London: The Amalgamated Press n.d., 4to, 2 vols., new shorter edition, vol.1 : Abyssinia to Iceland, 724pp., ill., maps, vol.2 : India to Yugoslavia, pp.725-1444, ill., maps, index

0743   n.d.   ENG 1402

Carpenter, Frank N. The Koreans at Home

pp.391-396 out of unknown magazine, 8vo, ill.

0744   n.d.   GER 168

Gleichen-Russwurm, Alexander von. Kultur- und Sittengeschichte aller Zeiten und Völker [History of the Culture and Customs of all Times and Peoples]

Wien: Gutenberg Verlag Christensen & Co., n.d., 8vo, 24 volumes in 12, ill., c. 450pp. per volume

IV.j) GEOLOGY & METEOROLOGY

0745   1886   GER 76

Gottsche, C. Geologische Skizze von Korea [Geological Sketch of Korea]

in: Sitzungsberichte der Königlich Preussischen Akademie der Wissenschaften zu Berlin, 1886, pp.857-873; Gompertz 1712; Domschke/Goossmann 368

0746   1886   GER 76

Roth, J. Beiträge zur Petrographie von Korea [Contributions to the Petrography of Korea]

in: Sitzungsberichte der Königlich Preussischen Akademie der Wissenschaften zu Berlin, 1886, pp.875-881; Gompertz 1713; Domschke/Goossmann 874

0747   n.d. (c.1888)   ENG 869

Aston, W.G. Earthquakes in Korea

3pp., taken out of a magazine, 8vo

0748   1920   ENG 944

Froc, Louis, O.S.J. Zikawei Observatory. Atlas of the Tracks of 620 Typhoons 1893-1918

Shanghai: l'Orphelinat de T'ou-se-we, 1920. 4to, 3pp., 23 maps

0749   1926   ENG 1000
Home Office, Bureau of Social Affairs. Companion maps and diagrams to the Great Earthquake of 1923 in Japan
Tokyo: Home Office 1926. 8vo, xi, large, folded maps

0750   1929   GER 24 Vol.75
Ruud, Ingolf. Eine Theorie über die Entwicklung der ostasiatischen Gebirgsbögen [A Theory on the Development of East Asian Mountain Ranges]
in: Petermanns Geographische Mitteilungen Vol.75, 1929, pp.230-234; Domschke/Goossmann 879

0751   1934   ENG 1377
Kobayashi, Teiichi. The Cambro-Ordovician Formations and Faunas of South Chosen Paleontology. Part I : Middle Ordovician Fauna. Part II : Lower Ordovician Fauna.
in: Journal of the Faculty of Science, Imperial University of Tokyo, Section II : vol.III pt.8 1934 pp.329-519, plates (= Part I); vol.III pt.9 1934 pp.521-585 (= Part II)

IV.k) ASTRONOMY

0752   1856   ENG 178 : 3
Jones, George. United States Japan Expedition. Observations on the Zodiacal Light from April 2 1853 to April 22 1856, made chiefly on Board the United States Steam-Frigate Mississippi, during her Late Cruise in Eastern Seas, and her Voyage homeward with Conclusions from the Data thus Obtained.
Washington: A.O.P. Nicholson, 1856. vol.3 out of 3 volumes, 4to, xliii, 705pp., ill.

0753   1897   FRE 301.3
Chevalier, Henri and Hong, Tyong-Ou. Guide pour Rendre Propice l'Etoile qui Garde Chaque Homme et pour Connaitre les Destines de l'Annee [Guide how to Make Favourable the Star which Guides every Man and for Knowing his Fate in the Year]
in: Annales de Musee Guimet vol.26, Paris 1897. 4to, 123pp.; translated from the Korean by Henri Chevalier and Hong Tyoung-Ou

0754 　　　　　　　　　　　　　　1936　　　ENG 1282
Rufus, W.C.　Korean Astronomy
n.pl.: Chosen Christian College 1936. 8vo, 52pp., plates

V.) HISTORY

V.a) WORLD HISTORY

0755   1652   LAT 14
Horni, Georgii. De Originibus Americanis Libri Quattuor [Four Books on the Origins of the Americans]
Hagae Comitis (Den Haag): Adr. Vlacq 1652; lib.iv chapters vi-viii pp.240-246 speculation on similarity of names Corea

0756   1698   FRE 280e8 : 1-4
Morery, Louis. Le grand dictionnaire historique ou le melange curieux de l'histoire sacree et profane ... Subtitle : ou l'on a mis le Supplement dans le meme ordre Alphabetique
[Grand Historical Dictionary, or Curious Blending of Holy and Profane History... Supplement in Alphabetical Order]
Amsterdam: George Gallet 1698. folio, 4 vols., bound in 2, vol.1-2 A-B 523pp., C-F 572pp., vols.3-4 G-M 582pp., N-Z 588pp.; contents: on Korea vol.2 p.263

0757   1727   FRE 346e3
Huet, M. Pierre Daniel) Histoire du Commerce et de la Navigation des Anciens [History of Trade and Navigation of the Ancients]
Paris: Antoine-Urbaine Coustelier, 3rd edition, 1727. 12mo, 400pp., contents: not on Korea

0759   1759   ENG 580 : 2/4, 8, 16
The Modern Part of the Universal History, compiled from the original writers by the authors of the antient
London: T. Osborne 1759, 1765, 1769, folio, vol.2 : 1759, 747pp., on the Arabs, Mongols etc., vol.3

1759, 759pp., on India, China etc., vol.4 1759, 668pp., on Japan, Cape of Good Hope, European East India Companies, vol.8, on China, 1769, 544pp.; vol.16 1765, 332pp., general index; contents: on Korea vol.3 pp.748-759 and vol.8 pp.520-544

0760   1859   FRE 53

Lostalot-Bachoue, M.E. de. Le Monde. Histoire de Tous les Peuples depuis les Temps les plus Recules [The World History of All Peoples since the Most Distant Times]

Paris : Freres Lebigre-Duquesne 1859. 4to, 10 volumes; contents: volume 9 includes chapters on the history of China and Japan, c. 490pp. per volume

0761   1867   ENG 473e2

Townsend, George H. The Manual of Dates : a Directory of Reference to the Most Important Events in the History of Mankind to be Found in Authentic Records.

London: Frederick Warne 1867. 8vo, viii, 1067pp.

0762   1899   ENG 810 : 1/2

Suetonius. History of the Twelve Caesars translated into English by Philemon Holland. Anno 1606 with an introduction by Charles Whillbley

London: David Nutt in the Strand 1899. 2 vols., vol.1 283pp., vol.2 305pp.; contents: not on Korea

0763   1902   ENG 1133

Adams, Brooke. The New Empire

NY: MacMillan 1902. 12mo, 243pp., maps, index; contents: 2 Korea entries

0765   n.d. (c.1907)   ENG 791 : 1/51

Harmsworth. History of the World

London: Harmsworth n.d. (c.1907). 8vo, 51 vols., total 6576pp., ill., maps, index

0766   n.d.   ENG 1104

Hammerton, J.A. Universal History of the World

London: Amalgamated Press, n.d., 8 vols., vol.1 712pp., vol.2 pp.713-1400, vol.3 pp.1401-2028, vol.4 pp.2029-2860, vol.5 pp.2661-3292, vol.6 pp.3295-3916, vol.7 pp.3917-4552, vol.8 4553-5212, index; contents: several Korea entries

0767   1912   ENG 1459v.8
Anonymous. Historic Tales and Golden Deeds, Vol.8 of Boys' and Girls' Bookshelf
NY: University Society, 1912. large 8vo, pp.209-416, ill., no index; contents; on Korea pp.296-303.

0768   n.d. (c.1916)   ENG 889 : 1/2
Wells, H.G. The Outline of History. Being a Plain History of Life and Mankind
London: George Newnes n.d. (c.1916). 4to, 2 vols., total 780pp., ill., index

0769   1926   ENG 890e5
Williams, Henry Smith. The Historian's History of the World. A Comprehensive Narrative of the Rise and Development of Nations from the Earliest Times as Recorded by over Two Thousand of the Great Writers of All Ages. Edited with the Assistance of the Distinguished Board of Advisors and Contributors, Vols.26-27; Index to Vols. 1-26
London: Encyclopaedia Britannica (1904) 5th edition 1926. 8vo, vol.26 : xii, 695pp.; vol.27 : 662pp.; contents: on Korea vol.27 p.278

0770   1930   POR 1e2
Guerreiro, Pelo Fernao O.S.J. Relacao Anual das Coisas Que Fizeram os Padres da Companhia de Jesus nas Suas Missoes : do Japao, China, Cataio, Tidore, Ternate, Amboino, Malaca, Pegu, Bengala, Bisnaga, Madure, Costa da Pescaria, Manar, Ceilao, Travancor, Malabar, Sodomala, Goa, Salcete, Lahor, Diu, Etiopia-a-Alta ou Preste Joao, Monomotapa, Angola, Guine, Serra Leoa, Cabo Verde e Brasil nos anos de 1600 a 1609 e do processo da conversao e Cristandade daquelas partes Tirada das Cartas que os Missionarios de la escreveram [Annual Report on the Deeds of the Fathers of the Jesuit Order in their Missions in Japan, China, Tidore, Ternate, Ambon, Malacca, Pegu, Bengal, Bisnaga, Madoera, Costa da Pescaria, Manar, Ceylon, Travancore, Malabar, Sodomala, Goa, Salcete, Lahore, Diu, High Ethiopia and PresterJohn, Monomatapa, Angola, Guinea, Sierra Leone, Cape Verde and Brasil from the Year 1600 to the Year 1609, and of the Progress of Conversing and of the Christianity in those Parts, Drawn from Letters the Missionaries Wrote from these Places]. in the series: Scriptores Rerum Lusitanarum [Writers on

Portuguese Topics].
Coimbra: Imprensa de Universidade, 1930-1942. small folio, 2nd edition, 3 vols., vol.1 : 1600-1603, xiii, 422pp., vol.2 : 1604-1606, 434pp., vol.3 1607-1609, 440pp.; edited by Artur Viegas

0771 1931 ENG 815

Suetonius. The Historie of Twelve Caesars, Emperors of Rome

London: Oxford UP 1931, Written in Latin by C. Suetonius Tranquillus and newly translated into English by Philemon Holland. From the edition of 1606, 4to, 485pp.; contents: not on Korea

0772 1935 ENG 881

Marriott, John A.R. Concise History of the World (illustrated)

London: Associated Newspapers 1935. 8vo, 772pp., ill., index

0773 1935 ENG 1369e2

Sykes, Percy. A History of Exploration from the Earliest Times to the Present Day

London: Routledge, (1933) 2nd edition, 1935, 4to, 374pp..

0774 1936 FRE 228e3

Delage, Edmond. Chroniques de la Mer [Chronicles of the Sea]

Paris: Grasset 1936. 3rd edition, 12mo, 312pp.

0775 1938 ENG 1339

Campbell, Gordon, Vice Admiral. Abandon Ship !

London: Hodder & Stoughton 1938. 8vo, ill., 327pp., map, bibliography; contents: pp.95-226 on the Alceste, on Korea pp.107-124

0776 n.d. (c.1940) ENG 11497

Loon, Hendrik Willem van. The Home of Mankind. The Story of the World we Live in.

London: Odhams Press, n.d. (c.1940). 8vo, 506pp., contents: ch.38, Korea, Mongilia and Manchukuo, pp.348-352

0777 1944 ENG 1465

Mockford, Julian. Here are South Africans

London: Adam & Charles Black 1944. 12mo, 111pp., ill., maps

0778 1947 POR 8

Lagoa, Visconde de. A Peregrinacao de Fernao Mendes Pinto (Tentativa de

Reconstituicao Geografica) [The Travels of Ferdinand Mendez-Pinto, Attempt of a Geographical Reconstruction], Vol.1 in the series: Estudos de Historia e Geografia da Expansao Portuguesa. Ministerio de Colonias, Junta de Investigacoes Coloniais, Anais 1947 [Historical and Geographical Studies on Portuguese Expansion. Ministry of the Colonies, Office for Colonial Studies].

Lisboa: Junta das Missoes Geograficas e de Investigacoas Coloniais 1947. small 4to, 156pp., ill.; contents: chapter 3 almost entirely devoted to Korea, as well as entries on pages 62-68, 71, 72, 75, as well as many other references throughout the text. Pinto Portuguese 16th century traveller

0779   1949   FRE 208e2

Baumont, Maurice. L'Essor Industriel et L'Imperialisme Colonial (1878-1904) [Industrial Expansion and Colonial Imperialism, 1878-1904]. in the series: Peuples et Civilizations. Histoire Generale [Peoples and Civilizations. General History].

Paris: Presses Universitaires de France 1949. 8vo, 628pp.

V.a.1) EAST ASIA

0780   1588   LAT 7

Maffei, Giovanni Pietro O.S.J. Selectarum epistolarum ex India libri qvatvor [Selected Letters from Four Books on India]

Venetiis (Venezia): apud Damianum Zenarium, 1588. 8vo, only right pages counted, xviii, 211pp

0781   1589   LAT 8

Maffei, Giovanni Pietro O.S.J. Historiarum Indicarum libri XVI, selectarum item ex India epistolarum eodem interprete libri III [16 Books on the History of India, Selected Items from the Three Books of Indian Letters by the Same Author]

Venetiis (Venezia): apud Damianum Zenarium, 1589. 8vo, only right pages counted, xxvii, 282pp., index at front

0782   1729   DUT 15

Salmon, Th. Hedendaegsche Historie, of Tegenwoordige Staet van Alle Volkeren : in opzigte hunner Landsgelegenheit, Personen, Klederen, Gebouwen, Zeden, Wetten, Gewoontens, Godsdienst, Regering, Konsten en

Wetenschappen, Koophandel, Handwerken, Landbouw, Landziektens, Planten, Dieren, Mineralen en andere Zaken tot de natuurlyke Historie dienende.
Part 1 : Behelzende de Tegenwoordige staet der Keizerryken China en Japan, als mede van de Ladrones, Filippynsche en Molukkische Eilanden, en van Makassar. [Modern History and Present State of All Peoples : Regarding their Country's Location, Persons, Clothing, Buildings, Customs, Laws, Habits, Worship, Government, Arts and Sciences, Trade, Craftsmanship, Agriculture, Illnesses, Plants, Animals, Minerals and Other Things related to Natural History. Part 1 : About the Present State of the Empires of China and Japan, as well as the Ladrones, the Philippines and the Molucca Islands and of Makassar]
Amsterdam: Isaak Trinion 1729. 12mo, 574pp., ill., maps; translated from the English and added to by M. van Goch

0783   1735   DUT 15e2
Salmon, Th. Hedendaegsche Historie, of Tegenwoordige Staet van Alle Volkeren : in opzigte hunner Landsgelegenheit, Personen, Klederen, Gebouwen, Zeden, Wetten, Gewoontens, Godsdienst, Regering, Konsten en Wetenschappen, Koophandel, Handwerken, Landbouw, Landziektens, Planten, Dieren, Mineralen en andere Zaken tot de natuurliyke Historie dienende.
Part 1 : Behelzende de Tegenwoordige staet der Keizerryken China en Japan, als mede van de Ladrones, Filippynsche en Molukkische Eilanden, en van Makassar. [Modern History and Present State of All Peoples : Regarding their Country's Location, Persons, Clothing, Buildings, Customs, Laws, Habits, Worship, Government, Arts and Sciences, Trade, Craftsmanship, Agriculture, Illnesses, Plants, Animals, Minerals and Other Things related to Natural History. Part 1 : About the Present State of the Empires of China and Japan, as well as the Ladrones, the Philippines and the Molucca Islands and of Makassar]
Amsterdam: Isaak Trinion, second edition 1736. 12mo, xviii, 645, xvii pp.; see DUT 15

0784   1742   LAT 12
Maffei, Giovanni Pietro O.S.J. Jo. Petri Maffeji Bergomatis e Societate Jesu Opera Omnia Latine Scripta, nunc primum in unum corpus collecta, variisque illustrationibus exornata [J.P. Maffei of Bergamo and the Jesuit Society's Collected Works Written in Latin, now for the First Time Compiled in one

Edition, Ornated with Various Illustrations]
Bergamo: Lancellotus, Vol.I : 1742. 4to, 458pp., index; Vol.II : 1742, 514pp., index, 64 pp.,; contents: mostly about Japan

0785 1755 FRE 340

Rollin, M. Histoire Moderne des Chinois, des Japonnais, des Indiens, des Persans, des Turcs, des Russiens etc. [Modern History of the Chinese, the Japanese, the Indians, the Persians, the Turks, the Russians etc.]

Paris: Desaint et Saillant 1755-1778. 12mo, 30 vols., vol.1 MDCCLV (1755) 486pp., vol.2 MDCCLV (1755), 485pp., vol.3 MDCCLVI (1756), 496pp., vol.4 MDCCLVI (1756), 486pp., vol.5 MDCCLVI (1756), 496pp., vol.6 MDCCLVII (1758), 488pp., vol.7 MDCCLX (1760), 567pp., vol.8 MDCCLX (1760), 478pp., vol.9 MDCCLXII (1762), 612pp., vol.10 MDCCLXII (1762), 476pp., vol.11 MDCCLXIV (1764) 515pp., vol.12 MDCCLXIV (1764) 558pp., vol.13 MDCCLXXII (1772) 530pp., vol.14 MDCCLXXII (1772) 474pp., vol.15 MDCCLXVIII (1768) 446pp., vol.16 MDCCLXXII (1772) 461pp., vol.17 MDCCLXX (1770) 458pp., vol.18 MDCCLXX (1770) 468pp., vol.19 MDCCLXXI (1771) 478pp., vol.20 MDCCLXXI (1771) 468pp., vol.21 MDCCLXXI (1771) 476pp., vol.22 MDCCLXXI (1771) 467pp., vol.23 MDCCLXXIII (1773) 480pp., vol.24 MDCCLXXIII (1773) 469pp., vol.25 MDCCLXXIV (1774) 462pp., vol.26 MDCCLXXIV (1774) 478pp., vol.27 MDCCLXXVI (1776) 500pp., vol.28 MDCCLXXVI (1776) 488pp., vol.29 MDCCLXXVIII (1778) 488pp., vol.30 MDCCLXXVIII (1778) 297, 224pp., index; contents: on Coree vol.1 pp.445-486

0787 1756-1758 FRE 337

Deguignes, M. Histoire Generale des Huns, des Turcs, des Mongols et des Autres Tartares occidentaux, & C. [General History of the Huns, Turks, Mongols and Other Oriental Tatars]

Paris: Desaibnt & Saillant 1756-1758. small 4to, vol.1 MDCCLVI (1756), 471pp.; vol.1.2 MDCCLVI (1756) 522pp., vol.2 MDCCLVI (1756), 292pp., vol.3 MDCCLVII (1757), 542pp., vol.4 MDCCLVIII (1758), 517pp., index

0788 1764 GER 153

Semler, Johannes Salomon (ed.). Allgemeine Geschichte der Ost- und Westindischen Handlungsgesellschaften in Europa [General History of the European East and West India Companies]

Halle 1764. 2 vols., translated by J.S. Semler, large 8vo, 600, 706pp., ill., no index

0789 1858 GER 66

Kaeuffer, Johann Ernst Rudolph. Geschichte von Ost-Asien. für Freunde der Geschichte der Menschheit dargestellt [History of East Asia, Described for

Friends of the History of Mankind]
Leipzig: Brockhaus 1858-1860. 8vo, 3 vols., vol.1 1858 485pp., vol.2 1859 814pp., vol.3 1860 727pp., map, index

0790 1876 ENG 1054
Balfour, Frederic Henry. Waifs and Strays from the Far East, Being a Series of Disconnected Essays on Matters Relating to China
London : Trübner 1876. 8vo, 223pp.; pp.63-70, contents: on Korea

0791 1893 DEN 8
Konow, Henrik. I Asiens Farvande [Sailing in Asia's Waters]
København: Philipsen 1893, 409pp.

0792 1900 ENG 310
Hannah, Ian C. A Brief History of Eastern Asia
London: T. Fisher Unwin, 1900. 12mo, xvi, 303pp., index; contents: on Korea pp.250-253

0793 1904 ENG 449
Douglas, Robert K. Europe and the Far East
Series title : Cambridge Historical Series
Cambridge: UP 1904. 12mo, vol.1 : vii, 450pp., vol.2 : vii, 487pp., maps, bibliography, index

0794 1904 ENG 504 : 2
Helmolt, H.F. (ed.). The World's History : a Survey of Man's Record. Vol.II : Oceania, Asia and the Indian Ocean.
London: William Heinemann 1904. small 4to, x, 642pp., ill., maps, index; contents: on Korea pp.114-121

0795 n.d. (c.1914) ENG 1420:2
Bryce, Viscount. The Book of History. A History of All Nations. Vol.III : The Far East.
N.Y.: Grolier, n.d., illustrated. 8vo, 885pp.; contents: pp.857-885 : Angus Hamilton, Korea, The Land of the Morning Calm

0796 1911 ENG 310e2
Hannah, Ian C. Eastern Asia : A History. Being the Second Edition of a Brief History of Eastern Asia. Entirely Rewritten.
London & Leipsic: T. Fisher Unwin 1911. 8vo, 327pp., index

0797   1912   ENG 449e2

Douglas, Robert K. Europe and the Far East.
Series title : Cambridge Historical Series.

Cambridge: UP (1904) 1912. 12mo, 487pp., maps, bibliography, index. Revised and corrected with an additional chapter (1904-1912) by Joseph H. Longford

0798   1914   ENG 317

Tappan, Eva March (ed.). A History of the World in Story, Song and Art, Vol.1 : China, Japan and the Islands of the Pacific. Series title : The World's Story in 14 Volumes.

Boston & NY: Houghton Mifflin (Riverside) 1914. 8vo, xxx, 570pp., ill.; contents: on Korea pp.255-278, by Homer B. Hulbert

0799   1918   FRE 307

Maspero, Henri. Etude d'Histoire d'Annam [Study of the History of Annam]

in: Bulletin de l'Ecole Fraçaise d'Extreme Orient, Hanoi : Imprimerie d'Extrem Orient 1918, large 8vo, 36pp.

0800   1921   FRE 8 : 1/3

Grousset, R. Histoire de l'Asie [History of Asia]

Paris: G. Cres & Cie 1921-1922, 8vo, 3 vols., vol.1 : L'Orient, vi, 308pp., vol.2 : L'Inde et la Chine, viii, 400pp., vol.3 : Le Monde Mongol, le Japon, ii, 486pp.; contents: no chapter on Korea

0801   1923   FRE 255

Cordier, Henri. Melanges d'Histoire et de Geographie Orientale [Essays on Eastern Geography and History]

Paris: Jean Maisonneuve & Fils, 1923. 8vo, 273pp.

0802   1923   ENG 1075

Webster, Hutton. History of the Far East

Boston: D.C. Heath, 1923. 8vo, 173pp.

0803   1923   DEN 4

Karlgren, Bernhard. Østasien I det Nittende Aarhundrede [East Asia in the 19th Century]

København: Gyldendal 1923. 96pp.

0804 1925 GER 134
Krause, F.E.A., Geschichte Ostasiens [History of East Asia]
Göttingen: Vandenhoeck & Ruprecht, 2 vols., 1925. 8vo, 400, 488pp., map, bibliography; on Korea vol.I pp.262-276, vol.II pp.244-264, 400-454; Domschke/Goossmann 612

0805 1926 ENG 272
Steiger, G.N., Beyer, H.O. and Benitez, C., A History of the Orient
Boston etc.: Ginn and Company 1926. 12mo, ix, 469pp., ill., maps, bibliography, index

0806 1928 ENG 287 (2 ex.)
Treat, Payson J. The Far East : a Political and Diplomatic History. in the series: Harper's Historical Series.
NY and London: Harper & Brothers 1928. 8vo, xi, 549pp., maps, bibliography, index

0807 1928 ENG 621
Vinacke, Harold M. A History of the Far East in Modern Times. in the series: Borzoi Historical Series.
NY: Alfred A. Knopf MCMXXVIII (1928). 8vo, xx, 479pp., maps, index

0808 1929 FRE 14 (2 ex.)
Grousset, Rene. Histoire de l'Extreme Orient [History of the Far East]
Paris: Librairie Orientaliste Paul Geuthner 1929. 8vo, 2 vols., vol.1 : xvii, 402pp., vol.2 : pp.403-770, ill., maps, bibliography, index

0809 1937 ENG 112 (2 ex.)
Park, No-Young. Retreat of the West. The White Man's Adventure in Eastern Asia
Boston: Hale (1937). 8vo, xiv, 336pp., bibliography. Introduction by Prof. Blakeslee. comment: author historian (Ph.D., Harvard), Korean-American. The book covers all periods of history.

0810 1937 ENG 1437
Cable, Boyd. A Hundred Year History of the P & O Peninsular and Oriental Steam Navigation Company.
London: Ivar Nicholson & Watson 1937. large 8vo, 289pp., ill., index; contents: not on Korea

0811 1941 ENG 621e4(2 ex.)
Vinacke, Harold M. A History of the Far East in Modern Times
NY: Crofts 1941. 8vo, 643, 15pp., maps, index

0812 1942 ENG 708
Bishop, Carl Whiting. Origin of the Far Eastern Civilizations : a Brief Handbook. Smithsonian Institution War Background Studies No.1
Washington: Smithsonian Institution 1942. 8vo, 53pp., ill., map

0813 1947 ENG 1073
Latourette, Kenneth Scott. A Short History of the Far East
NY: MacMillan 1947. 8vo, 665pp., index

0814 1948 ENG 1147
Eckel, Paul E. The Far East since 1500
London: George Harrap 1948. 8vo, 820pp., index; contents: numerous Korea entries

0815 1950 GER 71
Waldschmidt, Ernst. (ed.). Weltgeschichte in Einzeldarstellungen. Geschichte Asiens [World History in Monographs. History of Asia]
München: Bruckmann 1950. 8vo, 767pp.; contents: maps on Japan and Korea pp.545-714, by Oskar Kressler

0816 n.d. FRE 77 : 1
Coubertin, Pierre de. Histoire Universelle. Les Empires d'Asie [Universal History. The Empires of Asia]
Aix en Provence, Societe de l'Histoire Universelle, n.d., 8vo, 92pp.; contents: Korea pp.35-37

V.a.2) CHINA

0817 1588 ITA 9 : 2
Mendoza, Juan Gonzalez de, O.S.A. Dell'Historia della China, Pt.2 [Of the History of China, Pt.2]
Venezia: Andrea Muschio MDLXXXVIII (1588). 12mo, pp. (lxxii) 462 (ii), translated from the Spanish by Francesco Auanzo

0818 1654 LAT 3
Martini, Martin O.S.J. De bello Tartarico historia : in qua, quo pacto Tartarihacnostra ætate Sinicum imperium inuaserint, ac fere totum occuparint,

narratur, eorumque mores breuiter describuntur [On the Tartarian War : in which is reported, how the Tartars in our days invaded the Chinese Empire and occupied all of it, their customs also briefly described]

Köln: Kalckhoven 1654. small 16mo, 131, 49pp., map

0819 1655 LAT 1

Mendoza, Juan Gonzalez de, O.S.A. Rerum morumque in regno Chinensi maxime notabilium historia .. Item PP. Augustinianorum & Franciscanorum in illud ingressus... Ex Hispanica Lingua in Latinam transtulit [Most Notable History of the Things and Customs in the Chinese Empire, and how the Augustinian and Franciscan Monks entered it; translated from the Spanish into the Latin Language]

Antverpiae (Antwerpen): Francisci Fickaert 1655. 8vo, 2 parts in 1, (4), 176, 222, (14) pp.

0820 1658 LAT 9

Martini, Martin O.S.J. Sinicae historiae decas prima : Res a gentis origine ad Christum natum in extrema Asia, sive Magno Sinarum imperio gestas complexas [Book 1 of Chinese History : Things happended in Farthest Asia from the Origin of the People to the Birth of Christ, or the Complex History of the Great Chinese Empire]

Monachi (München): L. Straub für J. Wagner MDCLVIII (1658). small 8vo, 362pp., ill., index

0821 1670 FRE 180

Palafox, Juan de. Histoire de la Conqueste de la Chine par les Tartares. Contenant plusieurs choses remarquables, touchant la Religion, les Moeurs, & les Coutumes de ces deux Nations, & principalement de la derniere [History of the Conquest of China by the Tatars. Containing several remarkable Subjects, touching the Religion, Customs & Habits of both Nations, mainly the latter]

Paris: Bertier 1670. 8vo, xvi, 478pp.; Palafox worked on reports sent to him in Mexico from the Philippines; translated from the Spanish. 'Tatars' refer to Manchus.

0822 1673 LAT 5

Rougemont, Francisco de, O.S.J. Historia Tartaro-Sinica nova : Curiose complectens ab anno 1660. Aulicam Bellicamque inter Sinas disciplinam. Sacrorum Jura, &c Sacrificulorum; Christianae Religionis prospera adversaque, singulari fide, elegantia facili, idoneis testimoniis breviter & clare describens [New Tartarian-Chinese History. Curiosities completing since 1660. Military and Civil Service Discipline in China. Of Holy Laws and Sacrifices. Brief and Clear Description of the Prospering and Suffering of the Christian Religion, the Singular Faith, after elegantly made, fitting testimonies]

Lovanii (Leuven): Martini Hullegaerde MDCLXXIII (1673). 16mo, 328pp., map

0823   1741   ENG 584e3 (2 ex.)
Halde, Peter du, O.S.J. General History of China

London: J. Watts and B. Dod 1741. 4 vols., 8vo, vol.1 : 509pp., vol.2 : 438pp., vol.3 : 496pp., vol.4 : 464pp., ill., maps, translated from the French; contents: on Korea vol.4 pp.381-428

0824   1754   FRE 219
Brunem, Vojeu de O.S.J. Histoire de la conquete de la Chine par les Tartares Mancheoux ; a laquelle on a joint un accord chronologique des Annales de la Monarchie Chinoise, avec les epoques de l'ancienne histoire sacree & profane, depuis le Deluge jusqu'a Jesus-Christ [History of the Conquest of China by the Manchu Tartarians, to which is added a Chronological Account of Annals of the Chinese Empire, with Sacred and Profane Epochs of the Ancient History, from the Flood until Jesus Christ]

Lyon: Chez les Freres Duplain 1754. 2 vols., 12mo, vol.1 : 345pp., vol.2 : 318pp.; comment: Author's name an anagram of his real name Jouve de Embrun, a Jesuit Father born at Embrun Nov. 1st 1701, died at Lyon April 2 1758.

0825   1755   ENG 1423
Rollin. The History of China upon the Plan of Mr. Rollin's Antient History, translated from the French

London: J. and P. Knapton 1755. 8vo, 382pp., contents: pp.349-382 History of Corea

0826   1837   FRE 58
Pauthier, M.G. L'Univers Histoire et description de tous Les Peuples.
Chine ou description historique, geographique et litteraire de ce vaste empire, d'apres documents chinois, Premiere Partie [Universal History and Description of all Peoples. China or Historical, Geographical and Literary Description of that Empire, from Chinese Documents, First Part]

Paris: Firmin Didot Freres, MDCCCXXXVII (1837). 8vo, 493pp., ill., map

0827　　　　　　　　　　　　　　　　1852　　　　　DUT 3
Gützlaff, Karl. Güetzlaff's Geschiedenis van het Chinesche Rijk, van de Oudste Tijden tot op den Vrede van Nanking [Gützlaff's History of the Chinese Empire, from the Oldest Times to the Peace of Nanking]
's-Gravenhage: K. Fuhri 1852. 8vo, 2 vols., vol.1 : 395pp., map, vol.2 : 435pp., ill., translated from the English by K.N. van Meppen

0828　　　　　　　　　　　　　　　　1860　　　　　FRE 10
A. S. et D. Histoire complete de l'empire De La Chine : Depuis son Origine Jusqu'a nos Jours [Complete History of China, from its Origin until our Days]
Paris: Parent Desbarres 1860. 16mo, 2 vols. bound in 1, 336+310pp., ill., continued to our days by M. P. D

0829　　　　　　　　　　　　　　　　1884　　　　　GER 143
Fries, Sigmund Ritter von. Abriss der Geschichte Chinas seit seiner Entstehung [Sketch of the History of China since its Emergence]
Wien: Wilhelm Frick; Hong Kong & Shanghai: Kelly & Walsh 1884. 8vo, 284pp.

0830　　　　　　　　　　　　　　　　1893　　　　　ENG 147
Boulger, Demetrius Charles. A Short History of China : Being an Account for the General Reader of an Ancient Empire and People
London: W.H. Allen & Co. 1893. 8vo, 436pp., map, index

0831　　　　　　　　　　　　　　　　1897　　　　　ENG 252
Williams, S. Wells et al. A History of China, Being the Historical Chapters from "The Middle Kingdom".
NY : Scribner's 1897. 8vo, 474pp., map, index. With concluding chapter by Frederick W. Williams

0832　　　　　　　　　　　　　　　　1899　　ENG 327 (2 ex.)
Douglas, Robert K. The Story of the Nations, vol.51. China.
London: T. Fisher Unwin, MDCCCXCIX (1899). 12mo, xlx, 456pp., ill., map, index

0833　　　　　　　　　　　　　　　　n.d.　　　　ENG 327e3
Douglas, Robert K. The Story of the Nations, vol.51. China
London: T. Fisher Unwin, (1899) n.d., 12mo, xlx, 476pp., ill., map, index

0834   1912   ENG 327e4
Douglas, Robert K. The Story of the Nations, vol.51. China.
London: T. Fisher Unwin, (1899) 1912. 12mo, xx, 492pp., ill., map, index. Brought up to date by Ian C. Hannah

0835   1913   ENG 689
Gowen, Herbert H. An Outline History of China : Part 1. From the Earliest Times to the Manchu Conquest, A.D. 1644.
Boston: Sherman, French & Company 1913. 8vo, 208pp., ill., appendix, bibliography, index

0836   1914   ENG 1223
Backhouse, E., Bland, J.O.P. Annals & Memoirs of the Court of Peking (from the 16th to the 20th Century)
London: W. Heinemann 1914. large 8vo, 531pp., ill., index; contents: on Korea pp.143-147

0837   1914   ENG 1209
Li, Ung Bing. Outlines of Chinese History
Shanghai: Commercial Press 1914. large 8vo, 644pp., index; contents: on Korea p.585

0838   1921   ENG 1195
Bau, Mingchien Joshua. The Foreign Relations of China
NY: Fleming H. Revell 1921. 8vo, 508pp., no index

0839   1925   ENG 1345
Carter, Thomas Francis. The Invention of Printing in China and its Spread Westward
NY: Columbia UP 1925. small 4to, 282pp., ill., index; contents: several Korea entries

0840   (1925)   ENG 901e2
Soothill, W.E. China and the West. A Sketch of their Intercourse.
London: Curzon Press (1925) new impression 1974. 8vo, 216pp., index

0841   1927   ENG 356
Grantham, A.E. Hills of Blue. A Picture-roll of Chinese History. From Far Beginnings to the Death of Chien Lung, A.D. 1799
London 1927. 8vo, 643pp., ill., index, written to the general public

0842　　　　　　　　　　　　　　　1929　　　　ENG 790
Wilhelm, Richard. A Short History of Chinese Civilization
London etc.: George C. Harrap & Co. 1929. translated from the German by Joan Joshua, 8vo, 284pp., ill., maps

0843　　　　　　　　　　　　　　　1931　　　　ENG 165
Sansom, G.B. Japan : A Short Cultural History
London: Cresset Press 1931, xvi, 344pp., ill.

0844　　　　　　　　　　　　　　　1931　　　　ENG 1086
Hudson, G.F. Europe and China.
London: Edward Arnold 1931. 8vo, 336pp., maps, index; contents: 2 Korea entries

0845　　　　　　　　　　　　　　　1932　　　　DEN 7
Larsen, Kay. Den Danske Kinafart [Danish Traders Sailing to China]
København: Gads 1932. large 8vo, 104pp.

0846　　　　　　　　　　　　　　　1933　　　　ENG 1298e2
Fitzgerald, C.R. Son of Heaven. A Biography of Li Shih-Min, founder of the Tang Dynasty
Cambridge: UP (1933) Reprint 1971. 8vo, 232pp., index; contents: has Korea entries

0847　　　　　　　　　　　　　　　1934　　　　ENG 1198
Elwell-Sutton, A.S. The Chinese People. Their Past, Present and Future.
London: Ivar Nicholson & Watson 1934. 12mo, 264pp., index; contents: several Korea entries

0848　　　　　　　　　　　　　　　1937　　　　ENG 895
Hughes, E.R. The Invasion of China by the Western World
London: Adam and Charles Black 1937. 8vo, 324pp., map, index; contents: on Korea p.37

0849　　　　　　　　　　　　　　　1939　　　　ENG 618
Kiernan, E.V.G. British Diplomacy in China 1880 to 1885
Cambridge: UP 1939, 8vo, xi, 327pp., bibliography, index; contents: on Korea pp.73-85, 101-112, 160-171

0850　　　　　　　　　　　　　　n.d. (1942)　　ENG 1084e2
Green, O.M. The Foreigner in China
London etc.: Hutchinson, n.d. (1942). 8vo, 190pp., index, ill.

0851   1943   ENG 681
Chi, Tsui. A Short History of Chinese Civilization
NY: Putnam 1943. 8vo, xix, 388pp., maps, bibliography, appendices, index, Preface by Laurence Binyon

0852   1943   ENG 1067
Williamson, H.R. China among the Nations,
London: Student Christian Movement Press 1943. 12mo, 125pp., ill.

0853   1943   ENG 165e2
Sansom, G.B. Japan : A Short Cultural History
NY: Appleton-Century-Crofts, revised edition, 1943. xviii, 554pp., ill.

0854   1947   ENG 839e3
Latourette, Kenneth Scott. The Chinese. Their History and Culture
NY: MacMillan, 3rd edition, 1947. 8vo, 847pp.

0856   1950   ENG 855
Yang, Lien-Sheng. Topics in Chinese History
Cambridge, Mass.: Harvard UP 1950. Harvard Yenching Institute IV, 8vo, 57pp.

V.a.3) MANCHURIA, TURKESTAN

0857   1913   FRE 348
Cordier, H. Les Conquetes de l'Empereur de la Chine (17th-18th Century, in Central Asia)
Paris: Ernest Leroux 1913. folio, 18pp., 4 plates

0858   1931   ENG 595 (2 ex.)
Li Chi. Manchuria in History, a Summary
Peiping: Peking Union Bookstore 1932. 12mo, 43pp., ill., maps

0859   1938   ENG 1284
Hedin, Sven. The Silk Road
NY: Dutton 1938. 8vo, 322pp., ill., map, index; contents: not on Korea

0860 1941 ENG 1283
Lamb, Harold. The March of the Barbarians
London: Robert Hale 1941. 8vo, 347pp.; contents: on Korea p.207

V.a.4) RUSSIAN SIBERIA

0861 1925 ENG 1214e2
Mavor, James. An Economic History of Russia.
London: J.M. Dent, (1914) 1925. 8vo, 2 vols.; contents: vol.1, 614pp. : 1st half 19th century, vol.2, xxii, 630pp. : until Russian Revolution

0862 1937 ENG 1248e2
Pares, Bernard. A History of Russia
London: Jonathan Cape (1926) 1937. 8vo, 570pp.

0863 1944 ENG 1197
Marriott, J.A.R. Anglo-Russian Relations 1689-1943
London: Methuen 1944. 12mo, 227pp.; contents: on Korea p.154

0864 1948 ENG 876
Lengyel, Emil. Secret Siberia
London: The Travel Book Club (1947) 1948. 8vo, 285pp., ill., index; contents: actually a history of Siberia

0865 1949 ENG 1177
Mitchell, Mairin. The Maritime History of Russia 848-1948
London: Sidgwick & Jackson 1949. 8vo, 543pp., maps, index; contents: on Korea p.425

V.a.5) JAPAN

0866 1598 ITA 8
Frois, Luigi O.S.J. Ragguaglio della Morte di Quabacondono, dal Giappone nel Mese d'Ottobre del 1595 [Report on the Death of Quabacondono, of Japan, in the Month of October in 1595]
Rome: Zannetti 1598. 16mo, 61pp.

0867   1598   ITA 20
Frois, L. Copia d'una lettera annua scritta dal Giappone nel MDXCV al R.P. Claudio Acquaviva Generale della Compagnia di Giesu [Japan in 1595, to Claudio Acquaviva, General of the Jesuit Order]
Roma: Zannetti 1598. 16mo, 62pp.

0868   1599   ITA 13
Frois, L. Trattato d'Alcuni prodigii occorsi l'anno MDXCVI nel Giappone [Treatise of Events which happened in Japan in the Year 1596]
Roma: Zannetti 1599. 16mo, 88pp.

0869   1732   FRE 312
Kämpfer, Engelbert. Histoire naturelle, civile et ecclesiastique de l'empire du Japon [Natural, Civil and Ecclesiastic History of the Japanese Empire]
La Haye (= Den Haag): Gosse & Neaulme (1729) 1732. 12mo, 3 vols., 312, 416, 379pp., map

0870   1736   FRE 188
Charlevoix, Pierre-François-Xavier de, O.S.J. Histoire et description generale du Japon ou l'on trouvera tout ce qu'on a pu apprendre de la nature & des productions du pays, du caractere & des coutumes des habitans du gouvernement & du commerce, des revolutions arrivees dans l'empire & dans la religion, & l'examen de tous les auteurs, qui ont ecrit sur le meme sujet, avec les fastes chronologiques de la decouverte du nouveau monde [History and General Description of Japan or one finds all what one can learn about the Nature and Production of that Country, its Character, the Customs of its Inhabitants, the Government and Trade, the Innovations which reached this Empire, the Religion, the Examination of all Authors which have written about the same Subject, with chronological .. on the Discovery of the New World]
Paris: Gandouin etc., 1736. 9vols., 12mo, vol.1 418pp., vol.2 586pp., vol.3 590pp., vol.4 493pp., vol.5 575pp., vol.6 432pp., vol.7 475pp., vol.8 407pp., index, vol.9 442pp., ill., maps; contents: on Korea : vol.4 pp.447-493. Note : we have one complete set of 9 vols., and another set missing vol.1

0871   1869   ENG 41
Dickson, Walter. Japan : Being a Sketch of the History, Government and Officers of the Empire

London and Edinburgh: William Blackwood and Sons 1869. 8vo, vii + 489pp., ill., index

0872   1880   ENG 286

Reed, Edward J. Japan : its History, Traditions, and Religions. With a Narrative of a Visit in 1879

London: John Murray 1880. 8vo, 2 vols., vol.1 : iii, 366pp., vol.2 : x, 356pp., ill., map, index

0873   1893   ENG 214 (2 ex.)

Kuwasaburo, Takatsu (Comp.). History of the Empire of Japan : compiled and translated for the Imperial Japanese Commission of the World's Columbian Exposition, Chicago, U.S.A. 1893

Tokyo: Dai Nippon Tosho Kabushiki Kwaisha 1893. 8vo, vi, 428pp., ill., map, translated by Captain Brinkley

0874   1897   ENG 206

Bergen, R. van. The Story of Japan

NY etc.: American Book Company 1897. 12mo, 294pp., ill., index

0875   1904   ENG 139eR

Cary, Otis (Rev.). Japan and its Regeneration

Layman's Missionary Movement 1904. 12mo, viii, 160pp., ill., map, index. History of Japan and of missionary endeavours - meant as a textbook for missionaries.

0876   1904   ENG 1487

Brinkley, Captain F. Japan. Its History, Arts and Literature.

London: T.C. and E.C. Jack, 1904. 8vo, vol.5, 260pp., ill.

0877   1904   GER 159

Koch, Wilhelm. Japan : Geschichte nach japanischen Quellen und ethnographische Skizzen [Japan : History after Japanese Sources and Ethnographic Sketches]

Dresden: Wilhelm Baensch 1904. 8vo, v, 410pp.

0878   1906   POR 7

Ayres, Christovam. Fernao Mendes Pinto e o Japao : Pontos Controversos. - Discussao - Informacoes Novas. Com a repreducsao de quatro cartas geographicas portuguezas, ate hoje ineditas, e de uma carta representando o

Japao no secule XVI [Fernando Pinto in Japan : Controversial Points - Discusion - New Informations. With a Reproduction of four Portuguese Maps, so far inedited, and a Map featuring Japan in the 16th Century]
Lisboa: Typographia da Academia Real des Sciencias 1906. small folio, 156pp., ill., map

0879　　　　　　　　　　　　　　　1910　　　ENG 898e2
Longford, Joseph H. The Story of Old Japan
London: Chapman and Hall, 1910. 8vo, 409pp., map, index

0880　　　　　　　　　　　　　　　1910　　　GER 179v.2
Wirth, A. and Dirr, Adolf. Die Erschliessung Japans. Erinnerungen des Admirals Perry von der Fahrt der amerikanischen Flotte 1853-1854 [The Opening of Japan. Memories of Admiral Perry of the Journey of the American Fleet 1853-1854]
Hamburg: Gutenberg 1910. 8vo, 375pp., ill., no index

0881　　　　　　　　　　　　　　　1912　　　GER 53
Saito, Hisho. Geschichte Japans [History of Japan]
Berlin: Ferdinand Dummlers Verlagsbuchhandlung 1912. 8vo, x, 262pp., ill.; Foreword by Viscount S. Chinda & Yonekichi Miyake

0882　　　　　　　　　　　　　　　1912　　　ENG 1261
Saito, Hisho. A History of Japan
London: Kegan, Paul, Trench, Trübner 1912; translated by Elizabeth Lee, 8vo, 260pp., ill., index; contents: numerous Korea entries

0883　　　　　　　　　　　　　　　1914　　　ENG 283
Brinkley, F.R.A. A History of the Japanese People : from the Earliest Times to the End of the Meiji Era
NY & London: Encyclopaedia Britannica, 1914. small 4to, xii, 786pp., ill., maps, index. An official Japanese history, in collaboration with Baron Kikuchi (former President of the Imperial University at Kyoto)

0884　　　　　　　　　　　　　　　1916　　ENG 104　(2 ex.)
Davis, F. Hadland. Japan : from the Age of the Gods to the Fall of Tsingtau. in the series: The Nations' Histories.
London: T.C. and E.C. Jack, 1916. 12mo, x, 323pp., ill., maps, bibliography, index

0885 1916 ENG 265
Yamada, Nakaba. Ghenko : the Mongol Invasion of Japan
NY: Dutton 1916. 8vo, xx, 276pp., maps, bibliography, index; Introduction by Lord Armstrong

0886 1917 ENG 1406
Nishimura, Shinji. A Study of the Ancient Ships of Japan. Pt.1 : The Kumano-No-Morota-Bune or the Many-Oared Ship of Kumano
Tokyo: Waseda University 1917. large 8vo, 43pp., ill.

0887 1919 ENG 106 Vol.19
Griffis, W.E. Japan's Debt to Korea
in: Asia. The American Magazine on the Orient, Vol.19, 1919, pp.742-748

0888 1920 ENG 64eR (2 ex.)
Longford, Joseph H. The Story of the Nations : Japan
London: T. Fisher Unwin, 1920. 8vo, vo, 495pp., ill., map, index. New edition, revised, supplementary chapters by David Murray

0889 1921 ENG 303 (2 ex.)
Ballard, G.A. The Influence of the Sea on the Political History of Japan
London: Murray 1921. 8vo, xviii, 311pp., ill., map, appendices

0890 1923 FRE 135 : 7
Mazeliere, Marquis de la. Le Japon. Histoire et Civilisation. Le Japon comme Grande Puissance, la Transformation de l'Asie [Japan, History and Civilization. Japan as a Great Power. The Transformation of Asia]
Paris: Plon 1923. 12mo, 576pp.; Introduction : La Civilisation au debut du XXe siecle.

0891 1926 ENG 926e2
Murdoch, James. A History of Japan. Vol.1 : From the Origins to the Arrival of the Portuguese in 1542 A.D., Vol.2 : During the Century of Early Foreign Intercourse (1542-1651), Vol.3 : The Tokugawa Epoch (1652-1868)
NY: Greenberg 1926. 8vo, 3 vols., vol.1 : 667 pp., index; vol.2 : 743pp., map, index; vol.3 : 823pp., index; revised and edited by Joseph H. Longford

0892 1927 ENG 1069
Gowen, Herbert H. An Outline History of Japan

NY: Appleton 1927. 8vo, 458pp., index, map

0893　　　　　　　　　　　　　　1928　　　ENG 241
Boxer, C.R. A Portuguese Embassy to Japan (1644-1647). Translated from an unpublished Portuguese Manuscript and other contemporary Sources, with Commentary and Appendices
London: Kegan, Paul, Trench & Trübner 1928. 8vo, viii, 64pp., ill.

0894　　　　　　　　　　　　　　1929　　GER 36 : 2.1/2.2
Nachod, O. Geschichte von Japan. Vol.2 : Die übernahme der Chinesischen Kultur 645 bis ca. 850 [History of Japan. Vol.2 : The Adoption of Chinese Culture 645 until c.850]
Leipzig: Asia Major 1929-1930. 8vo, 1 vol. in two books, 1179, 64pp., map

0895　　　　　　　　　　　　　　1931　　　ENG 165
Sansom, G.B. Japan : a Short Cultural History
London: the Crescent Press 1931. 8vo, xvi, 344pp., ill., map, bibliography, index

0896　　　　　　　　　　　　　　1933　　　FRE 83
Gowen, Herbert H. Histoire du Japon : des origines a nos jours [History of Japan : From the Origins to Our Days]
Paris: Payot 1933. 8vo, 448pp.; translated from the English by S. Jankelevich

0897　　　　　　　　　　　　　　1937　　　ENG 1047e3
Akagi, Roy Hidemichi. Japan's Foreign Relations 1542-1936. A Short History
Tokyo: Hokuseido 1937. 8vo, 560pp., ill., index

0898　　　　　　　　　　　　　　1938　　　ENG 291
Mazeliere, M. le Marquis de la. Japan : History and Civilization.
Paris: Plon 1938-1939. 8 vols., 8vo, vol.1 : Old Japan, cxii, 490pp., vol.2 : Feudal Japan, 358pp., vol.3 : Japan under the Tokugawas, 356pp., vol.4 : Modern Japan : Revolution and Restoration 1854-1869, cxcvii, 310pp., vol.5 : Modern Japan : The Transformation of Japan 1869-1910, 410pp., vol.6 : Modern Japan : The Transformation of Japan, Continuation, 732pp., vol.7 : Japan as a Great Power : the Transformation of Asia, 396pp., vol.8 : Japan actually becoming a Great Power. The Transformation of Asia - the Revision of Treaties - The Sino-Japanese War, 270pp., translated from the French by Marc Loge

0899　　　　　　　　　　　　　　1938　　　FRE 49
Sansom, G.B. Le Japon. Histoire de la Civilisation Japonaise [Japan, History

of Japanese Civilisation]
Paris: Payot 1938. large 8vo, 634pp., ill.; Preface by Joseph Hackin, conservateur Musee Guimet

0900 1938 GER 158
Buschan, Georg. Kulturgeschichte Japans [Cultural History of Japan]
Wien: Bernian 1938. 8vo, 278pp., plates

0901 1939 FRE 314
Bernard, Henri O.S.J. Infiltrations occidentales au Japon avant la recouverture du dix-neuvieme siecle [Western Infiltrations of Japan prior to the 19th Century Recovery]
in: Bulletin de la Maison Franco-Japonaise vol.II no.1-4

0902 1940 ENG 544
Nourse, Mary A. Kodo. The Way of the Emperor. A Short History of the Japanese
Indianapolis: Bobbs-Merritt 1940. 8vo, 350pp., ill., maps, index

0903 1946 ENG 259
Walworth, Arthur. Black Ships off Japan. The Story of the Opening up of Japan by Commodore Perry in 1853
NY: Alfred A. Knopf 1946. introduction by Sir George Sansom, 8vo, xviii, 277pp., ill., maps, index

0904 1950 ENG 2r
Sansom, G.B. The Western World and Japan. A Study in the Interaction of European and Asian Cultures
NY: Alfred A. Knopf 1950. xvi, 504, xi pp., maps

V.a.6) KOREA

0905 1868 GER 166r
Pfizmaier, A. Nachrichten von den alten Bewohnern des heutigen Corea [Information of the Ancient Inhabitants of Present-Day Korea]
in: Sitzungsberichte der Philosophisch-Historischen Classe der Kaiserlichen Akademie der Wissenschaften, Siebenundfunfzigster Band. Jahrgang 1867 - Heft I Bis III. Wien, 1868, pp.462-523. large 8vo, xerocopy; Domschke/Goossmann 814

0906   1877   FRE 63
Koei-Ling. Journal d'une Mission en Coree [Journal of a Mission to Korea]
Paris: Ernest Leroux, 1877. large 8vo, 62pp., map, translated from the Chinese by F. Scherzer. Author was Chinese ambassador to Korea in 1866

0907   1879   FRE 293
Rosny, Leon de. Les successeurs de Zin-Min. Jusqua l'epoque de la Guerre de Coree [The Successors of Zin-Min. Until the Era of the Korean War]
in: Revue Orientale et Americaine 1879, pp.89-112

0908   1886   FRE 335
Rosny, Leon de. Les Coreens aperçu ethnographique et historique [The Koreans, an Ethnographic and Historic Outline]
Paris: Maisonneuve Freres et Ch. Leclerc, Editeurs, 1886, 16mo, 91pp.; cfr. Gompertz 757, listed under 1866, aperçu ethngraphique, 144pp.

0909   1887   ENG 1472*v.23
Carles, W.R. A Corean Monument to Manchu Clemency
in: Journal of the China Branch of the Royal Asiatic Society 1887, p.1, 285; Gompertz 1399, under 1888, attributed to W.R. Carles

0910   1888   ENG 1472*v.22
Nocentini, Ludovico (com.). Names of the Sovereigns of the Old Corean States, and Chrongical Table of the Present Dynasty.
in: Journal of the China Branch of the Royal Asiatic Society 1888, pp.90-100, 8vo

0911   1889   ENG 1472*v.22
Anonymous. The Miryeks or "Stone Men of Corea"
in: Journal of the China Branch of the Royal Asiatic Society 1888, pp.224-226, 8vo; Gompertz 1398; attributes it to Prof. Terien de Lacouperie

0912   1891   ENG 150 (2 ex.)
Ross, John. History of Corea. Ancient and Modern with Description of Manners and Customs, Language and Geology
London: J. and R. Parlane (1878) 1891. 8vo, xii, 404pp., ill., maps; Gompertz 126

0913   1894   ENG 597 (2 ex.)

Griffis, William E. Corea Without and Within. Chapters on Corean History, Manners and Religion with Hendrick Hamel's Narrative of and Travels in Corea. Annotated. Covering the Origin of the Coreans, who they are, Three Kingdoms of Ko-Rai, Land of the Morning Calm, Government, Captives in Seoul, Southern Provinces, Escape to Japan, Morals, Punishments, Festivals, Temples, Domestic Life, Houses, Marriage, Education, Mourning and Burial. Also covering their national Traits, Habits, Writing, Religion, Christianity, Americans in Corea 1867-82, native Products, Food, Clothing, Commerce, Art, Eight Provinces & a Host of Others

NY: Scribner's 1894. 12mo, 474pp., index, appendix, map; Gompertz 159-45

0914   1895   FRE 305
Sainson, Camille. Les Origines de la Coree. Extrait du Tong-kouo-thong-kieun [The Origins of Korea. Extract from Tong-kouo-thong-kieun]

Peking: Pe-T'ong 1895, 8vo, 28pp.

0915   1898   FRE 342
Gaubil, Antoine O.S.J. De la Situation de la Japon et de la Coree [On the Situation of Japan and Korea]

Leide: Brill 1898. T'oung Pao 1898, large 8vo, 16pp. comment : Manuscrit inedit du Pere A. Gaubil O.S.J. (unedited manuscript by father A. Gaubil, O.S.J.; of 1729), edited by Henri Cordier

0916   1898   FRE 206 v.19
Courant, Maurice. Stele Chinoise du Royaume de Ko Kou Ryo [Chinese(-Script) Pillar of the Kingdom of Goguryeo]

Paris: Imprimerie Nationale 1898. 8vo, 31pp.; Gompertz 1404 (= Journal Asiatique 1898 pp.210-238)

0917   1898   FRE 191 (3 ex.)
Chevalier, Henri. Ceremonial de l'achevement des travaux de Hoa Syeng (Coree)=華城城役儀執 [Ceremonial on the Achievements of the Works of Hoa Syeng (Korea)]

Leiden: E.J. Brill 1898. large 8vo, translated and summarized by Henri Chevalier, 16pp., plates

0918   1903   FRE 323
Bourdaret, Emile. Note sur les dolmes de la Coree [Note on the Menhirs of Korea]

Lyon, Societe d'Anthropologie de Lyon, vol.XXI, 1905. 12mo, 3pp.; Gompertz 1408

0919   1904   FRE 322
Bourdaret, E. Rapport sur une mission scientifique en Coree [Report on a Scientific Mission in Korea]
Extract of : Nouvelles archives des missions scientifiques

0920   1905   ENG 122 : 1/2 (2 ex.)
Hulbert, Homer B. The History of Korea
Seoul : Methodist Publishing House 1905. 2 vols., 8vo, vol.1 : vii, 409pp., vol.2 : 374pp., index

0921   1906   ENG 120 (3 ex.)
Hulbert, Homer B. The Passing of Korea
NY: Doubleday, Page & Co., 1906 / London : William Heinemann 1906. 8vo, xii, 473pp., ill., index

0922   1910   GER 165
Bälz, E. Korea von seinen Anfängen bis zu seinem Ende [Korea from its Beginnings to its End]
Frankfurt: Frankfurter Societäts-Druckerei 1910. small 8vo, 24pp., Domschke/Goossmann 65

0923   1910   GER 164
Bälz, E. Dolmen und alte Königsgräber in Korea [Menhirs and Old Royal Tombs in Korea]
Berlin: Berliner Anthropologische Gesellschaft 1910. pp.776-781; Domschke/Goossmann 63; has Zeitschrift für Ethnologie vol.42, 1911, pp.776-781 as source

0924   1911   ENG 7 (4 ex.)
Longford, Joseph H. The Story of Korea
London: T. Fisher Unwin 1911. 8vo, vii, 400pp., ill., map, bibliography, index

0925   1927   ENG 181 (4 ex.)
Gale, James Scarth. A History of the Korean People
Published serially in "The Korean Mission Field", July 24 1924 to Sept. 1927
  Seoul: Korea Mission Field 1927. large 8vo, without pagination (209pp.)

0926   1931   ENG 1410
Sekino, Tadashi. Ancient Remains and Relics in Korea. Efforts toward their Research and Preservation
Japan Council of the Institute of Pacific Relations 1931. 12mo, 31pp.

0927 1937 ENG 693:14
Sadler, A.L. The Naval Campaign in the Korean War of Hideyoshi (1592-1598)
in: Transactions of the Asiatic Society of Japan, 2nd Series, Vol.14, pp.179-208

V.b) CONTEMPORARY HISTORY & POLITICS

V.b.1) WORLDWIDE

0928 ENG 1291
The Annual Register. A Review of Public Events at Home and Abroad for the Year
London: Longman; 8vo, we have volumes 188 (1947; on 1946, 504pp.), 189 (1948, on 1947, 568pp.), 190 (1949, on 1948, 515pp.), 191 (1950, on 1949, 524pp.); on Korea vol.188 vol.189 pp.364-366, pp.320-321, vol.190 pp.331-333, vol.191 pp.335-337

0929 1887 ENG 1322
Brassey, Lord. The Naval Annual
Portsmouth: Griffin 1887. 8vo, frontispiece missing, 781pp., index; contents: not on Korea

0930 1901 ENG 1419
Creelman, James. On the Great Highway
Boston: Lothrop 1901. 12mo, 418pp., ill., index; contents: 2 chapters on Korea

0931 1906 ENG 1471 Vol.11
The World's Work. A History of Our Time
NY: Doubleday, Page & Co. 1906. Vol.XI : Nov. 1905-April 1906, pp.6800-7466, ill., large 8vo, index; has two Korea entries

0932 1907 ENG 485
Murray, A.M. Imperial Outposts : from a Strategical and Commercial Aspect, with Special Reference to the Japanese Alliance
London: John Murray 1907. 8vo, xxiv, 210pp., ill., maps. With a preface by Field Marshall Earl Roberts

0933 1907 ENG 760
Manson, Marsden. The Yellow Peril in Action. A possible Chapter in History
San Francisco: Britton & Rey 1907. 8vo, 28pp.; dedicated to the Men who Train and Direct the Men Behind the Guns. Contents: Racist, anti-Asian

0934　　　　　　　　　　　　　　1925　　　　ENG 294
Willoughby, W.W. Opium as an International Problem : the Geneva Conferences
Baltimore: Johns Hopkins Press 1925. 8vo, xvi, 585pp., appendices, index

0935　　　　　　　　　　　　　　1930　　　　ENG 1319e2
Fay, Sidney Bradshaw. The Origins of the World War
NY: MacMillan (1928) 1930. printing 1964, 12mo, 577pp.; contents: not on Korea

0936　　　　　　　　　　　　　　1938　　　　ENG 1289
Young, Eugene J. Looking behind the Censorships
London: Peter Davies 1938. small 8vo, 350pp.; contents: on Korea p.117

0937　　　　　　　　　　　　　　1941　　　　ENG 1299
Butler, Harold Beresford. The Lost Peace
London: Faber and Faber 1941. 8vo., 224pp.

0938　　　　　　　　　　　　　　1942　　　　ENG 1249
Mowrer, E.A., Rajchman, M. Global War. An Atlas of World Strategy
London: Faber & Faber 1942. large 8vo, 128pp., maps, index; contens: on Korea pp.16-17

0939　　　　　　　　　　　　　　1944　　　　ENG 1107e3
Vernadsky, George. A History of Russia. A Series of the New Home Library
Philadelphia: Blakiston (1929) 1930, 1944. 12mo, 517pp., index; contents: on Korea p.180

0940　　　　　　　　　　　　　　1944　　　　ENG 1351
Britannica Book of the Year 1944. A Record of the March of Events in 1943
Chicago: Encyclopedia Britannica 1944. small 4to, 812pp.; contents: on Chosen pp.374 and 612

0941　　　　　　　　　　　　　　1945　　　　ENG 1211
Dallin, David J. Soviet Russia's Foreign Policy 1939-1942
New Haven: Yale UP (1942) 1945. 8vo, 452p., index; contents: on Korea p.338:tr.by Leon Dennen.

0942　　　　　　　　　　　　　　1945　　　　ENG 1316
Welles, Sumner. An Intelligent American's Guide to the Peace
NY: Dryden Press 1945. 4to, 370pp., maps; contents: on Korea pp.295-298

0943　　　　　　　　　　　　　　1948　　　　ENG 1436

The Story of Our Time
NY: Grolier Society, Encyclopaedic Yearbook 1948. Thorstein V. Kalijarvi (ed.)

0944   1948   ENG 1292

Sellin, Thorsten (ed.). Peace Settlements of World War II
in : the Annals of the American Academy of Political and Social Sciences, vol.257
Philadelphia 1948. 8vo, 271pp.; contents: on Korea pp.27-29, 69-70

0945   1948   ENG 1485

Bern, Gregory. Behind the Red Mask
LA: Bern Publications 1948. small 4to, 324pp., no index, no Table of Contents; contents: chapter 13 : (Soviet/Communist atrocities); in Korea and Manchuria, pp.59-62

0946   1949   ENG 1108

Sherwood, Robert E. The White House Papers of Harry L. Hopkins, Vol.II, 1942-1945
London: Eyre & Spottiswoode 1949. 8vo, 971pp., index; contents: on Korea p.877

0947   1949   FRE 208e2

Baumont, Maurice. L'Essor Industriel et L'Imperialisme Colonial 1878-1904
Paris: Presses Universitaires de France, 1949. 8vo, 628pp., index; contents: several Korea entries

0948   1950   ENG 1238

Mallory, Walter H. Political Handbook of the World. Parliaments, Parties and the Press
NY: Harper & Brothers 1950. large 8vo, 224pp.; contents: not on Korea

0949   1950   ENG 1163

Stettinius, Edward P. Roosevelt and the Russians
London: Jonathan Cope 1950; 8vo, 320pp.; contents: on the Yalta Conference, on Korea p.96

0950   1950 ENG 1293e4 (2 ex.)

Gathorne-Hardy, G.M. A Short History of International Affairs 1920-1939
Oxford: UP 1950. 8vo, 540p., maps, index; contents: on Korea pp.310-314

0951   1950   ENG 1403

Americana Annual. An Encyclopedia of the Events in 1949
NY: Americana 1950. large 8vo, 788pp., ill., index; contents: on Korea pp.382-384

0952   1950   ENG 1342
Peterson, Maurice. Both Sides of the Curtain. An Autobiography
London: Constable 1950. 8vo, 314pp., index; contents: on Korea pp.59-60

V.b.2) FAR EAST

0953   1861   FRE 319
Chassiron, Ch. de. Notes sur le Japon, la Chine et l'Inde, 1858-1860
Paris: E. Dentu 1861. 8vo, 356pp., no index

0954   1872   ENG 1405
Papers Relating to the Foreign Relations of the United States
Washington: GPO 1873,. 8vo, xxiv., pp.125-138; contents: on China and Japan. in TOC page : Corea - see China

0955   1894   ENG 94 (5 ex.)
Curzon, George N. Problems of the Far East : Japan - Korea - China
London: Longmans, Green 1894. 8vo, xx, 441pp., ads, ill., map, index; contents: on Korea pp.81-233

0956   1894   ENG 1443
Richthofen, Baron Ferdinand von. China, Japan and Korea
in: Journal of the Royal Geographic Society, 1894. translated from Berliner Geographische Gesellschaft pp.556-572; Gompertz 225

0957   1895   ENG 69 (4 ex.)
Norman, Henry. The Peoples and Politics of the Far East
London: T. Fisher Unwin / NY: Scribner MDCCCXCV (1895). 8vo, xvi, 608pp., ill., maps, index; contents: on Korea pp.323-371; Gompertz 254

0958   1896   ENG 1088
Chirol, Valentine. The Far Eastern Question
London: MacMillan 1896. 8vo, 196pp., ill., maps, no index

0959   1896   ENG 94e2 (2 ex.)
Curzon, George N. Problems of the Far East : Japan - Korea - China
Edinburgh: Archibald Constable & Co., 1896. 8vo, xxiv, 444pp., ill., maps, index

0960 1896 GER 93
Brandt, Max von. Die Zukunft Ostasiens : Ein Beitrag zur Geschichte und zum Verständnis der ostasiatischen Frage [East Asia's Future. A Contribution to the History and Understanding of the Far Eastern Question]
Stuttgart: Strecker und Moser 1896. 12mo, 80pp.

0961 1897 GER 167
Brandt, Max von. Ostasiatische Fragen [East Asian Questions]
Berlin: Gebrüder Pätel 1897. 8vo, viii, 359pp.; Domschke/Goossmann 136

0962 1899 ENG 166 vol.46
Hallett, Holt S. The War Cloud in the Farthest East
in: The Nineteenth Century, vol.46, 1899, pp.988-995

0963 1900 ENG 529
Griffis, William E. America in the East. A Glance at Our History, Prospects, Problems, and Duties in the Pacific Ocean
NY: Narnes 1900. 12mo, 224pp., ill., index

0964 1900 FRE 60
Leroy-Beaulieu, Pierre. La Renovation d'Asie. Siberie, Chine, Japon [The Renovation of Asia. Siberia, China, Japan]
Paris: Armand Colin 1904. 12mo, xxvii, 482pp.

0965 1900 ENG 551
S., D.W. European Settlements in the Far East : China, Japan, Corea, Indo-China, Straits Settlements, Malay States, Siam, Netherlands India, Borneo, The Philipines etc.
London: Sampson Low, Manston & Co. 1900. 12mo, xii, 331pp., ill., map, index; contents: on Korea pp.41-56

0966 1900 ENG 196 (2 ex.)
Walton, Joseph. China and the Present Crisis. With Notes on a Visit to Japan and Korea
London: Sampson Low, Manston & Co. 1900. 8vo, xii, 319pp., map

0967 1900 ENG 71e3 (3 ex.)

Diosy, Arthur. The New Far East
London: Cassell (first edition, 1898) 1900. 12mo, xx, 374pp., ill., index, with illustrations from special designs by Kubota Beisen, of Tokyo. Author vice president of the Japan Society of London; contents: on Korea p.92

0968   1900   ENG 1035
Bancroft, Hubert Howe. The New Pacific
NY: Bancroft 1900. 8vo, 788pp., index, map

0969   1901   GER 22 (2 ex.)
Brandt, Max von. Dreiunddreissig Jahre in Ostasien. Erinnerungen eines deutschen Diplomaten [33 Years in East Asia. Memoires of a German Diplomat]
Leipzig: Georg Wigand 1901. 3vols., 8vo, vol.1 : xi, 319pp., vol.2 : xv, 333pp., vol.3 : xvii, 333pp.; Domschke/Goossmann 134

0970   1902   ENG 480
Temple, Richard. The Nineteenth Century Series. Progress of India, Japan and China in the Century
Toronto and Philadelphia: Linscott ; London and Edinburgh : W. & R. Chambers 1902. 8vo, xxxiv, 510pp., index

0971   1902   ENG 1383
Agreement between the United Kingdom and Japan Relative to China and Corea signed at London, Jan. 30th 1902
London: HMSO 1902, 8vo, unpaginated (2pp.); Treaty Series No.3

0972   1903   ENG 29e2 (2 ex.)
Krausse, Alexis. The Far East : its History and its Question
London: Grant Richards (first edition, 1900), MDCCCCIII (1903). 8vo, xiv, 372pp., maps, index

0973   1903   ENG 21 (2 ex.)
Foster, John W. American Diplomacy in the Orient
Boston: Houghton, 1903, 8vo, xiv, 498pp., index, articles typed in, some staining the paper

0974   1904   ENG 71e4 (2 ex.)
Diosy, Arthur. The New Far East

London: Cassell (first edition, 1898) MCMIV (fourth edition, 1904) / MCMV (reprinting 1905). 12mo, 4th edition, 8th impression, xx, 374pp., ill., index

0975 　　　　　　　　　　　　　　　　1904　　　　FRE 60e4
Leroy-Beaulieu, Pierre. La Renovation d'Asie. Siberie, Chine, Japon [The Renovation of Asia. Siberia, China, Japan]
Paris: Armand Colin 1904. 12mo, xxvii, 482pp.

0976　　　　　　　　　　　　　　　　　1905　　　　FRE 238
Metin, Albert. Etudes sur la Politique Exterieure des Etats. Vol.4 : L'Extreme Orient. Chine - Japon - Russie [Studies on the Foreign Policy of States. The Far East : China - Japan - Russia]
Paris: Librairie de "Pages Libres" 1905. 12mo, 126pp.

0977　　　　　　　　　　　　　　　1905　　ENG 284　(3 ex.)
Little, Archibald. The Far East
Oxford: Clarendon 1905. 8vo, viii, 333pp., ill., maps, index; contents: on Korea pp.243-257; Gompertz 397

0978　　　　　　　　　　　　　　　1905　　ENG 302 : 1/2　(3 ex.)
Weale, B.L. Putnam. The Re-Shaping of the Far East
London: MacMillan 1905. 8vo, 2 vols., vol.1 : xvi, 548pp., vol.2 : 524pp., map, appendices

0979　　　　　　　　　　　　　　　　　1905　　　　ENG 980
Asakawa, K. Japan and Korea
Originally published in : The Dartmouth Bi-Monthly, Vol.I, No.I, Oct. 1905, pp.29-35　several loose leaf articles bound in : K. Asakawa, Russo-Japanese War Articles, 8vo

0980　　　　　　　　　　　　　　　　　1905　　　　ENG 980
Asakawa, K. Korea and Manchuria under the New Treaty
in: Atlantic Monthly, Nov.1905, pp.3-15; several loose leaf articles bound in : K. Asakawa, Russo-Japanese War Articles, 8vo

0981　　　　　　　　　　　　　　　1906　　ENG 186　(3 ex.)
Millard, Thomas F. New Far East. An Examination into the New Position of Japan and her Influence upon the Situation of the Far Eastern Question, with Special Reference to the Interests of America and the Future of the Chinese Empire

NY: Scribner's / London: Hodder & Stoughton 1906. 8vo, xiv, 319pp., 2pp. ads, maps

0982　　　　　　　　　　　　　　1906　　　　SWE 8
Cassel, Hjalmar. Det Nya Östasien [The New Far East]
Stockholm: Albert Bonnier 1906. 8vo, 363pp.

0983　　　　　　　　　　　　　　1907　　ENG 365 (2 ex.)
Weale, B.L. Putnam. The Truce in the East and its Aftermath. Being the Sequel to 'The Re-Shaping of the Far East'
NY: MacMillan 1907. 8vo, 647pp., ill., map, index, appendices; contents: on Korea pp.40-140

0984　　　　　　　　　　　　　　1907　　ENG 132 (2 ex.)
Cotes, Everard. Signs and Portents in the Far East
London: Methuen & Co. (1907) 2nd edition 1907. 8vo, xii, 308pp., 40pp. ads, ill., index

0985　　　　　　　　　　　　　　1907　　　ENG 69e7
Norman, Henry. The Peoples and Politics of the Far East
NY: Scribner; London: T. Fisher Unwin, 7th edition, 1907. 4to, xvi, 608pp., ill., map

0986　　　　　　　　　　　　　　1908　　　ENG 304
Weale, B.L. Putnam. The Coming Struggle in Eastern Asia
London: Macmillan 1908. 8vo, xiv, 656pp., ill., map, index

0987　　　　　　　　　　　　　　1908　　ENG 233 (3 ex.)
Angier, A. Gordon. The Far East Revisited : Essays on Political, Commercial, Social, and General Conditions in Malaya, China, Korea and Japan
London: Witherby 1908. 8vo, xii, 364pp., ill., map, index; with a preface by Robert Hart

0988　　　　　　　　　　　　　　1909　　ENG 212 (2 ex.)
Millard, Thomas F. America and the Far Eastern Question. An Examination of Modern Phases of the Far Eastern Question, Including the New Activities and Policy of Japan, the Situation of China, and the Relation of the United States of America to the Problems involved.
NY: Moffat 1909. 8vo, 576pp., ill., maps, 13 appendices

0989　　　　　　　　　　　　　　1909　　　ENG 133

Hamilton, Angus et al. Problems of the Middle East
London: Eveleigh Nash, 1909. 8vo, xvi, 484pp., ads, charts, index; pp.293-365

0990   1909   ENG 40e2

Millard, Thomas F. The Far Eastern Question. An Examination of Modern Phrases of the Far Eastern Question Including the New Activities and Policy of Japan and the Situation of China
London: T. Fisher Unwin 1909. 8vo, xxiv, 576pp., ill., map; contents: on Korea pp.128-162

0991   1910   ENG 351

Harrison, E.J. Peace or War East of Baikal ?
Yokohama: Kelly & Walsh 1910. 8vo, 563pp., ill., map, index; contents: on Korea pp.364-427

0992   1910   ENG 35 (3 ex.)

Blakeslee, George H. (ed.). China and the Far East. Clark University Lectures
NY: Thomas Y. Crowell 1910. 8vo, xxii, 455pp.; A collection of essays on the Far East and the consequences of modern developments for U.S. policy; contents: on Korea pp.369-455

0993   1911   ENG 270 (6 ex.)

Collier, Price. The West in the East from an American Point of View
NY: Scribner's / London: Duckworth 1911, 8vo, 534pp.; contents: on Korea pp.463-517

0994   1911   GER 174

Franke, O. Ostasiatische Neubildungen [New Formations in East Asia]
Hamburg: Boyen 1911. large 8vo, xi, 396pp.; Gompertz 459

0995   1912   ENG 82 (3 ex.)

Lawton, Lancelot. Empires of the Far East : A Study of Japan and of her Colonial Possessions, of China & Manchuria and of the Political Questions of Eastern Asia and the Pacific
London: Richards 1912. 8vo, 2 vols., vol.1 : x, 731pp., vol.2 : vii, pp.733-1598; contents: on Korea pp.1025-1108

0996   1913   GER 35

Grünfeld, Ernst. Hafenkolonien und kolonieähnliche Verhältnisse in China, Japan und Korea : eine kolonialpolitische Studie [Harbour Colonies and Conditions similar to Colonies in China, Japan and Korea : A Study in Colonial

Politics]
Jena: Gustav Fischer 1913. 8vo, vii, 236pp., index; Domschke/Goossmann 386

0997   1913   ENG 88
Eddy, Sherwood. The New Era in Asia
NY: Missionary Education Movement of the United States and Canada 1913. 16mo, xiv, 215pp., map, 3pp.; contents: pp.57-84 : The New Era in Korea

0998   1914   ENG 17
Eliot, Charles W. Some Roads Toward Peace : A Report to the Trustees of the Endowment on Observations made in China and Japan in 1912. Carnegie Endowment for International Peace, Division of Intercourse and Education, No.1
Washinton: Carnegie Endowment 1914. large 8vo, (6) + 88pp.

0999   1918   ENG 389
Coleman, Frederic. The Far East Unveiled : an Inner History of Events in Japan & China in the Year 1916.
Boston: Houghton 1918. 8vo, 304pp., index; contents: on Korea pp.151-158

1000   1918   ENG 372
Dennett, Tyler. The Democratic Movement in Asia
NY: Association 1918. 12mo, 252pp., ill.; missionary agenda, no index, not organised by country

1001   1919   ENG 78
Brown, Arthur Judson. Mastery of the Far East : the Story of Korea's Transformation and Japan's Rise to Supremacy in the Orient
NY: Scribner's 1919. 8vo, xi, 671pp., ill., map, index

1002   1919 ENG 339 (2 ex.)
Weale, B.L. Putnam (Simpson, Bertram Lenox). The Truth about China and Japan
NY: Dodd, Mead 1919 / London: George Allen & Unwin 1921. 8vo, 248pp., appendices; contents: among the appendices app. G : Manifesto of the Korean People issued to the World on March 1st 1919 (pp.191ff); in the British edition the manifesto is not included.

1003   1919   ENG 1056

Hyndman, H.M. The Awakening of Asia
London etc.: Cassell 1919. small 8vo, 291pp.; contents: on Korea pp. 24, 74, 109, 137, 147

1004   1919   ENG 1125
MacDonald, A.J. The War and Missions in the East
London: Robert Scott 1919. 8vo, vi, 178pp.; no index

1005   1919   ENG 1081
Millard, Thomas F. Democracy and the Eastern Question
NY: Century 1919. 8vo, 446pp., appendices; no index

1006   1920   ENG 685
Fahs, Charles H. America's Stake in the Far East. World Problem Discussion Series
NY: Associated Press 1920. 8vo, 170pp.

1007   1920   ENG 1072
Sherrill, Charles H. Have we a Far Eastern Policy ?
NY: Scribner's 1920. 8vo, 397pp.

1008   1920   ENG 1258
Peace Handbooks Issued by the Historical Section of the Foreign Office. Vol.XII : China, Japan, Siam
London: H.M.S.O. 1920. 8vo, China 140pp., Mongolia 24pp., Manchuria 87pp., Tibet 75pp., Kiaochow and Weihaiwei 62pp., Japan 109pp., Siam 21pp., index 41pp.; contents: numerous Korea entries

1009   n.d. (c.1920)   ENG 1130
Harris, Norman Dwight. Europe and the East
London: George Allen & Unwin, n.d. (c.1920). small 8vo, 677pp.; contents: chapter xv : The Korean Tangle, pp.503-541

1010   1921   ENG 585
Bland, J.O.P. China, Japan and Korea
NY: Scribner's 1921. 8vo, x, ill., 327pp.; contents: pp.192-208 on Independence Movement of Korea

1011   1921   ENG 342
Hornbeck, Stanley K. Contemporary Politics in the Far East

NY: Appleton 1921. 8vo, 466pp., index, appendix, biographical notes

1012　　　　　　　　　　　　　　　1922　　ENG 434　(2 ex.)
Powell, E. Alexander. Asia at the Crossroads : Japan, Korea, China, Philippine Islands
London: T. Fisher Unwin / NY: Century 1922. 8vo, xxi, 369pp., ill.; contents: on Korea pp.101-180

1013　　　　　　　　　　　　　　　1922　　　　ENG 288
Dennett, Tyler. Americans in Eastern Asia
NY: MacMillan 1922. 8vo, xvi, 725pp.

1014　　　　　　　　　　　　　　　1922　　　　ENG 316
Hunt, Frazier. The Rising Temper in the East : Sounding the Human Note in the World-Wide Cry for Land and Liberty
Indianapolis: Bobbs-Merrill 1922. 8vo, 248pp., ill.; contents: pp.115-126 on Korea

1015　　　　　　　　　　　　　　　1922　　　　ENG 1057
Weale, Putnam. An Indiscreet Chronicle from the Pacific
N.Y.: Dodd & Mead 1922. 8vo, 320pp.

1016　　　　　　　　　　　　　　　1922　　　　FRE 329
Amar, Isaac A. Les Capitulations en Turquie, dans le Levant et en Extreme-Orient [The Concessions in Turkey, the Levant and the Far East]
Geneva: Faculte de Droit de l'Universite, dissertation 1922. 8vo, 115pp.

1017　　　　　　　　　　　　　　　1923　　　　GER 172
Franke, O. Die Grossmächte in Ostasien von 1894 bis 1914, ein Beitrag zur Vorgeschichte des Krieges [The Great Powers in East Asia from 1894 to 1914, a Contribution to the Pre-History of the War]
Braunschweig: Westermann 1923. xxiv, 8vo, 407pp.

1018　　　　　　　　　　　　　　　1924　　　　GER 55
Rohde, Hans. Der Kampf um Asien [The Fight for Asia]
Stuttgart etc.: Deutsche Verlags-Anstalt, 1924-1926. 8vo, 2 vols., vol.1 : Der Kampf um Orient und Islam [The Struggle for Orient and Islam], 270pp., maps, 1924, vol.2 : Der Kampf um Ostasien und den Stillen Ozean [The Struggle for East Asia and the Pacfic Ocean], 368pp., maps, 1926

1019   1924   ENG 1210

Millard, Thomas F. Conflict of Policies in Asia

NY: Century 1924. 8vo, 507pp., index; contents: on Korea p.53

1020   1925   ENG 335

Soyeshima, Michimasa and Kuo, P.W. Oriental Interpretations of the Far Eastern Problem

Chicago: University of Chicago 1925. 12mo, 219pp., ill., index; Lectures at the Harris Foundation 1925

1021   1925   ENG 1180

Dutcher, George Matthew. The Political Awakening of the East

NY: Abingden 1925. 8vo, 372pp., index; contents: includes Egypt; chapter IV : Japan, pp.174-237; has numerous Korea references

1022   1926   ENG 548

Morley, Felix. Our Far Eastern Assignment

NY: Doubleday, Page & Co. 1926. 12mo, 185pp.; introduction by Henry Morgenthau

1023   1926   GER 111

Hagemann, Walter. Das Erwachende Asien [Awakening Asia]

Berlin: Germania 1926. 12mo, 159pp.

1024   1928   ENG 412

Roosevelt, Nicholas. The Restless Pacific

NY & London: Scribner's 1928. 8vo, x, 291pp., ill., map, index

1025   1928   ENG 1253

Harrison, Marguerite. Asia Reborn

NY: Harper & Brothers 1928. 8vo, 389pp., index; contents: on Korea pp.305-309

1026   1930   ENG 438 (2 ex.)

Sands, William Franklin. Undiplomatic Memories. The Far East 1896-1904

NY: Whittlesey 1930 / London: Jon Hamilton n.d. (1930). 8vo, 238pp., ill.

1027   1931   ENG 1230

Morse, Hosea Ballou and MacNair, Henry Farnsworth. Far Eastern International Relations

Boston: Houghton Mifflin 1931. 8vo, 846pp., index; contents: numerous Korea entries

1028   1932   FRE 107
Tsurumi, Yusuke. Le conflit Sino-Japonais [The Sino-Japanese Conflict]
Paris: Recueil Sirey 1932. 8vo, 60pp.

1029   1932   FRE 74
Le Mouvement Japonophobe Chinois. Le Conflit Sino-Japonais. Histoire des operations militaires en Mandchourie et a Changhai en 1931 et 1932. [The Sino-Japanese Conflict]
n.pl., Le Mouvement Japanophobe Chinois, 1932. 12mo, 427, vi pp.

1030   1932   ENG 732
Eddy, Sherwood. The World's Danger Zone : China, Russia, Japan, Manchuria
NY: Farrar [1932]. 8vo, 119pp., appendix

1031   1932   ENG 893
Datta, S.K. Asiatic Asia
London: Faber & Faber 1932. 12mo, 194pp., index

1032   1932   ENG 1381
Koo, V.K. Wellington. Memoranda Presented to the Lytton Commission
NY: Chinese Cultural Society 1932. 2 vols., 8vo, together 940pp., 29 documents in English translation, no index

1033   1932   ENG 1082
Whyte, Frederick. The Future of East and West
London: Sidgwick & Jacobson 1932. 12mo, 180pp., index; contents: on Korea p.125

1034   1932   ENG 1213
Sokolsky, George W. The Tinderbox of Asia
London: George Allen & Unwin 1932. 8vo, 376pp., map, index; contents: numerous Korea entries

1035   1932   POR 5
Schwalbach, Luiz. A Forja do Extremo-Oriente [In the Forge of the Far East]
Lisboa: Emprensa Nacional 1932. 12mo, 69pp; comment: forge referring to Japan as the most industrialized nation in the region

1036   1934   ENG 246

Barnes, Joseph. Empire in the East

NY: Doubleday, Doran & Co., 1934. 8vo, 322pp., map. Contributions by O. Lattimore, J.E. Orchard, J. Barnes, G. Clark, F.V. Field, H.F. Bain, C.L. Alsberg, P.S. Buck, T. Dennett, N. Peffer

1037   1934   ENG 1244

Bodley, R.V.C. The Drama of the Pacific. Being a Treatise on the Immediate Problems which face Japan in the Pacific

Tokyo: Hokuseido 1934. 12mo, 218pp., map, index-table of contents at end, reaches far back into history

1038   1934   ENG 1444

Rasmussen, O.D. The Reconquest of Asia

London: Stanhope 1934. 363pp., map

1039   1934   ENG 1148

Treat, Payson J. China and Korea 1885-1894

in: Political Science Quarterly, vol.XLIX, No.4, 1934, pp.506-543

1040   1934   ENG 1040

Carr, Harry. Riding the Tiger. An American Newspaper man in the Orient

Boston, NY: Houghton Mifflin 1934. 8vo, 262pp.

1041   1935   FRE 164

Levy, Roger. Extreme Orient et Pacifique [The Far East and the Pacific]

Paris: Armand Colin 1935. 12mo, 220pp.

1042   1935   ENG 923

Ross, I. Clunies (ed.). Australia and the Far East. Diplomatic and Trade Relations

Sydney: Angus & Robertson 1935. 8vo, 310pp.

1043   1935   ENG 1296

Willoughby, Westel W. The Sino-Japanese Controversy and the League of Nations

Baltimore: Johns Hopkins 1935. 8vo, 733pp., index; contents: 2 Korea entries

1044　　　　　　　　　　1935　　　ENG 1186
Mogi, Sobei and Redman, H. Vere. The Problem of the Far East
London: Victor Gollancz 1935. 12mo, 348pp., index; contents: several Korea entries

1045　　　　　　　　　　1936　　　ENG 537
Das, Taraknath. Foreign Policy in the Far East
NY: Longman 1936. 12mo, 272pp., index, appendices, Foreword by Herbert Wright; contents: on Korea pp.103-137

1046　　　　　　　　　　1936　　　ENG 1274
Stimson, Henry L. The Far Eastern Crisis, Recollections and Observations
NY: Harper & Brothers 1936. 8vo, 293pp., index; contents: several Korea entries

1047　　　　　　　　　　1937　　　ENG 690
Hudson, G.F. The Far East in World Politics : a Study in Recent History
Oxford: Clarendon Press 1937. 12mo, vii, 276pp., ill., map, index

1048　　　　　　　　　　1937　　　ENG 1315
Paton, William. Christianity in the Eastern Conflicts. A Study of Christianity. Nationalism and Communism in Asia
London: Edinburgh House 1937. 12mo, 224pp., index; contents: 2 Korea entries

1049　　　　　　　　　　1938　　　FRE 138
Chalux (pseudonym). Autour du conflit Sino-Japonais [Around the Sino-Japanese Conflict]
Bruxelles: Office du Publicite 1938. 12mo, 241pp., ill.

1050　　　　　　　　　　1938　　　FRE 144
Farrere, Claude. Le grand drame de l'Asie [The Great Drama of Asia]
Paris: Flam 1938. 12mo, 197pp.

1051　　　　　　　　　　1938　　　FRE 111
Levy, Roger. Relations de la Chine et du Japon [Relations of China and Japan]
Paris: Hartmann 1938. small 8vo, 133pp., map, bibliography

1052　　　　　　　　　1938　ENG 130 (2 ex.)
Griswold, A. Whitney. The Far Eastern Policy of the United States

New Haven: Yale UP, 1938. 8vo, 530pp., ill., map, index, bibliography

1053   1938   ENG 1426
Auden, W.H. and Isherwood, Christopher. Journey to a War
London: Faber & Faber 1938. 8vo, 381pp., map. ill., no index. contents: London-Hong Kong-Macao; seemingly not on Korea

1054   1938   ENG 859
MacNair, Henry Farnsworth. The Real Conflict between China and Japan
Chicago: University of Chicago Press 1938. 4to, xvi, 216pp.

1055   n.d. (c. 1938)   FRE 112
Duboscq, Andre. Extreme Orient, 1931-1938 [Far East 1931-1938]
Paris: Fournier n.d. (c.1938). 12mo, 198pp.

1056   1939   ENG 508
British Far Eastern Policy. Information Department Papers No.24
London: The Royal Institute of International Affairs 1939. 8vo, v, 53pp., map

1057   1939   ENG 709
Bisson, T.A. American Policy in the Far East 1931-1940. Institute of Pacific Relations, Inquiry Series
NY: Institute of Pacific Relations 1939. 8vo, 146pp., index

1058   1939   FRE 247
Raynaud, Jean. Guerre en Asie [War in Asia]
(Paris): Braun et Liorit 1939. 12mo, 256pp.

1059   1939   ENG 501e2
Gunther, John. Inside Asia
London: Hamish Hamilton 1939. 8vo, 411pp.

1060   1939   FRE 152
Farrere, Claude. L'Europe en Asie [Europe in Asia]
Paris: Flammarion 1939. 12mo, 100pp., no index

1061   1940   FRE 125
Duboscq, Andre. Unite de l'Asie [The Unity of Asia]

Bibliography of Western Language Publications on Korea

Lyon: Ed. du Fleuve 1940. 12mo, 93pp., new edition

| 1062 | 1940 | ENG 1222 |

Abend, Hallett. Chaos in Asia

London: Bodley Head 1940. 8vo, 313pp., index; contents: one Korea entry

| 1063 | 1940 | ENG 909 |

Mitchell, Kate. Problems of the Pacific 1939. Proceeding of the Study Meeting of the Institute of Pacific Relations, Virginia Beach, Virginia, Nov.18-Dec.2 1939

NY: Institute of Pacific Relations 1940. 8vo, 299pp., index; co-edited by W.L. Holland

| 1064 | 1940 | ENG 1251 |

Smith, Robert Aura. Our Future in Asia

NY: Viking Press 1940. small 8vo, 306pp., map, index; contents: chapter XIII : Japanese Expansion and Aggression, pp.239-277, has reference to Korea

| 1065 | 1940 | ENG 481 |

Samson, Gerald. Warning Lights of Asia

London: Robert Hale 1940. 8vo, 317pp., ill., maps

| 1066 | 1941 | ENG 1217 |

Gayn, Mark J. The Fight for the Pacific

London: Bodley Head 1941. 8vo, 378pp., map, index; one Korea entry

| 1067 | 1941 | ENG 1166 |

Buss, Claude A. War and Diplomacy in Eastern Asia

NY: MacMillan 1941. 8vo, 570pp., index, bibliography; contents: 2 Korea entries

| 1068 | 1941 | ENG 1463 |

Snow, Edgar. The Battle for Asia

NY: Random House 1941. 8vo, 431pp., ill., map, index; contents: 2 Korea entries

| 1069 | 1942 | ENG 769 |

Hudson, G.F. and Rajchman, Marthe. An Atlas of Far Eastern Politics

NY: John Day 1942. 8vo, 207pp., maps, index. Enlarged edition, with a supplement for the years 1938 to 1942 by George E. Taylor. Published under the auspices of the International Secretariat, Institute of

Pacific Relations

| 1070 | 1942 | ENG 1272e2 |

Peffer, Nathaniel. Basis for Peace in the Far East
NY: Harper & Brothers 1942, 8vo, 277pp.

| 1071 | 1942 | ENG 501e3 |

Gunther, John. Inside Asia
NY: Harper & Brothers 1942. 8vo, xii, 637pp.

| 1072 | 1943 | FRE 155 |

Duboscq, Andre. Presence de l'Asie [The Presence of Asia]
Lyon: Ed. du Fleuve 1943. 12mo, 78pp.

| 1073 | 1943 | ENG 1077 |

Lattimore, Owen. America and Asia. Problems of Today's War and the Peace of Tomorrow
Claremont: Claremont College 1943. 8vo, 52pp.

| 1074 | 1943 | ENG 1346 |

Buck, Pearl S. Asia and Democracy
London: MacMillan, 1943. 12mo, 91pp.

| 1075 | 1943 | ENG 1250 |

Greenbie, Sydney. Asia Unbound
NY: Appleton - Century 1943. 8vo, 393pp., map, index; contents: several Korea entries

| 1076 | 1943 | ENG 1241 |

Keaton, George W. China, the Far East and the Future
London: Jonathan Cope 1943. 8vo, 296pp., index; contents: several Korea entries

| 1077 | 1944 | ENG 432 |

Abend, Hallett. Treaty Ports. A Rich Pageant of Life where East and West Agreed to Meet
NY: Doubleday, Doran 1944. 8vo, viii, 271pp., map, index

| 1078 | 1945 | ENG 724 |

Lasker, Bruno. Asia on the Move. Population Pressure, Migration and

Resettlement in Eastern Asia under the Influence of Want and War

NY: Henry Holt 1945. 8vo, 207pp., map, index, issued under the auspices of the American Council, Institute of Pacific Relations; Gompertz 1101

1079   1945   ENG 626
Jaffe, Philip. New Frontiers in Asia : a Challenge to the West

NY: Alfred Knopf 1945. 8vo, vi, 375pp., index; contents: on the Korean People's Emancipation League pp.286-287

1080   1945   ENG 629 (2 ex.)
Lattimore, Owen. Solution in Asia

London: The Cresset Press 1945. 12mo, 143pp., maps, index

1081   1945   ENG 481e2
Samson, Gerald. The Far East Ablaze

London: Herbert Joseph (1940) 1945. 8vo, 183pp., ill., map, index. Previously published in 1940 by Robert Hale Ltd. under the title "Warning Lights of Asia". The present edition has been revised, partly re-written, and brought up-to-date.

1082   1945   ENG 1281
Mathews, Basil. Unfolding Drama in South-East Asia

London: Livingstone Press 1945. 12mo, 135pp., index; contents : missionary bias, not on Korea

1083   1945   ENG 1242
Bisson, T.A. America's Far Eastern Policy

NY: Institute of Pacific Relations 1945. 8vo, 235pp., index, 26 documents attached (pp.165-230); contents: several Korea entries

1084   1945   ENG 1212
Moore, Harriet L. Soviet Far Eastern Policy 1931-1945.

Princeton: UP 1945. 12mo, 284pp., index, contents: several Korea entries

1085   1946   FRE 93
Renouvin, Pierre. La question d'Extreme Orient 1840-1940 [The Far Eastern Question, 1840-1940]

Paris: Hachette 1946. 8vo, 439pp., map, index

1086   1947   ENG 679

Isaacs, Harold R. No Peace for Asia
NY: MacMillan 1947. 8vo, 295pp., index

1087　　　　　　　　　　　　　　　　1947　　　　ENG 627
Thompson, Warren S. Population and Peace in the Pacific
Chicago: UP 1947. 8vo, 397pp., index, bibliography, maps

1088　　　　　　　　　　　　　　　　1947　　　　ENG 834
Cole, Taylor and Hallowell, John H. Post-War Governments of the Far East
in : The Journal of Politics, 1947, 8vo, pp.473-744

1089　　　　　　　　　　　　　　　　1948　　　　FRE 120
Prostoi, Michel. Tempete d'Asie [Asian Storm]
Paris: Ed. Liberte 1948. 12mo, 384pp.

1090　　　　　　　　　　　　　　　　1949　　　　ENG 531
Tompkins, Pauline. American-Russian Relations in the Far East
NY: MacMillan 1949. 8vo, xiv, 426pp., map, bibliography, index

1091　　　　　　　　　　　　　　　　1949　　　　ENG 1445
Lattimore, Owen. The Situation in Asia
Boston: Little & Brown & Co. 1949. 12mo, 249pp., index; contents: several Korea entries

1092　　　　　　　　　　　　　　　　1950　　ENG 318 (2 ex.)
MacNair, Henry Farnsworth and Lach, Donald F. Modern Far Eastern International Relations
Toronto etc.: van Nostrand 1950. 8vo, 681pp., ill., maps, bibliography, index

1093　　　　　　　　　　　　　　　　n.d.　　　　GER 10
Brosius, Hans. Fernost formt seine neue Gestalt [The Far East is Reshaping itself]
Berlin: Deutsche Verlasgs-Anstalt, n.d. (c.1940). 8vo, 240pp., ill.; contents: on Korea pp.97-99

V.b.3) CHINA

1094　　　　　　　　　　　　　　　　1880　　　　ENG 251
Ross, John. The Manchus, or the Reigning Dynasty of China
London: Paisley 1880. 8vo, xxxii, 751pp., ill., maps

1095   1896   ENG 145 : 1/2
Hertslet, Edward. Treaties &c. between Great Britain and China : and between China and Foreign Powers, and Orders in Council, Rules, Regulations, Acts of Parliament, Decrees, and Notifications Affecting British Interests in China
London: Harrison & Sons 1896. 8vo, 2 vols., vol.1 : map, 421pp., ill., vol.2 : pp.423-768, ill., index

1096   1898   ENG 247
Krausse, Alexis. China in Decay : a Handbook to the Far Eastern Question
London: Chapman & Hall 1898. 8vo, ix, 400pp., ill., maps, index

1097   1899   FRE 273
Anonymous. La Chine. Expansion des Grandes Puissances en Extreme-Orient (1895-1898) [China. Expansion of the Great Powers in the Far East, 1895-1898]
Paris: Librairie Militaire R. Chapelot 1899. large 8vo, preface signed by M.S.; contents: on Korea pp.29-47

1098   1899   ENG 1246
Beresford, Charles. The Break-up of China with an Account of its Present Commerce, Currency, Waterways, Armies, Railways, Politics and Future Prospects
London: Harper & Brothers 1899. 8vo, 509pp., ads, index; contents: 2 Corea entries

1099   1900   ENG 202
Pott, F.L. Hawks. The Outbreak in China, its Cause
NY: James Pott, 1900. 12mo, vii, 124pp.

1100   1900   ENG 1235
Krausse, Alexis. The Story of the Chinese Crisis
London: Cassell 1900. 12mo, 237pp., index, ads; cntents: 2 Korea entries

1101   1900   ENG 1448
Miller, J. Martin. China. The Yellow Peril. At War with the World
no place : no publisher, 1900. large 8vo, 490pp., ill., no index; contents: the book is a general history of China; the title, published in the year of the climax of the Boxer Rebellion, seems to be chosen to attract readers.

1102   1901   FRE 50
Cordier, Henri. Histoire des Relations de la Chine avec les Puissances Occidentales 1860-1900 [History of China's Relations with the Western Powers, 1860-1900]

Paris: Felix Alcan, 1901-1902. 8vo, 3 vols., vol.1 : l'Empereur T'oung Tche (1861-1875), 570pp., 1901, vol.2 : L'Empereur Kouang-Siu, Premiere Partie, 1875-1887, 650pp., 1902, vol.3 : L'Empereur Kouang-Siu, Deuzieme Partie, 1888-1902, 598pp., 1902, maps, index

1103   1901   ENG 785
Bigham, Clive. A Year in China 1899-1900

London: MacMillan 1901. 8vo, 234pp., ill., map, index

1104   1901   FRE 194
Saint-Ives, G. A l'Assaut de l'Asie. La conquete Europeenne en Asie [The Attack on Asia. The European Conquest of Asia]

Tours: Alfred Mame et Fils, 1901. 4to, 398pp., ill., maps; author Laureat de l'Institut de France

1105   n.d. (c. 1901)   ENG 1407
Northrop, Henry Davenport. China, the Orient and the Yellow Man

n.p., no publisher (privately published ?)_n.d. (c.1901). 8vo, 420pp., ill., no index, no t.o.c.; map; contents: pp.289-356 : Corea and the War between China and Japan

1106   n.d. (c. 1901)   FRE 281
Pellier, A. L'Europe et la Chine [Europe and China]

Limoges: Librairie du XXe siecle, no date (c. 1901). folio, 325pp., ill.

1107   1904   ENG 1036e2
Brown, Arthur Judson. New Forces in Old China. An Inevitable Awakening

NY: Fleming H. Revell 2nd edition 1904. 8vo, 370pp., map, ill.

1108   1904   ENG 1162
Ular, Alexandre. A Russo-Chinese Empire

Westminster: Constable 1904. translated from the French, small 8vo, 336pp., index; contents: 2 Corea and 1 Korea entry

1109   1907   ENG 281 (2 ex.)
Martin, William Alexander Parsons. The Awakening of China

NY: Doubleday, Page & Co. 1907. 4to, xvi, 328pp., ill.

Bibliography of Western Language Publications on Korea

1110   1909   ENG 1169
Conger, Sarah Pike. Letters from China with Particular Reference to the Empress Dowager and the Women of China
London: Hodder & Stoughton 1909. 8vo, 392pp., ill., index; contents: 3 Korea entries

1111   1910   ENG 114
Morse, Hosea Ballou. The International Relations of the Chinese Empire, 1834-1911
London: Longmans, Green and Co. 1910-1918. 8vo, vol.1 : 39, 727pp., ill., maps. The Period of Conflict, 1834-1860. 1910, vol.2 : 45, 479pp., ill., maps. The Period of Submission, 1861-1893. 1918. vol.3 : xvii, 530pp., ill., maps, index. The Period of Subjection, 1894-1911 : 1918

1112   1910   ENG 854
Gascoyne-Cecil, Lord William. Changing China
London: James Nisbet & Co., 1910. 8vo, x, 217pp., ill, map, index

1113   1911   ENG 854e4
Gascoyne-Cecil, Lord William. Changing China
London: James Nisbet & Co., 1911. 8vo, vii, 342pp., ill, map, index

1114   1912   ENG 452
Brown, Arthur Judson. The Chinese Revolution
NY: Student Volunteer Movement 1912. 8vo, x, 217pp., ill., map, index

1115   1912   ENG 91
Giles, Herbert A. China and the Manchus. Cambridge Manuals of Science and Literature
Cambridge: UP 1912. 16mo, viii, 148pp., ill., map, index.

1116   1912   ENG 1045
Colquhoun, Archibald R. China in Transformation
NY: Harper & Brothers 1912. 8vo, 298pp., glossary, maps

1117   1912   ENG 1062
Headland, Isaac Taylor. China's New Day, A Study of Events that have Led to its Coming
West Medford: Central Committeeon the United Study of Missions 1912. 12mo, 263pp., index

1118　　　　　　　　　　　　　　　　　1913　　　　ENG 624
Thomson, John Stuart. China Revolutionized
Indianapolis: Bobbs-Merrill n.d. (c.1913). 8vo, 589pp., ill., index

1119　　　　　　　　　　　　　　　　　1913　　　　ENG 564
McCormick, Frederick. The Flowery Republic
London: John Murray 1913. 8vo, xiv, 489pp., ill., maps, index

1120　　　　　　　　　　　　　　　　　1913　　　　ENG 198
Pott, F.L. Hawks. The Emergency in China
NY : Missionary Education Movement of the U.S. and Canada 1913. 12mo, xii, 310pp.

1121　　　　　　　　　　　　　　　　　1914　　　　ENG 33e2
Bland, J.O.P. and Backhouse, E. China under the Empress Dowager : being the History of the Life and Times of Tzu Hsi. Compiled from State Papers and the Private Diary of the Comptroller of her Household.
London: William Heinemann (1910) 1914. 8vo, xxvi, 322pp.

1122　　　　　　　　　　　　　　　　　1917　　　ENG 72 (2 ex.)
Latourette, Kenneth Scott. The Development of China
Boston etc.: Houghton & Mifflin 1917. 8vo, xii, 273pp., bibliography, index, map

1123　　　　　　　　　　　　　　　　　1917　　　　GER 144
Ling, Pyau. Beiträge zur neuesten Geschichte Chinas [Contributions to the Newest History of China]
Berlin: Curtius 1917. 8vo, 157pp.

1124　　　　　　　　　　　　　　　　　1918　　　　ENG 1144
Weale, B.L. Putnam. The Fight for the Republic in China
London: Hurst & Blackett / NY: Dodd, Mead & Co. (1917) 1918. 8vo, 490pp.

1125　　　　　　　　　　　　　　　　　1919　　　　ENG 910
Tomimas, Shutaro. The Open-Door Policy and the Territorial Integrity of China
NY: A.G. Seiler 1919. 8vo, 161pp., ill., appendix with Japanese language verses

1126　　　　　　　　　　　　　　　　　1920　　　　ENG 1199

Smith, C.A. Middleton. The British in China and Far Eastern Trade
London: Constable 1920. 8vo, 295pp., index; contents: several Korea entries

1127   1920   ENG 1364
Parker, E.H. The Present Position of China
n.pl.: no publisher, 1920. 8vo, 7pp.

1128   1921   ENG 1190e3
Morse, Hosea Ballou. The Trade and Administration of China
Shanghai: Kelly & Walsh 1921. 8vo, 505pp., ill., maps, appendices, index; contents: several Korea entries

1129   1921   ENG 226
MacMurray, John V.A. Treaties and Agreements with and Concerning China, 1894-1919
NY: Oxford UP 1921. 2 vols., xlvi, 1729pp., index, ill., maps, vol.1 : Manchu Period (1894-1911), vol.2 : Republican Period (1911-1919), Carnegie Endowment for International Peace publication

1130   1922   ENG 1112
Russell, Bertrand. The Problem of China.
London: George Allen & Unwin 1922. 12mo, 260pp., index; contents: several Korea entries

1131   1924   ENG 1488
Widler, Elly. Six Months Prisoner of the Szechwan Military
China Press 1924. 8vo, 170pp., ill., no index

1132   1926   ENG 603 (2 ex.)
Hsue, Shuhsi. China and her Political Entity : A Study of China's Foreign Relations with Reference to Korea, Manchuria and Mongolia.
NY : Oxford UP 1926. 2mo, xxiv, 438pp., index

1133   1926   FRE 237
Duboscq, Andre. La Chine en face des Puissances. Bibliotheque d'Histoire et Politique [China facing the Powers. Historical and Political Library]
Paris: Delagrave 1926. 12mo, 125pp.

1134   1926   ENG 1229

Gilbert, Rodney. What's Wrong with China ?
London: John Murray 1926. 8vo, 315pp., map, index; contents: several Korea entries. On Soviet relations with Korean exile / resistamce

1135 1927 ENG 429
Pratt, John T. China and Britain
London: Collins Publishers 1927. 8vo, 127pp., ill., map

1136 1927 ENG 242
Whyte, Sir Frederick. China and Foreign Powers. An Historical Review of their Relations
London: Oxford UP and Humphrey Milford, 1927. 8vo, viii, 78pp.

1137 1927 ENG 617
Baker, John Earl. Explaining China
NY: van Nostrand 1927. 8vo, 312pp., ill., index

1138 1928 ENG 1061
Monroe, Paul. China : A Nation in Evolution
NY: MacMillan 1928. 8vo, 447pp., ill., index

1139 1928 ENG 1067
Soothill, W.E. China and England
Oxford : UP 1928. 8vo, 228pp., index

1140 1928 ENG 1219 Vol.2
Keeton, G.W. The Development of Extraterritoriality in China
London: Longmans, Vol.II, 1928. 8vo, 422pp., index; contents: several Korea entries

1141 1928 ENG 1168
Joseph, Philip. Foreign Diplomacy in China 1894-1900
London: George Allen & Unwin 1928. 8vo, 458pp.

1142 1929 ENG 1058
Gilbert, Rodney. The Unequal Treaties. China and the Foreigner
London: John Murray 1929. 8vo, 248pp., index

1143 1931 ENG 676

Peffer, Nathaniel. China : The Collapse of a Civilization
London: George Routledge & Sons 1931. large 8vo, viii, 306pp., bibliography

| 1144 | 1931 | ENG 1208 |

Gull, E. Manico. Facets of the Chinese Question
London: Ernest Benn 1931. 8vo, 198pp., index

| 1145 | 1931 | ENG 1171e2 |

Holcombe, Arthur N. The Chinese Revolution
Cambridge, Mass.: Harvard UP 1931. 8vo, 401pp., index; contents: several Korea entries

| 1146 | 1931 | ENG 563 |

Japanese Association in China. Presenting Japan's Side of the Case
Shanghai: Japanese Association in China, 1931. 12mo, 77pp., contains 9 articles previously published in the "Far Eastern Review" or the "Shanghai Evening Post & Mercury"

| 1147 | 1932 | ENG 682e5 |

Williams, Edward Thomas. China Yesterday and Today
NY: Thomas Y. Crowell, reprint 5th ed., revised, 1932. 8vo, xxiv, 743pp., map, bibliography, index

| 1148 | 1932 | ENG 684 (2 ex.) |

Curtis, Lionel. The Capital Question of China
London: MacMillan 1932, 8vo, xix, 322pp., 2 ads, maps, appendices, index

| 1149 | 1932 | ENG 108eR |

Japan Foreign Office. The Present Condition of China. With Reference to Circumstances Affecting International Relations and the Good Understanding between Nations upon which Peace Depends
n.p.. (1932). large 8vo, 142 + 446 pp., tables, map, appendix, revised edition. A white paper

| 1150 | 1934 | FRE 92 |

Backhouse, E. and Bland, J.O.P. Les Empereurs Mandchous. Memoires de la Cour de Pekin. [The Manchu Emperors. Memoires from the Peking Court]
Paris: Payot 1934. small 8vo, 329pp., translated from the English by L.M. Mitchell; foreword by Henri Maspero, Prof. College de France

| 1151 | 1935 | FRE 249 |

Marques-Riviere, Jean. La Chine dans le monde : La Revolution Chinoise de 1912 a 1935 [China in the World. The Chinese Revolution 1912-1935]
Paris: Payot 1935. large 8vo, 280pp., ill., maps, Preface by Rev. P.J. Reviers de Mauny

| 1152 | 1936 | ENG 1161 |

Forster, Lancelot. The New Culture in China
London: George Allen & Unwin 1936. 12mo, 240pp., index; contents: 1 Korea entry

| 1153 | 1937 | ENG 878e2 |

May, Henry John. Little Yellow Gentlemen
London etc.: Cassell (1937), 2nd edition 1937. 12mo, 269pp.; contents: about Japanese activities in China 1934-1937

| 1154 | 1938 | ENG 1245 |

Isaacs, Harold R. The Tragedy of the Chinese Revolution
London: Secker & Warburg 1938. 8vo, 502p., index; contents : not on Korea

| 1155 | 1938 | ENG 1191 |

Chester, Wilfred L. China at Bay
Shanghai: Kelly & Walsh 1938. 8vo, 214pp., index, contents: 2 Korea entries

| 1156 | 1939 | ENG 1170 |

Andersson, J. Gunnar. China Fights for the World
London: Kegan, Paul, Trench & Trübner (1938) 1939. translated from the Swedish, 8vo, 272pp., map, index; contents: 1 Korea entry

| 1157 | 1939 | ENG 1225 |

Epstein, Israel. The People's War
London: Victor Gollancz 1939. 8vo, 384pp., index; contents: several Korea entries

| 1158 | 1942 | ENG 1234 |

Maurer, Herryman. The End is not yet. China at War.
London : W. Heinemann 1942. 12mo, 224pp., map, index; contents : 2 Korea entries

| 1159 | 1943 | ENG 678 |

Smedley, Agnes. Battle Hymn of China
NY: Alfred A. Knopf 1943. 8vo, 528, xvi pp., map, index

| 1160 | 1943 | ENG 1295 |

Prott, John J. War and Politics in China
London: Jonathan Cape 1943. large 12mo, 290pp., map, index; contents: several Korea entries

1161　　　　　　　　　　　　　1944　　　　ENG 1256
China Ministry of Information. China Handbook 1937-1944. A Comprehensive Survey of Major Developments in China in Seven Years of War
Chungking: Chinese Ministry of Information, 1944. 8vo, 626pp., xvi pp. index, pp.81-112 missing; contents: 2 Korea entries;

1162　　　　　　　　　　　　　1945　　　　ENG 1256e3
China Ministry of Information. China Handbook 1937-1945. A Comprehensive Survey of Major Developments in China in Eight Years of War
Chungking: Chinese Ministry of Information, 1947. 8vo, 862pp., xvi pp. index

1163　　　　　　　　　　　　n.d. (1944)　　ENG 1165
Green, O.H. The Story of China's Revolution
London: Hutchinson n.d. (1944). 8vo, 240pp., ill., index; contents: 2 Korea entries

1164　　　　　　　　　　　　　1945　　　　ENG 630
Rowe, David Nelson. China among the Powers
NY: Harcourt, Brace and Co., 1945. 12mo, x, 205pp., maps, index

1165　　　　　　　　　　　　　1945　　　　ENG 530
Pan, Chao-Ying. China Fights on
NY: Revell (1945). 8vo, 188pp., ill., index

1166　　　　　　　　　　　　　1945　　　　ENG 1143
Lattimore, Owen. The Making of Modern China
N.Y. : W.W. Norton & Co. 1945, 12mo, 212pp., index; contents: 1 Korea entry

1167　　　　　　　　　　　　　1947　　　　ENG 306
Chiang, Monlin. Tides from the West : A Chinese Autobiography
New Haven: Yale UP 1947. 8vo, vi, 282pp., index. Joint publication of Yale UP and the China Institute of Pacific Relations

1168　　　　　　　　　　　　　1947　　　　ENG 1220
Chiang, Kai-Shek. China's Destiny & Chinese Economic Theory

London: Dennis Dobson 1947. 8vo, 347pp., index, map (which expresses a Chinese claim on Korea); contents: 2 Korea entries in index

1169   1947   ENG 1237
Epstein, Israel. The Unfinished Revolution in China
Boston: Little, Brown & Co. 1947. 8vo, 442pp., index, map; contents: several Korea entries

1170   1947   ENG 1059
Payne, Robert. China Awake
London: Heinemann 1947. 8vo, 424pp., a diary

1171   1948   ENG 675
Pelcovits, Nathan A. Old China Hands at the Foreign Office
n.pl.: Kings Crown Press 1948. 8vo, xi, 349pp., map, bibliography, index. Published under the auspices of the American Institute of Pacific Relations

V.b.4) MANCHURIA, MONGOLIA, TURKESTAN

1172   ENG 369
The Japan-Manchoukuo Year Book
Tokyo: The Japan-Manchukuo Year Book, vols. 1935, 1940, small 4to, vol.1935 1131pp., 63pp.ads, vol.1940 1232pp., 93pp. ads

1173   1904   ENG 418
Weale, B.L. Putnam. Manchu and Muscovite. Being Letters from Manchuria Written during the Autumn of 1903, with an Historical Sketch
London: MacMillan 1904. 8vo, 552pp., ill., map, appendices

1174   1904   ENG 669e2
Browne, Brevet-Colonel, G.F. Military Report on Manchuria. Compiled for the Intelligence Department, War Office, in 1902; Corrected to January 1904
London: Probsthain & Co. 1904. 12mo, 140pp., map, index, confidential

1175   1908   ENG 980
Asakawa, K. Japan in Manchuria
in: Yale Review, August 1908, pp.185-214 and pp.268-302 several loose leaf articles bound in : K. Asakawa, Russo-Japanese War Articles, 8vo

1176　　　　　　　　　　　　　　1909　　　ENG 980
Asakawa, Kanichi. The Manchurian Conventions
in: Yale Review, Nov.1909, pp.3-15 several loose leaf articles bound in : K. Asakawa, Russo-Japanese War Articles, 8vo

1177　　　　　　　　　　　　　　1924　　　ENG 1156
Rea, George Bronson. The Greatest Civilizing Force in Eastern Asia. The Real Mission of the South Manchurian Railway Company
pamphlet, no place (probably Dairen : South Manchurian Railway Company), 1924. 8vo, 15pp.

1178　　　　　　　　　　　　　　1928　　　ENG 269e2
Clyde, Paul Hibbert. International Rivalries in Manchuria, 1689-1922
Columbus: Ohio State UP 1928. 8vo, xi, 311pp., index

1179　　　　　　　　　　　　　　1929　　　ENG 705
Young, C. Walter. The International Relations of Manchuria : a Digest and Analysis of Treaties, Agreements, and Negotiations Concerning the Three Eastern Provinces of China
Chicago: UP 1929. 8vo, 307pp., index, appendix, bibliography. Prepared for the 1929 Conference of the Institute of Pacific Relations in Kyoto, Japan

1180　　　　　　　　　　　　1930　ENG 106 Vol.30-1
Elliston, Herbert B. Latest Turn of the Manchurian Wheel : Russia "comes back" along the Chinese Eastern and among the Barga Mongols
in : Asia. The American Magazine on the Orient, vol.30 pt.1, 1930, pp.325-331

1181　　　　　　　　　　　　　　1930　　　ENG 526
Kinney, Henry W. Manchuria Today
Dairen: Hamada 1930, 8vo, 100pp., ill., maps

1182　　　　　　　　　　　　　　1931　　　ENG 783 : 1
Young, C. Walter. Japan's Special Position in Manchuria. Its Assertion, Legal Interpretation and Present Meaning
Baltimore etc.: Johns Hopkins UP 1931. 8vo, xxxii, 412pp., index; contents: several Chosen entries

1183　　　　　　　　　　　　　　1931　　　ENG 783 : 2
Young, C. Walter. The International Legal Status of the Kwantung Leased

Territory
Baltimore etc.: Johns Hopkins UP 1931. 8vo, xvii, 249pp., index, bibliography; contents: 2 Chosen entries

1184   1931   ENG 783 : 3
Young, C. Walter. Japanese Jurisdiction in the South Manchuria Railway Areas
Baltimore etc.: Johns Hopkins UP 1931. 8vo, xxii, 332pp., index; contents: 1 Chosen entry

1185   1932   ENG 766
South Manchuria Railway. Third Report on Progress in Manchuria 1907-1932. The Twenty-Fifth Anniversary Number Containing a Survey of the Manchurian Incident and League Council's Proceedings
Dairen : S,M.R. 1932. small 4to, 235pp., ill., maps, appendices

1186   1932   FRE 225
Levy, Roger. A Qui la Mandchourie? Le Droit International et l'Actualite [To Whom Belongs Manchuria ? International Law and Actuality]
Paris: A. Padone 1932. 12mo, 276pp., map

1187   1932   ENG 51
Penlington, John N. The Mukden Mandate. Acts and Aims in Manchuria
Tokyo: Maruzen 1932. 8vo, v + 246, vii pp., index. Illustrations by courtesy of Tokyo Asahi Shimbun. A survey and record of the important features of the Sino-Japanese conflict in Manchuria; pro-Japanese

1188   1933   ENG 102
Kawakami, K.K. Mandchoukuo : Child of Conflict
NY: MacMillan 1933. 8vo, 311pp., ill., index

1189   1933   FRE 114 No.3
Escarra, Jean. Le conflit sino-japonais et la Societe des Nations [The Sino-Japanese Conflict and the League of Nations]
Paris : Publications de la Conciliation Internationale No.3, 1933. 8vo, pp.207-327

1190   1933   FRE 114 No.4
Ray, Jean. La position, l'oeuvre et la politique du Japon et Mandchourie [The Position, Work and Policy of Japan in Manchuria]
Paris : Publications de la Conciliation Internationale No.4, 1933. 8vo, pp.333-482

1191 1934 ENG 393
Etherton, P.T. and Tiltman, H. Hessell. Manchuria the Cockpit of Asia
NY: Stokes (1932) 1934. 8vo, 327pp., ill., map

1192 1934 FRE 75
Yong, Thaddee Ann-Yuen. Aux origines du conflit Mandchou : Chine-Japon-Paix de Versailles [To the Origins of the Manchurian Conflict : China-Japan-the Land of Versailles]
Paris: Librairie Orientaliste Paul Geuthner, 1934. large 8vo, viii, 304pp., map, bibliography. Foreword by Dr. V.K. Wellington Koo, ex Chinese Foreign Minister, Chinese Ambassador in France

1193 1934 ENG 13
Cutlack, F.M. The Manchurian Arena : An Australian View of the Far Eastern Conflict
Sydney: Angus & Robertson 1934. 12mo, lx + 76pp., map

1194 1935 ENG 347
Rea, George Bronson. The Case for Manchoukuo
NY: Appleton 1935. 8vo, 425pp., ill., index, appendices

1195 1935 ENG 371 (2 ex.)
Anonymous. The Puppet State of "Manchukuo". China Today Series No.4
Shanghai: China United Press 1935. 8vo, 278pp., index, appendix, map; official Chinese publication

1196 1936 ENG 559
South Manchuria Railway Co. Answering Questions on Manchuria 1936
Tokyo: Herald Press 1936. 8vo, 84pp., ill., map

1197 1936 ENG 1476e2
Department of Foreign Affairs, Manchoukuo Government, Hsinking. General Survey of Conditions in Manchoukuo, with Special Emphasis on Economic Developments
Hsinking: Manchoukuo Government, 2nd revision 1936. 8vo, 59pp.

1198 1939 FRE 48
Tcheng Kui-I. La Cie Chemin de fer sud-mandchourien et L'emprise Japonaise en Mandchourie. [The South Manchurian Railway Co. and the Japanese

Enterprise in Manchuria]
Paris: Pierre Bossuet 1939. large 8vo, 316pp., bibliography, preface by Dr. Wellington Koo, Chinese Ambassador in France, author dr., Univ. de Paris

V.b.5) RUSSIAN FAR EAST

1199 1904 ENG 184
Beveridge, Albert J. The Russian Advance
NY: Harper 1904. 8vo, 486pp., maps, appendix

1200 1904 ENG 410e2
Drage, Geoffrey. Russian Affairs
London: John Murray 1904. large 8vo, xv, 738pp., maps, index,; contents: on Korea pp.456-458

1201 1905 ENG 1146
Berard, Victor. The Russian Empire and Czarism
London: David Nutt 1905 (Armenian Massacre Baku 1905). 8vo, xxiv, 299pp., map, translated by G. Fox-Davies and G.O. Pape, introduction by Frederick Greenwood; not on Korea

1202 1920 ENG 1258
Historical Section of the Foreign Office (British). Peace Handbooks, Vol.IX : The Russian Empire
London: H.M.S.O. 1920. 8vo, Courland, Livonia and Esthonia 86pp., Bessarabia 50pp., Ukraine 110pp., Don & Volga Basin 108pp., Caucasia 95pp., Eastern Siberia 96pp., Sakhalin 46p., index 55pp.

1203 1923 ENG 1216
Norton, Henry Kittredge. The Far Eastern Republic of Siberia
London: George Allen & Unwin 1923. 8vo, 316pp., map, index; contents: 3 Korea entries

1204 1924 ENG 84
Ossendowski, Ferdinand. Man and Mystery in Asia
NY: Dutton (1924). 8vo, xvi, 343pp., index, maps, ill., in collaboration with Lewis Stanton Palen; comment: author educated Pole, who stayed extensively in the Russian Far East

1205 1925 FRE 235
Ossendowski, Ferdinand. L'Homme et le Mystere en Asie [Man and Mystery in Asia]

Paris: Plon 1925. 12vo, 306pp., translated from the English by Robert Renard

1206   1943   ENG 1314

C.C. of the C.P.S.U. History of the Communist Party of the Soviet Union (Bolsheviks)

London: Cobbett 1943. 8vo, 345pp. (Central Committee of the Communist Party of the Soviet Union)

1207   1950   ENG 1183e2

Dallin, David. The Rise of Russia in Asia

London: Hollis & Carter 1950. small 8vo, 293pp., index; contents: numerous Korea entries

V.b.6) JAPAN

1208   ENG 366

The Japan Year Book

Tokyo: Japan Year Book Office; 8vo, vols. 1910, 1913-1914, 1916, 1926-1927, 1929-1930, 1931, 1938-1939

1209   ENG 369

The Japan-Manchoukuo Year Book

Tokyo: The Japan-Manchukuo Year Book, large 8vo, vols. 1935, 1940

1210   1923   ENG 282e3

The Japan Times Year Book

Tokyo: Japan Times; 4to, vol.1933

1211   1855   ENG 816

Pierce, Franklin (ed.). Message of the President of the United States. Transmitting a Report of the Secretary of the Navy, in Compliance with a Resolution of the Senate of December 6 1854, Calling for Correspondence, &c., Relative to the Naval Expedition to Japan

[Washington] Committee on Foreign Relations 1855. small 8vo, 195pp., U.S. Senate publication

1212   1870   ENG 1331

Letter from the Secretary of the Navy in Answer to a Resolution of the House of March 2 Calling for Information Regarding the Loss of the United States Steamer Oneida (in Yedo Bay)

Washington: G.P.O. 1870. small 8vo, 86, 30pp., map. torn out of larger publication, no frontispiece

1213   1890   ENG 458
Inagaki, Manjiro. Japan and the Pacific : And a Japanese View of the Eastern Question
London: T. Fisher Unwin MDCCCXC (1890). 8vo, 265, 24pp., maps

1214   1891   ENG 1154
Nitobe, Inazo. The Intercourse between the U.S. and Japan
Baltimore: Johns Hopkins UP 1891. 8vo, 198pp., index; contents: several Korea entries

1215   1896   ENG 357e2
Morris, J. Advance Japan : A Nation Thoroughly in Earnest
London: W.H. Allen (1895) 1896. 8vo, xxii, 443pp., ill., maps, index

1216   1898   ENG 189
Morris, J. What will Japan do ? A Forecast
London: Lawrence 1898. 12mo, xii, 190pp., map

1217   1899   ENG 470
Ransome, Stafford. Japan in Transition : A Comparative Study of the Progress Policy, and Methods of the Japanese since their War with China
London and NY: Harper & Brothers MDCCCXCIX (1899). 8vo, xix, 339pp., ill., maps, index

1218   1899   ENG 866
Foreign Office (Japanese). Treaties and Conventions between the Empire of Japan and other Powers
Tokyo: Z.P. Maruya 1899. 2 vols., vol.1 388pp., appendix, 8vo, vol.2 in Chinese, 604pp., ill., map

1219   1904   ENG 1226
Okakura, Kakuzo. The Awakening of Japan
NY: Century 1904. 12mo, 227pp., no index; contents: on history; chapter X : Japan and Peace (modern history, concerning relations between Japan and Korea) pp.201-224

1220   1904   ENG 980, end
Correspondence Regarding the Negotiations between Japan and Russia 1903-1904, presented to the Imperial Diet, March 1904
several loose leaf articles bound in : K. Asakawa, Russo-Japanese War Articles, 8vo

1221 1904 GER 142
Krahmer, Gustav. Die Beziehungen Russlands zu Japan [Relations of Russia with Japan]
Leipzig: Zuckschwerdt 1904. 8vo, viii, 221pp., map; Gompertz 390; Domschke/Goossmann 607

1222 1905 ENG 779e2
Hildreth, Richard. Japan as it Was and Is
Boston etc.: Philip Samson & Co. 1905. 8vo, 610pp., map, index

1223 1905 ENG 300
Hishida, Seiji G. The International Position of Japan as a Great Power
NY: Columbia UP 1905. 8vo, 289pp., bibliography; contents: covering the entire history of Japan's international relations

1224 1905 ENG 54
McCarthy, Michael J.F. The Coming Power : A Contemporary History of the Far East, 1898-1905
London: Hodder & Stoughton 1905. 8vo, xv, 400pp., ill., maps, two books printed in one; contents: book II, from page 153 onward, deals with the Russo-Japanese War

1225 1905 ENG 22
Suyematsu, Baron. A Fantasy of Far Japan or Summer Dream Dialogues
London: Archibald Constable & Co. 1905. 8vo, xii + 337 pp., index; contents: dialogues on a very wide range of subjects, e.g. the issue of the war, peace prospects, Japanese art and the west, commerce and industry, superstition etc., founded on actual conversations. Korea/Chosen not listed in index.

1226 1905 ENG 50 (3 ex.)
Suyematsu, Baron. The Risen Sun
London: Archibald Constable & Co. 1905. 8vo, xi, 355pp., index; contents: a volume of speeches given and articles published in America and Europe in the aftermath of the outbreak of the Russo-Japanese War

1227 1905 ENG 1124
Dyer, Henry. Dai Nippon, The British of the East. A Study in National Evolution
London: Blackie & Son 1905. 8vo, 450pp., index; contents: several Korea entries

1228 1908 FRE 341
M. Jules. Petit Jap deviendra grand [Small Japan Becomes Great]

Myongji-LG Korean Studies Library

Paris: Berger-Levrault 1908. 12mo, 598pp., ill., map, no index; contents: chapters II to VII on Korea, pp.29-228

1229   **1908**   **FRE 316**

Iwaya. Sazanami, L'Ambassade du Japon a Paris [The Japanese Embassy in Paris]

Tokyo 1908. 8vo, 34pp. French language text + unpaginated Chinese language text

1230   **1909**   **ENG 1137**

Dyer, Henry. Japan in World Politics

London: Blackie & Son 1909. 8vo, 425pp., bibliography, index; contents: several Korea entries

1231   **1911**   **FRE 136**

Labroue, Henri. L'Imperialisme Japonais [Japanese Imperialism]

Paris: Delagrave (1911). 12mo, 332pp.

1232   **1913**   **ENG 899 (2 ex.)**

Longford, Joseph H. The Evolution of New Japan

Cambridge: UP 1913. 12mo, 166pp., ill., map, index

1233   **1915**   **ENG 524**

Griffis, William Elliot. The Mikado. Institution and Person

Princeton: UP 1915. 12mo, viii, 346pp.

1234   **1915**   **ENG 424**

Porter, Robert P. Japan : The New World Power. Being a Detailed Account of the Progress and Rise of the Japanese Empire.

London etc.: Humphrey Milford, Oxford UP 1915. 8vo, xxiv, 789pp., map, index. First published as "The Full Recognition of Japan" in 1911; contents: on Korea pp.605-653

1235   **1916**   **ENG 1262**

McLaren, Walter Wallace. A Political History of Japan during the Meiji Era, 1867-1912

London: George Allen & Unwin 1916. 8vo, 380pp., index, ads; contents: numerous Korea entries

1236   **1917**   **ENG 215**

Pooley, A.M. Japan at the Cross Roads

London: George Allen & Unwin 1917. 8vo, 362pp., ads

1237   1918   ENG 382
Sunderland, Jabez T. Rising Japan : is She a Menace or a Comrade to be Welcomed by the Fraternity of Nations ?
NY and London: Putnam's 1918. 12mo, xii, 220pp., index, ads. With a foreword by Lindsay Russell; comment: author Billings lecturer (1913-1914) in Japan, China, India

1238   1918   ENG 268 (2 ex.)
Clarke, Joseph I.C. Japan at First Hand : Her Islands, their People, the Picturesque, the Real, with Latest Facts and Figures on their War-Time Trade Expansion and Commercial Outreach
NY: Dodd and Mead 1918. 8vo, 482pp., ill., index; contents: on Korea pp.339-365

1239   1918   ENG 274 (2 ex.)
Porter, Robert P. Japan : the Rise of a Modern Power
Oxford: Clarendon 1918. 12mo, xii, 362pp., ill., maps, index. Includes pen drawings by Elizabeth Keith

1240   1918   FRE 234
Roux, Hugues le. L'heure du Japon (Pacifique - Japon - Chine). La France et le Monde [The Hour of Japan. (Pacific - Japan - China). France and the World]
Paris: Plon-Nourrit 1918. 12mo, 336pp.

1241   1918   ENG 1046
Latourette, Kenneth Scott. The Development of Japan
NY: MacMillan 1918. 8vo, 237pp., index; contents: numerous Korea-entries

1242   1918   ENG 1396e2
Wilson, Woodrow. The State. Elements of Historical and Practical Politics
Boston: D.C. Heath 1918. 8vo, 554pp.; contents: ch.20 : The Gout of Japan, pp.526-533

1243   1918   ENG 1279
Anonymous. The Problem of Japan. A Political Study of Japan and of her Relations with Russia, Great Britain, China, Germany, the United States, the British Colonies and the Netherlands and of the World Politics of the Far East and the Pacific
Amsterdam: C.L. van Langenhuysen 1918. large 8vo, 272pp.; pp.229-272 appendices of documents

| 1244 | 1919 | ENG 61 |

Chung, Henry. The Oriental Policy of the United States

NY etc.: Fleming H. Revell 1919. 8vo, 306pp., bibliography, introductory note by Jeremiah W. Jenks, Director of Far Eastern Bureau, Research Prof. of Government and Public Administration, NY Univ.; contents: anti-Japanese and pro-Korean in outlook

| 1245 | 1921 | ENG 535 |

Gleason, George. What Shall I Think of Japan ?

NY: MacMillan 1921. 8vo, 284pp., bibliography, index, map; contents: on Korea pp.137-166

| 1246 | 1921 | ENG 385 |

Osborne, Sidney. The New Japanese Peril

London: Allen (1921). 12mo, 184pp.

| 1247 | 1921 | ENG 387 |

Kuno, Yoshi S. What Japan Wants

NY: Crowell (1921). 12mo, 154pp.; contents: pp.67-84 on Korea

| 1248 | 1921 | ENG 1079 |

Treat, Payson J. Japan and the United States 1853-1921,

Boston: Houghton & Mifflin 1921. 8vo, 283pp.

| 1249 | 1922 | ENG 161 |

Ono, Giichi. Expenditures of the Sino-Japanese War

NY: Oxford UP (American Branch) 1922. large 8vo, xv, 330pp., index. A Carnegie Endowment for International Peace Foundation publication

| 1250 | 1922 | ENG 991 |

Gubbins, J.H. The Making of Modern Japan. An Account of the Progress of Japan from Pre-Feudal Days to Constitutional Government & the Position of a Great Power, with Chapters on Religion, the Complex Family System, Education etc.

Philadelphia: J.B. Lippincott 1922. 8vo, 316pp., ill., index

| 1251 | 1923 | ENG 735 |

Fujisawa, Rikitaro. The Recent Aims and Political Development of Japan

New Haven: Yale UP 1923. 8vo, xi, 222pp., index, Publication of the Institute of Political Publications, Williams College

1252 1923 ENG 558
Dennis, Alfred P. The Anglo-Japanese Alliance
Berkeley: University of California 1923. 8vo, 111pp., bibliography, appendices. Prepared to be published prior to the meeting of the Conference on Limitation of Armament and Pacific and Far Eastern Questions

1253 1923 ENG 1138
Fisher, Galen M. Creative Forces in Japan
London: Church Missionary Society 1923. 12mo, 208pp., ill., index; contents: several Korea entries

1254 1926 ENG 976
Tsurumi, Yusuke. Present Day Japan
NY: Columbia UP 1926. 12mo, 114pp.

1255 1927 ENG 939
Kwong, Kwang Lee. The Tanaka Memorial. An Outline Presented to the Japanese Emperor on July 25th 1927, by Premier Tanaka, for the Conquest of China and Other Nations
no place, no publisher, 8vo, 14pp.; comment: this item published as a historic document is now believed to be a propaganda forgery; see article "Tanaka Memorial" in the Wikipedia (http://en.wikipedia.org/wiki/Tanaka_Memorial)

1256 1928 ENG 437
Young, A. Morgan. Japan under Taisho Tenno, 1912-1926
London: Allen (1928). 8vo, 347pp., index

1257 1929 ENG 341
Young, A. Morgan. Japan in Recent Times, 1912-1926
NY: Morrow 1929. 8vo, 347pp., index

1258 1931 GER 85 (2 ex.)
Brown, Arthur Judson. Japan. Aufstieg zur Weltmacht. Der Aufbau moderner Staaten [Japan, Ascendancy to a World Power. The Organisation of Modern States]
Zürich etc.: Orell Fuessli 1931. 8vo, 294pp., timetable, index. Translated from the English by Prof. Dr. Hermann Schoop, timetable added by the translator; contents: on Korea pp.109-127; Domschke/Goossmann 140

1259 1931 ENG 892
Chang, Chung-Fu. The Anglo-Japanese Alliance
Baltimore: Johns Hopkins UP 1931. 8vo, 315pp.; contents: ch.VI (pp.200-224) on Korea, China and the Alliance

1260 1931 ENG 1276
Nitobe, Inazo. Japan. Some Phases of her Problems and Development
NY: Scribner 1931. 8vo, 397pp., map, bibliography, index; contents: numerous Korea entries

1261 1932 ENG 406
Bälz, Erwin. Awakening Japan : the Diary of a German Doctor, Erwin Bälz
NY: Viking 1932. 8vo, 406pp., ill., edited by his son, Toku Bälz. Translated from the German by Eden and Cedar Paul

1262 1932 ENG 688
Kawakami, K.K. Japan Speaks on the Sino-Japanese Crisis
NY: MacMillan 1932. 8vo, 184pp., appendices, map. Introduction by Tsuyoshi Inukai, Prime Minister of Japan

1263 1932 ENG 1
Taft, Henry W. Japan and America. Journey and a Political Survey
NY: MacMillan 1932. 8vo, 359pp., index, 14 appendices of documents; contents: Korea not listed in index

1264 1932 FRE 165
Matsui, Iwane. L'armee Japonaise et le conflit d'extreme Orient [The Japanese Army and the Far Eastern Conflict]
Geneve: Kundig 1932. 12mo, 30pp.

1265 1932 ENG 1393
Treat, Payson J. Diplomatic Relations between the U.S. and Japan, 1853-1895
Stanford: UP 1932. 2 vols. 8vo, 592, 600pp., maps, index in vol.2; contents: numerous Korea entries

1266 1933 ENG 266
Eldridge, F.R. Dangerous Thoughts on the Orient
NY: Appleton-Century 1933. 8vo, 232pp., ill., index, Contents: mostly on Japan, pro-Japanese

Bibliography of Western Language Publications on Korea

1267   1933   FRE 151
Viollis, Andree. Le Japon et son Empire [Japan and its Empire]
Paris: L Grasset 1933. 12mo, 264pp.

1268   1933   ENG 57
O'Conroy, Taid. The Menace of Japan
London: Hurst & Blackett 1933. 8vo, 294pp., ill., index; contents: on Korea pp.176-191

1269   1934   FRE 123
Grande, Julien. La Place du Japon dans le Monde [Japan's Place in the World]
Paris: Parisis-Editions 1934. 12mo, 228pp., index; translated from the English by Ed. Corribe

1270   1934   ENG 894
Grande, Julien. Japan's Place in the World
London: Wymans & Sons 1934. small 8vo, 253pp., ill., index

1271   1934   ENG 446
Scherer, James A.B. Japan's Advance
Tokyo: Hokuseido Press 1934. 8vo, xvii, 347pp., ill., index

1272   1934   ENG 44
Wildes, Harry E. Japan in Crisis
NY: MacMillan 1934. 8vo, 300pp., index; contents: on Korea pp.228-238

1273   1934   ENG 1158 (2 ex.)
Close, Upton. Challenge : Behind the Face of Japan
NY: Farrar & Rinehart 1934. 8vo, 325pp., ill., maps, appendix, no index

1274   1935   FRE 105
Zischka, Antoine. Le Japon dans le Monde. L'Expansion Nippone 1854-1934 [Japan in the World. Japanese Expansion 1854-1934]
Paris: Payot 1935. 8vo, 325pp.

1275   1935   ENG 402
Saito, Hirosi. Japan's Policies and Purposes : Selections from Recent Addresses and Writings
Boston: Jones 1935. 8vo, 231pp., appendix

1276 1935 ENG 355
Kennedy, Malcolm D. The Problem of Japan
London: Nisbet & Co. 1935. 8vo, xvi, 287pp., ill., maps, bibliography, index

1277 1935 ENG 1120
Ireland, Tom. War Clouds in the Skies of the Far East
NY: G.P. Putnams 1935. 8vo, 925pp., ill., index; contents: several Korea entries

1278 1935 ITA 4
Tomaselli, Cesco. Ecco il Giappone [Here Comes Japan]
Milano: Mondadori 1935. large 8vo, 258pp., ill.

1279 c. 1935 ENG 702
Takeuchi, Tatsuji. War and Diplomacy in the Japanese Empire
London: George Allen & Unwin, n.d. (c. 1935). 8vo, xix, 505pp., appendix, bibliography, index; introduction by Quincy Wright

1280 1936 GER 113
Zischka, Anton. Japan in der Welt. Die Japanische Expansion seit 1854 [Japan in the World. Japanese Expansion since 1854]
Leipzig etc.: Goldmann 1936. 8vo, 388pp.; contents: on Korea pp.219-238

1281 1936 ENG 257
Venables, E.K. Behind the Smile in Real Japan
London: George G. Harrap & Co. 1936. 8vo, 320pp., ill.; contents: on Korea pp.27, 117, 201-202, 284

1282 1936 ENG 263
Pickering, Ernest H. Japan's Place in the Modern World
London: Harrap (1936). 8vo, 326pp., ill., index

1283 1936 ENG 99
Yakhontoff, Victor A. Eyes on Japan
NY: Coward-McCann 1936. 8vo, xvii, 330pp., ill.

1284 1936 ENG 58
Nohara, Komakichi. The True Face of Japan : A Japanese upon Japan
London: Jarrolds 1936. 8vo, vii, 288, viii pp., ill., index; contents: on Korea pp.25ff

1285 1936 ENG 543
Falk, Edwin A. Togo and the Rise of Japanese Sea Power
London etc.: Longmans, Green & Co. 1936. 8vo, xiii, 508pp., ill., maps, bibliography, index

1286 1936 ENG 1071
Ishimaru, Tota. Japan Must Fight Britain
London: Hurst & Blackett 1936. 8vo, 288pp.

1287 1936 ENG 1243
Causton, Eric E. Militarism and Foreign Policy in Japan
London: George Allen & Unwin 1936. 8vo, 207pp., map, bibliography; contents: several Korea entries

1288 1936 ENG 1221
Fujihara, Gunjiro. The Spirits of Japanese Industry (History of the Japanese Industrialization)
Tokyo: Hokuseido 1936. 8vo, 149pp., ill., index; contents: several Korea entries

1289 1936 POR 6
Brasil, Jaime. O Japao Actual [Present-day Japan]
Lisboa: Cosmos 1936. 12mo, 48pp.

1290 1937 FRE 209
Haushofer, Karl. Le Japon et les Japonais : Geopolitique du Japon [Japan and the Japanese. Geopolitics of Japan]
Paris: Payot 1937. 8vo, 299pp., ill., maps. Translated from the German by George Mantandon, Prof. of Ethnology at l'Ecole d'Anthropologie.

1291 1937 FRE 104
Utley, Freda. Le Japon aux Pieds d'Argile. Bibliotheque Pacifique et Economique [Japan's Feet of Clay. Pacific and Economic Library]
Paris: Payot 1937. small 8to, 475pp., Translated from the English by M. Vaneix

1292 1937 ENG 228:1 (2 ex.)
Kuno, Yoshi S. Japanese Expansion on the Asiatic Continent : A Study in the History of Japan with Special Reference to Her International Relations with China, Korea and Russia
Berkeley: UP 1937. 8vo, 373pp., ill., maps, appendices, bibliography, index; we have only vol.1 of 3

1293 1937 ENG 103e2
Utley, Freda. Japan's Feet of Clay
[London]: (1937). 8vo, viii, 408pp., index; contents: on Korea pp.11, 14, 38, 39, 42, 91 and 351

1294 1938 ENG 360
Young, A. Morgan. Imperial Japan 1926-1938
London: Allen (1938). 8vo, 328pp., index

1295 1938 ENG 773 (2 ex.)
Chamberlin, William Henry. Japan over Asia
Boston: Little, Brown 1937 (395pp.) / London: Duckworth, 1938 (328pp.). 8vo, 395/328pp., ill., index

1296 1938 ENG 388
Bisson, T.A. Japan in China
NY: MacMillan 1938. 8vo, 417pp., ill., maps, index

1297 1938 ENG 97
Shepherd, Charles R. The Case against Japan, A Concise Survey of Historical Antecedents of the Present Far Eastern Imbroglio
NY: Ryerson (1938). 8vo, viii, 242pp., index, appendix, bibliography; contents: on Korea pp.3-16

1298 1938 ENG 98
Price, Willard. Japan Reaches out
Sydney: Angus & Robertson 1938. 8vo, xii, 322pp., index, map; contents: on Korea pp.145-169

1299 1938 ENG 37 (2 ex.)
Scherer, James A.B. Japan Defies the World
Indianapolis: Bobbs-Merrill (1938). 8vo, 311pp., index, appendix; contents: essentialy focussed on betrayal of Japan by the militarists; causes and effects of the runaway war machine, ill-effects of Korean controls in 1931 etc.

1300 1938 ENG 32
Kawai, Tatsuo : The Goal of Japanese Expansion
Tokyo: Hokuseido 1938. 8vo, 120pp. index, charts, ill., map. Translated from the Japanese

1301 1938 ENG 872
Dilts, Marion May. The Pageant of Japanese History
NY: Longmans (1938) 1942. 8vo, 380pp., ill., index

1302   1938   ENG 1341
Price, Willard. Where Are You Going, Japan ?
London: W. Heinemann 1938. 8vo, 369pp., ill., index; contents: pp.167-238 : Japan in Korea

1303   1938   ENG 939r
Chinese Student Patriot Association of America. The Tanaka Memorial. An Outline Presented to the Japanese Emperor on July 25th 1927 by Premier Baron Giichi Tanaka for the Japanese Conquest of China and Other Nations
NY : Chinese Students' Patriotic Association of America 1938. 8vo, 14pp., reprint from Far Eastern Magazine vol.1 no.7, May 1938; comment: this item published as a historic document is now believed to be a propaganda forgery

1304   n.d. (1938)   ENG 1083
Johns, Leslie W. Japan : Reminiscences and Realities
London: Stanley Paul n.d. (1938). 8vo, ill., 256pp., index, 32pp. ads; contents: ch.viii : Japan Rejuvenates Korea, pp.165-183

1305   1940   ENG 545
Hishida, Seiji. Japan among the Great Powers; A Survey of Her International Relations
London: Longmans 1940. 8vo, 405pp., map, index

1306   1940   ENG 1037
Borton, Hugh. Japan since 1931. Its Political and Social Development
NY: Institute for Pacific Relations, Inquiry Series, 1940. 8vo, 149pp., index

1307   1941   ENG 736
Wang, Ching-Chun. Japan's Continental Adventure
London: George Allen & Unwin 1941. 8vo, 224pp., index; contents: with a chapter by Owen Lattimore, What Korea pays for Japanese rule

1308   1942 ENG 525e2; ENG 1441 (2 ex.)
Rhee, Syngman. Japan Inside Out; The Challenge of Today
NY: Fleming H. Revell, 2nd ed., n.d. (c.1941). 8vo, 208pp., ill., index

1309   1941   ENG 1206
Whyte, Frederick. Japan's Purpose in Asia

London: Royal Institute of International Affairs 1941. 12mo, 61pp., no index

1310   1941   GER 160

Haushofer, Karl. Japan baut sein Reich [Japan Constructs its Empire]

Berlin: Zeitgeschichte-Verlag 1941. 8vo, 330pp., plates

1311   1942   ENG 533

Crow, Carl (ed.). Japan's Dream of World Empire : The Tanaka Memorial

NY: Harper (1942). 8vo, 118pp.; comment: a military and political plan called "Mein Kampf" of Japan. In 1927, Emperor Hirohito was allegedly informed of this grand scheme to control all of Asia; today it is regarded a Chinese propaganda forgery

1312   1942   ENG 1218

Barber, Noel. How Strong is Japan ?

London: George C. Harrap 1942. 12mo

1313   1943   ENG 1167

Byas, Hugh. Government by Assassination

London: George Allen & Unwin 1943. 12mo, 369pp., viii pp. index; contents: 2 Korea entries

1314   1944   ENG 346

Patric, John. Why Japan Was Strong : Adventurous Investigations of a Yankee Hobo in Japan, Manchuria, Korea and China

NY: Doubleday (1943) 1944. 8vo, 313pp., maps

1315   1944   ENG 1182

Mendelssohn, Peter de. Japan's Political Warfare

London: George Allen & Unwin 1944. large 12mo, 192pp., index; contents: 2 Korea entries

1316   1944   ENG 1468

Newman, Barclay Moon. Japan's Secret Weapon

[New York]: Current Publishing Co. 1944. 12mo, 223pp., index; contents: 1 Korea entry

1317   1945   ENG 523

Eldridge, F.B. The Background of Eastern Sea Power

Melbourne: Georgian House 1945. 8vo, 386pp., ill., map, bibliography, index

Bibliography of Western Language Publications on Korea

1318 1945 ENG 1099
Price, Willard. The Son of Heaven. The Problem of the Mikado
London: W. Heinemann 1945. 12mo, 209pp., index; contents: several Korea entries

1319 1945 ENG 1024
Price, Willard. Japan and the Son of Heaven
NY: Duell, Sloan and Pearce 1945. 8vo, 231pp., index

1320 1945 ENG 1164
Johnstone, William C. The Future of Japan
Oxford: UP 1945. 12mo, 162pp., map, index; contents: several Korea entries

1321 1945 ENG 1354
Supreme Commander for the Allied Powers. Summation of Non-Military Activities in Japan and Korea
Washington D.C.: Supreme Commander for the Allied Powers 1945. 4to, Vols.3 and 5, 206, 299pp., maps

1322 1946 ENG 712
Wheeler, Post L. Dragon in the Dust. An Inside Story of the Japanese Conspiracy
Hollywood: Marcel Rodd 1946. 8vo, 253pp., index

1324 1948 ENG 1231
Horner, Francis J. A Case History of Japan
London: Sheed & Ward 1948. 12mo, 227pp., index; contents: several Korea entries

1325 1948 ENG 1447
Political Reorientation of Japan September 1945 to September 1948
Washington : US GPO 1948, on behalf of the Government Section, Supreme Commander for the Allied Forces, 8vo, xxxvi, 401pp.

1326 n.d. FRE 89
Utley, Freda and Wils, David. On peut arreter le Japon [Japan Ought to be Arrested]
Geneve: News Chronicle n.d., 8vo, 61pp.

Myongji-LG Korean Studies Library

1327   n.d.   ENG 774
Goette, John. Japan Fights for Asia
London: MacDonald & Co. n.d., small 8vo, 190pp., index

1328   n.d.   ENG 57e2
O'Conroy, Taid. The Menace of Japan. Paternoster Library No.8
London: Hurst & Blackett n.d. (c. 1938). 8vo, 268pp., ill., index; contents: on Korea pp.176-191

1329   n.d.   FRE 124
Escarra, Jean. Reflexions sur la politique du Japon a l'egard de la Chine et sur quelques aspects juridiques du conflit actuel [Reflections on Japanese Policy regarding China and about the Juridical Aspects of the Present Conflict]
Paris: no publisher, small 8vo, 27pp.

1330   n.d.   FRE 88 : 2
Anonymous. L'agression japonaise et la Conference des Neuf Puissances a Bruxelles II [Japanese Aggression and the Conference of New Powers at Brussels, II]
Bruxelles: Delegation Chinoise n.d., 8vo, 50pp.

V.b.7) KOREA

1331   1894   FRE 288 Vol.CIV
Chaille-Long. Le Corps Diplomatique en Coree [The Diplomatic Corps in Korea]
in: L'Illustration Vol.CIV 1894, pp.151-152

1332   1897   ENG 592
Wilkinson, W.H. The Corean Government : Constitutional Changes, July 1894 to October 1895. With an Appendix on Subsequent Enactments to 30th June 1896
Shanghai: Statistical Department of the Inspectorate General of Customs 1897. 4to, xi, 192pp., maps, index+

1333　　　　　　　　　　　　　　　1900　　FRE 72 : 1900
Laguerie, Villetard de. La Russie et le Japon en Coree [Russia and Japan in Korea]
in: A Travers le Monde, 1900, p.39

1334　　　　　　　　　　　　　　　1900　　FRE 72 : 1900
Laguerie, Villetard de. La Coree depuis le traite de Chimonoseki [Korea since the Treaty of Shimonoseki]
in: A Travers le Monde, 1900, pp.157-159

1335　　　　　　　　　　　　　　　1904　　ENG 832
Rockhill, William Woodville. Treaties and Conventions with or Concerning China and Korea 1894-1904, together with various State Papers and Documents affecting Foreign Interests.
Washington: Government Printing Office 1904. large 8vo, 565pp.

1336　　　　　　　　　　　　　　　1904　　FRE 72 : 1904
Zenzinoff, B. de. Situation politique et economique actuelle de la Coree [The Actual olitical and Economic Situation of Korea]
in: A Travers le Monde, 1904, p.61

1337　　　　　　　　　　　　　　　1904　FRE 288 Vol.CXXIV
Balet, J. La Coree Japonaise [Japanese Korea]
in: L'Illustration vol.CXXIV, 1904, p.106

1338　　　　　　　　　　　　　　　1904　　ENG 1382
Hulbert, Homer B. Korea, the Bone of Contention
in: Century Magazine, Vol.V., 1904, pp.151-154

1339　　　　　　　　　　　　　　　1906　　ENG 507 : 1906
McKenzie, F.A. The Colonial Policy of Japan in Korea
in: Proceedings of the Central Asian Society, 1906, pp.1-27

1340　　　　　　　　　　　　　　　1908　　ENG 73 (4 ex.)
McKenzie, F.A. The Tragedy of Korea
London: Hodder & Stoughton MCMVIII (1908) / NY: E.P. Dutton, n.d., 8vo, xii, 312pp., ill.

1341　　　　　　　　　　　n.d. (after 1905)　　　　ENG 1150
Hulbert, Homer B. Japan's Object Lesson in Korea
in: Pacific Monthly pp.167-175

1342　　　　　　　　　　　　　1910　　　　　　GER 193
Backhausen, Alfred. Die japanische Verwaltung in Korea und ihre Tätigkeit [The Japanese Administration in Korea and her Work]
Berlin: Dietrich Reimer 1910. small 8vo, 79pp., documents in appendix, map; Domschke/Goossmann 62

1343　　　　　　　　　　　　　1910　　　　　　FRE 308
Perrinjaquet. Coree & Japon. Annexion de la Coree au Japon. Traite du 22 aout 1910 et ses consequences [Korea and Japan. Annexion of Korea by Japan. The Treaty of August 22nd 1910 and its Consequences]
Paris: A. Pedone 1910. 8vo, 16pp., extract from Revue Generale du Droit International

1344　　　　　　　　　　　　　1911　　　　FRE 68 : 1911
Balet, J.C. Sous la domination japonaise : La renaissance de la Coree [Under Japanese Domination : The Renaissance of Korea]
in: Journal des voyages et avontures de terre et de mer, 1911, pp.159-160

1345　　　　　　　　　　　　　1913　　　　　　ENG 840
Special Correspondent of the "Japan Chronicle". The Korean Conspiracy Trial. Full Report on the Proceedings in Appeal
Kobe: Office of the "Japan Chronicle" 1913. 8vo, 309pp.

1346　　　　　　　　　　　　　1919　ENG 160e2 (2 ex.)
Kendall, Carlton Waldo. The Truth about Korea
San Francisco: Korean National Association 1919. 16mo, 104pp., map, bibliography

1347　　　　　　　　　　　　　1919　　　　　ENG 1023
Irwin, Spencer Dunshee. Korea and Her Oppressor
Granville, Ohio: Times Print 1919. 16mo, not paginated (8pp.)

1348　　　　　　　　　　　　　1919　　ENG 106 Vol.19
Barstow, Marjorie and Greenbie, Sydney. Korea Asserts Herself
in: Asia. The American Magazine on the Orient, vol.19, 1919, pp.921-926

1349   1919   ENG 106 Vol.19
Chung, Henry. Korea Today
in: Asia. The American Magazine on the Orient, vol.19, 1919, pp.467-474

1350   1920   ENG 137 (2 ex.)
McKenzie, F.A. Korea's Fight for Freedom
London: Simpkin, Marshall & Co. 1920. 8vo, 320pp.; contents: an eyewitness account of Korea under the Japanese

1351   1920   ENG 1121 (2 ex.)
Graves, Joseph Waddington. The Renaissance of Korea
Philadelphia: P. Jaison & Co. 1920. 12mo, 73pp., map, ill., appendix with documents, a.o. Korean declaration of independence

1352   1920   ENG 1016
Smith, Frank Herron. The Other Side of the Korean Question. Fresh Light on Some Important Factors
Reprinted by the Seoul Press from the Japan Advertiser, 1920. 12mo, 33pp.

1353   1921   ENG 395 (2 ex.)
Chung, Henry. The Case of Korea. A Collection of Evidence on the Japanese Domination of Korea, and of the Development of the Korean Independence Movement
NY / Chicago: Fleming H. Revell 1921. 8vo, 265pp., map, index. Foreword by Selden P. Spencer, US Senator from Missouri

1354   1921   ENG 1491
Rhee, Syngman et al. Korea's Appeal to the (American Delegation to the) Conference on Limitation of Armament, 1921
no place, no publisher, 1921, small 8vo, 61pp., map, mostly appendix of documents

1355   1921   ENG 106 Vol.21-2
Reinsch, Paul S. Secret Diplomacy and the Twenty-One Demands
in: Asia, The American Magazine on the Orient, Vol.21 Part 2 pp.937-943

1356   1924   GER 194
Li, Kolu. Unabhängigkeitsbewegung Koreas und japanische Eroberungspolitik

[Korea's Independence Movement and Japanese Policy of Conquest]
Berlin: no publisher 1924. 8vo, 32pp.; Domschke/Goossmann 693

1357   1924   ENG 1464
Moriya, Sakau. Development of Chosen and Necessity of Spiritual Enlightenment
Seoul: Government-General of Chosen, Sept. 1924. small 8vo, 41pp.; comment: author Director of General Affairs Department;

1358   1931   ENG 728 (2 ex.)
Wang, Whitewall. Wanpaoshan Incident and the Anti-Chinese Riots in Korea
Nanking: International Relations Committee n.d. (c 1931). 8vo, 111pp., ill.

1359   1935   ENG 1484
Government-General of Chosen. Thriving Chosen. A Survey of Twenty-Five Years' Administration
Seoul: Government-General of Chosen Oct. 1935. large 8vo, 94pp., numerous plates, maps

1360   1944   ENG 903
Oliver, Robert T. Korea, Forgotten Nation : with an introduction by Syngman Rhee
Washington: Public Affairs Press 1944. 12mo, 138pp.

1361   See 1321

1362   1945   ENG 1344
World Topics Quarterly
World Topics Quarterly, Fall issue 1945 (no.74), 8vo, ill.; contents: Korea, p.20

1363   1946   ENG 1392
Pauley, Edwin W. Report on Japanese Assets in Soviet-Occupied Korea to the President of the United States, June 1946
typoscript bound as a book, large 8vo, 141pp., ill.

1364   1947   ENG 267 (2 ex.)
Chung, Henry. The Russians Came to Korea
Seoul: Korean Pacific Press 1947. 8vo, 212pp., ill., appendices

1365 1947 ENG 821
U.S. Department of State. Korea's Independence
Washington D.C.: G.P.O. 1947. 8vo, 60pp., map

1366 1948 ENG 245 (2 ex.)
Bristol, Horace. Korea. A Photographic Record on a Country .. Whose Fate is Being Decided Today .. and Some of the People Who Will Decide it
Tokyo: Toppan Press 1948. square 8vo, 77 plates

1367 1948 ENG 845
National Economic Board. South Korean Interim Government Activities
Seoul: U.S. Army Military Government 1948. 4to, iv, 192pp.

1368 1949 ENG 373
Pyun, Y(ong) T('ae). Korea, My Country
Seoul: International Cultural Association 1949. 12mo, 224pp., maps. Collection of essays and newspaper articles by Y.T. Pyun on the political situation

1369 1949 ENG 1401
Strong, Anna Louise. In North Korea. First Eye-Witness Report
NY: Soviet Russia Today 1949. 49pp.

1371 1950 ENG 738
Oliver, Robert T. Why War Came in Korea
NY: Fordham UP 1950. small 8vo, 260pp., no index

1372 1950 ENG 641
Tewksbury, Donald G. (comp.). Source Materials on Korean Politics and Ideologies. Source Books on Far Eastern Political Ideologies.
NY: Institute of Pacific Relations 1950. 4to, 190pp.

1373 1950 ENG 822 (2 ex.)
Anonymous. New Korea
Canton: Librairie "Min Chu", March 1950. 8vo, 76pp., ill.; contents: about North Korea. English and Chinese Text

1374 1950 ENG 707
Green, A. Wigfall. The Epic of Korea

Washington D.C.: Public Affairs Press 1950. 8vo, 136pp., map

| 1375 | 1950 | ENG 10778 |

Winnington, Alan. I Saw the Truth in Korea
London: People's Press 1950. 8vo, 15pp.

| 1376 | 1950 | ENG 942 |

One Year in Korea
Seoul: United Nations Command 1950. folio, 20pp., maps

V.c) ON ASIAN EMIGRANTS

| 1377 | 1877 | ENG 759 |

Gibson, O. The Chinese in America. Spine Title : T'ong Yan Choi Kum Shan
Cincinnati: Hitchcock & Walden 1877. 16mo, 403pp.

| 1378 | 1934 | ENG 1152 |

Palmer, Albert W. Orientals in American Life
NY: Friendship Press 1934. 12mo, 212pp., index; contents: several Korea entries

| 1379 | 1938 | ENG 982 |

Ichikawa, Haruko. Japanese Lady in America
Tokyo: Kenkyusha 1938. small 8vo, 347pp., no index

V.d) MILITARY HISTORY

V.d.1) SECOND OPIUM WAR, 1859-1860

| 1380 | 1861 | FRE 272 |

Lucy, Armand. Lettres Intimes sur la Campagne de Chine en 1860 : Souvenirs de Voyage [Intimate Letters about the Campaign in China 1860 : Souvenirs of a Journey]
Marseille: Imprimerie et Lithographie Jules Barile 1861. 8vo, 204pp., ill., map. Letter of General Montauban at end

V.d.2) FRENCH EXPEDITION OF 1866

1381   1873   FRE 67 Vol.25
Zuber, M.H. Une expedition en Coree (1866) [An Expedition to Korea (1866)]
in: Le Tour du Monde vol.25, 1873, pp.401-416; comment: also FRE 185 (2 ex.); listed under 1866

V.d.3) U.S. EXPEDITION OF 1871

1382   1871   ENG 1332
Rodgers, John. Expedition to Corea
in: Report of the Secretary of the Navy, Washington: GPO 1871, 8vo, pp. 275-315

1383   1922   ENG 1357
Schroeder, Seaton. A Half Century of Naval Service
NY: D. Appleton & Co. 1922. 8vo, 444pp., ill., index; contents: pp.47-55 on the expedition to Korea

1384   1948   ENG 1425
Bauer, K. Jack. The Korean Expedition of 1871
in: United States Naval Institute Proceedings Vol.74 No.540, Feb. 1948, pp.197-204

V.d.4) SINO-JAPANESE WAR 1894-1895

1385   1894   ENG 591e2
Morris, J. War in Korea : a brief Treatise upon the Campaign now in Progress : its Origin, and probable Results
London: Ward, Lock and Bowden 2nd edition 1894. 12mo, viii, 108pp., ill., map

1386   1894   FRE 70 : 1894
Lefort, Albert. Le Conflit entre la Chine et le Japon [The Conflict between China and Japan]
in: Revue Encyclopedique, 1894. back, pp.243, 283

1387   1894   ENG 798
Anonymous. A Photographic Album of the Japan-China War = 日清戰爭寫眞圖 : Part 1, Corea and Manchuria. The Campaign in Corea.
n.p. 1894. folio, no paging, ill., bilingual Japanese & English

1388   1895   ENG 285   (2 ex.)
White, Trumbull. The War in the East, Japan, China and Corea
Philadelphia: Eliot 1895. 8vo, 673pp., ill., with an introduction by Julius Kumpei Matumoto, with illustrations by Teitoku Morimoto; Gompertz 255

1389   1895   FRE 288 Vol.CVI
Laguerie, Villetard de. Le drame coreen [The Korean Drama]
in: L'Illustration vol.cvi, 1895, p.359

1390   1896   FRE 304
Bei-Sen, Han-Ko et al. Guerre Sino-Japonaise. Recueil d'Estampes [The Sino-Japanese War, a Collecion of Prints]
Tokyo: P. Barboutev 1896. images i-v on Korea; a collection of ilustrations, 8vo, not paginated

1391   1896   ENG 301
Vladimir. The China-Japan War : Compiled from Japanese, Chinese and Foreign Sources
London: Sampson 1896. 8vo, x, 449pp., ill., maps, index, appendices

1392   1898   ENG 758
Allan, James. Under the Dragon Flag. My Experiences in the Chino-Japanese War
NY: Frederick A. Stokes 1898. 12mo, 122pp.

1393   1902   GER 135
Richthofen, Freiherr Wilhelm von. Chrysanthemum und Drache. Vor und während der Kriegszeit in Ostasien. Skizzen aus Tagebüchern [Chrysanthemum and Dragon. Before and during Wartime in East Asia. Sketches from Diaries]
Berlin: Ferdinand Dümmler 1902. 8vo, 288pp., ill.; contents: on Korea pp.198-213

V.d.5) BOXER REBELLION 1897-1901

1394   1902   GER 192
Canera, Carl. Deutschlands Kämpfe in Ostasien [Germany's Fights in the Far East]
München 1902. 8vo, 245pp., ill., map, ads

V.d.6) RUSSO-JAPANESE WAR 1904-1905

1395 1904 ENG 262 (2 ex.)
Asakawa, K. The Russo-Japanese Conflict : its Causes and Issues
Boston: Houghton 1904; 8vo, xv, 383pp., ill., map, index. With an introduction by Frederick Wells Williams

1396 1904 ENG 404
Anonymous. Russo-Japanese War Fully Illustrated
Tokyo: Kinkodo 1904. large 8vo, 3 vols., vol.1 424pp., ads, ill., vol.2 pp.425-848, ads, ill., maps, vol.3 pp.849-1274, ads; we have one copy of vol.1.2 pp.140-282

1397 1904 ENG 23
Story, Douglas. The Campaign with Kuropatkin
London: T. Werner Laurie 1904. 8vo, xii, 301pp., ill.

1398 1904 ENG 39 (2 ex.)
Miller, J. Martin. Thrilling Stories of the Russo-Japanese War
Washington D.C.: n.d. (c.1904). large 8vo, plates, 473pp., map. Spine title : Official History of the Russo-Japanese War. Introduction by General Nelson A. Miles, Commander in Chief of the U.S. Army who travelled the Far East

1399 1904 ENG 390
Palmer, Frederick. With Kuroki in Manchuria
NY: Scribner's 1904. 8vo, 362pp., ill., maps

1400 1904 ENG 522
McCaul, Ethel. Under the Care of the Japanese War Office
London: Cassell 1904. 12mo, 256pp., index

1401 1904 FRE 66
Leroux, Gaston. Les Heros de Chemulpo [The Heroes from Chemulpo]
Paris: Felic Juven 1904. 4to, 151pp., ill.; contents: About the Russian sailors who defended against an assault of the Japanese, before war had been declared.

1402 1904 ENG 826 (2 ex.)
Wilson, H.W. Japan's Fight for Freedom : The Story of the War between Russia and Japan

London: Amalgamated Press 1904-1906. folio, 3 vols., vol.1 1904, 436pp., vol.2 1905, pp.437-868, vol.3 1906 pp.869-1444, ill., map

1403 1904 ENG 1184

Cowen, Thomas. The Russo-Japanese War. From the Outbreak of Hostilities to the Battle of Liaoyang.

London: Edward Arnold 1904. 8vo, 343pp., ill., maps, no index

1404 1904 FRE 13

Lynch, George. Coree, Chine et Mandchourie : les convoitises Russes et Japonaises (The Path of Empire) [Korea, China and Manchuria : The Covets of the Russians & Japanese]

Paris: Dujarric 1904. 16mo, xii, 344pp., translated from the English by G. Giluncy

1405 1904 ENG 66e2 (2 ex.)

Lawrence, T.J. War and Neutrality in the Far East

London: MacMillan, second, enlarged edition 1904. 8vo, xiii, 301pp., index

1406 1904 ENG 1260

Linthicum, Richard. War between Japan and Russia. The Complete Story of the Desperate Struggle between Two Great Nations

n.pl., W.R. Vansant 1904. 8vo, pp.25-40, 45, 65-66, 97-98, 114-115, 131-132, 153-155, 169-171, 179-183, 195, 197, 209, 226-227, 239-240, 253-259, 273, 283, 297, 303, 331, 347, 352, 359, 369-370, 387, 408, 421, 429, 437, 447; many illustrations

1407 1904 ENG 1153

Stratemeyer, Edward. Under the Mikado's Flag, or Young Soldiers of Fortune

Boston: Lothrop, Lee & Shepard / Norwood Press 1904. 12mo, 305pp., no index

1408 1904 ENG 1132

Sedgwick, F.R. The Russo-Japanese War. Special Campaign Series

London: George Allen & Unwin 1904. 12mo, 192pp., large maps in folder

1409 1904 FRE 352

Donnet, Gaston. Histoire de la Guerre Russo-Japonaise [History of the Russo-Japanese War]

Paris: Ch. Delagrave 1904. small 4to, 402pp., ill., maps, no index

1410   1904   FRE 325
Anonymous. Blancs & Jaunes. La Guerre Russo-Japonais 1904. Recits d'un temoin oculaure [Whites and Yellow Guys. The Russo-Japanese War 1904. Recollections of an Eyewitness]
Paris: Tallandier 1904. 2 vols., large 8vo, 1346pp., ill., maps

1411   1904 FRE 288 Vol.CXXIII
Balet, J. Lettres du Japon. Le theatre et la guerre. La mission du Marquis Ito en Coree mise a la scene [Letters from Japan. The Theater and the War. The Misson of Marquis Ito to Korea, Sent from the Scene]
in: L'Illustration, vol.CXXIII 1904 pp.394-395

1412   1904   FRE 71 : 1904
Beguin, C. Le conflit russo-japonais. [The Russo-Japanese Conflict]
in: Revue Universelle, 1904, pp.121-126

1413   1904   ENG 980
Asakawa, K. Some of the Issues of the Russo-Japanese Conflict
in: Yale Review, May 1904, pp.16-50

1414   1904   ENG 980
Asakawa, K. Some of the Events Leading up to the War in the East
in: Yale Review, August 1904, pp.125-158

1415   1904   FRE 72 : 1904
Laguerie, Villetard de. L'enjeu de la Guerre Russo-Japonaise [The Stakes in the Russo-Japanese War]
in: A Travers le Monde 1904, pp.126-127

1416   1905   ENG 477 (2 ex.)
Strang, Herbert. Kobo : A Story of the Russo-Japanese War
London etc.: Blackie & Son 1905. 8vo, xi, 370pp., ill., maps

1417   1905   ENG 49 (2 ex.)
McKenzie, Frederick Arthur. From Tokyo to Tiflis : Uncensored Letters from the War

London: Hurst & Blackett 1905. 8vo, x, 340pp., ill., maps, index. An informal account of the author's experiences during the Russo-Japanese War; contents: on Korea pp.16-159

1418　　　　　　　　　　　　　　　1905　　　　ENG 344
Taburno, J. The Truth about the War
Kansas City: Hudson 1905. 12mo, 144pp., map, index. Translated from the Russian by Victoria von Kreuter.

1419　　　　　　　　　　　　　　　1905　　　　ENG 784
Oakley, Jane H. A Russo-Japanese War Poem
Brighton: Standard Press 1905. 12mo, 248pp., poem in 86 cantos

1420　　　　　　　　　　　　　　　1905　　　　ENG 804
Hare, James H. (editor). Photographic Record of the Russo-Japanese War.
NY: P.F. Collier & Son 1905. folio, 256pp., ill., with an account of the Battle of the Sea of Japan by A.T. Mahan, U.S. Navy captain

1421　　　　　　　　　　　　　　　1905　　　　FRE 143
Klado, N.L. La Marine Russe dans la Guerre Russo-Japonaise, "Apres le depart de la deuxieme escadre du Pacifique" [The Russian Navy in the Russo-Japanese War. After the Departure of the Second Pacific Squadron]
Paris: Berger Levrault 1905. 12mo, 326pp., translated from the Russian by Rene Marchand

1422　　　　　　　　　　　　　　　1905　　　　FRE 243
Kann, Reginald. Japon, Mandchourie, Coree. Journal d'un Correspondant de Guerre en Extreme Orient [Japan, Manchuria, Korea. Journal of a War Correspondent in the Far East]
Paris: Calmann-Levy 1905. 12mo, 374pp., maps

1423　　　　　　　　　　　　　　　1905　　　　ENG 234
Villiers, Frederic. Port Arthur : Three Months with the Besiegers. A Diurnal of Occurrents
London: Longmans, Green & Co. 1905. 8vo, vi, 176pp., ill., map, 40pp. ads

1424　　　　　　　　　　　　　　　1905　　　　ENG 383
Barry, Richard. Port Arthur : A Monster Heroism
NY: Moffat 1905. 8vo, 344pp., ill., comment: for a general readership

1425　　　　　　　　　　　　　　1905　　　　FRE 311
Recouly, Raymond. Dix mois de guerre en Mandchourie [Ten Months of War in Manchuria]
Paris: Felix Juven 1905. 12mo, 333pp., ill., maps, no index

1426　　　　　　　　　　　　　　1905　　　　ENG 450
Greener, William. A Secret Agent in Port Arthur
London: Archibald Constable 1905. small 8vo, viii, 316pp., ill.

1427　　　　　　　　　　　　　　1905　　　　ENG 52
Brooke, Lord. An Eye-Witness in Manchuria
London: Eveleigh Nash 1905. 8vo, viii, 312pp.

1428　　　　　　　　　　　　　　1905　　　　ENG 53
Baring, Maurice. With the Russians in Manchuria
London: Methuen & Co. 1905. 8vo, xv, 205pp., 40pp. ads

1429　　　　　　　　　　　　　　1905　　　　ENG 63
Richardson, Teresa Eden. In Japanese Hospitals during War-Time : Fifteen Months with the Red Cross Society of Japan (April 1904-July 1905)
Edinburgh and London: William Blackwood & Sons MCMV (1905). 8vo, xiv, 294pp., ill.

1430　　　　　　　　　　　　　　1905　　　　ENG 131
Unger, Frederic William. Russia and Japan and a Complete History of the War in the Far East
NY: Brown Brothers 1905. 8vo, 2 vols., vol.1 : 176pp., ill., maps, assisted by Charles Morris; contents: vol.2 begins with August 24th 1904, events in Manchuria

1431　　　　　　　　　　　　　　1905　　ENG 352 (3 ex.)
The Military Correspondent of the Times. The War in the Far East 1904-1905
London: John Murray 1905. 8vo, xvi, 656pp., maps, index

1432　　　　　　　　　　　　　　1905　　　　ENG 463
Lloyd, Arthur. Admiral Togo
Tokyo: Kinkodo 1905. 12mo, 160pp., ill.

1433　　　　　　　　　　　　　　1905　　　　ENG 534

Myongji-LG Korean Studies Library

Seaman, Louis Livingston. From Tokio through Manchuria with the Japanese
NY: Appleton 1905. 8vo, 268pp., ill., ads

1434   1905   ENG 1044
Burleigh, Bennet. Empire of the East, or Japan and Russia at War, 1904-1905
London: George Bell 1905. 8vo, 458pp., ill.

1435   1905   ENG 1052
Tyler, Sydney. The Japan-Russia War. An Illustrated History of the War in the Far East. The Greatest Conflict of Modern Times
Philadelphia: Ziegler 1905. 8vo, 568pp., ill.

1436   1905   ENG 1215
Smith, F.E. International Law as Interpreted during the Russo-Japanese War
London: T. Fisher Unwin 1905. large 8vo, 494pp., index, ads; contents: several Korea entries

1437   1905   ENG 1202
O. The Yellow War
Edinburgh: William Blackwood & Sons 1905. small 8vo, 302pp., 25pp., ads, no index

1438   1905   ENG 1135
Fraser, David. A Modern Campaign, Or War and Wireless Telegraphy in the Far East
London: Methuen 1905. 12mo, 356pp., index, 40pp. ads; contents: 2 Korea entries

1439   1905   ENG 1474
Collier's War Correspondents. The Russo-Japanese War. A Photographic and Descriptive Review of the Great Conflict in the Far East
NY: P.F. Collier & Son MCMV(1905). folio, 144pp., ill.

1440   1905   FRE 68 : 1905
Balet, J.C. Les captifs de Matsuyama. La Guerre Russo-Japonais [The Captives of Matsuyama. The Russo-Japanese War]
in : Journal des voyages et avontures de terre et de mer 1905, pp.116-117

1441   1905   GER 120
Reventlow, E. Graf zu. Der Russisch-Japanische Krieg [The Russo-Japanese

War]
Berlin-Schömeberg: Internationaler Welt-Verlag, 1905-1906. 4to, 3 vols., 1660pp., ill., maps; Domschke/Goossmann 859

1442　　　　　　　　　　　　1905　　　　　FRE 186
Galli, Henri. La guerre en extreme-orient [The War in the Far East]
Paris: Garnier Freres 1905. 4to, 954pp., ill.

1443　　　　　　　　　　　　n.d. (1905)　　　ITA 10
Matania, Fortunio. La guerra nell'estremo oriente [The War in the Far East]
Milan: n.d. (1905). 384, 280pp., ill., map

1444　　　　　　　　　　　　n.d. (c. 1905)　　ENG 170
Everett, Marshall. Exciting Experiences in the Japanese-Russian War Including a Complete History of Japan, Russia, China and Korea. Relation of the United States to the Other Nations. Cause of the Conflict.
anonymous, n.p. n.d. (c. 1905). 8vo, 494pp., ill.; publisher's preface, but publishing company not names. Author 'the greatest descriptive writer the world has ever known'

1445　　　　　　　　　　　　n.d. (c. 1905)　　ENG 768
Cassell's History of the Russo-Japanese War
London etc.: Cassell Co. n.d. (c. 1905). large 8vo, 6 vols., total 1370pp., introduction by Arthur Diosy

1446　　　　　　　　　　　　n.d. (c. 1905)　　FRE 207 : 5
Rouskii Invalid. Les Batailles d'Octobre sur le Cha-Ho. vol.5, from : Comptes rendus publies par le Rouskii Invalid de conferences sur la Guerre Russo-Japonaise faites a l'Academie d'Etat Major Nicolas [The Battles on the Cha-Ho, in October; from Explanations published by the Rouski Invalid (Invalid Russian) on the Conferences on the Russo-Japanese War, held at the Academy of Staff Major Nicolas]
Paris: Charles Lavauzelle n.d. (c. 1905). 8vo, 238pp., maps, 5th fascicle, translated from the Russian

1447　　　　　　　　　　　　n.d. (c. 1905)　　FRE 213
Niessel, Capitaine brevete. Enseignements tactiques decoulant de la Guerre Russo-Japonaise [Tactical Training after the Russo-Japanese War]
Paris: Henri-Charles Lavauzelle, n.d. (c.1905). 8vo, 181pp.

1448   n.d. (c. 1905)   ENG 949e2
A Neutral. The Russo-Japanese War. Englands Responsibilities.
London: S. Sidders & Co., 2nd edition, n.d., 12mo, 17pp., pro-Japanese

1449   1906   ENG 219
Negrier, de. Lessons of the Russo-Japanese War
London: Hugh Rees 1906. 12mo, 88pp., map, index, translated from the French by E. Louis Spiers

1450   1906   ENG 778
Seaman, Louis Livingston. The Real Triumph of Japan. The Conquest of the Silent Foe
NY: Appleton 1906. 12mo, 291pp.

1451   1906   ENG 475
Klado, Captain Nicolas. The Battle of the Sea of Japan
London: Hodder and Stoughton 1906. 4to, xvii, 306pp., ill., map, index; translated from the Russian by J.H. Dickinson and F.P. Marchant

1452   1906   FRE 239
Niox, General. La Guerre Russo-Japonaise. Chroniques [The Russo-Japanese War. A Diary]
Paris: Ch. Delagrave 1906. 12mo, 171pp., map

1453   1906   GER 17
Barzini, Luigi. Mukden
Leipzig: Dieterich 1906. 8vo, 181pp., ill., map, translated from the Italian into the German by Emil Kerbs

1454   1906   ENG 47
Semenoff, Captain Vladimir. The Battle of Tsu-Shima : between the Japanese and Russian Fleets, fought on 27th May 1905. Translated by Captain A.B. Lindsay
London: John Murray 1906. 8vo, xxx, 165pp., map

1455   1906   FRE 30
Mahon, Patrice. L'Armee Russe apres la Campagne de 1904-1905 [The Russian Army after the Campaign of 1904-1905]

Paris: R. Chapelot 1906. small 8vo, 215pp., published under the direction of the 2e Bureau de l'Etat Major de l'Armee

1456   1906   ENG 158
Politovsky, Eugene S. From Libau to Tsushima ; A Narrative of the Voyage of Admiral Rojdestvensky's Fleet to Eastern Seas, Including a Detailed Account of the Dogger Bank Incident
London: John Murray 1906. 12mo, xvi, 305 pp., translated by Major F.R. Godfrey

1457   1906   GER 54
Spaits, Alexander. Mit Kosaken durch die Mandschurei : Erlebnisse im Russisch-Japanischen Kriege [With Cossacks through Manchuria. Adventures in the Russo-Japanese War]
Wien: Verlagsbuchhandlung Carl Konegen 1906. 8vo, 334pp., ill., maps

1458   1906   ENG 1041
Maxwell, William. From the Yalu to Port Arthur. A Personal Record.
London: Hutchinson 1906. 8vo, 407pp., ill.

1459   1906   FRE 327
Cheradame, Andre. Le Monde et la Guerre Russo-Japonaise [The World and the Russo-Japanese War]
Paris: Plon 1906. 8vo, 566pp., maps, no index

1460   1906   FRE 296
Cordonnier. Les Japonais en Mandchourie [The Japanese in Manchuria]
Paris: Henri-Charles Lavouzelle 1906. 8vo, 286pp., ill. cut out, maps still there; no index

1461   1906   ENG 1490
Ashmead-Bartlett, Ellis. Port Arthur. The Siege and Capitulation
Edinburgh: William Blackwood & Sons, MCMVI (1906). 8vo, 511pp., index, maps in folder

1462   1906   SPA 5
Schoenmeyr, Alfredo. Informe sobre la Guerra Ruso-Japones 1904-1905 [Sober Information on the Russo-Japanese War 1904-1905]
Santiago: Litografia Universo 1906. 4to, 2 vols., 162, 32pp.

1463 1906 GER 146
Noerregaard, B.W. Die Belagerung von Port Arthur [The Siege of Port Arthur]
Leipzig: Dieterich 1906. 8vo, vi, 292, 50, 137pp., ill., maps

1464 1907 ENG 68
Scidmore, Eliza Ruhamah. As the Hague Ordains. Journal of a Russian Prisoner's Wife in Japan
NY: Henry Holt & Co. 1907. 8vo, viii + 359pp. + ads, ill.

1465 1907 DUT 12e2
Wijnaendts, H. and Ridder, P.H.A. de. Studien betreffende de veldoorlog tusschen Rusland en Japan [Studies relating to the Land War between Russia and Japan]
Bergen-op-Zoom: Gebroeders Juten 1907. 4to, 247pp., maps

1466 1907 ENG 210 (2 ex.)
Hamilton, Ian. A Staff Officer's Scrap Book during the Russo-Japanese War
London : Arnold 1907. 8vo, 2 vols., vol.1 : 362pp., vol.2 : 387pp., index, ill., maps

1467 1907 ENG 65
Sakurai, Tadayoshi. Human Bullets : A Soldier's Story of Port Arthur
London: Archibald Constable & Co. 1907. 8vo, xvi, 270pp., ill., translated by Masujiro Honda, edited by Alice Mabel Bacon, with an introduction by Count Okuma

1468 1907 ENG 1141e2
Grant, R. (translator). Before Port Arthur in a Destroyer. The Personal Diary of a Japanese Naval Officer
London: John Murray 1907. translated from the Spanish / from the Japanese, 8mo, 243pp., map, index; contents: not on Korea

1469 1907 FRE 303
Matignon, J.J. Souvenirs de campagne en Mandchourie avec l'armee japonais [Souvenirs of the Campaign in Manchuria with the Japanese Army]
in: Bulletin de la Societe Franco-Japonais de Paris, 1907, small 4to, 61pp.

1470 1907 GER 145 (2 ex.)
Tettau, Eberhard Freiherr von. Achtzehn Monate mit Russlands Heeren in der

Mandschurei [18 Months with Russia's Armies in Manchuria]
Berlin: Mitter, 1907-1908. 2 vols., 8vo, 398, 483pp., maps

1471   1908   ENG 777
Asiaticus. Reconnaissance in the Russo-Japanese War
London: Hugh Rees 1908. 8vo, 147pp., translated from the German by J. Montgomery

1472   1908   FRE 39
Kvitka, Colonel A. Journal d'un cosaque du Transbaikal : Guerre Russo-Japonaise 1904-1905 [Diary of a Cossack from Transbaikalia : the Russo-Japanese War 1904-1905]
Paris: Librairie Plon 1908. 4to, 403pp., ill., map

1473   1908   GER 49
Marstrand-Mechlenburg, K. Das Japanische Prisenrecht in seiner Anwendung im japanisch-russischen Kriege : Eine Sammlung der Japanischen Prisenrechtsbestimmungen und der Entscheidungen der Japanischen Prisengerichte [The Japanese Law of Prize and its Adaptation during the Russo-Japanese War : A Collection of Japanese Regulations on Prizes and of the Decisions of Japanese Prize Courts]
Berlin: Ernst Siegfried Mittler und Sohn 1908. large 8vo, vi, 937pp., author Dr. jur., he translated and edited the documents with the assistance of Auswärtiges Amt and Reichs-Marine-Amt (Foreign Office and Navy Office)

1474   1908   ENG 216
Nojine, Mosieur E.K. The Truth about Port Arthur
London: John Murray 1908. 8vo, xxii, 395pp., (6)pp. ads, plates, map, index. translated and abridged by Captain A.B. Lindsay, edited by Major E.S. Swinton

1475   1908   ENG 1128e2
Sedgwick, F.R. The Russo-Japanese War on Land. A Brief Account of the Strategy and Major Tactics of the War
London: Forster Groom 1908. 8vo, 166pp., maps, no index

1476   1909   ENG 430
Historical Section, German General Staff. The Russo-Japanese War. The

Battle of Liao-Yan
London: Hugh Rees 1909. 8vo, xvi, 235pp., maps, translated by Karl von Donat

1477   1909   ENG 495
Anderson, J.H. The Russo-Japanese War on Land 1904-1905 : Up to the Battle of Liao-Yang
London: Hugh Rees 1909. 8vo, 105pp., map

1478   1909   FRE 220
Farrere, Claude. La bataille [The Battle]
Paris: Les Inedits de Modern-Bibliotheque / Artherm Fayard 1909. 8vo, 187pp., ill.; fiction

1479   1909   ENG 24
Kuropatkin, General. The Russian Army and the Japanese War : being Historical and Critical Comments on the Military Policy and Power of Russia and on the Campaign in the Far East. translated by Captain A.B. Lindsay
NY: Dutton 1909. 8vo, 2 vols., 309 + 348pp., edited by E.D. Swinton, appendix, index, maps

1480   1909   ENG 101
Semenoff, Wladimir. Rasplata (The Reckoning) : His Diary during the Blockade of Port Arthur and the Voyage of Admiral Rojestvensky's Fleet
London: John Murray 1909. 8vo, xv, 489pp., index

1481   1909   GER 163
Einzelschriften über den Russisch-Japanischen Krieg [Individual articles on the Russo-Japanese War]
Wien: L.W. Seidel & Sohn 1909-1911. 5 vols. + 5 vols. supplements, 8vo, vol.1 328pp., 2nd edition 1909, vol.2 616pp., 1910, vol.3 146pp., 2nd edition 1910, vol.4 153pp., 1910, vol.5 314pp., 1911

1482   1910   GER 109
Hamilton, Ian. Tagebuch eines Generalstabsoffiziers während des Russisch-Japanischen Krieges [A Statt Officer's Diary during the Russo-Japanese War]
Berlin: Karl Siegismund 1910. large 8vo, 391pp., ads, maps, translated by Paul von Heydebreck and Georg Schröder

1483   1910   FRE 31e2
Semenoff, Wladimir. Apres Tsoushima. Le Prix du Sang. Carnet de notes du

Commandant Semenoff, de l'Etat Major de l'Amiral Rojestvensky [After Tsushima. The Price of Blood. Notebook of Commandant Semenoff, Staff Officer under Admiral Rojestvensky]

Paris: Augustin Challamel (1909) 1910. 12mo, 308pp., about Russo-Japanese War. Revised and corrected translation of the articles published by Semenoff in "Vlestnik Evropy" by Commandant de Balincourt, French officer

1484   1910   GER 115:1

Breit, Josef. Der Russisch-Japanische Krieg 1904-1905. Teil 1 : Vom Ausbruch des Krieges bis zum übergang der Japaner über den Jalu [The Russo-Japanese War 1904-1905. Part 1 : From the Outbreak of the War until the Japanese Crossing of the Yalu]

Wien: L.W. Seidel & Sohn 1910. 8vo, 358pp., maps

1485   1911   FRE 82

Witte, Comte Serge. La Guerre avec le Japon. Declarations Necessaires. Reponse a l'Ouvrage du General Kouropatkine [The War with Japan. Necessary Declarations. An Answer to the Publication by General Kuropatkin]

Paris: Nancy, Berger-Levrault 1911. small 8vo, 75pp., translated from the Russian by E. Duchesne. Author Russian prime minister 1903-1906

1486   1912/1913   ENG 209

Hurst, C.J.B. and Bray, F.E. Russian and Japanese Prize Cases, being a Collection of Translations and Summaries of the Principal Cases Decided by the Russian and Japanese Prize Courts Arising out of the Russo-Japanese War 1904-1905

London: H.M.S.O. 1912, 1913. 8vo, 2 volumes, vol.1 : Russian cases, xi, 382pp., vol.2 : Japanese cases, xxvi, 475pp.

1487   1913   ENG 1343

Strang, Herbert. Jack Brown in China. A Story of the Russo-Japanese War

Oxford: UP, Reprint 1913. 12mo, 370pp., glossary

1488   1913   FRE 204 : 5 : 1/2

Etat Major General de l'Armee Russe. Guerre Russo-Japonaise 1904-1905. Historique redige a l'Etat Major de l'Armee, 2e Bureau. Volume 5 : Bataille de

Moukden, 1st Part : Evenements ayant precede immediatement la Bataille de Moukden. La Bataille elle-meme jusqu'a l'Ordre du Commandant en Chef prescrivant la Retraite des 2e et 3e Armees sur le Houenho. 2nd Part : Recul des IIIe et Iere Armee sur les Positions du Houenho. Trouee des Japonais a Kiouzang, Retraite des Armees de Mandchourie sur Tieling et les Positions de Sseupingkai [The Russo-Japanese War 1904-1905. The Official Account of its History by the General Staff of the Russian Army, translation published under the direction of Army Staff Headquarters, 2nd Bureau, Vol.5 : The Battle of Mukden. Part 1 : Events which immediately preceded the Battle of Mukden. The Battle itself until the Commander-in-Chief's Order to retreat to the 2nd and 3rd armies on the Houenho.

Part 2 : Retreat of the 3rd and 1st armies to positions on the Houenho. A breach of the Japanese at Kiouzang. Retreat of the Manchurian armies on Tieling and the positions of Sseupingkai]

Paris: R. Chapelot 1913. 8vo, 2 parts, part 1 828pp., part 2 515pp., translation published under the direction of the l'Etat Major de l'Armee (French), 2e Bureau

| 1489 | 1922 | ENG 477e2 |

Strang, Herbert. Kobo : A Story of the Russo-Japanese War

London etc.: Blackie & Son 1922. 8vo, xi, 370pp., ill., maps

| 1491 | 1937 | ENG 362 |

Thiess, Frank. The Voyage of Forgotten Men (Tsushima)

NY: Bobbs Merrill 1937. 8vo, 415pp., ill., index, translated by F. Salangar

| 1492 | 1940 | GER 175 |

Thiess, Frank. Tsuschima

Berlin: Paul Zsolnay 1940. 8vo, 514pp., map

| 1493 | 1942 | FRE 218 |

Thiess, Frank. Tsoushima. Une poignante epopee de la mer [Tsushima, A Touching Epic of the Sea]

Paris: Flammarion 1942. small 8vo, 311, xvii pp., translated from the German by D. Geneix

| 1494 | n.d. | FRE 186 |

Galli, Henri. La Guerre en Extreme Orient. Russes et Japonais. De Tchemulpo

a Liao-Yang [The War in the Far East. Russians and Japanese. From Chemulpo to Liaoyang]
Paris: Garnier Freres, n.d. (c.1905). large 8vo, 954pp., ill., maps

1495 n.d. ENG 1042 (2 ex.)
Grew, E. Sharpe. War in the Far East. A History of the Russo-Japanese Struggle.
London: Virtue, n.d. (c.1905). 6 vol., large 8vo, 240, 240, 240, 240, 240, 240pp.

V.d.7) WORLD WAR I, 1914-1918

1496 1916 GER 184
Leonhardi, Prof. Sonnenschein und Sturm in Osten. Erlebnisse eines Sechzigjährigen auf einer Weltreise während des Weltkrieges [Sunshine and Storm in the East. Adventures of a Sixty-Year-Old on a Journey around the World during the World War]
Hollesen: Huwaldsche Buchhandlung 1916. 12mo, 262pp.

1497 1919 GER 189
Bruggen, C.J.A. van. Das Reich Gottes in Sibirien [God's Realm in Siberia]
Zürich: Max Rescher 1919. 12mo, 427pp.

V.d.8) SINO-JAPANESE WAR 1937-1945, AND WORLD WAR II 1941-1945

1498 1937 ENG 741
Japanese Chamber of Commerce of New York. The Sino-Japanese Crisis of 1937. First Comprehensive, Authentic, Factual Statement, with Official American and Japanese Documents
NY: Japanese Chamber of Commerce [1937]. 12mo, 59pp.

1499 1937 ENG 516
Press Bureau of the Chinese Delegation. Japanese Aggression and World Opinion (July 7 to October 7 1937)
Geneva: Press Bureau of the Chinese Delegation (Bureau de Guomintang) 1937. 8vo, 127pp.

1500   1937   FRE 87

Bureau de Presse de la Delegation Chinoise. L'agression japonaise et la Societe des Nations [Japanese Aggression and the League of Nations]

Geneve: Bureau de Presse de la Delegation Chinoise 1937-1940. 8vo, 5 vols. out of 8, vol.1 : 37pp., 1937, vol.2 : 93pp., 1937, vol.5 : 130pp., 1938, vol.7 : 94pp., 1939, vol.8 : 123pp., 1940

1501   1938   ENG 319

The Royal Institute of International Affairs. China and Japan : Information Department Papers, No.21

London: The Royal Institute of International Affairs 1938. 8vo, 130pp., 2 maps

1502   1943   GER 196

Kaiserlich Japanische Militärmission. Japanisches Kriegstagebuch. Vol.II : Von Singapur bis Mandalay und Corregidor [Imperial Japanese Military Mission (in Germany) : Imperial War Diary : Vol.II : From Singapore to Mandalay and Corregidor]

Berlin: E.S. Mittler 1943. 8vo, 103pp., ill.

V.d.9) THE KOREAN WAR 1950-1953

1503   1950   DUT 9

Kadt, J. de. De consequenties van Korea. Een pleidooi voor vrede door kracht [The consequences of Korea. A plea for peace (secured) by power]

Amsterdam: G.A. van Oorschot 1950. 12mo, 299pp.

1504   1950   ENG 729

MOFA, DPRK. Ministry of Foreign Affairs, Democratic People's Republic of Korea. Documents and Materials Exposing the Instigators of the Civil War in Korea

Pyongyang: Ministry of Foreign Affairs 1950. 8vo, iv, 25pp.

1505   1950   ENG 743

Soviet News. American Armed Intervention in Korea. A Soviet News Booklet.

London: Soviet News 1950. 12mo, 28pp.

1506   n.d.   GER 103
United Nations, Department of Public Information. Vereint im Kampf in Korea [United in the Struggle for Korea]
München: United Nations Department of Public Information, n.d., small 4to, 24pp., ill.

1507   n.d.   ENG 931
Morris, Richard. What's Happening in Korea
NY: New Century Publishers, n.d., 12mo, 23pp.; contents: anti-U.S. account of the start of the war

V.d.10) OTHER MILITARY HISTORY

1508   1872   ENG 1273
Low, Lt. Charles R. The Great Battles of the British Navy
London: Routledge 1872. 12mo, 496pp.

1509   1894   FRE 59
Bujac, E. L'Armee Russe. Son Histoire. Son Organisation Actuelle [The Russian Army, its History, its Present Organisation]
Paris: Charles Lavauzelle 1894. 8vo, 428pp., bibliography

1510   1894   FRE 288 Vol.CIV
Toucy. L'Armee Chinoise [The Chinese Army]
in: L'Illustration, vol.CIV, 1894, p.171

1511   n.d. (c.1900)   FRE 183
Draner. Types Militaires Etrangeres [Foreign Military Types]
Paris: Librairie Illustree n.d. (c.1900). folio, 40pp., ill.; contents: caricatures, not on Korea

1512   1904   FRE 72
Yi, Tai Tjo. L'Armee Coreenne [The Korean Army]
in: A Travers le Monde, 1904, pp.117-118

1513   1904   ENG 1365
Parker, E.H. Artillery in the Far East
essay, revision sheet, double 4to, folded; 1904

1514 n.d. ENG 871
Wilson, H.W. Battleships in Action
London: Sampson Low, n.d., 2 vols., 337+384pp., 8vo; contents: covers naval warfare from 1861 to the end of WW I

1515 1921 ENG 16
Ogawa, Gotaro. Conscription System in Japan
NY: Oxford UP 1921. large 8vo, xiii, 245pp., Series : Carnegie Endowment for International Peace

1516 1921 ENG 1233e3
Bywater, Hector C. Sea-Power in the Pacific. A Study of the American-Japanese Naval Problem.
London: Constable 1921. 8vo, 334pp., ill., maps

1517 1922 ENG 162
Ono, Giichi. War and Armament Expenditures of Japan
NY: Oxford UP 1922. large 8vo, xvii, 315pp., index; Series : Carnegie Endowment for International Peace

1518 1922 ENG 163
Kobayashi, Ushisaburo. War and Armament Loans of Japan
NY: Oxford UP 1922. large 8vo, xv, 221pp., bibliography, index, Series : Carnegie Endowment for International Peace

1519 1948 ENG 1297
Blackett, P.M.S. Military and Political Consequences of Atomic Energy
London: Turnstile 1948. 8vo, 216pp.

1520 1950 ENG 727
Seversky, Alexander P. de. Air Power
NY: Simon & Schuster 1950. 8vo, xxiv, 376pp., ill., maps

VI.) BIOGRAPHY

VI.a) BIOGRAPHICAL DICTIONARIES

1521   1899   ENG 1312
Who's Who 1899
London: Adrian & Charles Black 51st issue, 1899. 12mo, 1014pp., 64pp. ads, edited by Douglas Sladen

1522   1907   ENG 1100e3
Maunder, Samuel. The Biographical Treasury. A Dictionary of Universal Biography
London: Longman, Green 1907. 16mo, 719pp.

1523   1943   ENG 1320
Webster's Biographical Dictionary
Springfield Mass.: Webster's 1943. 8vo, 1698pp., 1st edition

VI.b) COMPILATIONS OF BIOGRAPHIES BY TOPIC

1524   1883   ENG 271
Lanman, Charles. Leading Men of Japan, with an Historical Summary of the Empire
Boston: Lothrop [1883]. 12mo, 421pp., bibliography; contents: a detail study with biographies of 58 important Japanese men during the Meiji era

1525   1929   ENG 1483

Hall, Josef Washington. Eminent Asians. Six Great Personalities of the New East

NY: D. Appleton & Co. 1929. 8vo, 511pp., no index; contents: chapter 3 pp.101-246 on Yamagata, Prince Ito

VI.c) BIOGRAPHIES OF HISTORICAL FIGURES

1526   1890   ENG 203

Dening, Walter. The Life of Toyotomi Hideyoshi

Tokyo: Hakubunsha 1890. 12mo, 417pp., appendix, ill.

1527   1931   ENG 891

Lamb, Harold. Genghis Khan. The Emperor of All Men

London: Thornton Butterworth 4th impression 1931. 8vo, 287pp., ill., index

1528   1937   ENG 987

Sadler, A.L. The Maker of Modern Japan. The Life of Tokugawa Ieyasu

London: Allen & Unwin 1937. 8vo, 430pp., ill., index

1529   1949   ENG 1145

Waley, Arthur. The Life and Times of Po Chü-I 772-846

London: George Allen & Unwin 1949. 8vo, 237pp., map

VI.d) BIOGRAPHIES OF POLITICAL FIGURES

1530   1894   ENG 255

Lane-Poole, Stanley. The Life of Sir Harry Parkes : Sometime Her Majesty's Minister to China & Japan

London: MacMillan 1894. 2 vols., vol.1 : xxvi, 512pp., map; vol.2 : xx, 477pp., map, appendices, index

1531   1894   FRE 288 Vol.CIV

Bryois, Henry. Li Hong-Tchang

in: L'Illustration vol.CIV 1894 p.272

1532 1895 ENG 188
Douglas, Robert K. Public Men of To-day. Li Hung Chang
NY: Warne [1895]. 12mo, 251pp., 16pp. ads, ill.

1533 1901 ENG 466
Lane-Poole, Stanley. Sir Harry Parkes in China
London: Methuen 1901. 8vo, xxv, 386, 47pp., map, index

1534 1909 ENG 1196 (2 ex.)
Stead, W.T. The M.P. for Russia. Reminiscences and Correspondence of Mme Olga Novikoff
London: Andrew Melroze 1909. 4to, 536pp.; contents: not on Korea

1535 1915 ENG 497
Pooley, A.M. (ed.). The Secret Memoirs of Count Tadasu Hayashi
NY and London: G.P. Putnam's Sons 1915. 8vo, v, 331pp., ill., map; comment: Tadasu Hayashi studied in England, became Japanese ambassador in China, Britain, later Japanese Foreign Minister

1536 1915 GER 182
Hagen, Gräfin M. von. Memoiren des Vizekönigs Li Hung Chang [Memoires of Viceroy Li Hung Chang]
Berlin: Karl Sigismund 1915. 8vo, 243pp.

1537 1917 ENG 1068
Bland, J.O.P. Li Hung-Chang (Masters of the Nineteenth Century)
N.Y.: Holt 1917. 8vo, 327pp., ill., index

1538 1918 ENG 456
Lawrence, Mary Viola Tingley. A Diplomat's Helpmate : How Rose F. Foote, Wife of the First U.S. Minister to Korea, Served her Country in the Far East
San Francisco: Crocker 1918. 8vo, ix, 50pp., ill.

1539 1921 ENG 106 Vol.21-1
Graves, Louis. Willard Straight in Far Eastern Finance. Part VI of An American in Asia
in: Asia. The American Masgazine on the Orient, vol.21-1 1921, pp.160-166

1540   1923   ENG 1078

Mannix, William Francis. Memoirs of Li Hung Chang, with the story of a literary forgery by Ralph D. Parne

Boston: Houghton Mifflin 1923. 8vo, 298pp.

1541   1926   ENG 578 : 1/2

Buckle, Earl George. The Letters of Queen Victoria : Second Series. A Selection from Her Majesty's Correspondence and Journal between the Years 1862 and 1878

London: John Murray 1926. 2 vols., 8vo, ill., vol.I : 1862-1869, vol.2 : 1870-1878

1542   1928   ENG 1308 (2 ex.)

Ronaldshay, Earl of. The Life of Lord Curzon

London: Ernest Benn 1928-1929. 3 vols., 8vo, 457, 318, 424pp., index in volume 3; contents: 1 Korea entry

1543   1929   ENG 8 : 1

Gwynn, Stephen (ed.). The Letters and Friendships of Sir Cecil Spring Rice, a Record

London: Constable 1929. 8vo, only vol.1, second impression, vi, 504pp., ill.; comment: Sir Spring Rice was a British poet; he corresponded a.o. with Theodore Roosevelt. Spring Rice travelled to Japan (1892, pp.121-152; content: on Korea pp.125-138, 146-147, 388-389, 420-421, 445, 479)

1544   1933   ENG 435

Allen, Bernard M. The Rt. Hon. Sir Ernest Satow, G.C.M.G. : a Memoir

London: Kegan Paul, Trench, Trubner 1933. 8vo, vii, 152pp., index; comment: Satow scholar of Japanese, British diplomat

1545   1940   ENG 721

Hedin, Sven. Chiang Kai Shek : Marshal of China

NY: John Day 1940. 8vo, xiv, 290pp., index; translated from the Swedish by Bernard Norbelie

1546   1948   ENG 1240

Hsiung, S.I. The Life of Chiang Kai Shek

London: Peter Davies 1948. 12mo, 398pp., ill., map, index; contents: 2 Korea entries

VI.e) BIOGRAPHIES OF MILITARY FIGURES

1548   1904   ENG 1408
Schley, Winfried Scott. Forty-Five Years under the Flag
NY: Appleton & Co. 1904. 8vo, 439pp.; contents: chapter 9 : Opening Communication with Korea, pp.88-96

1549   1935   ENG 806
Nakamura, Koya. Admiral Togo : a Memoir
Tokyo: Togo Gensui Hensankai 1935. 4to, 347pp., ill.

1550   1935   ENG 1205
Bodley, R.V.C. Admiral Togo. The authorized Life of Admiral of the Fleet, Marquis Heikachiro Togo
London: Jarrolds 1935. 8vo, 288pp.

1551   1941   ENG 604
Nym, Wales. Song of Ariran : The Life of a Korean Rebel
NY: John Day 1941. 8vo, xxvi, 258pp., ill., map, index; contents: Kim San, Communist Korean resistance fighter; Nym Wales met him in Yenan

VI.f) BIOGRAPHIES OF MISSIONARIES

1552   1867   FRE 176
Anonymous. Vie de Monseigneur Pierre-Andre Retord, Eveque d'Acanthe [The Life of Mr. Pierre Andre Retord, Bishop of Acanthe]
Lyon: Louis Perin 1859. small 8vo, 327, 40pp.; contents: last 40 pages : Euloge de Mr. Daveluy, eveque d'Acone, coadjuteur de Coree, martyrise en Coree le vendredi saint 1866, prononce dans la Cathedrale d'Amiens par mgr Mermillod, Lyon, Bauchu, 1867 (Eulogy on Mr. Daveluy, Bishop of Acone, Coadjutor of Korea, martyrized in Korea in 1866, pronounced in the Carthedral of Amiens by Mr. Mermillod, Lyon, Bauchu 1867)

1553   1888   FRE 9
Hulst, M. d' Vie de Just de Bretenieres : Missionaire Apostolique Martyrise en Coree en 1866 [Life of Just de Bretenieres : Apostolic Missionary martyrized

in Korea in 1886]
Paris: Librairie Poussielque Freres 1888. 16mo, ill., 347pp.

1554 c.1890 FRE 94e3
Piacentini, Abbe Arthur. Mgr. Ridel, Eveque de Philippopolis, Vicaire Apostolique de Coree d'apres sa Correspondence [Mgr. Ridel, Bishop of Philippopolis, Apostolic Vicar of Korea, according to his Correspondence]
Lyon: Librairie Generale Catholique et Classique n.d. (c.1890). 8vo, 374pp., map

1555 1892 FRE 9e2
Hulst, M. d' Vie de Just de Bretenieres : Missionaire Apostolique Martyrise en Coree en 1866 [Life of Just de Bretenieres : Apostolic Missionary martyrized in Korea in 1886]
Paris: Librairie Poussielque Freres 1892. 12mo, ill., 348pp., no index

1556 1893 ENG 586e7
Anonymous. Martyrs in Corea. The New Glories of the Catholic Church.
Baltimore: Murphy 1893. 12mo, 331pp., translated from the Italian by the fathers of the London Oratory, preface by Cardinal Wiseman; contents: focus on Korea, discusses the acts of several Korean martyrs in the persecution of 1839

1557 1899 ENG 1189
Bickersteth, Samuel. Life and Letters of Edward Bickersteth, Bishop of South Tokyo
London: Sampson Low, Marston & Co. 1899. 8vo, 496pp., masp, index; contents: 1 Korea entry

1558 1903 ENG 1450
McCully, Elizabeth A. A Corn of Wheat, or the Life of Rev. W.J. McKenzie of Korea
Toronto: Westminster 1903. 12mo, 290pp., ill.

1559 1910 FRE 351
Anonymous. Just de Bretenieres, Martyr en Coree (1839-1866) [Just de Bretenieres, Martyr in Korea, 1839-1866]
in: Les Contemporaines, vol.19 no.948 pp.1-16

1560 1912 ENG 1076 (2 ex.)

238

Griffis, William Elliot. A Modern Pioneer in Korea. The Life Story of Henry G. Appenzeller
NY: Fleming H. Revell 1912. 8vo, 298pp., index

1561   1912   ENG 1098e2
Taylor, Howard. Hudson Taylor in Early Years. The Growth of a Soul
London: Morgan Scott, 2nd ed., for China Inland Mission 1912. 8vo, ill., 511pp., map, index; contents: not on Korea

1562   1914   ENG 772
Christie, Dugald. Thirty Years in Moukden, 1883-1913, being the Experiences and Recollections of Dugald Christie, C.M.G.
London: Constable & Co. MCMXIV (1914). 8vo, 303pp., ill., map, index, edited by his wife

1563   1917   ENG 192
Hart, E.I. Virgil C. Hart, Missionary Statesman. Founder of the American and Canadian Missions in Central and Western China
London: Hodder & Stoughton, Doran 1917. 12mo, 34pp., ill.

1564   1918   ENG 222
Appert, C. For the Faith : Life of Just de Bretenieres
Maryknoll: Catholic Foreign Mission Soc. [1918]. 12mo, 170pp., ill., appendix, translated from the French by Florence Gilmore

1565   1918   ENG 863 (2 ex.)
Underwood, Lilias H. Underwood of Korea
NY: Fleming H. Revell 1918. 350pp.

1566   1922   ENG 1347
Walsh, James A. In the Homes of Martyrs. Just de Bretenieres
NY: Maryknoll 1922. 12mo, 151pp.; contents: describes places in France where Martyrs came from

1567   1924   FRE 57
Mutel, G. Documents relatifs aux Martyrs de Coree, de 1839 a 1846. Missions de Seoul [Documents relating to the Martyrs of Korea, from 1839 to 1846. The Seoul Mission]
Hong Kong: Imprimerie de Nazareth (Societe des Missions Etrangeres de Paris) 1924. 8vo, vii, 145pp.

1568 1925 FRE 80
Launay, Adrien. Martyrs Français et Coreens 1838-1846, Beatifies en 1925 [French and Korean Martyrs, 1838-1846, beatified in 1925]
Paris: Tequi 1925. 8vo, xii, 272pp., ill.

1569 1929 FRE 103
Launay, Adrien. Les Bienheureux Martyrs de la Societe des Missions Etrangeres [The Blessed Martyrs of the Society of Foreign Missions]
Paris: Tequi / Societe des Missions Etrangeres 1929. 8vo, 251pp.

1570 1930 GER 197
Weber, Norbert O.S.B. P. Lukas Etlin O.S.B., Ein kurzes Lebensbild [Father Lukas Etlin, a brief biography]
St. Ottilien : Missionsverlag 1930. 12mo, 99pp., ill.

1571 1932 ENG 34
Christie, Mrs. Dugald. Dugald Christie of Manchuria : Pioneer and Medical Missionary. The Story of a Life with a Purpose
London: Clarke n.d. [c.1932]. 8vo, 231pp., ill., index. Foreword by Sao-Ke Alfred Sze, late Chinese Minister to Great Britain

1572 1933 ENG 1454
Noble, M.W. Victorious Lives of Early Christians in Korea
Seoul: Christian Literature Society of Korea 1933. 12mo, 174pp.

1573 1936 ENG 455
Trollope, Constance. Mark Napier Trollope : Bishop in Corea 1911-1930
London: Society for Promoting Christian Knowledge 1936. small 8vo, xii, 187pp., ill., with a foreword by the Bishop of Brechin

1574 1938 ENG 900 Vol.21
Kim, Francis. Father Daniel McMenamin. An Appreciation
in: The Far East Vol.21, 1938, p.57

1575 1938 ENG 900 Vol.21
Duffy, Gavan. The Perfect Knight. Father Chargebeouf
in: The Far East, vol.21, 1938, pp.78-80

1576   1938   ENG 1173
Chinese Artists. The Life of Christ
Westminster: Society for the Propagation of the Gospel 1938. 8vo, 53pp.

1577   1938   ENG 900 Vol.21
Anonymous. The Late Monsigneur Demange. Vicar Apostolic of Taikou, Korea
in: The Far East, vol.21, 1938, p.108

1578   1939   ENG 900 Vol.22
Monaghan, Patrick. A Korean Apostle
in: The Far East, vol.22, 1939, p.77

1579   1939   ENG 900 Vol.22
McPolin. The New Vicar Apostolic of Taikou, Korea, Monsigneur Mousset, Successor to the Late Bishop Demange, is Consecrated in Taikou
in: The Far East, vol.22, 1939, p.197

1580   1939   ENG 900 Vol.22
Quinlan, Thomas. The First Martyrs of Korea. How Three Heroic French Missionaries Gave Their Life for Christ in Korea
in: The Far East, vol.22, 1939, pp.222-223

1581   1943 ENG 136e2 (2 ex.)
Cowman, Lettie B. Charles E. Cowman, Missionary Warrior
LA: Oriental Missionary Society (1928) 1943. 8vo, 433pp., ill., maps

1582   1944   ENG 368
Harrington, Fred H. God, Mammon and the Japanese. Dr. Horace N. Allen and Korean-American Relations 1884-1905
Madison: Univ. of Wisconsin 1944. 8vo, 362pp., ill., maps, index, bibliography

1583   1950   ENG 474
Wright, Stanley F. Hart and the Chinese Customs
Belfast: Wm. Mullan &Son 1950. large 8vo, xvi, 940pp., ill., bibliography, index

VI.g) BIOGRAPHIES OF OTHERS

1584 1904 ENG 1372
Diffendorfer, Ralph E. Pai Chai Hakdong (Korean Child), in : Ralph E. Diffendorfer, Child Life in Mission Lands
NY: Methodist Book Concern, 1904. 12mo, 180pp., pp.132-148

1585 1908 ENG 218e3
Stoddart, Anna M. The Life of Isabella Bird [Mrs. Bishop], Hon. Member of the Oriental Society of Pekin
London: Murray 1908. 8vo, 416pp., ill., maps, appendix, index; Gompertz 416

1586 1912 ENG 460 : 1/2
Chaille-Long, Colonel. My Life in Four Continents
London: Hutchinson 1912. 2 vols., vol.1 : xxi, 308pp., vol.2 : pp.309-616, ill., map; contents: on Korea: pp.340-386

1587 1920 ENG 608
Villiers, Frederic. Villiers : His Five Decades of Adventure
NY & London: Harper & Brothers 1920. 8vo, 2 vols., 315, 338pp., ill.

1588 1920 ENG 1415
Gurney, W.N. Soo Pokki and In Sunny. The Story of the Pak Family of Corea
London: Society for the Propaganda of the Gospel in Foreign Parts 1920. 8vo, 59pp.

1589 1922 ENG 613
Graves, Louis. Willard Straight in the Orient
NY: Asia Publishing Co. 1922. 4to, 74pp., ill.; contents: pp.27-35 on Korea

1590 1924 ENG 1022
Croly, Herbert. Willard Straight
NY: MacMillan 1924. 8vo, 569pp., ill.

1591 1928 ENG 761
Hornby, Edmund. Sir Edmund Hornby, an Autobiography
Boston: Houghton Mifflin Co. 1928. 2 vols., 8vo, xiv, 396pp., ill., index, introduction by D.L. Murray

1592 1931 ENG 1287

Crewe, Marquess of. Lord Roseberry
London: John Murray 1931. 2 vols., 8vo, together 756pp., index; contents: not on Korea

1593   1941   DEN 6
Petersen, Josef. Søfareren Vitus Bering [Seafarer Vitus Bering]
København: Hagerup 1941. 233pp.

VI.h) DIARIES, MEMOIRS OF WESTERN RESIDENTS OF THE FAR EAST

1594   1849   ENG 350
Lowrie, Walter Macon. Memoirs of the Rev. Walter M. Lowrie, Missionary to China, edited by his father
NY: Robert Carter 1849. 8vo, 460pp.

1595   1863   ENG 123
Alcock, Sir Rutherford. The Capital of the Tycoon : a Narrative of a Three Years' Residence in Japan
London: Longman, Green 1863. 2 vols., 8vo, vol.1 xxxi, 469pp., ill., map, vol.2 x, 539pp., ill., map, index; comment: author British Envoy and Minister Plenipotentiary in Japan

1596   1887   FRE 44
Aubry, J.B. Les Chinois chez eux [The Chinese among themselves]
Lille: Societe St. Augustin, Desclee, De Brouwer 1887. small 4to, 294pp.

1597   1887   ENG 1048
Balfour, Frederic Henry. Leaves from my Chinese Scrapbook
London: Trübner 1887. 8vo, 215pp.; contents: on Korea pp.167-170

1598   1894   ENG 171 (2 ex.)
Carles, W.R. Life in Corea
NY and London: MacMillan (1888) 1894. 8vo, xiv, 317pp., plates, map; Gompertz 186

1599   1895   ENG 975
Laurie, Andre. Schoolboy Days in Japan

Boston: Esks and Laurient 1895. translated by Laura E. Kendall, 8vo, 270pp., ill.; contents: not on Korea

1600   **1897**   **ENG 616**

Hearn, Lafcadio. Gleanings in Buddha Fields : Studies of Hand and Soul in the Far East

London and NY: Harper & Brothers 1897. 12mo, 296pp.

1601   **1898**   **ENG 86 (4 ex.)**

Gale, James Scarth. Korean Sketches

Chicago: Fleming H. Revell 1898 / NY: Young People's Missionary Movement of the United States and Canada n.d., 16mo, 256pp., ill.; Gompertz 285

1602   **1901**   **FRE 336**

Ridel, M. Ma captivite dans les prisons de Seoul [My Captivity in the Prisons of Seoul]

Lille 1901. 8vo, 189pp.; contents: with a biography of M. Ridel by Adrien Launay

1603   **1904**   **ENG 476**

Farrer, Reginald J. The Garden of Asia : Impressions from Japan

London: Methuen 1904. 8vo, xi, 296, 40pp., contents: on Korea pp.56-78; Gompertz 363

1604   **1904 ENG 86e2 (2 ex.)**

Gale, James Scarth. Korean Sketches

Edinburgh: Oliphant Anderson & Ferrier (1898) 1904. 16mo, 256p., ill., ads; Gompertz 285

1605   **1904 ENG 200eR (2 ex.)**

Scidmore, Eliza Ruhamah. Jinrikisha Days in Japan

NY: Harper & Brothers (1891) 1904. 12mo, ix, 386pp., ill., index

1606   **1904 ENG 589 (2 ex.)**

Underwood, Lilias H. Fifteen Years among the Top-Knots; Life in Korea

NY: American Tract Society 1904. 8vo, xviii, 271pp., ill.; Gompertz 353

1607   **1905 ENG 1400 (2 ex.)**

Barnes, Annie M. An American Girl in Korea

Philadelphia: Penn 1905. 12mo, 392pp.

1608   **1908**   **ENG 623e3**

Thompson, R. Wardlaw. Griffith John : The Story of Fifty Years in China
London: Religious Tract Society 1908. 8vo, popular revised edition, xvi, 552pp., ill., maps, index

1608a   1908   ENG 830 (2 ex.)
Allen, Horace N. Things Korean. A Collection of Sketches and Anecdotes, Missionary and Diplomatic
NY: Fleming H. Revell 1908. 8vo, 256pp., ill.

1609   1909   ENG 1011
Lloyd, Arthur. Every-day Japan, Written after Twenty-Five Years' Residence and Work in the Country
London: Cassell etc. 1909. introduction by Count Hayashi, 8vo, 381pp., ill., index; contents: several Korea entries

1610   1910   ENG 897
Little, Archibald. Gleanings from Fifty Years in China
London: Sampson Low, Marston & Co. 1910. 8vo, 330pp., index; contents: on Korea p.212

1611   n.d. (c.1910)   ENG 1066
Daly, Mrs. de Burgh. An Irishwoman in China
NY: Frederick A. Stokes, n.d., 8vo, 295pp.

1612   1912   ENG 886
Anethan, Albert d'. Fourteen Years of Diplomatic Life in Japan, Leaves from the Diary of Baroness Albert d'Anethan, with an introduction by Baron Kato
London: Stanley Paul & Co. 1912. 8vo, 471pp., ill., no index; contents: diary entries cover the years 1893-1906

1613   1912   ENG 1070e2
Ballard, Susan. Jottings from Japan
Westminster: Society for the Propagation of the Gospel in Foreign Parts 1912. 12mo, 96pp., ill.

1614   1913   ENG 211
Wilkes, Paget. Missionary Joys in Japan. Or Leaves from my Journal
London: Morgan & Scott MCMXIII (1913). 8vo, 321pp., ill. "With Christian poems. Travel and autobiography of a missionary hero in Japan and Korea". Introduction by Rev. Barclay F. Buxton

BIOGRAPHY

1615 1913 ENG 1050
Foster, John W. (ed.). Memoirs of the Viceroy Li Hung Chang
London: Constable 1913. 8vo, 314pp., ill.

1616 1916 ENG 503e8 : 1/2
Redesdale, Lord. Memories
London: Hutchinson 1916. 8vo, 2 vols., vol.1 : 396pp., ill., vol.2 : pp.397-816, ill., index; comment: author British nobleman, traveller, stayed extensively in Japan

1617 1919 ENG 376
Nisbet, Mrs. Anabel M. Day in and Day Out in Korea : Being Some Account of the Mission Work that has been Carried on in Korea since 1892 by the Presbyterian Church in the United States
Richmond: Presbyterian Committee, [n.d. c.1919]. 12mo, 199pp., ill., map, index

1618 1920 ENG 1034
Anderson, Isabel. The Spell of Japan
Boston: Page (1914) 1920. 8vo, 396pp., ill., index; contents: numerous Korea entries

1619 1926 ENG 614 (2 ex.)
Singer, Caroline and Baldridge, C. le Roy. Turn to the East
NY: Minton & Balch 1926. 4to, 72pp., ill., foreword by Nathaniel Peffer

1620 1926 ENG 1306
Marquess Curzon of Keddleston. Leaves from a Viceroy's Note-book and other Papers
London: MacMillan 1926. 8vo, 414pp., ill., index

1621 1930 FRE 97
Hugon, Joseph O.S.J. Mes Paysans Chinois [My Chinese Peasants]
Paris: Editions Dillen & Cie 1930. 8vo, 206pp., ill.

1622 1930 ENG 988
Cosenza, Mario Emilio (ed.). The Complete Journal of Townsend Harris, First American Consul General and Minister to Japan
NY: Doubleday, Doran & Co. 1930. published for the Japan Society, 8vo, 616pp., ill., index; contents: covers period 1855-1858; Korea not mentioned in index

1623 1931 GER 105
Bälz, Erwin. Das Leben eines deutschen Arztes im erwachenden Japan [The Life of a German Medical Doctor in Awakening Japan]
Stuttgart: J. Engelhorns Nachfahren 1931. 8vo, 454pp., ill., index; edited by Toku Bälz; Gompertz 596; Domschke/Goossmann 67

1624 1932 FRE 153
Boecher, Herbert. Chinois, Japonais et Brigands. Recit d'un familier du Marechal Tchan-Tsueliang [Chinese, Japanese and Brigands. Report of an Acquaintance of Marshal Chang Tso Lin]
Paris: Calevas MCMXXXII (1932). 12mo, 173pp., translated from the German by Maurice d'Aubigne

1625 n.d. (after 1933) ENG 1207
Barrow, George de S. The Fire of Life.
London : Hutchinson n.d. (after 1933). 8vo, 236pp., index; contents: memoirs of a British Officer, who served in India; Boxer Rebellion; 1 Korea entry

1626 1937 ENG 76
Crouch, Archie R. Riksha Rambles of Archie and Ellen or Adventures in Christian Service
Cambria CA: Cambrian Press 1937. 16mo, 108pp.

1627 1938 ENG 588 (2 ex.)
Chisholm, William H. Vivid Experiences in Korea, by a Missionary Doctor
Wheaton, Illinois: Van Kampen Press (1938). 12mo, 136pp., ill.

1628 1938 ENG 900 Vol.21
Marinan, Gerard. An Early Morning in Korea
in: The Far East, vol.21, 1938, pp.200-202

1629 1938 ENG 900 Vol.21
Monaghan, Patrick. Two Curious Episodes
in: The Far East, vol.21, 1938, p.11

1630 1939 ENG 900 Vol.22
Monaghan, Parick. The Pride of Moppo
in: The Far East vol.22, 1939, p.107

1631   1941   ENG 1055
Griscom, Lloyd C. Diplomatically Speaking
London: John Murray 1941. 8vo, 398pp., index, ill.; comment: author U.S. diplomat in Japan, 1902-1905

1632   1944   ENG 1116
Grew, Joseph C. Ten Years in Japan
London: Hammond, Hammond & Co. 1944. 8vo, 480pp., ill., index

1633   1946   FRE 20
Abend, Hallet. Mes Annees en Chine (1928-1941) [My Years in China, 1928-1941]
Paris: Jules Tallander 1946. 12mo, 318pp., translated from the English by Jeanne Fournier-Pargoire

1634   1947   ENG 706
Baldridge, Cyrus LeRoy. Time and Chance
NY: John Day 1947. 8vo, 432pp., ill.

1635   1947   ENG 723
Morris, John. The Phoenix Cup. Some Notes on Japan in 1946
London: Cresset Press 1947. 8vo, x, 224pp.

1636   1948   ENG 602
Gayn, Mark. Japan Diary
NY: Sloane 1948. 8vo, x, 517pp., index

1637   1948   GER 112
Abshagen, Karl Heinz. Im Lande Arimasen [In the Land of Arimasen]
Stuttgart: Deutsche Verlagsanstalt 1948. 8vo, 375pp.

1638   1948   ENG 276
Herlihy, Francis. Now Welcome Summer [autobiography of a Missionary active in Korea]
Dublin: Clonmore & Reynolds 1948. 255pp., ill.

1639   1949   ENG 135 (2 ex.)
Materi, Irma Tenant. Irma and the Hermit. My Life in Korea
NY: Norton 1949. 8vo, 256pp.

VII.) CULTURE

VII.a) CULTURE : IN GENERAL

1640   1874   FRE 55
Congres International des Orientalistes. Comte-Rendu de la Premiere Session. Paris 1873, vol.1 [International Congress of Orientalists : Concerns of the First Session, Paris 1873, vol.1]
Paris: Maisonneuve et Cie, 1874. 8vo, 583pp., ill.

1641   1888   ENG 550
Lowell, Percival. The Soul of the Far East
Boston: Houghton Mifflin & Co. 1888. 12mo, 226pp.

1642   1898   ENG 220 (2 ex.)
White, Trumbull. Glimpses of the Orient : or the Manners, Customs, Life and the History of the People of Japan and Corea, the Philippine, Caroline and Ladrone Islands, with an Account of American Naval Operations in the Philippines
[Philadelphia: Franklin Book] 1898. 8vo, 437pp., ill., contents: pp.317-390 on Korea

1643   1899   FRE 318
Courant, Maurice. Notes sur les etudes Coreennes et Japonaises [Notes on Korea and Japan Studies]
extract from Les Actes du Congres des Orientalistes, Paris 1899, large 8vo, pp.67-94

1644   1903   ENG 1348

Clodd, Edward. The Story of the Alphabet
NY: Appleton 1903. 12mo, 209pp., index; contents: pp.75-80 on Oriental scripts

1645   1903   FRE 294 v.1
Congres international des etudes d'extreme orient [International Congress on Studies of the Far East]
Hanoi: F.H. Schneider 1903. 4to, vol.1, 137, iii pp.

1646   1907   ENG 81
McKenzie, F.A. The Unveiled East
NY: E.P. Dutton & Co. 1907. 8vo, viii, 347pp., ill., maps, index; contents: on Korea pp.31-74, 325-342

1647   1924   ENG 309
King-Hall, Stephen. Western Civilization and the Far East
London: Methuen 1924. 8vo, xxv, 385pp., maps, index

1648   1932   ENG 737
Saunders, Kenneth. The Heritage of Asia
London: Student Christian Movement [1932]. 12mo, 224pp., ill., bibliography, index

1649   1941   ENG 433
Saunders, Kenneth. A Pageant of Asia : A Study of Three Civilizations
London: Oxford UP (1934) 1941. 8vo, xii, 452pp., ill.; contents: the civilizations of India, China and Japan

1650   1949   ENG 628
Northrop, F.S.C. The Meeting of East and West : An Inquiry Concerning World Understanding
NY: MacMillan 1949. 8vo, xxii, 531pp., bibliography, index

VII.a.1) CHINESE CULTURE

1651   1869   FRE 51
Girard, O. France et Chine. Vie Publique et Privee des Chinois Anciens et Modernes. Passe et Avenir de la France dans l'Extreme Orient [France and China. Public and Private Life of the Ancient and Modern Chinese. The Past and the Arrival of the French in the Far East]

Paris: Hachette 1869. 2 vols. bound in 1, 8vo, 434, 472pp.

1652   1916   ENG 232
Bashford, James W. China, an Interpretation
NY: Abington 1916. 8vo, 620pp., index

1653   1946   ENG 739 (2 ex.)
Cable, Mildred and French, Francesca. China : Her Life and Her People
London: University of London Press 1946. small 8vo, 160pp., ill., maps, bibliography, index

VII.a.2) JAPANESE CULTURE

1654   1904   POR 3
Batalha, Ladislau. O Japao por Dentro : Esboço analitico da civilisacao Niponica [Japan from the Inside. Analytical Sketch of the Japanese Civilization]
Lisboa: Paroeria Antonio Maria Pereira 1904. small 8vo, xvi, 402pp., ill., preface by Dr. Theofilo Braga

1655   1913   ENG 56e2
Redesdale, Lord. A Tragedy in Stone and Other Papers by Lord Redesdale
London: John Lane the Bodley Head 1913. 8vo, 344pp.

1656   1937   ENG 279
Shepherd, K.M. The Land and Life of Japan
London: Edinburgh House Press 1937. 12mo, 144pp., ill., map, bibliography, index

1657   1950   ENG 2
Sansom, G.B. The Western World and Japan
London: The Cresset Press 1950. 8vo, xvi, 544pp., ill., maps, index

VII.a.3) KOREAN CULTURE

1658   1946   ENG 719
Korean American Cultural Association. The Culture of Korea
Printed in the U.S.A, by the Korean American Association 1946. 8vo, xvi, 334pp., ill., edited by Changsoon Kim

VII.b) CULTURE : LANGUAGE

VII.b.1) LANGUAGES OTHER THAN KOREAN

1659 1898 ENG 1280e3
Chamberlain, Basil Hall. A Handbook of Colloquial Japanese
Yokohama: Kelly & Walsh 1898. 12mo, 565pp.

1660 1904 GER 156 : 19
Lange, Rudolf. Übungs und Lesebuch zum Studium der Japanischen Schrift [Reader and Exercises for the Study of Japanese Script]
Berlin: Georg Reimer 1904. 8vo, 529pp. in Lehrbücher des seminars für orientalische Sprachn zu Berlin Band, 19.

1661 1920 ENG 1080e2
Hillier, Walter. An English-Chinese Dictionary of Peking Colloquial
Shanghai: American Presbyterian Mission Press 1920. small 8vo, 1030pp.

1662 1929 ENG 850
Karlgren, Bernhard. Sound and Symbol in Chinese
London: Oxford UP (1923) 1929. 12mo, 112pp., ads; translated from the Swedish

1663 1937 ENG 837e2
Roget, Peter Mark. Thesaurus of English Words and Phrases, Classified and Arranged so as to Facilitate the Expression of Ideas and to Assist in Literary Composition
NY: Grosset & Dunlap, revised American edition 1937. 8vo, 705pp.; contents: not on Korea

1664 1947 ENG 851
Pike, Kenneth L. Phonemics. A Technique for Reducing Language to Writing
Ann Arbor: University of Michigan Press 1947. Univ. of Michigan Publications, Linguistics Vol.III, 4to, 254pp.; contents: not on Korea

1665 1950 ENG 860
Vaccari, Oreste. Pictorial Chinese-Japanese Characters. A New and Fascinating Method to Learn Ideographs
NY: Brentano's 1950. 8vo, 264pp., ads

VII.b.2) KOREAN LANGUAGE

1666   1832   ENG 126 Vol.1
Gützlaff, Charles. Remarks on the Corean Language
in: Chinese Repository, vol.1, pp.276-279

1667   1833   ENG 126 Vol.2
Gützlaff, Charles. The Corean Syllabory
in: Chinese Repository, vol.2, 1833, pp.135-138

1668   1889   FRE 202 (2 ex.)
Imbault-Hauart, Camille. Manuel de la langue Coreenne parlee a l'usage des Français [Manual of Spoken Korean for the Use of Frenchmen]
Paris: Imprimerie Nationale MDCCCLXXXIX (1889). large 8vo, 108pp.

1669   1889   FRE 295
Les Missionaires de Coree. Grammaire Coreenne [Korean Grammar]
Yokohama: Levy and Solebelle 1889. large 8vo, 196pp., 54, 39pp. exercises

1670   1890   ENG 142:1
Underwood, H.G. and Gale, J.S. A Concise Dictionary of the Korean Language
Yokohama: Kelly & Walsh 1890. 2 vols., we have only vol.1, x, 196pp.

1671   1901   FRE 29 (2 ex.)
Aleveque, Charles. Petit Dictionnaire Français-Coreen [Small French-Korean Dictionary]
Seoul: Seoul Press 1901. 12mo, vi, 374pp.

1672   1903   ENG 1479e3
Baird, Annie L.A. Fifty Helps for the Beginner in the Use of the Korean Language.
Yokohama: Fukuin 3rd edition 1903. 16mo, 100pp.

1673   1904   ENG 28 : 1904
Hulbert, Homer B. The Korean Language
in: Annual Report of the Board of Regents of the Smithsonian Institution, Washington: G.P.O. 1904,

large 8vo, pp. 793-810

1674   1911 ENG 1336 (2 ex.)
Gale, James Scarth. A Korean-English Dictionary
Yokohama: Fukuin 1911, 8vo, 1154pp.

1675   1914 ENG 856e2 (2 ex.)
Underwood, Horace Grant. An Introduction to the Korean Spoken Language
NY: MacMillan 2nd edition 1914. 16mo, 475pp.

1676   1921 ENG 1479*e5
Baird, Annie L.A. Fifty Helps for the Beginner in the Use of the Korean Language
Yokohama: Fukuin 5th edition 1921. 16mo, 100pp.

1677   1923 GER 62 : 2 (2 ex.)
Eckardt, Andreas O.S.B. Koreanischen Konversations-Grammatik [Korean Conversation Grammar]
Heidelberg: Julius Groos 1923. 12mo, 422pp.; Domschke/Goossmann 219

1678   1923 GER 62 : 1
Eckardt, Andreas O.S.B. Schlüssel zur Koreanischen Konversations-Grammatik [Key to the Korean Conversation Grammar]
Heidelberg: Julius Groos 1923. 12mo, 204pp.; Domschke/Goossmann 219

1679   1924 ENG 1478
Gale, James Scarth. Present-Day English-Korean (Three Thousand Words)
n.p.: Christian Literature Society of Korea 1924. 16mo, 77pp.

1680   1925 ENG 1149
Wade-Koone, Edward and Oh, Seung Kun(rev.) by late Horace Grant Underwood, D.D., L.L.D. and Horace Horton Underwood. An English-Korean Dictionary
Seoul: YMCA 1925. small 16mo, 721, 18pp.

1681   1933 FRE 347
Haguenauer, M. Systeme de transcription de l'alphabet coreen [Transcription System for the Korean Alphabet]

extract of Journal Asiatique, 1933, pp.145-161

1682 1935 GER 154 : 38
Figulla, H.H. Prolegomena zu einer Grammatik der Koreanischen Sprache [Prolegomena for a Grammar of the Korean Language]
in: Mitteilungen des Seminars für Orientalische Sprachen an der Friedrich-Wilhelms-Universität zu Berlin, vol.xxxviii, pp.101-121; Domschke/Goossmann 303

1683 1936 GER 27
Roth, Lucius O.S.B. Koreanische Grammatik [Korean Grammar]
Tokwon, Hamkyung Namdo: Abtei Tokwon 1936. 8vo, viii, 562pp.

1684 1939 ENG 1477
Ramstedt, G.J. A Korean Grammar
Helsinki: Suomalais-Ugrilainen Seura 1939. 8vo, 200pp.

1685 1944 ENG 1159
Sunoo, Harold H.W. A Standard Colloquial Korean Text Book for University Students, Book I
Seattle: University Book Store 1944. 8vo, 111pp.

1686 1944 ENG 560 (2 ex.)
Pai, Edward W. Conversational Korean
Washington: Korean Affairs Institute Inc. 1944. 8vo, xiv, 171pp.; comment: this textbook was conceived to help the wartime need and to quickly teach the Korean language to Americans

1687 1945 ENG 852
Park, K.D. Oral Korean for Beginners
Honolulu: Tongg 1945. small 8vo, 111pp.

1688 1947 ENG 744
Lukoff, Fred. Spoken Korean : Books 1 and 2
NY: Holt 1947. large 16mo, viii, together 832pp, edition prepared for the U.S. Armed Forces Institute

1689 1949 ENG 801
Ramstedt (G.T.). Studies in Korean Etymology
In the series : Memoires de la Societe Finno-Ougrienne, XCV, Helsinki : Suomlais-Ugriainen Seura 1949, 8vo, 292pp.

1690   n.d.   ENG 858
Methodist Episcopal Church, Korea Mission. Language Course of Korea Mission
no place: M.E. Church South no date. 8vo, 6pp., English and 17pp. Chinese text

VII.c) CULTURE : NAMES

1691   1939   ENG 996
Gillis, I.V. and Pai, Ping Ch'i. Japanese Surnames
Peking: Hwa Hsing Press 1939. 4to, 171pp. + appendix

1692   1940   ENG 997
Gillis, I.V. and Pai, Ping Ch'i. Japanese Personal Names
Peking: no publisher 1940. 4to, 70pp.

1693   1943   ENG 825
Manual Chinese Manchurian Names
Tokyo: Times, 1943. 8vo, 223pp., text in Chinese, title in English

VII.d) CULTURE : LITERATURE

VII.d.1) MYTHS, LEGENDS, FAIRY TALES

1694   1914   FRE 313
Collection Coreenne [Koran Collection]
edited by Victor Segalen, containing translations from the Arabic by J.C. Mardrus Paris: Presses du P'ei-Tang; in stock two volumes, 1914, large 8vo, unpaginated

1695   1888   ENG 992
Kobunsha (ed.). The Mouse's Wedding. Japanese Fairy Tale Series No.6
translated by David Tamsen Tokyo: Kobunsha (1885) 2nd edition 1888. small 16mo, ill., unpaginated (16pp.)

1696   1889   ENG 1462
Allen, H.N. Korean Tales, Being a Collection of Stories translated from the Korean Folk Lore

NY: G.P. Putnam's Sons 1889. 12mo, 193pp.

1697 1893 GER 141 (2 ex.)
Arnous, H.G. Korea. Märchen und Legenden, nebst einer Einleitung über Land und Leute, Sitten und Gebräuche [Korea. Fairy Tales and Legends, with an Introduction on Country and Inhabitants, Customs and Habits]
Leipzig: W. Friedrich 1893. 146pp., ill.; Domschke/Goossmann 27

1698 1900 ENG 870
Aston, W.G. Chhoi-Chung. A Korean Märchen [A Korean Fairy Tale]
[Tokyo]: Asiatic Society of Japan 1900. 8vo, 30pp.

1699 1911 ENG 174e2
Griffis, William Elliot. Korean Fairy Tales
NY: Thomas Y. Crowell 1911. 8vo, xii, 212pp., ill., plates

1700 1912 ENG 290 (2 ex.)
Davis, F. Hadland. Myths & Legends of Japan
London: George G. Harrap & Co. 1912. 8vo, 432pp., ill., bibliography, index

1701 1913 ENG 699 (2 ex.)
Im, Bang and Yi, Ryuk. Korean Folk Tales : Imps, Ghosts and Fairies
London: J.M. Dent & Sons 1913. 12mo, x, 233pp., translated from the Korean by James Scarth Gale

1702 1919 ENG 1388 (3 ex.)
Taylor, Charles M. Winning Buddha's Smile. A Korean Legend
Boston: Richard G. Bodger 1919. small 8vo, 153pp.

1703 n.d. (1922) ENG 520
Griffis, William Elliot. The Unmannerly Tiger and Other Korean Fairy Tales
NY: Thomas Y. Crowell (1911) n.d. (c.1922). small 8vo, second edition, vii, 212pp., ill.

1704 n.d. (1922) ENG 1376 (2 ex.)
Kim, Man Choong. The Cloud Dream of the Nine,
Boston : Small, Hayward & Co. n.d. (1922). 8vo, 307pp., translated by James Scarth Gale,

1705 1925 ENG 77 (3 ex.)
Hulbert, Homer B. Omjee the Wizard. Korean Folk Stories

Springfield: Milton Bradley Co. 1925. 8vo, ii, 156pp., illustrated by Hildegard Lupprian

1706　　　　　　　　　　　　　　　　1925　　　　ENG 857
Miller, Oliver Beaupre. Little Pictures of Japan
Chicago: The Book House for Children 1925. pictures by Katherine Sturges, small 4to, 192pp.

1707　　　　　　　　　　　　　　　　1927　　ENG 577 (2 ex.)
Miller, Lilian May. Grass Blades from a Cinnamon Garden
Tokyo: Japan Advertiser Press 1927. 8vo, 88pp., ill.; contents on Korea p.30

1708　　　　　　　　　　　　　　　n.d. (c. 1928)　　　GER 151
Eckardt, Andreas O.S.B. Zwischen Halla und Päktusan. Koreanische Märchen und Erzählungen [Between Halla and Paekdusan. Korean Fairy Tales and Stories]
St. Ottilien: Missionsverlag, n.d. (c. 1928). 8vo, vii, 135pp., ill.; Domschke/Goossmann 222

1709　　　　　　　　　　　　　　　　1932　　　ENG 1391
Metzger, Berta. Tales Told in Korea
NY: Frederick Stokes 1932. 12mo, 247pp., ill.

1710　　　　　　　　　　　　　　　　1947　　ENG 489 (2 ex.)
Carpenter, Frances. Tales from a Korean Grandmother
NY: Doubleday & Co. 1947. 8vo, 287pp., ill.; comment: we have one ex. printed in 1947, one ex. reprint of 1973

1711　　　　　　　　　　　　　　　　1948　　ENG 374 (2 ex.)
Pyun, Yong T'ae. Tales from Korea
[Seoul]: Cultural Association International (1948). 12mo, 180pp., ill., map, illustrated by C.J. Lee, introduction by Horace H. Underwood

1712　　　　　　　　　　　　　　　　n.d.　　　　FRE 229
Couchoud, Paul Louis. Sages et Poetes d'Asie [Wise Men and Poets from Asia]
Paris: Calmann-Levy, n.d., 12mo, 299pp.

1713　　　　　　　　　　　　　　　　n.d.　　　　ENG 935
The International Library
no place, The nternational Library, no date, excerpt advertising a 20 volume edtion, with probes of novels etc., 8vo, ill., no index; contents: not on Korea

VII.d.2) NOVELS ETC.

VII.d.2.1) NOVELS ETC. ON THE FAR EAST

1714   1766   FRE 262e2 : 1/6

Argens, Marquis J.B. Boyer d' Lettres Chinoises ou correspondance philosophique, historique et critique, entre un chinois voyageur et ses correspondants a la Chine, en Moscovie, en Perse et au Japon. Nouvelle edition augmentee de nouvelles lettres & de quantitie de remarques [Chinese Letters or Philosophical, Historical and Critical Correspondence between a Chinese Traveller and his Correspondents in China, Muscovy, Persia and Japan. New edition, enlarged by new letters and lots of remarks]

La Haye ('s-Gravenshage, NL): Pierre Paupie 1766. 6 vols., 16mo, vol.1 : 352pp., vol.2 : 363pp., vol.3 : 376pp., vol.4 : 367pp., vol.5 : 356pp., vol.6 : 208pp.; comment: fictional correspondent of an 18th century Confucian Chinese who travelled; written by a Frenchman who did not reveal his name.

1715   1772   FRE 264e6

Delaporte, M. l'Abbe. Le Voyageur François, Ou la connoissance de l'ancien et de nouveu monde. Mis au jour par M. l'Abbe Delaporte [The French Voyager : or the Knowledge of the Old and the New World, written chronologically by Abbot Delaporte]

Paris: Celiot 1772. 12mo, 454pp., indices. covers Japan, Corea, Tartarie; contents: on Korea pp.266-298. Korea-chapter in form of a letter, dated King-Ki-Tau, capitale de la Coree, ce 15 fevrier 1747

1716   1810   FRE 269

Levis, M. de. Les voyages de Kang-Hi : ou nouvelles lettres chinoises [The Travels of Kang-Hi, or New Chinese Letters]

Paris: Imprimerie de P. Didot l'Aine 1810. 2 vols., 12mo, vol.1 : 238pp., vol.2 : 287pp.; contents: contains letters from a Chinese, addressed from Paris, to his correspondent in China

1717   1819   SWE 6

Bauer, Joh. Chr. Aug. Alexander Selkirchs sällsamma äfventyr [Alexander Selkirch's Strange Adventures]

Stockholm 1819-1828. 16mo, 12vols., bound in 6. Vol.1-2 Asien, 554pp., 1819/1820, vol.3-4 Asien, pp.555-798, 1820, Afrika, pp.1-279, 1820; vol.5-6 Afrika, pp.280-722, 1820/1821, vol,7-8 Polynesien, 476pp., 1822, vol.9-10 Polynesien, pp.477-711, 1823, America, pp.1-248, 1826, vol.11-12 America, pp.249-771, 1827/1828, cntents: on Korea vol.3 pp.765-772; comment: Actually a handbook on non-European geography, written around the skeleton of the travelogue of a fictional Alexander Selkirch, said to be a Russian citizen (obviously styled after Scottish sailor Alexander Selkirk, whose adventures inspired Daniel Defoe to write Robinson Crusoe)

| 1718 | 1890 | ENG 993 |

Shigemi, Shiukichi. A Japanese Boy, by Himself

NY: Henry Holt 1890. 12mo, 128pp.

| 1719 | 1904 | ENG 986 |

Watanna, Onoto. Daughters of Nijo. A Romance of Japan

NY: MacMillan 1904. 8vo, 397pp., ill.

| 1720 | n.d. (1907) | FRE 291 |

Blutel, Fernand. Roman d'un captif [Novel of a Captive (in the Russo-Japanese War)]

Paris: Gedalge n.d. (1907). 398pp., ill.

| 1721 | 1911 | ENG 1486 |

London, Jack. When God Laughs, and Other Stories

Cleveland: International Fiction Library 1911. 12mo, 319pp., no index

| 1722 | c. 1920 | ENG 426 |

Ozaki, Madame Yukio. Romances of Old Japan : Rendered into English from Japanese Sources

London: Smipkin Marshall n.d. (c. 1920). large 8vo, ix, 278pp., ill.

| 1723 | 1923 | FRE 37 |

Loti, Pierre. Madame Chrysantheme, Pecheur d'Islande [Madame Chrysantheme; The Island Fisher]

Paris: Pierre Lafitte 1923. 4to, 252pp., ill.; contents: about Japan

| 1724 | 1923 | FRE 38 |

Loti, Pierre. Les Desenchantees, Matelot [The Disenchanted. Matelot]

Paris: Pierre Lafitte 1923. 4to, 274pp., ill.; contents: not on Korea

| 1725 | 1923 | FRE 197 |

Loti, Pierre. La Troisieme Jeunesse de Madame Prune. Le Marriage de Loti [Madame Prune's Third Youth. Loti's Marriage]

Paris: Pierre Lafitte 1923. 4to, 239pp., ill.

1726   1923   ENG 825
Rolt-Wheeler, Francis. The Boy with the U.S. Diplomats
Boston: Lothrop, Lee & Shepard Co. 1923. 8vo, 349pp., ads, U.S. Service Series

1727   1931   FRE 310
Challaye, Felicien. Contes et Legendes du Japon [Tales and Legends of Japan]
Paris: Ferdinand Nathan 1931. 12mo, 303pp., bibliography, index; contents: 3 Chosen entries

1728   1936   FRE 245
Toulouse, Jean. Terre Jaune [Yellow Land]
Paris: Raoul Saillard 1936. 12mo, 224pp.; contents: novel, starts in Korea

1729   1939   ENG 1003
Kawai, Michi. My Lantern
Tokyo: Kyo Bum Kwan 1939. 8vo, 230pp., ill.

1730   1939   ENG 1227
Hsiung, S.I. The Professor from Peking. A Play in Three Acts
London: Methuen 1939. 12mo, 196pp.

1731   1940   ENG 1467
Basil, George C. Test Tubes and Dragon Scales
Chicago: John C. Winston Co. 1940. 8vo, 314pp., ill.; comment: author ex-superintendent, Syracuse-in-China hospital, Chungking; all names in this manuscript are ficticious

1732   1941   ENG 722
Collis, Maurice. The Great Within
London: Faber and Faber 1941. 8vo, 349pp., ill., map

1733   1948   ENG 687
Buck, Pearl S. Peony
NY: John Day 1948. 8vo, 312pp., ill.

VII.d.2.2) NOVELS ETC. ON KOREA

1734   1871   ENG 1268
Willis, George. R. Forecastly Echoes.

Yokohama 1871. large 12mo, 27pp.; contents: Corea, a Summer Dream pp.1-8 (ode)

1735   1886   FRE 189 Vol.7

Scherzer, M. F. (translator). Tchao-Sien-Tche. Memoire sur la Coree, par un coreen anonyme [Memoire of Korea, by a Korean]

in: Journal Asiatique Vol.7 1886 pp.1-192, translated from the Chinese by F. Scherzer; Gompertz 172

1736   1892   FRE 196

Printemps Parfume. Roman Coreen [Korean Spring. A Korean Novel]

Paris: Dentu 1892. 16mo, 209pp., ill., translated from the Korean by J.H. Rosny

1737   1895   FRE 328

Leroux, Ernest (ed.). Le bois sec refleuri. Roman Coreen [The dry Forest which blooms again]

Paris: Ernest Leroux 1895. translated from the Korean by Hong Tiyong ou. 8vo, 192pp.

1738   n.d. (c. 1900)   ENG 488

Perry, Jean. The Man in Grey, or more about Korea

London: S.W. Partridge n.d. (after 1895). 12mo, 138, 32pp., ill.

1739   n.d. (c. 1900)   ENG 331 (2 ex.)

Perry, Jean. Chilgoopie the Glad, a Story of Korea and Her Children

London: Partridge n.d. (after 1895). 12mo, 144, 32pp., ill.

1740   n.d. (c. 1900)   ENG 1424

Perry, Jean. Uncle Mac, the Missionary

London: Partridge n.d., 170, 32pp.

1741   1902   ENG 861

Hulbert, Archer Butler. The Queen of Quelparte

Boston: Little, Brown & Co. 1902. 12mo, x, 330pp.

1742   1903   ENG 924

Barnes, Anna M. The Red Miriok (Shan Folk Lore Stories)

Philadelphia: American Baptist Publication Society 1903. 12mo, 109pp.

1743   1904   ENG 173 (3 ex.)

Gale, James Scarth. The Vanguard. A Tale of Korea

NY: Revell 1904. 8vo, 320pp., ill.

1744 1904 ENG 598 (4 ex.)
Allen, Horace N. Korea : Fact and Fancy : being a republication of Two Books entitles "Korean Tales" and "A Chronological Index"
Seoul: Methodist Publishing House 1904. 8vo, 285pp., index

1745 1905 ENG 187 (3 ex.)
Underwood, Lilian H. With Tommy Tompkins in Korea
NY: Fleming H. Revell 1905. 8vo, 326pp., ads

1746 1906 ENG 587 (3 ex.)
Noble, W. Arthur. Ewa : A Tale of Korea
NY: Eaton & Mains 1906. 8vo, 354pp., ill.; contents: anti-Japanese perspective

1747 1909 ENG 454 (2 ex.)
Baird, Annie L.A. Daybreak in Korea : a Tale of Transformation in the Far East
NY: Fleming H. Revell 1909. 8vo, 123pp., ill.

1748 1909 ENG 582 (3 ex.)
Wagner, Ellasue Carter. Kim Su Bang, and Other Stories of Korea
Nashville: Church [1909]. 12mo, 99pp., ill.

1749 1909 GER 202
Spillmann, Joseph O.S.B. Die koreanischen Brüder. Ein Zug aus der Missionsgeschichte Koreas [The Korean Brothers. A Chapter in Korea's Mission History]
Freiburg im Breisgau: Herder 1909. 16mo, 101pp., ill.; Domschke/Goossmann 973

1750 1910 ENG 583
Pike, H. Lee M. Yung Pak : Our Little Korean Cousin
Boston: L.H. Page & Co. (1905) 1910. 12mo, 4th impression, vi, 96pp., ill., illustrated by L.J. Bridgman

1751 1911 ENG 514
Wagner, Ellasue Carter. Pokjumie : A Story from the Land of the Morning

Calm
Nashville: Church 1911. 12mo, 115pp.

1752 1911 ENG 223e2 (2 ex.)
Guthapfel, Minerva L. The Happiest Girl in Korea, and Other Stories from the Land of Morning Calm
NY: Fleming H. Revell [1911]. 12mo, 106pp., ill., author Methodist missionary

1753 1922 ENG 1397
Wagner, Ellasue Carter. Kumokie. A Bride of Old Korea
Nashville: Church 1922. small 8vo, 230pp.

1754 1926 ENG 333
Swinehart, Lois H. Sarangie : A Child of the Chosen
NY: Fleming H. Revell [1926]. 12mo, 157pp., ill.

1755 1927 ENG 565
Herbert, Agnes. A Girl's Adventures in Korea
London: A. & C. Black 1927. 8vo, 245pp., ill.

1756 1928 ENG 1453
New, Ilhan. When I was a Boy in Korea
Boston: Lothrop, Lee and Shepard 1928. 12mo, 190pp., ill.; Gompertz 1026

1757 1929 GER 200e2
Weber, Norbert O.S.B. Die Heilige Weide. Eine Erzählung aus dem Koreanischen Missionsleben [The Holy Meadow. A Tale from Korean Mission Life]
St. Ottilien: Missionsverlag 1929. 12mo, 221pp.; Domschke/Goossmann 1074 (which lists this title as "Die Heilige Weise" (The Holy Way)

1758 1929 FRE 145
Seu, Ring-Hai. Autour d'une Vie Coreenne [Around a Korean Life]
Paris: Editions Agence Korea 1929. 12mo, 189pp., contents: novel about Korea's fight for independence

1759 1930 ENG 1337
Benson, Stella. Tobit Transplanted (The Far Away Bride)

London: MacMillan 1930. 12mo, 362pp.

1760   1931 ENG 394 (6 ex.)
Kang, Younghill. The Grass Roof
NY: Scribner's 1931. 8vo, viii, 367pp., translated from the Korean by the author and by Frances Keely

1761   1931 ENG 740
Wagner, Ellasue. Korea : the Old and the New
NY: Fleming H. Revell [1931]. small 8vo, 160pp., ill., map

1762   1933 GER 201
Kang, Younghill. Das Grasdach. Ein Koreaner erzählt sein Leben [The Grass Roof. A Korean narrates his life('s story)]
Leipzig: Paul List 1933. 8vo, 330pp.; Gompertz 1061; Domschke/Goossmann 500

1763   1933 ENG 1460
Kang, Younghill. The Happy Grove
NY: Charles Scribner 1933. 8vo, 326pp., ill.

1764   1934 FRE 355
Seu, Ring-Hai. Miroir, cause de malheur ! et autres contes Coreens [The Mirror, Cause of Calamity ! and Other Korean Stories]
Paris: ed. Eugene Figuiere 1934. 12mo, 219pp.

1765   1936 ENG 1451
Miller, Frederick S. Korean Young Folks
NY: Fleming H. Revell 1936. 12mo, 189pp., ill.

1766   1937 ENG 109 (2 ex.)
Kang, Younghill. East goes West
NY: Charles Scribner's Sons 1937. 8vo, 401pp. The Korean American author's account of his move to America

1767   1937 FRE 167 (2 ex.)
Kang, Younhill. Au Pays du Matin Calme [In the Land of Morning Calm]
Paris: Plon 1937. 12mo, 285pp., novel, translated from the English by Claudine Decourcelle

1768   1939   ENG 1452
Miller, Frederick S. The Gospel in Korea
NY: Fleming H. Revell 1939. 12mo, 183pp.

1769   1939   FRE 309 v.42
Ri, Chai Uk. Sur la Novelle en Coree [On the Novel in Korea]
in : France-Japon, vol.42, 1939, 4to, pp.345-347

1770   1941   ENG 1018
Benson, Stella. The Far Away Bride
NY: Readers Club (1930) 1941. 8vo, 354pp.; contents: on Korea

1771   1947   ENG 843 (2 ex.)
Chu, Yosup. Kim Yusin. The Romances of a Korean Warrior of the 7th Century.
Seoul: The Mutual Publishers 1947. 12mo, 10pp.

1772   1947   ENG 1413
Fairfax, Virginia and Bure, Hallie. Ke Sooni. Books about Children in Other Lands.
NY: Friendship Press 1947. 8vo, 125pp., ill.

1773   1948   ENG 1349
Wagner, Ellasue. The Dawn of Tomorrow. True Stories from Old Korea
no publisher, 12mo, 88pp.

1774   1950   GER 150
Eckardt, Andre O.S.B. Unter dem Odongbaum [Under the Odong Tree]
Eisenach: Roeth 1950. 12mo, 181pp.

VII.d.3) POLITICS DISGUISED AS FICTION

1775   See No. 1225

1776   1933   ENG 725
Adachi, Kinnosuke. Tales of Three Cities in Manchuria
[Tokyo]: South Manchurian Railway Company 1933. 8vo, 27pp., ill.; contents: covers Darien, Mukden & Hsinking (formerly Changchun)

VII.d.4) FICTION, NOT RELATED TO KOREA

1777   1896   FRE 35
Loti, Pierre. Ramuntcho Aziyade
Paris: Pierre Lafitte 1896. 4to, 255p., ill.

1778   1916   FRE 242
Maurras, Charles. Les Amants de Venise. George Sand & Musset [The Lovers of Venice. George Sand and Musset]
Paris: E. de Boccard 1916. 12mo, 322pp.

1779   1923   FRE 36
Loti, Pierre. Le Roman d'Un Spahi. Mon Frere Yves [The Story of a Sepoy. My Brother Yves]
Paris: Pierre Lafitte 1923. 4to, 286pp., ill.

VII.e) CULTURE : ARTS

VII.e.1) ART HISTORY

VII.e.1.1) ART HISTORY : FAR EAST

1780   1942-1943   GER 127
Ostasiatische Zeitschrift [East Asian Magazine]
Publisher : Gesellschaft für Ostasiatische Kunst [Society for East Asian Art]
in stock: vol.28 no.5,6 (pp.156-197), 1942-1943, 4to, ill.

1781   1929-1931   ENG 1360
The Museum of Far Eastern Antiquities(Östasiatiatiska Samlingarna), Stockholm, Bulletin.
in stock: vol. 1-31929 large 8vo, (3 vols.), 191, 237, 176pp.

1782   n.d. (c. 1900)   FRE 306
Dupont, Maurice. Calme et sommeil dans l'art d'extreme orient [Calmness nd Sleep in the Art of the Far East]
Paris: Boulogne sur Seine n.d., 2 vols., large 8vo, vol.1 Inde et Perse, 8pp., plates, vol.2 Chine, Japon, 10pp., plates

1783　　　　　　　　　　　　　　　　　1906　　　GER 28
Graul, Richard. Ostasiatische Kunst, und ihr Einfluss auf Europa [East Asian Art, and Her Influence on Europe], vol.87 in the series : Aus Natur und Geisteswelt. Sammlung wissenschaftlich-gemeinverständlicher Darstellungen [From Nature and the World of Spirits. Collection of Scientific, yet Plainly Comprehensible Descriptions]
Leipzig: B.G. Teubner 1906. 12mo, 88, 16pp., ill., index

1784　　　　　　　　　　　　　　　　after 1910　　ENG 1026
Fenollosa, Ernest F. Epochs of Chinese and Japanese Art. An Outline History of East Asiatic Design
NY: Frederick A. Stokes, n.d. (after 1910). large 8vo, 2 vols., 204, 212p., ill., index; Gompertz 1240

1785　　　　　　　　　　　　　　　　　1912　　　GER 29
Kümmel, Otto. Ausstellung alter ostasiatischer Kunst : China-Japan, veranstaltet von der Königlichen Akademie der Künste zu Berlin, September/Dezember 1912 [Exhibition of Ancient East Asian Art : China-Japan, organized by the Royal Akademy of the Arts, Berlin]
Berlin: Julius Bard 1912, 12mo, xxxii, 128, 28pp., ill., preface by A. Kampf

1786　　　　　　　　　　　　　　　　　1913　　　GER 19
Glaser, Curt. Die Kunst Ostasiens : der Umkreis Ihres Denkens und Gestaltens [East Asian Art : The Circle of Its Thinking and Its Shaping]
Leipzig: Insel-Verlag 1913. 8vo, viii, 222pp., ill., glossary

1787　　　　　　　　　　　　　　　　　1922　　　GER 6
Kümmel, Otto. Die Kunst Ostasiens [The Art of East Asia], vol.IV in : Die Kunst des Ostens [The Art of the East]
Berlin: Bruno Cassirer 1922. small 4to, 48, 166pp., ill.

1788　　　　　　　　　　　　　　　　　1925　　　GER 47e2 : 2
Woermann, Karl. Die Kunst der Naturvölker und der übrigen nichtchristlichen Kulturvölker, einschließlich der Kunst des Islams [The Art of Primitive Peoples and of the Other Non-Christian Civilized Peoples, Including Islamic Art], in : Geschichte der Kunst aller Zeiten und Völker [History of the Art of all Peoples and all Times]

Leipzig: Bibliographisches Institut (1915) 1925. small 4to, xvi, 492pp., comment: on Korea pp.288-292; Gompertz 1245

1789   1926   GER 107
Feddersen, Martin. Führer durch das Hamburgische Museum für Kunst und Gewerbe, XIII : Ostasien. Vol.1; Chinesisches Kunstgewerbe, Koreanische Keramik, Buddhistische Bildwerke [Guide through the Hamburg Museum of Arts and Crafts. XIII : East Asia, Vol.1; Chinese Arts and Crafts. Korean Ceramics. Buddhist Sculptures]
Hamburg: Museum für Kunst und Gewerbe 1926. 12mo, 80pp., ill.

1790   1928   GER 31
Fischer, Otto. Die Kunst Indiens, Chinas und Japans [The Art of India, China and Japan]
Berlin: Propyläen 1928. 4to, 643pp., ill., index; Gompertz 1261

1791   1929   GER 99
Kümmel, Otto. Die Kunst Chinas, Japans und Koreas [The Art of China, Japan and Korea] in the series : Handbuch der Kunstwissenschaft [Handbook on the Science of the Arts]
Wildpark-Potsdam: Akademische Verlagsanstalt Athenaion 1929. 4to, 198pp., ill., index; Gompertz 1267

1792   1929   FRE 54
Grousset, R. Les civilisations de l'Orient [The Civilizations of the Orient]
Paris: G. Cres & Cie. 1929-1930. 8vo, 4 vols., vol.1 : l'Orient, ii, 362pp., vol.2 : l'Inde, ii, 370pp., vol.3 : la Chine, 360pp., vol.4 : le Japon, viii, 319pp.

1793   1929   GER 97
Cassirer & Helbing, (ed.). Sammlung Theodor E. Simon, Berlin : Chinesische Kunstgegenstände, verzeichnet von L. Reidemeister. Gemälde, Möbel und Europäische Porzellane des 18. Jahrhunderts, verzeichnet von C.F. Förster, [Collection Theodor E. Simon, Berlin : Chinese Pieces of Art, registered by L. Reidemeister; Paintings, Furniture and European Porcelain Items, registered by C.F. Förster]
Cassirer & Helbing, Berlin 1929. 4to, 44pp., xli plates, auction catalogue, bound together with 1793a

and 1793b in one volume; cover title : Katalogue Ostasiatischer Kunst [Catalogues East Asian Art]

1793a　　　　　　　　　　　　　　　1929　　　　GER 97
Cassirer & Helbing. Die Sammlung Dr. A. Breuer, Berlin : Ostasiatische Kunst, eingeleitet von Otto Kümmel. [Collection Dr. A. Breuer, Berlin : East Asian Art, with an introduction by Otto Kümmel]

Cassirer & Helbing, Berlin 1929. 4to, 82pp., xl plates; auction catalogue, bound together with 1793a and 1793b in one volume; cover title : Katalogue Ostasiatischer Kunst [Catalogues East Asian Art]

1793b　　　　　　　　　　　　　　　1930　　　　GER 97
Helbing. Ostasiatische Kunst aus dem Besitz des Herrn Hugo Meyl, München. [Far Eastern Art, Collection Hugo Meyl],

Helbing, München 1930. 4to, 55pp., 32 plates; auction catalogue, bound together with 1793a and 1793b in one volume; cover title : Katalogue Ostasiatischer Kunst [Catalogues East Asian Art]

1794　　　　　　　　　　　　　　　1934　　　　GER 6e2
Kümmel, Otto. Die Kunst Ostasiens [The Art of East Asia], vol.IV

in: Die Kunst des Ostens [The Art of the East], Berlin: Bruno Cassirer 1934, small 4to, 48, 166pp., ill.

1795　　　　　　　　　　　　　　　1935　　　　ENG 1009
Kahn, Ely Jacques. Design in Art and Industry

NY: Scribner's 1935. 4to, 204pp., ill.; contents: on Korea & Japan pp.67-102

1796　　　　　　　　　　　　　　　1936　　　　FRE 284
Grousset, Rene. Collection Iris. L'Art d'Extreme Orient. Paysages, Fleurs, Animaux [Collection Iris. The Art of the Far East. Sceneries, Flowers, Animals]

Paris: Plon 1938. folio, 10, xv pp.

1797　　　　　　　　　　　　　　　1937　　　　FRE 343
Morgenstern, Laure. Esthetique d'Orient et d'Occident [Oriental and Occidental Aesthetics]

Paris: Ernest Leroux 1937. small 4to, 282pp., ill., no index

1798　　　　　　　　　　　　　　　1941　　　　GER 1

Itten, Johannes. Asiatische Kunst : Indien, Tibet, China, Korea, Japan. Erinnerungen an die asiatische Ausstellung aus schweizer Sammlungen vom 17. Mai bis 7. September 1941 im Kunstgewerbemuseum Zürich [Asian Art : India, Tibet, China, Korea, Japan. Recollections of the Exhibition of Asiatic Pieces from Swiss Collections from May 17th till September 7th 1941 at the Zürich Museum of Arts and Crafts]

Zürich: Kunstgewerbemuseum 1941. 4to, xv, 132pp., ill., foreword by Johannes Itten, most pictures by Hans Fissler; contents: on Korea pp.109-111.

1799　　　　　　　　　　　　　1942　ENG 829　(2 ex.)
Toledo Museum of Art. Northeastern Asiatic Art. Korea, Manchuria, Mongolia and Tibet

Toledo: The Toledo Museum of Art 1942. 8vo, no paging, ill.; contents: the first half of the book is devoted to Korean art

1800　　　　　　　　　　　　　　　　1943　　　ENG 979
Alien Property Custodian. Collection of Chinese and Other Far Eastern Art, Assembled by Yamanaka & Company, In.c Now in Process of Liquidation under the Supervision of the Alien Property Custodian of the United States of America

N.Y. 1943. 4to, not paginated, 1683 items, ill.

1801　　　　　　　　　　　　　　　　1946　　　　GER 5
Speiser, Werner. Die Kunst Ostasiens [The Art of East Asia]

Berlin: Safari-Verlag 1946. small 4to, 355pp., ill.; Domschke/Goossmann 971

VII.e.1.2) ART HISTORY : CHINA

1802　　　　　　　　　　　　　　　　1910　　　　GER 32
Münsterberg, O. Chinesische Kunstgeschichte [The History of Chinese Art]

Esslingen: Neff Verlag 1910. 2 vols., small 4to, vol.1: xiii, 350pp., vol.2: xxi, 500pp., ill.; contents: vol.1 : Vorbuddhistische Zeit. Die hohe Kunst, Malerei und Bildhauerei [pre-Buddhist era; high art, painting and sculpture], vol.2 : Die Baukunst. Das Kunstgewerbe [architecture. arts as a craft].

1803　　　　　　　　　　　　　　　　1910　　　ENG 448e2
Bushell, Stephen W. Chinese Art. Victoria and Albert Museum Handbook

London: HMSO 1910. 2 vols., 8vo, vol.1 : xi, 148pp., ill., index, vol.2 : xiii, 158pp., index

1804   1931 ENG 1175 (2 ex.)
Morant, George Soulie de. A History of Chinese Art from Ancient Times to the Present Day
London: George G. Harrap 1931. large 8vo, 296pp., ill., index, translated from the French by G.C. Wheeler

1805   1935   ENG 1185
Yee Chiang. The Chinese Eye. An Interpretation of Chinese Painting
London: Methuen 1935. 16mo, 240pp., ill., index; contents: 2 Korea entries

1806   1935   ENG 1101
Jenyns, Soame. A Background to Chinese Painting
London: Sidgwick & Jackson 1935. 12mo, 209pp., ill., index; contents: 2 Korea entries

1807   1936   ENG 703
Carter, Dagny. China Magnificent : Five Thousand Years of Chinese Art
NY: John Day, Reynal & Hitchcock 1936. 8vo, xi, 225pp., ill., bibliography, index

1808   1948   ENG 1110
Cranmer-Byng, L. The Vision of Asia. An Interpretation of Chinese Art and Culture
London: Readers Union 1948. 16mo, 306pp., bibliography, index; contents: not on Korea

VII.e.1.3) ART HISTORY : JAPAN

1809   1949   FRE 333 v.1
Buhot, Jean. Histoire des Arts du Japon. Vol.1 : Des Origines a 1350 [History of Japanese Art. Vol.1 : From the Beginnings to 1350]
Paris: Vanoest 1949. folio, 267pp., 88 plates, index; contents: not on Korea

VII.e.1.4) ART HISTORY : KOREA

1810   1929   GER 72
Eckardt, Andreas O.S.B. Geschichte der Koreanischen Kunst [History of Korean Art]
Leipzig: Verlag Karl W. Hiersemann 1929. 4to, 119pp., clxvii plates; Gompertz 1266; Domschke/Goossmann 207

1811   1929   ENG 107
Eckardt, Andreas O.S.B. A History of Korean Art.
London: Edward Goldston 1929. 4to, 225pp., 168 plates, 1 map, translated from the German by J.M. Kindersley; Gompertz 1265

1812   1946   FRE 193
David, Madeleine. Musee Cernuschi. Exposition d'Art Coreen. Quelques Notes sur l'Histoire et l'Art de la Coree [Museum Cernuschi. Exhivition of Korean Art. Some Notes on the History and Art of Korea]
Paris: Enterprise de Presse 1946. 12mo, 23pp., bibliography, foreword by Rene Grousset, of the Academie Fraçaise, director of Musee Cernuschi

VII.e.2) PICTORIAL ARTS

1813   1886   ENG 809
Anderson, William. The Pictorial Arts of Japan : with a Brief Historical Sketch of the Associated Arts and some Remarks upon the Pictorial Art of the Chinese and Koreans
London: Sampson 1886. folio, 276pp., plates, index; Gompertz 1379

1814   1897   FRE 344
Anonymous. Objets d'art japonais et chinois. Peintures, estampes composant la collection des Goncourt [Japanese and Chinese Art Pieces. Paintings and Prints Composing the Goncourt Collection]
n.p., no publisher, 1897. 4to, 412pp., ill., no index

1815   1908   ENG 1013
Binyon, Laurence. Painting in the Far East. An Introduction to the history of Pictorial Art in Asia, Especially China and Japan
London: Edward Arnold 1908. 4to, 287pp., ill., index; contents: not on Korea

1816   1923   GER 41
Bernoulli, Rudolf. Ausgewählte Meisterwerke ostasiatischer Graphik in der Bibliothek für Kunst und Kunstgewerbe in Berlin [Selected Masterpieces of East Asian Graphic Art on the Library for Arts and Crafts in Berlin]

Plauen: Schulz 1923. 4to, 110pp., plates

1817　　　　　　　　　　　　　　　　　1933　　　　ENG 1489
Salaman, Malcolm (intro.). Masters of the Color Print, 9 : Elizabeth Keith
London: The Studio, 1933. 4to, unpaginated

VII.e.3) CERAMICS, POTTERY

1818　　　　　　　　　　　　　　　　　1881　　　　ENG 995
Audsley, George A. and Bowes, James L. Keramic Art of Japan
London: Henry Sotheran 1881. 4to, 304pp., ill., index

1819　　　　　　　　　　　　　　　　　1890　　　ENG 28 : 1890
Jouy, Pierre Louis. The Collection of Korean Mortuary Pottery in the U.S. National Museum
in: Annual Report of the Board of Regents of the Smithsonian Institute, 1890, pp.589-596; Gompertz 1308

1820　　　　　　　　　　　　　　　1891　ENG 28 : 1891 (2 ex.)
Hough, Walter. The Bernardou, Allen and Jouy Collections in the U.S. National Museum
in: Annual Report of the Board of Regents of the Smithsonian Institute, 1891, pp.429-488; Gompertz 773

1821　　　　　　　　　　　　　　　　　1899　　　　ENG 307
Bushell, S.W. Oriental Ceramic Art : Collection of W.T. Walters
NY: D. Appleton and Co. 1899. 8vo, xiii, 942pp., index; Gompertz 1310

1822　　　　　　　　　　　　　　　　1908　　ENG 615 (2 ex.)
Blacker, J.F. Chats on Oriental China
NY: Frederick A. Stokes Co. 1908 / London: Ernest Benn (1908) 1928. 8vo, 408pp., ill., index; on Chinese and Japanese porcelain and pottery

1823　　　　　　　　　　　　　　　　1914　　ENG 176 (3 ex.)
Hobson, R.L. and Morse, Edward S. Chinese, Corean and Japanese Potteries. Descriptive Catalogue of Loan Exhibition of Selected Examples, all Exhibited under the Auspices of the Japan Society, at the Galleries of M. Knoedler & Co., New York, March 2-21, 1914
NY: Japan Society 1914. 4to, x, 129pp., ill., with a report on early Chinese potteries, compiled from

original sources by Rose Sickler-Williams

1824 1918 ENG 748 (2 ex.)
Rackham, Bernard. Catalogue of the Le Blond Collection of Corean Pottery
London: His Majesty's Stationery Office 1918. large 8vo, 48pp., index, 48 plates, published by the Victoria and Albert Museum, Department of Ceramics; Gompertz 1328

1825 1924 ENG 882
Hobson, R.L. / British Museum. A Guide to the Pottery & Porcelain of the Far East in the Department of Ceramics and Ethnography
London: British Museum 1924. 8vo, 168pp., ill., index; Gompertz 1336

1826 1936 ENG 1385
Institute of Oriental Ceramics. Oriental Ceramics 1934-1935
n.p.: Institute of Oriental Ceramics 1936. large 8vo, 34pp., 10 plates; contents: pp.16-19 on Korean porcelain

1827 1944 ENG 1442
Honey, W.B. Corean Wares of the Yi Dynasty
from Transactions of the Oriental Ceramic Society 1944, pp.1-14, plates, 4to; Gompertz 1373 (on 1947)

1828 1946 ENG 700
Honey, William Bowyer. The Ceramic Art of China and Other Countries of the Far East
London: Faber 1946. 4to, vii, 238pp., ill., map, appendices, bibliography, index; Gompertz 1370 (on 1945)

1829 1946 ENG 797 : 1
Cox, Warren E. The Book of Pottery and Porcelain, vol.1
NY: Crown 1946. only vol.1, 558pp., ill., index; Gompertz 1368

1830 1947 ENG 824
Honey, William Bowyer. Corean Pottery
London: Faber & Faber 1947, 8vo, 19pp., index, plates; Gompertz 1374

1830a 1948 ENG 1053
Hobson, R.L. / British Museum. Handbook of the Pottery & Porcelain of the

Far East in the Department of Oriental Antiquities
London: British Museum 1948. 8vo, 179pp., ill., index

VII.e.4) ARTS AND CRAFTS - OTHERS

1831 1893 ENG 1269
Culin, Stewart. Chinese Games with Dice and Dominoes
in : Report of the National Museum, 1893, pp.471-537, large 4to

1832 1895 ENG 566 : 1
Lockhart, J.H. Stewart. The Currency of the Farther East : From the Earliest Times up to the Present Day, Vol.1 : Description of the Glover Collection of Chinese, Annamese, Japanese, Corean Coins : of Coins Used as Amulets : and Chinese Government and Private Notes
Hong Kong: Noronha 1895. 8vo, 216pp., bibliography; contents: pp.131-144 on Korean coins; Gompertz 1490

1833 1895 ENG 566 : 2
Glover, G.B. The Currency of the Farther East. Glover Collection. Vol.II : The Plates of the Chinese, Annamese, Japanese, Corean Coins ; of the Coins Used as Amulets, and of the Chinese Government and Private Notes
Hong Kong: Noronha 1895. large 8vo, 204pp., ill.; Gompertz 1490

1834 1895 ENG 667 (2 ex.)
Culin, Stewart. Korean Games : with Notes on the Corresponding Games of China and Japan
Philadelphia: University of Pennsylvania 1895. 8vo, xxxvi, 177pp., ill., index; Gompertz 789

1835 n.d. (c. 1895) ENG 941
Jenings, Foster H. Korean Headdresses in the National Museum
Smithsonian miscellaneous collections. pp.149-168; n.d., 8vo; Gompertz 869

1836 1896 ENG 28
Culin, Stewart. Chess and Playing Cards. Catalogue of Games & Implements for Divination Exhibited by the United States National Museum in Connection with the Department of Archaeology and Paleontology of the University of

Pennsylvania at the Cotton States and International Exposition, Atlanta, Georgia, 1895
in : Annual Report of the Board of Regents of the Smithsonian Institute 1896, pp.665-942; Gompertz 832

1837 1914 ENG 27 Vol.3.1
Ichihara, M. Coinage of Old Korea
in : The Numismatic and Philatelic Journal of Japan, Vol.3.1, 1914, pp.8-14, 47-50, 87-90, 133-136, 171-176, 212-214; cfr. Gompertz 1497

1838 n.d. (c. 1920) FRE 42 (2 ex.)
Dupont, Maurice. Decoration Coreenne [Korean Decoration]
Paris: Calavas n.d. (c.1920). 4to, 5pp., plates; Gompertz 1260, under 1927

1839 1923 ENG 1380
Canning-Wright, H.W. Peeps at the World's Dolls
London: A.C. Black 1923. 12mo, 87pp., ill.; contents: ch.ix pp.21-30 on Korea

1840 1925 GER 8
Kümmel, Otto. Die Kunst des Ostens, Vol.10 : Ostasiatisches Gerät ausgewählt und beschrieben. Mit einer Einführung von Ernst Grosse [The Art of the East. Vol.10 : East Asian Pieces of Equipment, Selected and described. With an Introduction by Ernst Grosse]
Berlin: Bruno Cassirer 1925. small 4to, vii, 62pp., plates

1841 1928 ENG 955
Hedemann, C.J. Catalogue of the Collection of Weapons, Honolulu Academy of Arts
Honolulu: Academy of Arts 1928. 12mo, 16pp.; contents: on Korea pp.9-10

1842 1929 ENG 1039
Schjöth, Fr. The Currency of the Far East. The Schjöth Collection at the Numismatic Cabinet of the University of Oslo, Norway
Oslo: Ascheberg 1929. 4to, 88pp., 132 plates; contents: on Korea pp.68-70

1843 1934 ENG 1375

Lasker, Edward. Go and Go-Moku. The Oriental Board Games and their American Versions
NY: Knopf 1934. 8vo, 214pp., ill., bibliography

1844 1936 ENG 912 (2 ex.)
Hunter, Dard. A Papermaking Pilgrimage to Japan, Korea, China
NY: Pynson 1936. 4to, 150pp., paper specimen, ill., index

1845 1941 ENG 1004
Sadler, A.L. A Short History of Japanese Architecture
Sydney: Angus & Robertson 1941. 4to, 133pp., 122 plates

VII.f) CULTURE : SPORTS

1846 1936 GER 205
Hoffmann, Heinrich & Ludwig. Die Olympischen Spiele 1936 [The Olympic Games of 1936]
Diessen: Raumbild-Verlag Otto Schönstein 1936. 4to, 54pp., numerous illustrations taped/inserted (photo album)

VII.g) CULTURE : PHILOSOPHY

1847 1881 ENG 195
Martin, W.A.P. The Chinese. Their Education, Philosophy and Letters
NY: Harper 1881. 12mo, 320pp., 8pp. ads, First published in China under the title : "The Hanlin Papers"

1848 1913 ENG 1239
Moule, G.H. The Spirit of Japan
London: Church Missionary Society 1913. 8vo, xii, 312pp., ill., map

1849 1917 FRE 113
Okakura, Kakuzo. Les Ideaux de l'Orient. Le Reveil du Japon [The Ideas of the Orient. The Awakening of Japan]
Paris: Payot 1917. 12mo, 360pp., translated by Jenny Serruys. Foreword by Auguste Gerard, French

ambassador in Japan

1850   1920   FRE 156
Hovelaque, Emile. Les Peuples d'Extreme Orient. La Chine. Series : Bibliotheque de Philosophie Scientifique [The Peoples of the Far East. China. Series : Library of Scientific Philosophy]
Paris: Flammarion 1920. 12mo, 286pp., Author inspecteur generale de l'instruction publique

1851   1921   FRE 236
Hovelaque, Emile. Les Peuples d'Extreme Orient. Le Japon. Series : Bibliotheque de Philosophie Scientifique [The Peoples of the Far East. Japan. Series : Library of Scientific Philosophy]
Paris: Flammarion 1921. 12mo, 344pp., comment: author inspecteur generale de l'instruction publique

1852   1922   GER 203
Lee, Kwanyong. Das Wollen als Grundtatsache des Bewusztseins [The Will as a Basic Fact of Consciousness]
Langensalza: Hermann Beyer & Söhne 1922. 12mo, 91pp.

1853   1934   ENG 1038
Saunders, Kenneth. The Ideals of East and West
Cambridge: UP 1934. 8vo, 246pp.

1854   1937   FRE 157 (2 ex.)
Farrere, Claude. Forces Spirituelles de l'Orient
Paris: Flammarion 1937. 12mo, 246pp.

VII.h) CULTURE : EASTERN SCIENCE & KNOWLEDGE

1855   1881   FRE 215
Rosny, Leon de. Les peuples orientaux connus des anciens chinois : d'apres les ouvrages originaux [The Eastern Peoples known to the Ancient Chinese. From Original Sources]
Paris: Ernest Leroux 1881. small 8vo, viii, 110pp., ill., maps

VII.i) CULTURE : RELIGION

VII.i.1) EASTERN RELIGION IN GENERAL

1856   **1729**   **DUT 16**

Moubach, O. Zesde verhandeling over de hedendaagsche godtsdienst-plichten en gewoontens der afgodische Oostindiaansche volkeren : vervattende den godtsdienst en de Plechtigheden der Japaneezen, en Coreanen, der Volkeren van Jesso, die der Tartaren en andere Noordere Gewesten [6th Reading on the Contemporary Worship and Habits of the Heathen East Indian Peoples : the Worships and Religious Customs of the Japanese, the Koreans, the Peoples from Hokkaido, those of the Tatars and of Other Adjacent Areas]

Amsterdam: H. Uytwert 1729. folio, pp.229-332, ill., taken from : O. Moubach, Naauwkeurige beschryving der uitwendige godtsdienst-plichten ... Vol.IV, Amsterdam : Hermanus Uytwert etc. 1729; contents: on Korea pp.288-289; comment: Author Jean Frederic Bernard Picard; translator Abraham Moubach.

1857   **1731**   **ENG 817**

Picart, Bernard. The Ceremonies and Religious Customs of the Several Nations of the Known World Represented in above an Hundred Copper Plates

London: Nicholas Prevost MDCCXXXI-MDCCXXXIX (1731-1739). folio, 5 vols. in 6, ill., indices, vol.I : The Ceremonies of the Jews &c, 1731, 412pp., vol.II : The Ceremonies of the Roman Catholics 1731, 345pp., vol.III : The Ceremonies of the Idolatrous Nations, 1731, 474pp., vol.IV.2 : Various Sects of Mahometans, with an Appendix of the Lives of Mohammed, Omar, and Ali, 1735, 514pp., vol.V : The Ceremonies of the Greeks and Protestants, 1736, 470pp., vol.VI pt.I : The Doctrine and Discipline of the Church of England, of the Presbyterians, Independents, Anabaptists, Quakers &c., 1737, 228pp., vol.VII : Various Sects of Mahometans, 1739, 162pp. (vol.VII is referred to as vol.II part II on front page); translated from the French; comment : vol.IV pt.I missing

1858   **1893**   **ENG 1119**

Barrows, John Henry (ed.). The World Parliament of Religions, Chicago 1893

London: Review of Reviews Office 1893. 8vo, 800pp., ill., no index

1859   **1895**   **ENG 377**

Griffis, William Elliot. The Religions of Japan, from the Dawn of History to the Era of Meiji

NY: Charles Scribner's Sons 1895. 12mo, xxi, 457pp., index

1860   1900   ENG 486
Geden, Alfred S. Studies in Eastern Religions. Series : Books for Bible Students
London: Charles H. Kelly 1900. 12mo, xiii, 378pp., index

1861   1903   FRE 321
Bourdaret, Emile. Religion et Superstition en Coree [Religion and Superstition in Korea]
Lyon: Societe d'Anthropologie de Lyon, transactions of 1903, printed Lyon 1904, small 8vo, 19pp.

1862   1910   ENG 539 (2 ex.)
Underwood, Horace Grant. The Religions of Eastern Asia
NY: MacMillan 1910. 8vo, ix, 267pp., index; Gompertz 1163

1863   1935   GER 169
Gundert, Wilhelm. Japanische Religionsgeschichte [History of Religion in Japan]
Tokyo / Stuttgart: Japanisch-Deutsches Kulturinstitut 1935. xviii, 267pp., ill.; Domschke/Goossmann 391

1864   1936   FRE 315
Levi, Sylvain. Etudes sur la pensee religieuse au Japon [Studies on Religious Thought in Japan]
in : Bulletin de la Maison Franco-Japonaise 1936, nos.2-4

VII.i.2) BUDDHISM

1865   1836   FRE 324
Anonymous. Foe Koue Ki, ou Relation des Royaumes Bouddhiques [Relations of Buddhist Kingdoms]
Paris: Imprimerie Royale 1836. folio, 424pp., index, translated by Abel Remuset; contents: has 2 pages on Korea

1866   1918   ENG 734 (2 ex.)
Starr, Frederick. Korean Buddhism. History - Condition - Art; Three Lectures
Boston: Marshall Jones 1918. small 8vo, xix, 104pp., ill.; Gompertz 1182

1867 1921 ENG 1074
Saunders, Kenneth J. Epochs in Buddhist History. The Haskell Lectures.
Chicago: Univ. of Chicago Press 1921. 8vo, 243pp., ill., index

1868 1922 GER 187e2
Hedin, Sven. Tsangpo Lamas Wallfahrt [Tsangpo Lama's Pilgrimage]
Leipzig: Brockhaus, 2nd edition 1922. 12mo, 346pp.

1869 1925 ENG 1008
Reischauer, August Karl. Studies in Japanese Buddhism
Tokyo: Methodist Publishing House (1917) 1925. 8vo, 361pp., ill., index; Gompertz 1175

1870 1925 GER 155
Cohn, William. Buddha
Leipzig: Klinkhardt & Biermann 1925. folio, lxiv, 253pp., plates

1871 1928 ENG 423
Pratt, James Bisset. The Pilgrimage of Buddhism and a Buddhist Pilgrimage
London: MacMillan 1928. 8vo, xii, 758pp., index; contents: on Korean Buddhism pp.417-436

VII.i.3) OTHER EASTERN RELIGIONS

1872 1895 ENG 985e4
Lowell, Percival. Occult Japan or the Way of the Gods. An Esoteric Study of Japanese Personality and Possession
Boston: Houghton & Mifflin, 4th edition, 1895. 8vo, 379pp., ill.

1873 1912 ENG 983e2
Hozumi, Nobushige. Ancestor-Worship and Japanese Law
Tokyo: Maruzu Kabushika-Kaisha, 2nd edition, 1912. 8vo, 198pp., index

1874 1914 ENG 1446
Armstrong, Robert Cornell. Light from the East. Studies in Japanese Confucianism
Toronto: University of Toronto Press 1914. large 8vo, xv, 326pp., ill.

1875 1923 GER 162

Schurhammer, Georg. Shin-to
Bonn & Leipzig: Kurt Schröder 1923. folio, 210pp., ill.

1876   1926   ENG 26
Kato, Genchi. A Study of Shinto, the Religion of the Japanese Nation
Tokyo: The Zaidan-Hojin-Meiji-Seitoku-Kinen-Gakkai 1926. 8vo, x, 255pp., ill., bibliography, index

1877   1929   FRE 357:2.1
Haguenauer, M.C. Sorciers et Sorcieres de Coree [Sorcerers in Korea]
in : Bulletin de la Maison Franco-Japonaise, Serie Fraçaise II.1 = 日佛會館學報:佛文編, 第二卷第一號, pp.47-65; Gompertz 1202

1878   1930   ENG 293
Anesaki, Masaharu. History of Japanese Religion, with Special Reference to the Social and Moral Life of the Nation
London: Kegan, Paul, Trench, Trübner & Co. 1930. 8vo, xxii, 423pp., ill., ads

1879   1935   ENG 999
Hepner, Charles William. The Kurozami Sect of Shinto
Tokyo: The Zaidan-Hojin-Meiji-Seitoku-Kinen-Gakkai (Meiji Japan Society) 1935. 8vo, 263pp., ill., index

1880   1938   ENG 1277
Holtom, D.C. The National Faith of Japan. A Study in Modern Shinto
London: Kegan, Paul, Trench, Trübner & Co. 1938. 8vo, 329pp., ill., index; contents: four Korea entries

VIII.) CHRISTIANITY AND MISSIONS

VIII.a) GENERAL WORKS

1881   ENG 305
Japan Christian Yearbook. The Christian Movement in Japan (1911-1912), The Christian Movement in Japan, including Korea, Formosa (1913). The Christian Movement in the Japanese Empire, Korea and Formosa (1916-1924), The Christian Movement in Japan & Formosa (1927-1939); since 1951 no subtitle
<small>Yokohama: Conference of Federated Missions, 12mo. vols.1911-1913, 1916-1919, 1923-1924, 1927-1931, 1938-1939, 1951, 1953-1970.</small>

1882   1913   FRE 210
Delpech, Jacques. Le Christianisme en Koree [Christianity in Korea]
<small>Paris: Societe Generale d'Impression 1913. 8vo, 101pp., dissertation, Faculty of Theology, Montauban</small>

1883   1948   DUT 23
Verkuyl, Johannes. Enkele aspecten van het probleem der godsdienstvrijheid in betrekking tot de plaats en arbeid der christelijke kerken in Azie [Several Aspects on the Problem of Freedom of Religion with Relation to the Location and Work of the Christian Churches in Asia]
<small>Kampen: J.H. Kok 1948. 8vo, 328pp.</small>

VIII.b) CATHOLIC CHURCH

VIII.b.1) GENERAL

1884   FRE 16
Annales de la Propagation de Foi [Annals of the Propagation of the Faith]
12mo, in stock : vols. 1-10 1825-1837/38, 12-61, 1840-1889, 61 1889, 71-72 1899-1900; contents: numerous articles on Korea

1885   ENG 513
Annals of the Propagation of the Faith
12mo, in stock : vol.14 1853; contents: has two articles on Korea

1886   GER 138
Die Katholischen Missionen. Illustrierte Monatsschrift [Catholic Missions. Illustrated Monthly]
4to, in stock : volumes 1873/1874-1879/1880, 1881/1882, 1883/1884, 1885/1886, 1887-1890, 1891/1892, 1893-1902

1887   ENG 900
Maynooth Mission to China. The Far East
Navan: Maynooth Mission to China, 4to, ill.; vols.1 (1918) - 76 (1993), 78 (1995) - 79 (1996)

1888   1641   LAT 15
Amiens, Jacques d'. Synopsis primi saeculi Societatis Iesu [A Summaric Description of the First Century of the Jesuit Order]
Tournai: Adrian Qunique 1641. 4to, 366pp.

1889   1863   SPA 3 : 1/4
Henrion, Baron de. Historia General de las Misiones : desde el siglo XII hasta nuestros dias por el Baron de Henrion [General History of the Missions, from the 12th Century until Our Days]
Barcelona: Juan Oliveres 1863. small 4to, 4 vols., vol.I 397pp., vol.II pp.398-706, vol.III 336pp., vol.IV pp.337-688, maps

1890   n.d. (c. 1900) FRE 2 : 3
Piolet, O.S.J. La France au dehors. Les missions Catholiques Françaises au

XIX siecle [France abroad. The French Catholic Missions in the 19th Century]
Paris: Colin, n.d. (c. 1900). small 4to, vol.3 (out of 6) : Chine et Japon, 503pp., ill.; contents: on Korea : pp.386-416, by A. Launay

1891   1923   ENG 695
Maryknoll Mission Letters
NY: MacMillan 1923. 2 vols., 1923, 1927, 8vo, 364, 402pp., indices; contents: 1 Korea entry in vol.1

1892   1936   FRE 45
Olichon, Armand. Les Missions. Histoire de l'Expansion du Catholicisme dans le Monde [The Missions. History of the Expansion of Catholicism in the World]
Paris: Bloud & Gay 1936. small 4to, 471pp.; contents: p.370 on Korea

1893   1937   FRE 251
Lesourd, Paul. Histoire des Missions Catholiques [History of the Catholic Missions]
Paris: De l'Arc 1937. 12mo, 491pp., foreword by Andre Boucher; contents: on Korea pp.270-272

1894   1939   FRE 150
Lavarenne, J. Petit Manuel Missionnaire [Small Manual for Missionaries]
Paris: Conseil Central de Lyon de la Propagation de la Foi 1939. 12mo, 115pp.

VIII.b.2) IN ASIA
1895   1615   LAT 6
Jarric, Pierre du, O.S.J. Thesavrvs Rervm Indicarvm. In quo Christianae ac Catholicae Religionis tam in India Orientali quam alijs regionib, Lusitanorum opera nuper detectis ortus, progress, incrementa & maxime quae APP Soc. Iesv ibid in dictae fidei plantatione ac propagatione ad annum usq M.D.C. gesta atq. exantlata sunt non minus vere quam eleganter recensetur. Addita sunt passim earunde regionum et eor quœ ad eas pertinet tam chorographicœ quam historiae descriptiones. Opus nunc primum a M. Martino Martinez e Gallico in Latinum sermonem translatum [Treasure of Indian Things. In which is Dealt with the Introduction, Propagation and Progress of the Christian Religion in East India and Other Areas Newly Discovered by the Portuguese until the Year

1600 .....]
Coloniae Agrippinae (Köln): Peter Henning MDCXV (1615). 12mo, xvi, 808pp. (recte 788), xxiv., ill., index, title of the original French edition : Histoire des choses plus mémorables advenues tant ez Indes Orientales; contents: on Korea p.583;

1896   1617   GER 119
Ricci, Matteo O.S.J. Historia von Einführung der Christlichen Religion in dass grosse Königreich China durch die Societat Jesu [History of the Introduction of the Christian Religion into the Chinese Kingdom by the Jesuit Order]
Augsburg: A. Hierat von Collen 1617. 8vo, xv, 527pp.

1897   1620   LAT 10
Orlandini, Nicolo. O.S.J. (and Iacobi Lainii and Francesco Sacchini) Historiae Societatis Iesv. Pars prima sive Ignativs (Pars secvnda, sive Lainivs) [History of the Jesuit Order, Pt.1 by Ignatius, Pt.2 by Lainius]
Antverpiae (Antwerpen): Filios Martini Nutij 1620. folio, 2 pts. in 1 vol., viii, 426, xxvi, xiii, 340, xxvii pp., Orlandini takes the story up to 1556 and in pt.II - a first edition - Sacchini continues the narrative to 1564; this section and pts.III-V all by Sacchini

1898   1655   LAT 3 appendix
Martini, Martino. Brevis Relatio de Numero et Qualitate Christianorum apud Sinas [Brief Account of the Number and Quality of the Christians among the Chinese]
Colonia (Köln): Ioannem Buseum 1655. 16mo, final 49 pages

1899   1665   LAT 4
Schall, Johann Adam O.S.J. Historica narratio de initio et progressu missionis Societatis Jesu apud Chineses, ac Præsertim in Regia Pequinensi, ex litteris R.P. Joannis Adami Schall ex eadem Societate. Supremi ac Regij Mathematum Tribunalis ibidem Praesidis [Historical Narrative of the Introduction and Progress of the Mission of the Jesuit Order among the Chinese, and presently in the Peking Region, from the letters of Johann Adam Schall O.S.J., the President of the Royal Mathematical Tribunal of Peking]
Vienna (Wien): Mattaeus Cosmerovius 1665. 16mo, 7, 267, 1pp.,ill. Revised and edited by Joanne Paulo Oliva, preapos. generalis O.S.J.

1900 1715 FRE 277e2
Crasset, O.S.J. Histoire de l'Eglise du Japon [History of the Church of Japan]
Paris: François Montalant 1715. small 4to, 2 vols., 659, 678pp.; Gompertz 11

1901 1738 GER 108
Crasset, Joanne, O.S.J. Ausführliche Geschicht der in dem äussersten Welt-Theil gelegenen Japonesischen Kirch, worinn ....ückliche Vertilgung der Abgötteren, Einführung, Fortpflanzung, Verfolgung und letztens gäntzliche Verbannung des heiligen Römisch Katholischen Glaubens in diesem grossen Reich nach denen besten Urkunden erzehlet wird [... History of the Japanese Church, located in the Remotest Part of the World, in which is narrated of the Extermination of the Pagan Gods, the Introduction, Spread, Persecution and Banning of the Sacred Roman Catholic Faith in this Great Empire, Based on the Best Documents]
Augsburg: Frantz Antoni Ilger 1738. 4to, 559pp., ill., translated into German

1902 1741 LAT 13
Moshemii, Laurentii. Historia Tartarorum Ecclesiastica [Church History of the Tartars]
Helmstedt: Fr. Chr. Weygand MDCCXXXXI (1741). 12mo, 216pp., index; contents: not on Korea

1903 1803 SPA 4
Pimentel, Mariano Lopez. Tribulaciones de los fieles en la partie oriental de la Asia. Dalas luz don Manuel Antonio Valdes [Tribulations of the Believers in the Eastern Part of Asia, Brought to the Light by Don Manuel Antonio Valdes]
Mexico: D. Mariano Joseph de Zuniga y Ontiveros 1803. small 8vo, 45pp.; comment: text on the Catholic missions to Korea during the second entrance of European missionaries, after a Korean noble, who has returned to his country under the name of Pedro Ly, and has started to spread the Catholic religion. This book tells the state of the missions from 1784 to 1797 and has some more data until 1800.

1904 1834 GER 124
Schall, Johann Adam von, O.S.J. Geschichte der Chinesischen Mission unter der Leitung des Pater Johann Adam Schall, Pristers aus der Gesellschaft Jesu [History of the Chinese Mission under the Direction of Father Johann Adam Schall, O.S.J.]
Wien: Mechitaristen-Congregations-Buchhandlung 1834. small 8vo, 461pp., translated from the Latin by Jg. Sch. von Mannsegg, the first German edition translated from the original (1685), Latin version

titled : Historica narratio de initio et progressu missionis Societatis Iesu apud Chinenses

1905   1860   SPA 6
Charlevoix, L. Historia de Japon y sus misiones [History of Japan and its Missions]
Valladolid: Questa 1860. 16mo, 294pp.

1906   1875   GER 138
Anonymous. Die Martern in China, Korea und Tongkin [The Martyrs in China, Korea and Tongking]
in : Die Katholischen Missionen. Illustrierte Monatsschrift 1874-1875, pp.17-24

1907   1888   FRE 254
Album des Missions Catholiques [Album of Catholic Missions]
Paris: Societe de Saint Augustin 1888. folio, vol.1 : Asie Orientale, 165pp., vol.2 : Asie Occidentale, 187pp.; contents: on Korea : vol.1 pp.125-130

1908   1909   ENG 419
Wolferstan, Bertram O.S.J. The Catholic Church in China : from 1860 to 1907
London and Edinburgh: Sands & Co. 1909. 8vo, xxxvii, 470pp., map, bibliography, index

1909   1921   FRE 300
Leclercq, R. (ed.). Les Martyrs. Vol.13 : La Revolution. L'Extreme Orient [The Martyrs. Vol.13 : The Revolution. The Far East]
Tours 1921. 12mo, 581pp., no index

1910   1923   ENG 695
Catholic Foreign Mission Society of America. Maryknoll Mission Letters : China. Extract from the Letters and Diaries of the Pioneer Missioners of the Catholic Foreign Mission Society of America
NY: MacMillan 1923-1927. 8vo, 2 vols., vol.I : 1923, xvi, 364pp., ill., map, index, vol.II : 1927, xvi, 402pp., ill., index

1911   1934   FRE 259
Elia, Pascal M. d'. Les Missions Catholiques en Chine. Resume d'histoire de l'eglise Catholique en Chine depuis les origines jusqu'a nos jours [The Catholic

Missions in China. Summary of the History of the Catholic Church in China from its Origins to our Days]
Shanghai: Tou se we 1934. large 8vo, 94pp.

1912   1938   ENG 900 Vol.21
Anonymous. Maynooth Mission to China, St. Columban's, Navan, Ireland
in : The Far East, Vol.21, 1938, pp.258-259

1913   1939   ENG 900 Vol.22
Anonymous. Where Our Priests are Working. Our Various Mission Territories in the East
in : The Far East, Vol.22, 1939, pp.49-50

1914   1940   GER 198
Tilmann, Klemens. Todesverächter. Ein Tatsachenbericht aus der Geschichte der Kirche in Fern-Ost [Those who Despise Death. A Report of Facts from the History of the Church in the Far East]
Freiburg im Breisgau: Herder 1940. 12mo, 155pp., map, ill.; Domschke/Goossmann 1018

VIII.b.3) IN KOREA

1915   1808   POR 4
Gouvea, Alexandre de. Carta do excellentissimo e reverendissimo Bispo de Pekim D. Fr. Alexandre de Gouvea ao illustrissimo e reverendissimo Bispo de Calandro. Sobre a introducçao, e progressos do Christianismo na peninsula da Corea, desde o anno de 1784 ate ao de 1797 [Letter by the Most Excellent and Reverend Bishop of Peking, Alexandre de Gouvea, to the Most Illustrious and Reverend Bishop of Calandro, about the Introduction and Progress of Christianity on the Korean Peninsula, from the Year 1784 to the Year 1797]
Lisboa: Joao Rodrigues Neves 1808. 16mo, 183pp.

1916   1874   FRE 266
Dallet, Ch. Histoire de l'eglise de Coree, precedee d'un introduction sur l'histoire, les institutions, la language, les moeurs et coutumes Coreennes [History of the Korean Church, Preceded by an Introduction in the History, the Institutions, the Language and the Customs of the Koreans]

Paris: Victor Palme 1874. 2 vols., 8vo, vol.1 : cxcii, 383pp., vol.2 594pp., ill., maps; Gompertz 114

1917　　　　　　　　　　　　1875　　ENG 14 : 1875
Goldie, F. The Early Days of the Korean Church. Part IV of Chronicles of Catholic Missions
in: The Month and Catholic Review 1875, pp.206-222

1918　　　　　　　　　　　　1875　　ENG 14 : 1875
Goldie, F. The Modern Church of Korea. Part V of Chronicles of Catholic Missions
in: The Month and Catholic Review 1875, pp.281-293

1919　　　　　　　　　　　　1875　　　　GER 138
Anonymous. Korea. II : Einführung des Christentums in Korea [Introduction of Christianity to Korea] (pp.159-163); III : Die Zeit der Verfolgung von 1839-1874 [The Time of Persecution, 1839-1874], pp.177-182
in: Die Katholischen Missionen, Illustrierte Monatsschrift, 1874-1875, pp.159-163, 177-182.
Note : Part I : Geographisches und Ethnographisches (ending with p.139) missing.

1920　　　　　　　　　　　　1875　　　　GER 138
Anonymous. Zwei junge Märtyrer aus Korea. [Two Young Martyrs from Korea]
in: Die Katholischen Missionen. Illustrierte Monatsschrift 1874-1875, pp.15-16

1921　　　　　　　　　n.d. (c.1894)　　　FRE 289
Launay, Adrien. La Coree et les missionaires Françases [Korea and the French Missionaries]
Tours: Alfred Mame, n.d. (before 1894)

1922　　　　　　　　　　　　1895　　FRE 231 Vol.29
Paquier, P. La Coree. Lettres d'un missionaire fribourgeois [Korea, Letters of a Fribourgian Missionary]
in: Nouvelles Etrennes Fribourgeoises Vol.29 1895 pp.36-44

1923　　　　　　　　　　　　1924　　　　ENG 540
The Catholic Church in Korea

Hong Kong: Societe des Missions Etrangeres 1924. 8vo, 108pp., ill., map

1924   **1924**   **FRE 192 (2 ex.)**

Mutel, G. Le Catholicisme en Coree. Son origine et ses progres [Catholicism in Korea. Its Origin and Progress]

Hong Kong: Imprimerie de la Societe des Missions Etrangeres de Paris 1924. 8vo, 41, 111pp., ill.

1925   **1931**   **FRE 353**

Vaudon, Chanoine Jean. Les Filles de Saint-Paul en Coree [The Daughters of St. Paul in Korea]

Chartres: Soeurs de St. Paul 1931, 16mo, 63pp., ill.

1926   **1938**   **ENG 900 Vol.22**

McPolin. The Year's Harvest. Report from Monsigneur McPolin

in: The Far East vol.22 1938 pp.266-267

VIII.c) PROTESTANT CHURCHES

VIII.c.1) IN GENERAL

1927   **1886**   **ENG 1470**

Gracey, J.T. Open Doors

Rochester NY: J.T. Gracey 1886. 16mo, 64pp.; contents: on Korea pp.60-61

1928   **1888**   **ENG 1366e4**

Marshall, T.W.M. Christian Missions. Their Agents and their Results.

NY: D. & J. Sadler 1888. 4th edition, 2 vols., small 8vo, 644pp., no index; contents: on Corea pp.113-120

1929   **1894**   **ENG 1371**

Lawrence, Edward A. Modern Missions in the East, their Methods, Successes and Limitations

NY: Fleming H. Revell 1894. 12mo, 340pp., ill., index

1930   **1899**   **ENG 1379e4**

Dennis, James S. Foreign Missions after a Century

Nashville: M.E. Church South, (1893) 4th edition 1899. 12mo, 368pp., index; contents: numerous Korea entries

1931   See No. 0060

1932   1902   ENG 509
Montgomery, Henry H. Foreign Missions. Series : Handbooks for the Clergy.
London: Longmans, Green 1902. 12mo, ix, 169, 24pp.; contents: ch.vi : Japan and Corea pp.55-69

1933   1906   GER 33 : 1/5
Richter, Julius. Allgemeine evangelische Missionsgeschichte. Ein Versuch [Universal History of Protestant Mission. An Attempt]
Gütersloh: C. Bertelsmann 1906-1932. 8vo, 5 vols., vol.1: 1906, iv, 445pp., ill., vol.2: 1908, viii, 316pp., ill., index, vol.3: 1922-1924, 813pp., ill., index, vol.4 1928, xvi, 584pp., ill., index, vol.5 1931-1932, 488pp., index; contents: vol.1 : Indische Missionsgeschichte [History of Mission in India], vol.2 : Mission und Evangelisation im Orient [Mission and Preaching in the Orient], vol.3 : Geschichte der evangelischen Mission in Afrika [History of Protestant Mission in Africa], vol.4 : Das Werden der evangelischen Kirche in China [Emergence of the Protestant Church in China] vol.5 : Die evangelische Mission in Niederländisch-Indien, Fern- und Südost-Asien, Australien, Amerika, [The Protestant Mission in the Netherlands Indies, in Far and Southeast Asia, Australia, America]

1934   1906   ENG 1374
Student Volunteer Movement. Students and the Modern Missionary Crusade
NY: Student Volunteer Movement for Foreign Missions 1906. 8vo, 713pp., index; contents: pp.391-413 on Korea

1935   1908   ENG 914 v.1908
Missionary Directory
Tokyo: Methodist Publishing House 1908. pp.463-518, 19pp. ads

1936   1909   ENG 237
Gordon, E.A. Messiah, the Ancestral Hope of the Ages, "The Desire of all Nations", as proved from the Records on the Sun-Dried Bricks of Babylonia, the Papyri and Pyramids of Egypt, the Frescoes of the Roman Catacombs, and on the Chinese Incised Memorial Stone at Cho-ang
Tokyo: Keiseisha 1909. 4to, ii, 212pp.; plates, index, esoteric work linking Christianity and Buddhism; spine title : In the Name of the Messiah

1937   1915   ENG 381
Montgomery, Helen Barrett. The King's Highway : a Study of Present Conditions on the Foreign Field
West Medford: CCUSFM [1915]. 12mo, 272pp., ill., index, bibliography; contents: on Korea pp.181-216

1938   1922   ENG 1456

Diffendorfer, Ralph E. The World Service of the Methodist Episcopal Church

Chicago: Methodist Episcopal Church 1922. large 8vo, 704pp., ill.; contents: on Korea pp.47-57

1939   1934   ENG 538

Eggleston, Margaret W. Forty Missionary Stories

NY: Harper 1934. 12mo, 162pp.

1940   1943   ENG 1051

Latourette, Kenneth Scott. A History of the Expansion of Christianity

London: Eyre and Spottiswoode 1943-1945. 8vo, Vol.1 : The First Five Centuries, 412pp., 1945; Vol.2 : The Thousand Years of Uncertainty, 492pp., 1943, Vol.3 : Three Centuries of Advance, 503pp., 1945, Vol.4 : The Great Century 1800-1914, Europe and the United States of America, 516pp., 1943, Vol.5 : The Great Century 1800-1914, in the Americas, Austral-Asia and Africa, 526pp., 1943, Vol.6 : The Great Century 1800-1914, in Northern Africa and Asia, 502pp., no date; on Korea ch.VII pp.412-430, Vol.7 : Advance through Storm. A.D. 1914 and after, with concluding Generalizations, 542pp., 1945.

1941   1943   ENG 1384e22

Cowman, Chas. E., Mrs. Streams in the Desert

LA: Oriental Missionary Society 1943. 12mo, 378pp., with handwritten text added. An almanac full of biblical phrases, arranged by calendar days; contents: not on Korea

VIII.c.2) IN ASIA

1942   1896   ENG 1363

American Presbyterian Mission. The China Mission Hand-Book

Shanghai: American Presbyterian Mission Press 1896. large 8vo, 336pp., map; contents: not on Korea

1943   1897   ENG 343

Reid, Gilbert. Seventh Report of the Mission among the Higher Classes in China

NY: Fleming H. Revell 1897. 12mo, 16pp.

1944   1908 ENG 464 (3 ex.)

Smith, Arthur H. The Uplift of China

London: London Missionary Society 1908. 12mo, x, 279pp., ill., map, index

1945   1913   ENG 1254
Continuation Committee. Conferences in Asia 1912-1913
NY: Chairman of the Continuation Committee 1913. 8vo, 159pp., ill., map, no index

1946   1918   ENG 932
The Kingdom of God in Japan. Observations and Recommendations of a Deputation appointed by the American Board of Commissioners for Foreign Missions
American Board of Commissioners for Foreign Missions, 1918. 12mo, 86pp.

1947   1923   ENG 1378 : 1923
Oriental Missionary Standard
Tokyo: Oriental Missionary Society 1923. folio, 4to, monthly issues paginated per month, issues of 1923, in xerocopy, bound together

1948   1926   ENG 1122e3
Donaldson, St. Clair. The Call from the Far East
Westminster: Missionary Council 1926. 8vo, 170pp., index; contents: several Korea entries

1949   1931   ENG 527 (3 ex.)
Eddy, Sherwood. The Challenge of the East (China, Korea, Japan etc.)
NY: Farrar & Rinehart 1931. 8vo, 265pp.; contents: on Korea pp.145-169

1950   1942   ENG 1188
Williamson, H.R. The Past Fifty Years in China of the Baptist Missionary Society, 1892-1942
London: Carey Press 1942. 16mo, 51pp., no index

VIII.c.3) IN KOREA

1951   ENG 1481
Korea Mission of the Presbyterian Church in the U.S.A: Minutes and Reports of the ...Annual Meeting of the Korea Mission of the Presbyterian Church
Seoul: Y.M.C.A. Press; 8vo, vol. 31 1915, 136pp., vol.32 1916, 136pp., vol.34 1918, 159pp., vol.43 1927, 123pp.

1952　　　　　　　　　　　　　　　1928　　　ENG 1390
Federal Council of Missions in Korea. Korea Missions Year Book
Seoul: Christian Literature Society of Korea; 8vo, in stock vol.1928

1953　　　　　　　　　　　　　　　1879　　ENG 749 (2 ex.)
M'Leod, N. Korea and the Ten Lost Tribes of Israel, with Korean, Japanese and Israelitish Illustrations
Tokyo: C. Levy and Sei Shi Bunsha Co., 1879. large 8vo, 23pp.

1954　　　　　　　　　　　　　　　1905　ENG 1421 (2 ex.)
Underwood, H.G. Twenty Years' Missionary Work in Korea
in : The Missionary Review of the World, Vol.XVIII, No.5, May 1905, pp.371-376

1955　　　　　　　　　　　　　　　1906　　　ENG 786
Corfe, C.J. (ed.). The Anglican Church in Corea. Being Documents, Original and Translated, Issued by Authority during the Episcopate of the First Bishop of the Church of England in Corea between 1889 and 1905
London : Rivingtons 1906. 12mo, 139pp.

1956　　　　　　　　　　　　　　　1907　　　ENG 952
Jones, George Heber and Noble, W. Arthur. The Korean Revival. An Account of the Revival in the Korean Churches in 1907
NY: Methodist Episcopal Church, Board of Foreign Missions 1907. 12mo, 45pp., ill.

1957　　　　　　　　　　　　　　　1908　ENG 75e3 (2 ex.)
Underwood, Horace G. The Call of Korea
NY: Fleming H. Revell n.d. (1908). 16mo, 204pp., map, ads, illustrations from photographs taken by Cameron Johnson

1958　　　　　　　　　　　　　　　1908　ENG 75e4 (2 ex.)
Underwood, Horace G. The Call of Korea : Political-Social-Religious
NY: Fleming H. Revell n.d. (1908). 16mo, 204pp., map, ads, illustrations from photographs taken by Cameron Johnson

1959　　　　　　　　　　　　　　　1909　　ENG 87 (5 ex.)
Gale, James Scarth. Korea in Transition
NY: Educational Department of the Board of Foreign Missions of the Presbyterian Church in the U.S. 1909 / NY: Young People's Missionary Movement of the United States and Canada 1909. (3 ex.),

16mo, 270pp., ill., map, bibliography, index

1960 1910 ENG 697
Davis, George T.B. Korea for Christ
London: Christian Worker's Depot 1910. 12mo, 71pp., ill.

1961 1910 ENG 1434
Jones, George Heber. The Korea Mission of the Methodist Episcopal Church
NY: Board of Foreign Missions of the Methodist Episcopal Church 1910. 60pp., ill.

1962 n.d. (c.1914) ENG 1151
Fowler-Willing, Jennie. The Lure of Korea
Boston: Women's Foreign Mission Society, n.d. (c.1914). 12mo, 69pp., ill.

1963 1915 ENG 491 (2 ex.)
Trollope, Mark Napier. The Church in Corea
London: Mowbray 1915. 16mo, 132pp., ill., map, index

1964 1917 ENG 1389
Anonymous. The English Church Mission in Corea, its Faith and Practices
Oxford: A.R. Mowbray 1917. 16mo, 80pp., no index. with a preface by C.J. Corfe(Bishop).

1965 1918 ENG 1449
Clark, Charles Allen. Digest of the Presbyterian Church of Korea (Chosen)
Seoul: Korean Religious Book & Tract Society 1918. 12mo, 261pp.

1966 1918 ENG 612
The Christian Gateway into Asia : Graphic Series-Korea.
NY: Centenary Commision of the Board of Foreign Missions of the Methodist Episcopal Church, (1918). 4to, (32)pp., ill.

1967 1919 ENG 1014 : 2
Commission on Relations with the Orient of the Federal Council of the Churches of Christ in America. The Korean Situation
NY: Federal Council of the Churches of Christ in America 1919. 8vo, 27pp.

1968 1921 ENG 224 (2 ex.)
Clark, Charles A. First Fruits in Korea : a Story of Church Beginnings in the

Far East
NY: Fleming H. Revell 1921. 8vo, 338pp., comment: author Presbyterian missionary

1969   1928   ENG 1414

Schweinitz-Brunner, Edmund de. Rural Korea : a Preliminary Survey of Economic, Social and Religious Conditions, pp.84-173 in : The Jerusalem Meeting of the International Missionary Church, 1928, Vol.VI : The Christian Mission in Relation to Rural Problems
n.p., International Missionary Church 1928. 16mo, 272pp., index

1970   1929   ENG 110 (3 ex.)

Paik, L. George. The History of Protestant Missions in Korea 1882-1910
Pyeng Yang, Korea: Union Christian College Press 1929. 8vo, x, 438, xvii pp., map, index, appendix, bibliography; comment: author Korean Protestant minister

1971   1929   ENG 332

Swinehart, Lois H. Korea Calls ! A Story of the Eastern Mission Field
NY: Fleming H. Revell [1929]. 12mo, 160pp.

1972   1938   ENG 717

Women's Foreign Mission Society. Fifty Years of Light
Seoul 1938. 8vo, 120pp., ill.

1973   n.d.   ENG 953

Scidmore, George H. et al. Competent Witnesses on Korea as a Mission Field. Statements from twelve men whose Province and Observation Qualify them to Speak with Authority
NY: Methodist Episcopal Church, Board of Foreign Missions, n.d., 12mo, 20pp., ill.; contributions by G.H. Scidmore, John R. Mott, W.J. Boyer, A.B. Leonard, Ch.W. Fairbanks, E. Cranston, R. Laidlaw, M.C. Harris, J.W. Chapman, M. Honda, J.B. Sleman, G.H. Jones

IX.) SCIENCE

IX.a) IN GENERAL

1974   1926   ENG 413
Third Pan-Pacific Science Congress. Scientific Japan : Past and Present
Kyoto: Pan-Pacific Science Congress [1926]. 8vo, 359pp., maps, ill., essays by N. Yamasaki, T. Okada, N. Kanehara, S. Kawasaki, B. Hayata, T. Kabunaki, Y. Koganei, A. Imamura, Y. Mikami, S. Shinjo, M. Shirai, Y. Fujikawa, A. Kuwaki, T. Terada

IX.b) MEDICINE, HEALTH

1975   1911   ENG 920
Jefferys, W. Hamilton and Maxwell, James L. The Diseases of China, including Formosa and Korea
Philadelphia: Blakiston's Son and Co. 1911. 8vo, 713pp., ill., index

1976   1911   FRE 68 : 1911
Charmelin, Andre. La Peste en Manchourie [The Plague in Manchuria]
in : Journal de voyages et aventures de terre et de mer, 1911, pp.192-196

1977   n.d.   ENG 951
Jones, George Heber. Christian Medical Work in Korea
NY: Methodist Episcopal Church, Board of Foreign Missions, n.d., 12mo, 16pp., ill.

1978   1925   ENG 292

Lim, Professor. Rontgenology
manuscript 1925, large 8vo, 336pp., drawings, entries in Korean and English. Notes taken by Chang Ho Kim, while studying at Taegu Medical College

1979   1938   ENG 900 Vol.21
Monaghan, Rev. Patrick. Our Leper Friends. The Story of Their Arrival.
in: The Far East, vol.21, 1938, pp.14-15

1980   1942   ENG 1259 (2 ex.)
Yui, John. Shanghai Co-operative Industrial Hygiene Center. Its Origin, Scope of Work and Future Prospects, 1942
Shanghai: Co-operative Industrial Hygiene Center 1942. pamphlet, 12mo, ill., contents: not on Korea

1981   1950   ENG 820
Balfour, Marshall C., Evans, Roger F., Notestein, Frank W., Taeuber, Irene B. Public Health and Demography in the Far East. Report of a Survey Trip, September 13-December 13 1948
NY: The Rockefeller Foundation 1950. 4to, 132pp., ill., maps; contents: on Korea pp.61-70

IX.c) BIOLOGY

1982   1886   ENG R 632
Forbes, Frances Blackwell and William, Botting Homesley. Index Florae Sinensis [Index of Chinese Flora]. An Enemeration of All Plants Known from China Proper, Formosa, Hainan, Corea, the Luchu Archipelago, and the Island of Hong Kong, together with Their Distribution and Synomy
in: The Journal of the Linnean Society. Botany. Vols.23, 26, 28, 1886-1905

1983   1890   ENG 1111
Baker, Samuel W. Wild Beasts and Their Ways
London etc.: Macmillan 1890. 2 vols., 419, 377pp.

1984   1902   GER 178
Kobelt, W. Die Verbreitung der Tierwelt [The Distribution of Fauna]
Leipzig: Christian Hermann Tauchnitz 1902. xiv, 576pp., ill.

1985   1910 ENG 936
Jouy, Pierre Louis. The Paradise Flycatchers of Japan and Korea
Proceedings of the United States National Museum Vol.37 pp.651-655; Gompertz 2002

1986   1914 ENG 805 v.6
Jordan, David Starr and Metz, Charles William. A Catalogue of Fishes known from the Waters of Korea, pp.1-56
in : W.J. Holland (ed.), Memoirs of the Carnegie Museum VI, 1913-1914,
Philadelphia: Carnegie Trust, n.d., folio; Gompertz 2007

1987   1917 ENG 956
Kuroda, Nagamichi. On One New Genus and Three New Species of Birds from Corea and Tsushima, reprinted from "Tori" (The Aves) No.5, 1917, pp.1-6
Tokyo: The Ornithological Society of Japan 1917. 6pp., ill.

1988   1919 GER 84
Schlechter, R. Orchideologiae Sino-Japonicae Prodromus. Eine Kritische Besprechung der Orchideen Ost-Asiens [Orchideologia Sino-Japonica Prodromus. A Critical Comment on the Orchids of East Asia]
Dahlem bei Berlin: Verlag des Repertoriums 1919. 8vo, 319pp.

1989   1924 ENG 934
Laufer, Berthold. Tobacco and its Use in Asia
Chicago: Field Museum of Natural History, Leaflet 18, 1924. 12mo, 39pp.; contents: on Korea pp.10 and 23

1990   1925 ENG 1019
Wilson, E.H. America's Greatest Garden. The Arnold Arboretum (Harvard University)
Boston: Stratford 1925. 8vo, 119pp., ill., index

1992   1931 ENG 828 (2 ex.)
Crane, Florence Hedleston. The Flowers and Folklore from Far Korea
Tokyo: Sanseido 1931. folio, 93, 4pp.; Gompertz 1654

1993   1933 GER 116 v.1

Klautke, P. Beitrag zur Pflanzenwelt der Diamantberge Koreas [Contribution to the Knowledge of the Flora of Korea's Diamond Mountains]

in : Jubiläumsband, ed. by the Deutsche Gesellschaft für Natur- und Völkerkunde Ostasiens, Teil I Tokyo 1933. pp.57-75; Gompertz 1667; Domschke/Goossmann 524

1994　　　　　　　　　　　　　　　　　1934　　　ENG 1377
Miduno, Tadamesa. Zytologische Untersuchungen der Bryophyte. I : Die Morphologie der Spermatozoiden einiger Hepaticeen [Zoological Examinations of Bryophytes. I : The Morphology of Spermatocoids of some Hepaticea]

in: Journal Faculty of Science, Imperial University of Tokyo, Section III : Botany, vol.IV pt.1, 1934, pp.367-387

1995　　　　　　　　　　　　　　　　　1935　　　GER 100
Bergman, Sten. Zur Kenntnis nordostasiatischer Vögel. Ein Beitrag zur Systematik, Biologie und Verbreitung der Vögel Kamtschatkas und der Kurilen [On the Knowledge of North East Asian Birds. A Contribution to the Systematic, Biology and Spread of the Birds of Kamchatka and of the Kuriles]

Stockholm: Albert Bonnier 1935. 4to, 268pp., ill.; contents: not on Korea

1996　　　　　　　　　　　　　　　　　1938　　ENG 436 (5 ex.)
Bergman, Sten. In Koreas Wilds and Villages

London: John Gifford / Travel Book Club 1938. 8vo, 232pp., ill., map, translated from the Swedish by Frederick Whyte

1998　　　　　　　　　　　　　　　　1948　ENG 710 Vol.101.1
Austin, Oliver L. The Birds of Korea

in: Bulletin of the Museum of Comparative Zoology at Harvard College, Vol.101.1, pp.1-302

IX.d) SOCIOLOGY

1999　　　　　　　　　　　　　　　　　1879　　　FRE 22e5
Jacolliot, Louis. Les Moeurs et les Femmes de l'Extreme Orient. Voyage au Pays des Perles [The Customs and the Women of the Far East. Voyage to the Land of Pearls]

Paris: E. Dentu 1879. 12mo, 346pp., ill. by E. Yon; contents: the book is on Ceylon / Sri Lanka; not on Korea

2000   1886   ENG 1469
Anonymous. Life in Korea,
pp.137-139 in : Children's Work for Children, 1886 issue, 8vo

2001   1898   ENG 862
Gifford, Daniel L. Everyday Life in Korea
Chicago etc.: Fleming H. Revell 1898. small 8vo, 231pp., ill., map

2002   1902   ENG 90eR
Bacon, Alice Mabel. Japanese Girls and Women
Boston: Houghton Mifflin Co. (1891) 1902. 16mo, revised and enlarged edition. xi, 478pp., index

2003   1905   ENG 1421
Underwood, Mrs. H.G. Women's Work for Women in Korea,
in: The Missionary Review of the World, vol.XVIII no.7, July 1905, pp.491-500

2004   1907   ENG 1416
Pollard, Edward B. Women : in All Ages and in All Counries. Vol.4 : Oriental Women
Philadelphia: George Barrie & Sons 1907. contents: ch.XII pp.291-316 : Women of China and Corea

2005   1911   ENG 1455
Moose, J. Robert. Village Life in Korea
Nashville: Smith & Lamar 1911. small 8vo, 242pp., il., frontispiece missing

2006   n.d. (c. 1920)   ENG 716
Tayler, Constance J.D. Koreans at Home : the Impressions of a Scotswoman
London: Cassell n.d. (c.1920). 8vo, 80pp., ill.

2007   n.d. (c. 1920)   ENG 751
Wagner, Ellasue Carter. Children of Korea
London: Oliphants n.d. (c.1920). 12mo, 93pp., ill.

2008   1924   ENG 1232
MacNair, Harley Farnsworth. The Chinese Abroad. Their Position and

Protection.
Shanghai: Commercial Press 1924. 8vo, 340pp., index; contents: several Korea entries

2009   1928   ENG 731
Parmelee, Maurice. Oriental and Occidental Culture, an Interpretation
NY: Century [1928]. 8vo, 379pp., ill., maps, index

2010   1933   ENG 1350
Woodsmall, Ruth Frances. Eastern Women - Today and Tomorrow.
Boston: Central Committee 1933. 12mo, 221pp., bibliography, index; contents: 3 Ewha College entries

2011   1946   ENG 1172
Embree, John F. A Japanese Village, Suye Mura
London: Kegan Paul, Trench & Trubner 1946. 8vo, 268pp.

X.) ADMINISTRATION

2012 ENG 1257
China Year Book
issues 1913, 1925-1926, 1926-1927; editor H.T. Montague Bell (1913), H.G.W. Woodhead (1925-1927), London : Routledge (1913), Tientsin : Tientsin Press (1926-1927), 8vo, 703, 1349, 1332pp., ill., maps

2013 1888 ENG 134
Outlines of the Modern Education in Japan
Tokyo: Department of Education, March 1888. 8vo, 184pp., translated and published by the DoE.; contents: not on Korea

2014 n.d. ENG 947
Jones, George Heber. Education in Korea
NY: Methodist Episcopal Church, Board of Foreign Missions, n.d., 12mo, 16pp., ill.

2015 1904 FRE 72 : 1904
Eude, Robert. L'ecole Française de Seoul [The French School in Seoul]
in : A Travers le Monde 1904, pp.373-374

2016 1924 ENG 596
Government-General of Chosen. History of Annexation and Present Condition of Chosen
Keijo: Government-General of Chosen, March 1924. 16mo, x, 30pp.

2017 1939 ENG 900 Vol.22
Neligan. Our School in Junten. The Story of its Beginnings and its Progress.

Some Remarks about the Korean Child. An Expensive Catechism Competition
in : The Far East, vol.22, 1939, pp.224-226

2018 1947 ENG 1355
U.S. Army Forces in Korea. South Korea Interim Government Activities
Seoul: United States Army Military Government 1947. 4to, 214pp., ill., maps

2019 1948 ENG 720 (3 ex.)
U.S. Department of State. Korea 1945 to 1948. A Report on Political Developments and Economic Resources with Selected Documents
NY: Greenwood Press 1948. 8vo, 124pp., map

2020 1948 ENG 844
UNTCOK. Report of the United Nations Temporary Commission on Korea
Lake Success: United Nations 1948. General Assembly, Official Records : 3rd Session, Supplement No.9, First Part : 3 vols., 4to, 47, 99, 304pp.; Second Part : 2 vols., 4to, 38, 14pp.

2021 1949 ENG 846
UNCOK. Report of the United Nations Commission on Korea
Lake Success: United Nations 1949. General Assembly, Official Records : 4th Session, Supplement No.9, 2 vols., 4to, 34, 63pp.

2022 1950 ENG 720eR
U.S. Department of State. Korea 1945 to 1948. A Report on Political Developments and Economic Resources with Selected Documents
NY: Greenwood Press (1948) 1950. 8vo, 124pp., map

XI.) ECONOMICS

XI.a) ECONOMIC STATISTICS

2023   1884   ENG 556
Her Majesty's Consul-General in Corea. Commercial Reports received at the Foreign Office from her Majesty's Consul-General in Corea 1884.
London: Harrison & Sons 1884. 8vo, 29pp.

2024   1889   ENG 1329
Foreign Office (British). Diplomatic and Consular Reports on Trade and Finance. Corea. Report for the Year 1888 on the Trade of Corea
Foreign Office, Annual Series No.565, 8vo, 12pp.

2025   1890   ENG 1329
Foreign Office (British). Diplomatic and Consular Reports on Trade and Finance. Corea. Report for the Year 1889 on the Trade of Corea
Foreign Office, Annual Series No.918, 8vo, 13pp.

2026   1891   ENG 225 (2 ex.)
China, Imperial Maritime Customs. Decennial Reports on the Trade, Navigation, Industries etc. of the Ports Open to Foreign Commerce in China and Korea, and on the Condition and Development of the Treaty Port Provinces 1882-1891
Shanghai 1891. 4to, lxxxiv, 694pp., maps; appendix II : Reports from Corean Ports : Jenchuan, Fusan, Yuensan, with 3 maps of the ports. Statistical Series No.6

2027   1894   ENG 662 : 1/5

Statistical Department of the Inspectorate General of Customs. Corea : Quarterly Returns of Trade for the Ports of Jenchuan, Fusan and Yuensan

Shanghai: Inspectorate General of Customs 1894-1903. 5 vols., large 8vo, vol.1 : reports and appendices on Korea bound together, individually paged, Oct.-Dec.1885-Oct.-Dec.1894. vol.2 : Jan-Mar. 1895-Jan-Mar. 1900, vol.3 : Apr-Jun. 1900- Oct.-Dec.1904, vol.4 : Korea. Imperial Maritime Customs, Returns of Trade and Trade Reports for the Year 1902, published by the order of the Chief Commisioner of Customs, Seoul : Seoul Press Hodge & Co. 1903, 209pp., vol.5 : Report on the Trade of Korea and Abstract of Statistics for the Year 1902, Seoul : Seoul Press Hodge & Co. 1903

2028   1909   ENG 747 : 1908-09

H.I.J.M. Residency General. Annual Report of Reforms and Progress in Chosen (1908-1909)

Keijo: H.I.J.M. Residency General 1909. large 8vo, viii, 215pp.

2029   1911   ENG 747 : 1910-11

Government General of Chosen. Annual Report of Reforms and Progress in Chosen (1910-1911)

Keijo: Government General of Chosen 1911. large 8vo, x, 268pp., ill.

2030   1913   ENG 1329

Foreign Office (British). Diplomatic and Consular Reports on Trade and Finance. Corea. Report for the Year 1912 on the Trade of Corea

Foreign Office, Annual Series No.5345, 8vo, 25pp.

2031   1914   ENG 1329

Foreign Office (British). Diplomatic and Consular Reports on Trade and Finance. Corea. Report for the Year 1913 on the Trade of Corea.

Foreign Office, Annual Series No.5520, 8vo, 29pp.

2032   1916   ENG 747 : 1914-15

Government General of Chosen. Annual Report of Reforms and Progress in Chosen (1914-1915)

Keijo: Government General of Chosen 1916. large 8vo, x, 183pp., ill.

2033   1917   ENG 747 : 1915-16

Government General of Chosen. Annual Report of Reforms and Progress in Chosen (1915-1916)

Keijo: Government General of Chosen 1917. large 8vo, x, 161pp., ill.

2034 1921 ENG 747 : 1918-21
Government General of Chosen. Annual Report of Reforms and Progress in Chosen (1918-1921)
Keijo: Government General of Chosen 1921. large 8vo, ix, ii, 232pp., ill., map

2035 1928 ENG 439 : 1926-27
Government General of Chosen. Annual Report on Administration of Chosen, 1926-1927
Keijo: Government General of Chosen 1928. 8vo, 201pp., appendix, ill.

2036 1929 ENG 439 : 1927-28
Government General of Chosen. Annual Report on Administration of Chosen, 1927-1928
Keijo: Government General of Chosen 1928. 8vo, 158pp., ill., map

2037 1931 ENG 439 : 1929-30
Government-General of Chosen. Annual Report on Administration of Chosen, 1929-1930
Keijo: Government General of Chosen, December 1931. 8vo, 183pp., ill., map

2038 1931-1932 ENG 359
Manchuria Year Book
Tokyo: Toa-Keizai Chosakyoku (East Asiatic Economic Intelligence Bureau), 8vo, 1931 : 347pp., index; 1932 : 530pp., index

2039 1936 ENG 95
Yano, Tsuneta and Shirasaki, Kyoichi. Nippon : A Chartered Survey of Japan, 1936
Tokyo: Kokusei-Sha 1936. large 8vo, xxxvi, 487pp., plates, index. An economic yearbook accounting for all fields of foreign trade and national activity. This is the fifth edition of the yearbook, but the first to be translated into English.

XI.b) ECONOMICS : ADDRESSBOOKS

2040　　　　　　　　　　　　　　　　　1938　　ENG 105 : 37-38
Mori, R. (森良治)(ed.). Asia Directory＝亞細亞年檻鑑 : A Complete and Up-To Date Guide to the Principal Manufacturers, Exporters, Importers, Merchants, Agents, Shipping Companies, Banks, Hotels, Commercial and Governmental Organizations etc., 1937-1938 edition
_{Yokohama: The Asia Directory Publishing Company 1938. 4to, 16pp. ads, xxviii, 262 (Japanese Empire Section) + a total of (253) pp. for other Asian countries}

XI.c) ECONOMICS : COUNTRY & AREA STUDIES

XI.c.1) THE WORLD

2041　　　　　　　　　　　　　　　　　　　　1939　　　　FRE 163
Allix, Andre, Leyritz, A., Merlier, A. Geographie Les Principales Puissances Economiques du Monde [Geography. The World's Major Economic Powers]
_{Paris: A. Hatier 1939. 12mo, 199pp.; contents: on Korea p.144}

XI.c.2) THE FAR EAST

2042　　　　　　　　　　　　　　　　　　　　1934　　　　ENG 445
Field, Frederick V. (ed.). Economic Handbook of the Pacific Area
_{NY: Doubleday, Doran & Co. 1934. 8vo, xl, 649pp., map, bibliography, index. Foreword by Newton D. Baker}

2043　　　　　　　　　　　　　　　　　　　　1949　　　　ENG 819
Institute for Pacific Relations, International Secretariat. The Development of Upland Areas in the Far East
_{NY: I.P.R. 1949-1951. 4to, 2 vols., vol.1 : China, the Philippines, Japan, 1949, iii, 82pp., vol.2 : Malaysia, Indochina, Indonesia & Western New Guinea, Korea, 1951, 121pp., maps. Utilization of Upland Areas in Korea by Shannon McCune vol.2 pp.103-121}

XI.c.3) JAPAN

2044　　　　　　　　　　　　　　　　n.d. (c.1910)　　　FRE 177e2

Dautremer, Joseph. L'Empire Japonais et sa vie economique [The Japanese Empire and its Economic Life]
Paris: Guilmoto new edition, n.d. (c.1910). 8vo, 308pp., ill., map

2045 1910 ENG 43

D'Autremer, Joseph. The Japanese Empire and its Economic Conditions
NY: Charles Scribner 1910. translated from the French, 8vo, 311pp., ill., map.; contents: Chapter xx (pp.301-311) on Korea

2046 1911 ENG 230

Porter, Robert P. The Full Recognition of Japan : Being a Detailed Account of the Economic Progress of the Japanese Empire to 1911
London: Oxford UP 1911. 8vo, 789pp., maps, index

2047 1928 ENG 296

Oinuma, Kazuo (ed.). Imperial Coronation and Japan's Industrial, Financial and Business Growth, 1924-1928
[Tokyo: Commercial Japan 1928]. 8vo, 200pp., ill., ads

2048 1932 ENG 10

Moulton, Harold G. Japan : An Economic and Financial Appraisal. With the Collaboration of Junichi Ko.
London: Faber & Faber Ltd. 1932. 8vo, xix, 645pp., map

2049 1939 ENG 31

Asahi, Isoshi. The Economic Strength of Japan
Tokyo: Hokuseido 1939. 8vo, xx, 323pp., charts, index; contents: an outline of the main changes that took place in Japanese trade and industry during the period 1930-1939, with particular attention to China's Open Door Policy

2050 1949 ENG 1178

Cohen, Jerome B. Japan's Economy in War and Reconstruction
Minneapolis: University of Minnesota Press 1949. small 4to, 545pp., ill., index; contents: numerous Korea entries

XI.c.4) KOREA

2051   1923   ENG 925
The Japan Times. Economic Development of Korea and Manchuria
Tokyo: Japan Times 1923. 4to, 319pp., ill.

2052   1926   ENG 172 (4 ex.)
Ireland, Alleyne. New Korea
NY: E.P. Dutton & Co. 1926. 8vo, xii, 354pp., map

2053   1944   ENG 298
Grajdanzev, Andrew J. Modern Korea. Her Economic and Social Development under the Japanese
NY: Institute of Pacific Relations 1944. 8vo, x, 330pp., bibliography, index

2054   1947   ENG 853
Shoemaker, James. Notes on Korea's Postwar Economic Position
NY: Institute of Pacific Relations, International Secretariat 1947. 4to, 29pp., typoscript, Secretariat Paper No.4

XI.d) ECONOMIC HISTORY

2055   1920   ENG 191 (3 ex.)
Bank of Chosen. Economic History of Chosen. Compiled on the Occasion of the Decennial of the Bank of Chosen
Seoul: Bank of Chosen 1920. 12mo, x, 268pp., ill., map, index

2056   1920   ENG 521
Bank of Chosen. Economic History of Manchuria. Compiled in Commemoration of the Decennial of the Bank of Chosen
Seoul: Bank of Chosen 1920. 12mo, 266pp., ill., index, appendices

2057   1946   ENG 1203
Allen, G.C. A Short Economic History of Japan, 1867-1937
London: George Allen & Unwin 1946. small 8vo, 200pp., index, several Korea entries

2058   1949   GER 181
Franke, Herbert. Geld und Wirtschaft in China unter der Mongolenherrschaft

[Money and Economy in China under Mongol Rule]
Wiesbaden: Harrassowitz 1949. 8vo, 171pp.

XI.e) AGRICULTURE, FORESTRY & FISHERY

2059　　　　　　　　　　　　　　　　1894　　　ENG 1418
Foreign Office (British). Corea. Report on the Cultivation of Cotton in Corea
London: HMSO 1894. 8vo, 4pp., Miscellaneous Series No.317

2060　　　　　　　　　　　　　　　　1904　　　GER 106
Brass, Emil. Nutzbare Tiere Ostasiens. Pelz- und Jagdtiere, Haustiere, Seetiere [Utilizable Animals of the Far East. Animals Prized for their Fur, Game, Domesticated Animals, Marine Animals]
Neudamm: J. Neumann 1904. small 8vo, 130pp.

2061　　　　　　　　　　　　　　　　1906　　　ENG 1418
Foreign Office (British). Corea. Report of the Result of Experiments in Cotton Culture in Corea. Diplomatic and Consular Reports. Cover tittle : Cotton Culture in Korea.
London : HMSO 1906. 8vo, 11pp., Diplomatic and Consular Reports No.654

2062　　　　　　　　　　　　　　　　1911　　ENG 190 (3 ex.)
King, F.H. Farmers of Forty Centuries or Permanent Agriculture in China, Korea and Japan
Madison, WS.: Mrs. F.H. King 1911. 12mo, ix, 441pp., ill., index; contents: on Korea pp.345-375

2063　　　　　　　　　　　　　　　　1912　　　ENG 549e2
Kains, M.G. Ginseng. Its Cultivation, Harvesting, Marketing and Market Value, with a short account of its History and Botany History and Botany
NY: Orange Judd Co., new edition, 1912. enlarged, 12mo, 144pp.

2064　　　　　　　　　　　　　　　　1913　　　GER 9
Hofmann, Amerigo. Aus den Waldungen des Fernen Ostens : Forstliche Reisen und Studien in Japan, Formosa, Korea und den angrenzenden Gebieten Ostasiens [From Far Eastern Forests : Forest Expeditions and Studies in Japan, Formosa, Korea and the Adjacent Areas of the Far East]

Wien etc.: Wilhelm Frick 1913. 8vo, viii, 225pp., ill., maps, ads; Gompertz 471; Domschke/Goossmann 470

2065   1923   ENG 462 Vol.XXXIX

Roxby, Percy M. Afforestation in Korea

in : The Scottish Geographical Magazine, vol.XXIX 1923 p.3-6

2066   1936   ENG 363 (3 ex.)

Lee, Hoon K. Land Utilization and Rural Economy in Korea. Report in the International Research Series of the Institute of Pacific Relations

Shanghai: Kelly & Walsh 1936. 8vo, 302pp., index, appendices

2067   1936   ENG 907

Ross, I. Clunies. A Survey of the Sheep and Wool Industry in North-Eastern Asia. With Special Reference to Manchukuo, Korea and Japan

Melbourne 1936. 8vo, 52pp., ill., maps

2068   1949   ENG 190e4

King, F.H. Farmers of forby Centuries : or Permanent Agriculture in China, Korea and Japan

London: Jonathan Cape (1927) 1949. 12mo, 379pp., index, 4th impression of the second edition of 1927. Edited by J.P. Bruce

XI.f) MINING, INDUSTRIES & TECHNOLOGY

2069   1914   ENG 1475

Seoul Mining Company. Tul Mi Chung Mine, Suan Mine, Collbran Contract. Consulting Engineer's Report

London: Waterlow & Son 1914. folio, 52pp.

2070   1922   ENG 532e2

Collins, William F. Mineral Enterprise in China

Tientsin: Tientsin Press (1918) 1922. 8vo, xiv, 410pp., appendix, index

2071   1925   ENG 425

Nishimura, Shinji. Ancient Rafts of Japan

Tokyo: Society of Naval Architects 1925. large 8vo, 180pp., ill., maps; Gompertz 1014

2072   1926   ENG 1236
Smith, Wilfred. A Geographical Study of Coal and Iron in China
Liverpool: UP 1926. 8vo, 83pp., map, index; contents: several Korea entries

2073   1927   ENG 248
Bain, H. Foster. Ores and Industries in the Far East : The Influence of Key Mineral Resources on the Development of Oriental Civilization
NY: Council on Foreign Relations 1927. 8vo, xii, 229pp., index. With a Chapter on Petroleum by W.B. Heroy. Preface by Edwin F. Gay

2074   1930   ENG 361
Orchard, John E. Japan's Economic Position : the Progress of Industrialization
NY: Whittlessey 1930. 8vo, 504pp., ill., maps, index, bibliography. With the collaboration of Dorothy Johnson Orchard. comment: author Columbia Univ. associated professor of Economic Geography

2075   1936   ENG 1221
Fujihara, Ginjiro. The Spirit of Japanese Industry＝工業日本精神
Tokyo: Hokuseido 1936. 8vo, 149pp., index; contents: several Korea entries

2076   1936   ENG 299
Mitsubishi Economic Research. Japanese Trade and Industry : Present and Future
London: Macmillan 1936. 8vo, 663pp., maps, index

2077   1938   ENG 680e2
Hubbard, G.E. Eastern Industrialization and its Effect on the West
Oxford: Oxford UP, London: Humphrey Milford (1935) 1938. 8vo, 418pp., bibliography, index. Conclusion by Professor T.E. Gregory, second edition, enlarged and revised

2078   1940   ENG 403
Schumpeter, E.B. The Industrialization of Japan and Manchukuo 1930-1940. Population, Raw Materials and Industry
NY: MacMillan 1940. 8vo, 944pp., index, appendix, glossary. Contributors G. Allen, M. Gordon, E. Penrose, A Harvard University, Bureau of International Research Publication

2079   1942   ENG 30
Mitchell, Kate L. Industrialization of the Western Pacific. Constituting Part III

of an Economic Survey of the Pacific Area
NY: Institute of Pacific Relations 1942. 8vo, xviii, 322pp., tables & map (I.P.R. Inquiry Series); contents: covers Japan, Korea, China, Southeast Asia, Australia, New Zealand and India.

2080 n.d. ENG 756
McCarthy, E.T. Further Incidents in the Life of a Mining Engineer
NY: E.P. Dutton & Co., n.d., 8vo, 400pp., index; contents: on Korea pp.194-257

XI.g) RAILWAY & TRANSPORTATION

2081 ENG 48 : 1916
Imperial Government Railways of Japan. (Also Privately-Owned Railways in Japan Proper and the South Manchuria Railway). Annual Report for the Year Ending March 31st 1916, English Edition.
Tokyo: Tokyo Tsukuji Type Foundry 1916. 4to, viii, 138pp., map; contents: also contains loose table of summary statistics for the year ending March 31st, 1917

2082 ENG 48 : 1923
Department of Railways, Government of Japan. Annual Report for the Year Ending March 31st 1923, English Edition
Tokyo: Tokyo Kenkyusha Printing Office 1923. 4to, vi, 97pp., map; contents: also contains loose table of summary statistics for the year ending March 31st 1924

2083 ENG 48 : 1935
Department of Railways, Government of Japan. Annual Report for the Year Ending March 31st, 1935. English Edition
Tokyo: Sanshusha Press 1935. large 8vo, viii, 321pp., chart, map

2084 1946 ENG 671
Korea. Seoul. Railroad Division. Department of Transportation. 1st May 1946, Schedule
Railroad Division, Seoul, Korea, 1946. 8vo, 74pp., index of destinations

XI.h) TRADE

2085 1847 ENG 1330 No.96
Palmer, Aaron H. Letter from the Secretary of State, Relative to the Productions, Trade and Commerce of the Oriental Nations with the United States
Washington: G.P.O. 1847. 8vo, 39pp., taken out of larger publication

2086 1894 ENG 1443
Agassiz, A.R. Our Commercial Relations with Chinese Manchuria
in : Journal of the Royal Geographic Society, 1894, pp.534-556

2087 1897 FRE 349
Anonymous. La Mission Lyonnaise d'Exploration Commerciale en Chine 1895-1897 [The Lyon Mission on the Commercial Exploration of China 1895-1897]
Lyon: A. Roy 1898. 4to, binding disintegrated, 4to, 473pp., ill., maps; contents: not on Korea

2088 1897 ENG 1418 (2 ex.)
Foreign Office (British). Miscellaneous Series. Reports on Subjects of General and Commercial Interest. Corea. Report on a Consular Journey to Ping-Yang and Chenampo. 1897
London : HMSO 1897. 8vo, 15pp., Miscellaneous Series No.433

2089 1901 ENG 164
Herod, Joseph Rogers. Favored Nation Treatment : An Analysis of the Most Favored Nation Clause, with Commentaries on its Uses in Treaties of Commerce and Navigation
NY: Banks Law 1901. 8vo, 136pp., index; contents: not on Korea

2090 1905 ENG 1139
Jernigan, T.R. China in Law and Commerce
London: MacMillan 1905. 8vo, 408pp., ads, index; contents: one Korea entry

2091 1906 GER 23
Passek, W. (ed.). Ein Deutscher Kaufmann in der Mandschurei : während des Russisch-Japanischen Krieges. Vol.1 of : Deutsche Kaufleute im Auslande.

Erfahrungen und Erlebnisse [A German Merchant in Manchuria, during the Russo-Japanese War. Vol.1 of : A German Merchant Abroad. Experiences and Adventures]
Berlin: Franz Siemenroth 1906. 8vo, vii, 186pp., ill., map

2092 1919 ENG 686
Irving National Bank. Trading with the Far East. How to sell in the Orient : Policies, Methods, Advertising, Credits, Financing, Documents, Deliveries.
NY: Irving National Bank [1919]. 12mo, 260pp., index

2093 1919 ENG 106 Vol.19
Dennett, Tyler. Business Side of Foreign Missions
in : Asia, The American Magazine on the Orient, vol.19, 1919, pp.687-691

2094 1931 ENG 1201
Utley, Freda. Lancashire and the Far East
London: George Allen & Unwin 1931. 8vo, 395pp., index; contents: 2 Korea entries

2095 1928 ENG 45
Thomas, James A. A Pioneer Tobacco Merchant in the Orient
Durham: Duke UP 1928. 8vo, 339pp., ill., index

2096 1930 ENG 606
Crocheron, B.H., Norton, W.J. Fruit Markets in Eastern Asia
Berkeley, CA: University of California Printing Office 1930. 8vo, 366pp., ill., Bulletin 493 (April 1930), contribution from the Giannini Foundation of Agricultural Economics

2097 1932 ENG 607e2
U.S. Department of Commerce, Bureau of Foreign and Domestic Commerce. Commercial Travelers' Guide to the Far East. Trade Promotion Series No.134
Washington: US GPO revised edition, 1932. 8vo, viii, 389pp., bibliography, index

2098 1936 ENG 299
Mitsubishi Economic Research. Japanese Trade and Industry. Present and Future
London: MacMillan 1936. 8vo, 663pp., maps, index

2099 1937 ENG 459e2

Greenbie, Sydney and Greemboe. Marjorie Barstow. Gold of Ophir : The China Trade in the Making of America
NY: Wilson-Erickson 1937. 8vo, xxii, 330pp., ill., bibliography, index

2100   n.d.   FRE 106
Matsuoka, Koji. L'etalon de change or en extreme-orient. Bibliotheque des sciences economiques franco-japonaises [The Standard of Gold Exchange in the Far East. Library of French-Japanese Economic Sciences]
Tokyo and Paris, n.d., small 8vo, 119pp.

XI.i) EXPOSITIONS

2101   1876   ENG 838
Leslie, Frank. Illustrated Historical Register to the Centennial Exposition 1876
folio, in box, 324pp.

2102   1900   FRE 171
Anonymous. Guide Lemercier publie par Les Concessionnaires du Catalorgue officiel Exposition Universelle de 1900.
Paris: Lemercier 1900. 12mo, 255pp., ill., maps, index; contents: on Korea p.226

2103   c.1900   FRE 41 : 1/2
Trousset, Jules. Les merveilles de l'exposition de 1900 [The Marvels of the Exposition of 1900]
Paris: Montgredien et Cie. n.d. (1900). 4to, 2 vols., 928, 800pp., ill., map

2104   c.1900   FRE 43
Gers, Paul. En 1900 [In 1900]
Corbeil: Ed. Crete, n.d. (c. 1900). 4to, 298pp.; contents: on Korea (Coree) pp.203-208

2105   c.1900   FRE 65
Quantin, J. L'exposition du siecle [The Exposition of the Century]
Paris: Le Monde Moderne, n.d., 4to, 367pp., ill., map

2106   c.1900   FRE 286
Anonymous. L'exposition de Paris 1900. Encyclopedie du siecle [The Paris

Exposition of 1900. Encyclopedia of the Century]
Paris: Montgredien et Cie., n.d. (c. 1900). folio, 3 vols., 324, 324, 320pp.; contents: on Korea vol.3 p.318

2107 1903 FRE 47
Raquez, A. Entree gratuite [Free Entry]
Saigon: Claude 1903. small 4to, 320pp., ill., catalogue on the Hanoi Exposition that year; contents: pp.48-50 relate to the Korea exhibit, with photo

2108 1915 ENG 835
Covertitle : San Francisco, Panama-Pacific International Exposition 1915. Views of China : P.P.I.E. 1915＝中國名勝.
no publisher, no place 1915. oblong 8vo, 53pp., ill., text in English and Chinese

2109 1915 ENG 672
H.I.J.M's Commission to the Panama-Pacific International Exhibition, San Francisco 1915. Japan as it is
Tokyo: Kokusai Tsushin-sa (International News Ageny). 1915. 8vo, 529pp.

2110 1915 ENG 278
Kyokwai, Hakurankwai. Japan and her Exhibits at the Panama-Pacific International Exhibition 1915
Tokyo: Societe des Expositions 1915. 12mo, 373pp., ill., map, index, 76pp., ads

XI.j) ECONOMY - OTHERS

2111 1901 ENG 204
Conant, Charles A. The United States and the Orient : the Nature of the Economic Problem
Boston: Houghton, Mifflin & Co. 1901. 12mo, x, 237pp., index

2112 1917 ENG 562
Kennan, George. E.H. Harriman's Far Eastern Plans.
Garden City: Country Life (1917). 12mo, 48pp., map. Harriman invested in Japan and its newly acquired territories

2113 1935 ENG 375e2
Stein, Guenther. Made in Japan
London: Methuen & Co. 1935. 8vo, ix, 206, 8pp. ads, ill.

XII.) RECREATION

XII.a) SPORTS

2114   1919   ENG 106 Vol.19
Andrew, Roy Chapman. Shooting Whales in the Far East
in : Asia. The American Magazine on the Orient Vol.19, 1919, pp.592-596

2115   1923   DEN 5
Madsen, Juel. Jagt og Krig [Hunt and War]
København: Nordisk Bokførlag 1923. large 8vo, 171pp.

2116   1924   ENG 106 Vol.24
Roosevelt, Kermit. After Tigers in Korea : An Elusive Hunt for the Finest of Their Race, in the Cold "Land of the Morning Calm"
In : Asia. he American Magazine on the Orient, Vol.24, 1924, pp.257-260

2117   1933   ENG 36
Bergman, Sten. Sports and Exploration in the Far East. A Naturalist's Experiences in and around the Kurile Islands.
London: Methuen & Co. 1933. 12mo, x, 246pp., ill., map, index, translated from the Swedish by Frederic Whyte

2118   n.d.   ENG 117
Spencer, Sidney (ed.). Mountaineering. The Lonsdale Library vol.18
Philadelphia: J.B. Lippincott, n.d. (c.1930es). 8vo, 383pp., ill., contains contributions by many authors. Includes two short articles by Walter Weston, one on Japan, the other on Korea.

XII.b) PHILATELY

2119   1923   FRE 24e27
Yvert & Tellier-Champion. Catalogue prin-courant de Timbres Poste [Catalogue of Stamps]
Paris: Yvert et Tellier 1923. 12mo, 1071pp., ads, xxxpp.; contents: Korea pp.237-239

XII.c) CUISINE

2120   1945   ENG 906
Bazore, Katherine. Hawaiian and Pacific Foods. A Cook Book of Culinary Customs and Recipes Adopted for the American Hostess.
NY: M. Barrows & Co. 1945. 8vo, 286pp., ill., index

XIII.) OTHERS

2121   1902   ENG 799
Lewis, Karl. Souvenir of the U.S.S. "Princeton", Asiatic Station, 1902
Yokohama: Karl Lewis 1902. oblong 8vo, 26pp., ill.

2122   1931   GER 34
Ross, Colin. Das Buch der fernen Welt. Asien, Afrika, Australien, Amerika [The Book of the Far World. Asia, Africa, Australia, America]
Berlin: Paul Franke 1931. 8vo, xvi, 336pp., ill., a collection of photos. contents: on Korea picture 41

2123   1946   ENG 182 (6 ex.)
Keith, Elizabeth. Old Korea : the Land of the Morning Calm
London etc.: Hutchinson 1946. 4to, 72pp., ill., pictures by Elizabeth Keith, text by her sister Elspet; Gompertz 1107

Chronological List of Titles published 1588-1850

1588	Maffei, G.P. : Selectarum epistolarum ex India	0780	LAT 7
1588	Mendoza, J.G. de : De'll Historia della China	0817	ITA 9
1589	Maffei, G.P. : Historiarum Indicarum libri XVI	0781	LAT 8
1598	Frois, L. : Ragguaglio della Morte di	0866	ITA 8
1598	Frois, L. : Giappone nel MDXCV al RP	0867	ITA 20
1599	Frois, L. : Trattado d'Alcuni prodigii	0868	ITA 13
1615	Jarric, P. du : Thesaurus Rerum Indicarum	1895	LAT 6
1617	Ricci, M. : Historia von der Einführung	1896	GER 119
1620	Orlandino, N. : Historiae Societatis Iesu	1897	LAT 10
1639	Ricci, M. : De Regno Chinae	0151	LAT 2
1641	Amiens, J. d' : Synopsis primi saeculi	1888	LAT 15
1652	Horn, G. : De Originibus Americanis Libri Quattuor	0755	LAT 14
1654	Martini, M. : De Bello Tartarico Historia	0818	LAT 3
1655	Mendoza, J.G. de : Rerum morumque in Regno Chinae	0819	LAT 1
1655	Martini, M. : Brevis Relatio de Numero et Qualitate	1898	LAT 3
1656	Martini, M. : Novus Atlas Absolutissimus	0054	GER 130
1658	Martini, M. : Sinicae historiae decas prima	0820	LAT 9
1665	Nieuhof, J. : Het Gezantschap der Nederlandtsche	0533	DUT 17
1665	Schall, J.A. : Historica Narratio de Initio et	1899	LAT 4
1666	Nieuhof, J. : Ambassade des Hollandois a la Chine	0534	FRE 317
1667	Kircher, A. : China monumentis qua sacris	0288	LAT 11
1668	Olearius, A. : Morgenländische Reisebeschreibung	0404	GER 123
1669	Kircher, A. : Special Remarks taken at large	0289	ENG 1439
1669	Nieuhof, J. : An Embassy of the East India Company	0535	ENG 1439
1670	Palafox, J. de : Histoire de la Conqueste	0821	FRE 180
1672	Arnold, Chr. : Wahrhaftige Beschreibungen	0119	GER 83
1673	Rougemont, F. de : Historia Tartaro-Sinica	0822	LAT 5
1692	The Voyages and Travels of Ferdinand	0405	ENG 813
1693	Nieuhof, J. : Het Gezantschap der Nederlandtsche	0536	DUT 17
1698	Le Comte, L. : Memoirs and Observations	0537	ENG 1473

1698	Morery, L. : Le Grand Dictionnaire Historique	0756	FRE 280
1701	Carletti, Francesco : Ragionamento	0343	ITA 6
1707	Pflug, H.O. : Den Danske Pillegrim	0100	DEN 10
1715	Bernard, J.F. : Recueil de Voyages au Nord	0329	FRE 260
1715	Crasset : Histoire de l'Eglise du Japon	1900	FRE 277
1727	Huet, M. : Histoire du Commerce et de la	0757	FRE 346
1729	Salmon, Th. : Hedendaagsche Historie of	0782	DUT 15
1729	Moubach, O. : Zesde Verhandeling over de	1856	DUT 16
1731	Picart, B.: The Ceremonies and Religious	1857	ENG 817
1732	Kämpfer, Engelbert : Histoire naturelle	0869	FRE 312
1735	Salmon, Th. : Hedendaagsche Historie of	0783	DUT 15
1736	Charlevoix, P.F.X. de : Histoire et description	0870	FRE 188
1737	Anville, J.B. d' : Nouvel Atlas de la Chine	0055	FRE 287
1738	Crasset, J. : Geschicht der in dem Äussersten	1901	GER 108
1740	Buffier, P. : Mouveaux Elements d'Histoire	0101	FRE 345
1741	Halde, P. de : General History of China	0823	ENG 584
1741	Moshemii, L. : Historia Tartarorum Ecclesiastica	1902	LAT 13
1742	Maffei, G.P. : Opera Omnia	0784	LAT 12
1744	Churchill's Voyages	0330	ENG 1285
1745	Astley, Th. : A New General Collection of	0331	ENG 570
1749	Exiles, A.F. Prevost d' : Histoire Generale des	0332	FRE 261
1750	Schwabe, J.J.: Allgemeine Historie der Reisen	0333	GER 117
1754	Samling af alle Rejsebeskrivelser	0334	DEN 2
1754	Brunem, V. de : Histoire de la Conquete	0824	FRE 219
1755	Rollin, M. : The History of China upon the Plan	0825	ENG 1423
1755-78	Rollin, M. : Histoire Moderne des Chinois	0785	FRE 340
1756-58	Deguignes, M. : Histoire Generale des Huns	0787	FRE 337
1759	The Modern Part of the Universal History	0759	ENG 580
1764	Semler, J.S. : Allgemeine Geschichte der	0788	GER 153
1766	Argens, Marquis J.B.B. d' : Lettres Chinoises	1714	FRE 262
1771	Voyage de Mons. Olof Toree	0538	FRE 339
1772	Delaporte : le Voyageur François	1715	FRE 264

1776-86	Missionaires de Pekin : Memoires Concernant	0048	FRE 283
1787	Grosier : Description Generale de la Chine	0152	FRE 28
1788	Tableau de l'Univers ou Geographie Universelle	0102	FRE 270
1790	Lesseps, J.B.B. Baron de : Journal Historique	0406	FRE 338
1792	Borheck, A.C. : Erdbeschreibung von Asien	0120	GER 69
1792	Forster, J.R. : Karl Peter Thunbergs Reisen	0606	GER 140
1792-94	Karl Peter Thunbergs Reise durch einen Theil von	0605	GER 190
1795	A Compendious Geographical Dictionary	0064	ENG 864
1796	Mavor, W. : Historical Account of the Most	0335	ENG 803
1796	Anderson, A. : Relation de l'Ambassade du Lord	0539	FRE 275
1797	Milet-Mureau, M.L.A. : Voyage de La Perouse	0407	FRE 278
1798	Milet-Mureau, M.L.A. : Voyage de La Perouse	0408	FRE 33
1798	Staunton, G. : An Authentic Account of an Embassy	0540	ENG 125
1798	Staunton, G. : Voyage dans l'interieur de la Chine	0541	FRE 274
1799	Resa omkring Jorden af Herr de la Perouse	0409	SWE 12
1800	Pennant, Th. : The Outlines of the Globe	0121	ENG 569
1800	Jean-François Galoup de la Perouse, Entdeckungs	0410	GER 118
1801	Laurie, R., Whittle, J.. : The Oriental Navigator	0081	ENG 908
1803	Pimentel, M.L. : Tribulaciones de los fieles	1903	SPA 4
1804	Broughton, W.R. : A Voyage of Discovery of the	0411	ENG 775
1805	Sprengel / Ehrmann : Bibliothek der Neuesten	0336	GER 125
1807	Broughton, W.R. : Voyage de Decouvertes dans	0412	FRE 265
1806	Pinkerton, J. : Modern Geography	0103	ENG 967
1808	Gouvea, A. de : Carta do excellentissimo	1915	POR 4
1809	Thunberg, K.P. : Thunberg's Voyages	0607	ENG 576
1810	Levis, M. de : Les voyages de Kang-Hi	1716	FRE 269
1811	Djurberg, D.: Geografiskt Lexicon	0065	SWE 9
1812	Lindner, F.L. : Neueste Länder- und Völkerkunde	0122	GER 110
1817	M'Leod, J.: Narrative of a Voyage in His Majesty's	0413	ENG 169
1817	Ellis, H. : Journal of the Proceedings of the late	0542	ENG 814
1818	M'Leod, J.: Narrative of a Voyage in His Majesty's	0414	ENG 169
1818	Hall, Basil : Account of a Voyage of Discovery	0415	ENG 567
1818	MacLeod, J. : Voyage du Capitaine Maxwell	0416	FRE 271

1818	Grosier, J.B. : De la Chine, ou Description	0153	FRE 28
1819	M'Leod : Voyage of his Majesty's Ship Alceste	0417	ENG 169
1819	Bauer, J.Chr.A. : Alexander Selkirchs sällsamma	1717	SWE 6
1820	McLeod, J. : Capitaine Maxwells Resa på Gula Havet	0418	SWE 3
1820	Hall, B. : Relazione d'un viaggio di scoperte alla	0419	ITA 2
1822	Hassel, G. : Vollständiges Handbuch der	0123	GER 26
1822	Zimmermann, E.A.W. : Jorden och dess Invånare	0124	SWE 7
1822	Manchao to Canton. Voyages and Travels	0543	ENG 431
1823	Vosgien : Dictionnaire Geographique	0066	FRE 263
c. 1823	Sage, A. le : Atlas Historique, Geographique	0056	FRE 298
1824	Stein, Chr.G.D. : Handbuch der Geographie und	0104	GER 136
since 1825	Annales de la Propagation de Foi	1884	FRE 16
1826	Palmblad, V.F. : Handbok I Physiska och Politiska	0105	SWE 2
1826	Dufay, J.: Bibliotheque Universelle des Voyages	0337	FRE 187
1827	Virtue, G. : The New London Universal Gazetteer	0067	ENG 483
1827	Brookes, R. : The General Gazetteer	0068	ENG 1090
1827	Timkovski, G. : Voyage a Peking a travers la	0420	FRE 268
1827	Timkovski, G. : Travels of the Russian Mission	0421	ENG 811
1827	Constable's Miscellany of Original and Selected	0422	ENG 1417
1829	Briand, P.C.: Les Jeunes Voyageurs en Asie	0338	FRE 250
1830	Ferraro, G. : I Costume Antico e Moderno	0701	ITA 1
1832	Hyakinth, A. : Denkwürdgkeiten über die	0573	GER 121
1832	San Kokf Tsou Ran To Sets, ou Aperçu General	0125	FRE 330
1832	Siebold, Ph.Fr. von : Nippon. Archief voor de	0195	DUT 18
1832	Gutzlaff, Ch. : Remarks on the Corean Language	1666	ENG 126
1832-51	Chinese Repository	0025	ENG 126
1833	Gutzlaff, Ch. : Journal of Two Voyages	0544	ENG 156
1833	Papers Relating to the Voyage undertaken by	0545	ENG 943
1833	Gutzlaff, Ch. : The Corean Syllabory	1667	ENG 126
since 1833	The Asiatic Journal and Monthly Register	0024	ENG 1458
1834	Brookes, R. : The London General Gazetteer	0069	ENG 1025
1834	Gutzlaff, Ch. : Journal of Three Voyages	0546	ENG 156

1834	Gutzlaff, Ch. : Journal of Three Voyages	0546	ENG 157
1834	Lindsay, H.H. : Report of the Proceedings on a	0548	ENG 496
1834	Schall, J.A. von : Geschichte der Chinesischen	1904	GER 124
1836	Foe Koue Ki, or Relation des Royaumes	1865	FRE 324
1837	Pauthier, M.G. : L'Univers Histoire est	0826	FRE 58
1838	Medhurst, W.H. : China. Its State and Prospects	0154	ENG 1270
1839	Eyries, J.B. : Voyage en Asie et en Afrique	0339	FRE 181
1839	Ennery & Hirth : Dictionnaire General de	0070	FRE 334
1840	Hall, B. : Narrative of a Voyage to Java, China	0423	ENG 1359
1841	Davis, J.F. : China en de Chinezen	0155	DUT 5
1841	Siebold, Ph.Fr. von : Manners and Customs of	0702	ENG 694
1842	Langdon, W.B. : Ten Thousand Things Relating to	0049	ENG 1224
1843	Allom, Th. : L'Empire Chinois	0290	FRE 282
since 1843	Illustrated London News	0012	ENG 795
1846	Balbi, A. : Abrege de Geographie	0106	FRE 279
1846	El Globo. Costumbres, Usos y Trajes de Todos	0703	SPA 1
1847	Martin, R.M. : China Political, Commercial and	0156	ENG 812
1847	Palmer, A.H. : Letter from the Secretary of State	2085	ENG 1330
1848	Gaultier : Elements de Geographie	0107	FRE 173
1848	Belcher, E. : Narrative of a Voyage of H.M.S.	0424	ENG 750
1849	Lowrie, W.M. : Memoirs of the Rev. Walter	1594	ENG 350

Index of Persons

Abend, Hallett	1062, 1077, 1633	Andrews, Roy Chapman	0382, 0398, 2114
Abraham, J. Johnston	0354	Anesaki, Masaharu	1878
Abshagen, Karl Heinz	1637	Anethan, Albert d'	1612
Adachi, Kinnosuke	0183, 1776	Angier, A. Gordon	0987
Adams, Arthur	0430	Anville, Jean Baptiste d'	0055
Adams, Brooke	0763	Appenzeller, Horace G.	1560
Agassiz, A.R.	2086	Appert, C.	1564
Akagi, Roy Hidemichi	0897	Argens, Marquis J.B. Boyer	1714
Akimoto, Shunkichi	0312	Armstrong, Robert Cornell	1874
Alcock, Sir Rutherford	1595	Arnold, Christoph	0119
Aleveque, Charles	1671	Arnold, Sir Edwin	0348
Allan, James	1392	Arnous, H.G.	1697
Allen, Bernard M.	1544	Arsenjew, Wladimir K.	0604
Allen, G.C.	2057	Asahi, Isoshi	2049
Allen, G.	2078	Asakawa, K.	0979, 0980, 1175, 1176, 1220, 1395, 1413, 1414
Allen, Horace N.	0050a, 1582, 1696, 1744		
Allen, Nellie B.	0140		
Allen, William C.	0476	Ashmead-Bartlett, Ellis	1461
Allix, Andre	2041	Asiaticus	1471
Allom, Thomas	0290, 0291	Astley, Thomas	0331
Allou	0572	Aston, W.G.	0747, 1698
Amar, Isaac A.	1016	Atwell, William Hawley	0399, 0493
Amezua y Mayo, Agustin G. de	0009	Auanzo, Francesco	0817
Amiens, Jacques d'	1888	Aubigne, Maurice d'	1624
Anderson, Aenaeas	0539	Aubry, J.B.	1596
Anderson, Isabel	1618	Auden, W.H.	1053
Anderson, J.H.	1477	Audsley, George A.	1818
Anderson, William	1813	Aunis, R. d'	0243, 0245
Andersson, J. Gunnar	1156	Austin, Major Herbert H.	0461

Austin, Oliver L.	1998	Barstow, Marjorie	1348, 2099
Ayres, Christovam	0878	Barton, Rexford W.	0517
Backhausen, Alfred	1342	Barzini, Luigi	1453
Backhouse, E.	0836, 1121, 1150	Bashford, James W.	1652
Bacon, Alice Mabel	1467, 2002	Basil, George C.	1731
Bain, H. Foster	2073	Batalha, Ladislao	1654
Baird, Annie L.A.	1672, 1676, 1747	Bau, Mingchien Joshua	0838
Baker, John Earl	1137	Bauer, Joh. Chr. Aug.	1717
Baker, Newton D.	2042	Bauer, K. Jack	1384
Baker, Samuel W.	1983	Baumont, Maurice	0947
Balbi, Adrien	0106	Bazalgette, L.	0671
Baldridge, Cyrus le Roy	1619, 1634	Bazore, Katherine	2120
Balet, J.C.	0185, 0715, 0716, 1337, 1344, 1411, 1440	Beach, Harlan P.	1931
		Beaton, Cecil	0524
		Beaton, Maude Hill	0397
Balfour, Frederic Henry	0790	Beaumont, Maurice	0779
Balfour, Marshall C.	1981	Beckmann, Frank Harrison	0516
Balincourt, Commandant de	1483	Beguin, C.	1412
Ball, J. Dyer	0052	Bei-Sen	1390
Ballard, G.A.	0889	Belcher, Edward	0424
Ballard, Susan	1613	Bell, Archie	0565, 0622
Bälz, Erwin	0922, 0923, 1261, 1623	Bell, H.T. Montague	2012
		Bell, John, Esq.	0335
Bamberger, Gustav	0379	Bellessort, Andre	0223, 0478, 0492
Bancroft, Hubert Howe	0968	Benitez, C.	0805
Barber, Noel	1312	Benson, Stella	0374, 0381, 1759, 1770
Baring, Maurice	1428		
Barnard, H. Clive	0724	Benyowski, Mauritius	
Barnes, Annie M.	1607, 1742	Augustus Count de	0451
Barnes, Joseph	1036	Berard, Victor	1201
Barrow, George de S.	1625	Berdrow, Wilhelm	0328
Barrows, John Henry	1858	Beresford, Charles	1098
Barry, Richard	1424	Bergen, R. van	0874

Berger, A.	0363		1037, 1550
Bergman, Sten	0690, 0696,	Boecher, Herbert	1624
	1995, 1996, 2117	Bonnetain, Paul	0129
Bering, Vitus	1593	Borg, Karl Friedrich von der	0573
Bern, Gregory	0945	Borheck, August Christian	0120
Bernard, Jean Frederic	0329	Borland, Beatrice	0510
Bernard, Henri O.S.J.	0901	Borton, Hugh	1306
Bernoulli, Rudolf	1816	Boucher, Andre	1893
Beuer, H.O.	0805	Bouillet, M.N.	0071
Beveridge, Albert J.	1199	Boulanger, Jacques	0507
Bickersteth, Edward	1557	Boulger, Demetrius Charles	0830
Bickersteth, Samuel	1557	Bourdaret, Emile	0659, 0711,
Bigelow, Poultney	0625		0712, 0713,
Bigham, Clive	1103		0918, 0919, 1861
Binyon, Laurence	1815	Bowes, James L.	1818
Birch, John Grant	0563	Boxer, C.R.	0893
Bishop, Carl Whiting	0812	Boyer, W.J.	1973
Bishop, Isabella L. Bird	0287, 0558,	Braga, Theofilo	1654
	0613, 0657,	Brandt, Max von	0960, 0961, 0969
	0658, 0669, 1585	Branom, Frederick K.	0063
Bisson, T.A.	1057, 1083, 1296	Brasil, Jaime	1289
Bitchurin, Nikita Yakovlevich	0573	Brass, Emil	2060
Blacker, J.F.	1822	Brassey, Lord	0929
Blackett, P.M.S.	1519	Bray, F.E.	1486
Blackie, W.G.	0073	Bredon, Juliet	0297
Blakeslee, Prof. George H.	0809, 0992	Breit, Josef	1484
Blakeney, William	0444	Bres, H.S.	0114
Bland, J.O.P.	0836, 1010,	Bretenieres, Just de	1553, 1555,
	1121, 1150, 1537		559, 1564, 1566
Blutel, Fernand	1720	Breuer, A.	1793
Bockenheimer, Ph.	0462	Briand, P.C.	0338
Bodley, R.V.C.	0401, 0632,	Brieux	0472

Brinkley, Captain F. R.A.	0204, 0873, 0876, 0883	Bushell, Stephen W.	1803, 1821
		Buskirk, James Dale van	0259
Bristol, Horace	1366	Buss, Claude A.	1067
Brodrick, Alan Houghton	0147	Butler, Frank Hedges	0375
Brooke, Lord	1427	Butler, Harold Beresford	0937
Brookes, R.	0068, 0069	Buxton, Barclay F.	1614
Brosius, Hans	1093	Buxton, L.H. Dudley	0175, 0485, 0729
Broughton, William Robert	0336, 0411, 0412	Byes, Hugh	1313
Broussenard, Louis	0580	Bywater, Hector C.	1516
Brown, Arthur Judson	0138, 1001, 1107, 1114, 1258	Cable, Boyd	0810
		Cable, Mildred	1653
Brown, Frank L.	0474	Campbell, Charles W.	0643, 0645, 0646
Browne, Brevet-Colonel, G.F.	1174	Campbell, Gordon, Vice Admiral	0775
Browne, George Waldo	0294		
Bruce, J.P.	2068	Campbell, P.D.	0561
Bruggen, C.J.A. van	1497	Canera, Carl	1394
Brunem, Vojeu de, O.S.J. (Jouve de Embrun)	0824	Canning-Wright, H.W.	1839
		Carles, W.R.	0240, 0640, 1598
Bryan, William Jennings	0352	Carletti, Francesco	0343, 0396
Bryce, Viscount	0795	Caron, François	0329, 0404
Bryois, Henry	1531	Carpenter, Frances	1710
Büchler, E.	0369	Carpenter, Frank G.	0134, 0568, 0628, 0629
Buck, Pearl S.	1074, 1733		
Buckle, Earl George	1541	Carpenter, Frank N.	0743
Buffier, P., O.S.J.	0101	Carr, Harry	1040
Buhot, Jean	1809	Carrington, Dorothy	0402
Bujac, E.	1509	Carter, Dagny	1807
Bunker, Frank F.	0142	Carter, Thomas Francis	0839
Bunsen, Marie von	0512	Cary, Otis	0875
Bure, Hallie	1772	Cassel, Hjalmar	0982
Burleigh, Bennet	1434	Castera, J.	0541
Burow, G.	0698	Causton, Eric E.	1287
Buschan, Georg	0727, 0736, 0900	Cavendish, A.E.J.	0648, 0649

Chablie, Jacques-Edouard	0383	Chisholm, Helen	0598
Chadourne, Marc	0391	Chisholm, William H.	1627
Chaille-Long	0650, 1331, 1586	Choutze, T.	0554
		Christie, Dugald	1562, 1571
Challaye, Felicien	0304, 1727	Chu, Yosup	1771
Chalux	1049	Chung, Henry	1244, 1349, 1353, 1364
Chamberlain, Basil Hall	0050, 0051, 0301, 0302, 1659	Clarette Henry	1228
		Clark, Charles Allen	1965, 1968
Chamberlin, William Henry	1295	Clark, James Hyde	0162
Chang, Chung-Fu	1259	Clarke, Joseph I.C.	1238
Chang, K.	0741	Clement, Ernest Wilson	0209
Chang Tso-Lin	1624	Clewell, Gladys D.	0734
Chantre, E.	0711	Clodd, Edward	1644
Chapman, J.W.	1973	Close, Upton	1273
Chargebeouf	1575	Clough, Ethlyn T.	0139
Charlevoix, L.	1905	Clune, Frank	0522
Charlevoix, Pierre-François-Xavier de, O.S.J.	0870	Clyde, Paul Hibbert	1178
		Coatsworth, Elizabeth J.	0682
Charmelin, Andre	1976	Cocks, Richard	0341
Chassiron, Ch. de	0953	Cohen, Jerome B.	2050
Chauvelot, Robert	0497	Cohn, William	1870
Cheradamue, Andre	1459	Cole, Taylor	1088
Chester, Wilfred L.	1155	Coleman, Frederic	0999
Chevalier, Henri	0753, 0917	Collier, D.M.B.	0187, 0188
Chi, Tsui	0851	Collier, Price	0993
Chiang, Kai-Shek	1168, 1545, 1546	Collins, Gilbert	0484
		Collins, Major Perry	0595
Chiang, Monlin	1167	Collins, William F.	2070
Chiang, Yee	1805	Collis, Maurice	1732
Childers, James Saxon	0500	Colquhoun, Archibald Ross	0556, 1116
Chirol, Valentine	0958	Comfort, Mildred Houghton	0519

Comte (Compte), Louis le, O.S.J.	0335, 0537	Croises, Feux	0691
		Croly, Herbert	1590
Conant, Charles A.	2111	Crouch, Archie R.	1626
Conger, Sarah Pike	1110	Crow, Carl	0295, 1311
Cook, Thomas	0279, 0280	Culin, Stewart	1831, 1834, 1836
Cordier, Henri	0002, 0003, 0058, 0801, 0857, 0915, 1102	Cutlack, F.M.	1193
		Cumming, C.F. Gordon	0557
		Curtis, Lionel	1148
Cordonnix	1460	Curzon, George N.	0955, 0959, 1542, 1620
Corfe, C.J.	1955		
Cornish, Vaughan	0117	Dallet, Ch.	1916
Corribe, Ed.	1269	Dallin, David	1207
Cosenza, Mario Emilio	1622	Daly, Mrs. de Burgh	1611
Coste, Eugene	0706	Daniel, Franz	0604
Cotes, Everard	0984	Darwent, C.E.	0296
Coubertin, Pierre de	0816	Das, Taraknath	1045
Couchoud, Paul Louis	1712	Datta, S.K.	1031
Coulson, Constance C.D.	0676	Dautremer, Joseph	2044, 2045
Courant, Maurice	0001, 0315, 0916, 1643	Daveluy	1552
		David, F.D.	0263
Cowen, Thomas	1403	David, Madeleine	1812
Cowman, Charles E.	1581	Davidson, Augusta M. Campbell	0219
Cowman, Lettie B.	1581, 1941		
Cox, Warren E.	1829	Davidson, Norman J.	0367
Cradock, Lt. C.	0433	Davidson, St. Clair	1948
Crane, Florence Hedleston	1992	Davis, F. Hadland	0884, 1700
Cranmer-Byng	1808	Davis, George T.B.	1960
Cranston, E.	1973	Davis, John Francis	0155, 0160
Crasset, O.S.J.	1900, 1901	Decourcelle, Claudine	1767
Creelman, James	0930	Deguignes, M.	0787
Cressey, George B.	0176	Delage, Edmond	0774
Crewe, Marquess of	1592	Delaporte	1715
Crocheron, B.H.	2096	Delpech, Jacques	1882

Demange, Msr.	1577	Ducrocq, Georges	0660, 0661
Demays, V.	0244	Dufay, Jules	0337
Dening, Walter	1526	Duffy, Gavan	1575
Dennett, Tyler	1000, 1013, 2093	Dupont, Maurice	1782, 1838
Dennis, Alfred P.	1252	Dutcher, George Matthew	1021
Dennis, James S.	1930	Dyer, Henry	1227, 1230
Deutsch, Leo	0598	Eckardt, Andreas O.S.B.	1677, 1678, 1708, 1774, 1810, 1811
Dickinson, J.H.	1451		
Dickson, Walter	0871		
Diffendorfer, Ralph E.	1584, 1938	Eckel, Paul E.	0814
Dilts, Marion May	1301	Eden, Charles H.	0197, 0292, 0293
Diosy, Arthur	0967, 0974, 1445	Eddy, Sherwood	0997, 1030, 1949
Dirr, Adolf	0880	Eggleston, Margaret W.	1939
Dix, Dorothy	0372	Ehlers, Otto Ehrenfried	0438
Dixon, G.C.	0489	Ehrmann, Theophil Friedrich	0336
Djurberg, Daniel	0065	Eickstedt, Egon Freiherr von	0740
Doegen, Wilhelm	0730	Eldridge, F.R.	1266, 1317
Dollin, David J.	0941	Elgin, Lord	0550, 0552
Domschke, R. Andreas	0010b	Elia, Pascal M. d'	1911
Donnet, Gaston	1409	Elias, Frank	0274
Dorosh, Elizabeth Gardner	0010	Eliot, Charles W.	0998
Dorosh, John T.	0010	Ellis, Henry	0542
Douglas, Robert K.	0793, 0797, 0832, 0833, 0834, 1532	Ellis, W., Rev.	0546, 0547
		Elliston, Herbert B.	1180
		Elwell-Sutton, A.S.	0847
Drage, Geoffrey	1200	Embree, John F.	2011
Drake, Henry Burgess	0258	Ennery	0070
Draner	1511	Epstein, Israel	1157, 1169
Dubosq, Andre	0236, 0529, 1055, 1061, 1072, 1133	Erdman, Charles R.	0483
		Escarra, Jean	1189, 1329
		Escayrac de Lauture, Comte d'	0159
Duchesne, E.	1485	Etherton, P.T.	1191

Etlin, P. Lukas	1570	Fleure, H.J.	0118
Eude, Robert	2015	Fochler-Hauke, Gustav	0189
Evans, Roger F.	1981	Foote, Rose F.	1538
Everett, Marshall	1444	Forbes, Frances Blackwell	1982
Evliya Effendi	0344	Ford, John D.	0439, 0453
Exiles, A.F. Prevost d'	0332	Forman, Harrison	0395
Exner, A.H.	0619	Formin, Victor	0723
Eyries, J.B.	0339	Förster, C.F.	1793
Fahs, Charles H.	1006	Forster, Johann Reinhold	0606
Fairbanks, Ch.W.	1973	Foster, Mrs. Arnold	0559
Fairfax, Virginia	1772	Foster, John W.	0973, 1615
Falk, Edwin A.	1285	Foster, Lancelot	1152
Fallex, M.	0135	Fox, Harry H.	0247
Farrer, Reginald J.	1603	Fowler-Willing, Jennie	1962
Farrere, Claude	0362, 0486, 0502, 1050, 1060, 1478, 1854	Franck, Harry A.	0635
		Frandin, Hippolyte	0641, 0699, 0700
		Frank, Harry A.	0566
Fawcett, C.B.	0116	Franke, Herbert	2058
Fay, Sidney Bradshaw	0935	Franke, O.	0994, 1017
Feddersen, Martin	1789	Fraser, David	1438
Fenollosa, Ernest F.	1784	Fraser, John Foster	0191
Ferraro, Giulio	0701	Frederic, Henry	1597
Field, Frederick V.	2042	Fremantle, Francis	0357
Figulla, H.H.	1682	French, Francesca	1653
Findlay, Alexander George	0084	Fries, Sigmund Ritter von	0829
Fischer, Otto	1790	Froc, Louis O.S.J.	0748
Fisher, Galen, M.	1253	Frois, Luigi O.S.J.	0341, 0866, 0867, 0868
Fitzgerald, C.R.	0846		
Fitzroy	0345	Fujihara, Gunjiro	1288
Fleming, George	0574	Fujikawa, Ginjiro	2075
Fleming, Peter	0594	Fujikawa, Y.	1974
Fletcher, Alfred C.B.	0366	Fujisawa, Rikitaro	1251

Gale, James Scarth	0247, 0925, 1601, 1604, 1670, 1674, 1679, 1701, 1704, 1743, 1959	Gleason, George	1245
		Gleichen-Russwurm, Alexander von	0744
		Glover, G.B.	1833
		Goan, Elizabeth	0725
Galli, Henri	1442, 1494	Goch, M. van	0782
Ganthorne-Hardy, G.M.	0950	Goette, John	1327
Gardner, Christopher Thomas	0247	Goldenring, Stefania	0672
Gardner, George Peabody	0470	Goldie, F.	1917, 1918
Gascoyne-Cecil, Lord William	1112, 1113	Goldschmidt, Richard	0630
Gaubil, A., O.S.J.	0915	Gompertz, G. StG. M.	0010a
Gaultier, l'Abbe	0107	Gonnel, Suzanne	0532
Gay, Edwin F.	2073	Gontscharow, Iwan A.	0490
Gayn, Mark J.	1066, 1636	Good, Dorothy	0232
Geden, Alfred S.	1860	Goold-Adams, H.E.	0648
Geneix, F.	1493	Goossmann, Rudolf	0010b
Genghis Khan	1527	Gordon, E.A.	1936
Gent, F.C.	0405	Gordon, Mrs. E.A.	0679
Genthe, Siegfried	0668	Gordon, M.	2078
Gerard, Auguste	0224, 1849	Gorst, Harold E.	0164
Gers, Paul	2104	Gottsche, C.	0745
Gibbons, Herbert Adams	0141	Gouvea, Alexandre de	1915
Gibbs, Philip	0268	Gowen, Herbert H.	0835, 0892, 0896
Gibson, O.	1377	Gowing, Lionel F.	0596
Gifford, Daniel L.	2001	Gracey, J.T.	1927
Gilbert, Rodney	1134, 1142	Grajdanzev, Andrew J.	2053
Giles, Herbert A.	1115	Grande, Julien	1269, 1270
Gillis, L.V.	1691, 1692	Grant, R.	1468
Gilmore, Florence	1564	Grant, Ulysses S.	0347
Gilmore, G.W.	0241	Grantham, A.E.	0841
Girard, O.	1651	Graul, Richard	1783
Glaser, Curt	1786	Graves, Joseph Waddington	1351

Graves, Louis	1539, 1589	Guerreiro, Pelo Fernao O.S.J.	0770
Grebst, W. A:son	0677	Guerville, A.B. de	0614
Greey, Edward	0612	Guimet, Emile	0610
Green, A. Wigfall	1374	Gull, E. Manico	1144
Green, O.H.	1163	Gundert, Wilhelm	1863
Green, O.M.	0850	Gundry, R.S.	0161
Greenbie, Sydney	1075, 1348, 2099	Gunther, John	1059, 1071
		Gurney, W.N.	1588
Greener, William	1428	Guthapfel, Minerva L.	1752
Gregory, T.E.	2077	Guzlaff, Karl	0544, 0545, 0546, 0547, 0548, 0549, 0827, 1666, 1667
Grenfell, Sir Wilfred Thomason	0498		
Grew, E. Sharpe	1495		
Grew, Joseph C.	0466, 1632		
Griffin, Gerald	0514		
Griffis, William Elliot	0196, 0216, 0238, 0887, 0913, 0963, 1233, 1560, 1699, 1703, 1859	Gwynn, Stephen	1543
		Habersham, A.W.	0425
		Hackmann, H.	0475
		Hagemann, Walter	1023
		Hagen, A.	0667
		Hagen, Gräfin M. von	1536
Griscom, Lloyd C.	1631	Haguenauer, M.C.	1681, 1877
Griswold, A. Whitney	1052	Halde, Peter du, O.S.J.	0335, 0823
Grootcurd, Christian Heinrich	0605	Halkin, Joseph	0447
Grosier, J.B.	0152, 0153	Hall, Basil	0345, 0415, 0419, 0422, 0423
Grosse, Ernst	1840		
Grousset, Rene	0800, 0808, 1792, 1796, 1812		
		Hall, Josef Washington	1525
		Hall, Mary Daniels	0403
Grünau, Freiherr von	0656	Hallett, Holt S.	0962
Grünfeld, Ernst	0996	Hallowell, John H.	1088
Gubbins, J.H.	1250	Hamel, Hendrik	0256, 0329, 0330, 0334
Gubernatis, A. de	0704		
Guebriant, Mgr. de	0508	Hamilton, Alexander	0503

Hamilton, Angus	0255, 0662, 0663, 0664, 0670, 0671, 0989	Hawks, Francis L.	0608
		Hayashi, Count Tadasu	1535, 1609
		Hayata, B.	1974
Hamilton, Ian	1466, 1482	Headland, Isaac Taylor	1117
Hammerton, J.A.	0078, 0717, 0726, 0733, 0742, 0766	Hearn, Lafcadio	0213, 1600
		Hedemann, C.J.	1841
		Hedin, Sven	0358, 0569, 0859, 1545, 1868
Han-Ko	1390		
Hannah, Ian C.	0792, 0796	Hellwald	0705
Hanstein, Otfrid von	0681	Helmolt, H.F.	0794
Hare, James H.	1420	Hendley, Charles M.	0487
Haring, Douglas Gilbert	0631	Henrion, Baron de	1889
Harmsworth, Cecil	0370	Hentgen, A.	0135
Harmsworth	0765	Hepner, Charles William	1879
Harmsworth, St. John	0370	Herbert, Agnes	0685, 1755
Harriman, E.H.	2112	Herlihy, Francis	1638
Harrington, Fred H.	1582	Herod, Joseph Rogers	2089
Hart	1583	Heroy, W.B.	2073
Harris, Audrey	0520	Hertslet, Edward	1095
Harris, M.C.	1973	Hesse-Wartegg, Ernst von	0615, 0651
Harris, Norman Dwight	1009	Hett, G.V.	0689, 0737
Harris, Townsend	1622	Hildreth, Richard	1222
Harrison, E.J.	0991	Hillier, Sir Walter	0657, 1661
Harrison, Marguerite	1025	Hirth	0070
Hart, Albert Bushnell	0356	Hishida, Seiji G.	1223, 1305
Hart, E.I.	1563	Hobson, R.L.	1823, 1825, 1830a
Hartshorne, Anna C.	0207		
Hassel, G.	0123	Hodge, John R.	0697
Hatch, Ernest F.G.	0450	Hodgkin, Henry T.	0173
Hattis, Walter B.	0511	Hoetinck, B.	0256
Haushofer, Karl	1290, 1310	Hoffmann, Heinrich	1846
Hawes, Charles H.	0597, 0600, 0602	Hoffmann, Ludwig	1846

Hofmann, Amerigo	2064	Hughes, E.R.	0848
Holcombe, Arthur N.	1145	Hughes, William	0127
Holland, Philemon	0762, 0771	Hugon, Joseph O.S.J.	1621
Holm, F.	0567	Hulbert, Archer Butler	1741
Holmes, Burton	0342, 0443, 0623, 0626	Hulbert, Homer B.	0038, 0253, 0798, 0920, 0921, 1338, 1341, 1673, 1705
Holtom, D.C.	1880		
Honda, Masujiro	1467		
Honda, M.	1973	Hulst, M. d'	1553, 1555
Honey, William Bowyer	1827, 1828, 1830	Humphrey, Seth K.	0495
Hong, Tiyong	1737	Hund, Archibald	0090
Hong, Tyoung-Ou	0753	Hunt, Frazier	1014
Hope, Moncrieff	0111	Hunt, J.H.	0247
Hopkins, Harold L.	0946	Hunter, Dard	1844
Hornbeck, Stanley K.	1011	Huntington, Ellsworth	0488
Hornby, Edmund	1591	Hürlimann, Martin	0284
Horner, Francis J.	1324	Hurst, C.J.B.	1486
Horni, Georgii	0755	Hyakinth, Archimandrite	0573
Hosie, Alexander	0181	Hyndman, H.M.	1003
Hough, Walter	1820	Ibanez, Vicente Blasco	0373, 0380
Hovelacque, Emile	1850, 1851	Ichihara, M.	1837
Hozumi, Nobushige	1873	Ichikawa, Haruko	1379
Hsiung, S.J.	1546, 1730	Imagawa, Ryoho Uichiro	0316
Hsue, Shuhsi	1132	Imamura, A.	1974
Hubbard, G.E.	2077	Imbault-Hauart, Camille	1668
Huber, Max	0454	Inagaki, Manjiro	1213
Huc, Evariste-Regis	0551, 0573a, 0573b, 0584, 0592	Ireland, Alleyne	2052
		Ireland, Tom	1277
		Irwin, Spencer Dunshee	1347
Huckel, Oliver	0728	Isaacs, Harold R.	1086, 1154
Hudson, G.F.	0844, 1047, 1069	Isherwood, Christopher	1053
Huet, M.	0757	Ishimaru, Tota	1286
Hugh, Robert	0113	Itten, Johannes	1798

Jacolliot, Louis	1999	Kaeuffer, Johann Ernst Rudolph	0789
Jaffe, Philip	1079	Kahn, Ely Jacques	1795
James, H.E.M.	0575, 0576	Kains, M.G.	2063
James, Neill	0636	Kalfe, S.	0252
Jarrad, Frederick W.	0083	Kampf, A.	1785
Jarric, Pierre du, O.S.J.	1895	Kämpfer, Engelbert	0869
Jartoux, Pere, O.S.J.	0329	Kanazawa, S.	0076
Jefferys, W. Hamilton	1975	Kanehara, N.	1974
Jeffries, W. Carey	0473	Kang, Younghill	0691, 1760,
Jenings, Foster H.	1835		1762, 1763,
Jenks, Jeremiah W.	1244		1766, 1767
Jenyns, Scame	1806	Kann, Reginald	1422
Jernigam, T.R.	2090	Karlgren, Bernhard	0803, 1662
Jerningham, Hubert	0457	Kato, Baron B.	0076, 1612
Jessen, Peter	0480	Kato, Genchi	1876
John, Griffith	1608	Katz, Richard	0384, 0386,
Johns, Leslie W.	1304		0388, 0390,
Johnson, Clifford	0590		0392, 0501,
Johnston, James D.	0427		0505, 0514
Johnstone, William C.	1320	Kawai, Michi	1729
Jones, George	0752	Kawai, Tatsuo	1300
Jones, George Heber	0139, 0247,	Kawakami, K.K.	1188, 1262
	0254, 1956,	Kawasaki, S.	1974
	1961, 1973,	Keane, Augustus H.	0133, 0705,
	1977, 2014		0708, 0719
Jordan, David Starr	1986	Keaton, George W.	1076
Joseph, Philipp	1141	Kedleston, Marquess Curzon	0686
Joshua, Joan	0842	Keely, Frances	1767
Jouy, Pierre Louis	1819, 1985	Keeton, G.W.	1140
Jurrius, J.	0074	Keith, Elizabeth	1239, 2123
Kabunaki, T.	1974	Keith, Elspet	2123
Kadt, J. de	1503	Kellermann, Bernhard	0051

Kemp, E.G.	0579	Knox, George William	0212
Kendall, Carlton Waldo	1346	Kobayashi, Teiichi	0751
Kendall, Laura E.	1599	Kobayashi, Ushisaburo	1518
Kendrew, W.G.	0175	Kobelt, W.	1984
Kenelly, M., O.S.J.	0168	Koch, W.	0877
Kennan, George	2112	Koei-Ling	0906
Kennedy, Malcolm D.	1276	Koganei, Y.	1974
Kerbs, Emil	1453	Kojine, E.K.	1474
Kerner, Robert J.	0007	Königsmarck, Graf Hans von	0206
Keyes, Sir Roger	0394	Konow, Ian C.	0791
Keyserling, Count Hermann	0376	Ko, Junichi	2048
Kiernan, E.V.G.	0849	Koo, V.K. Wellington	1032, 1192, 1198
Kikuchi, Baron	0883	Körber, Lili	0518
Kim, Chang Ho	1978	Konishio, Y.	0299
Kim, Changsoon	1658	Kotzebue	0345
Kim, Francis	1574	Krahmer, Gustav	1221
Kim, Man Choong	1704	Krause, F.E.A.	0804
Kim San	1551	Krausse, Alexis	0972, 1096, 1100
Kim, Yusin	1771	Kressler, Oskar	0815
King, F.H.	2062, 2068	Kreuter, Victoria von	1418
King, John W.	0082	Krieglstein, Eugen	0464, 0496
King-Hall, Stephen	1647	Kroebel, Emma	0675
Kinney, Henry W.	0184, 1181	Krusenstern	0345
Kirby, Elizabeth	0110	Kümmel, Otto	1785, 1787,
Kirby, Mary	0110		1791, 1793,
Kircher, Athanasius	0288, 0289		1794, 1840
Kirtland, Lucian Swift	0491	Kuno, Yoshi S.	1247, 1292
Kisak, Tamai	0031	Kuo, P.W.	1020
Klado, Nicolas L.	1421, 1451	Kuroda, Nagamichi	1987
Klaproth, J.	0125, 0420, 0421	Kuroki	1399
Klautke, Paul	0687, 1993	Kuropatkin, General	1479, 1485
Knapp, Arthur May	0215	Kuwaki, A.	1974
Knaur, Th.	0046	Kuwasaburo, Takatsu	0873

Kvitka, Colonel A.	1472		1602, 1890, 1921
Kwong, Kwan Lee	1255	Laurie, Andre	1599
Labbe, Paul	0601	Laurie, Robert	0081
Labroue, Henri	1231	Lautensach, Hermann	0262, 0265
Lach, Donald F.	1092	Lavarenne, J.	1894
Ladd, George Trumbull	0674	Lawrence, Edward A.	1929
Lafont, Renee	0380	Lawrence, James B.	0429
Lagoa, Visconde de	0778	Lawrence, Mary Viola Tingley	1538
Laguerie, Villetard de	0251, 1333, 1334, 1389, 1415	Lawrence, T.J.	1405
		Lawton, Lancelot	0995
Laidlaw, R.	1973	Leclercq, Julien	0465
Laini, Iacobo	1897	Leclercq, R.	1909
Lamb, Harold	0860, 1527	Lee, C.J.	1711
Lambert, J.	0523	Lee, Hoon K.	2066
Landenberger, E.	0506	Lee, Kwanyoung	1852
Lane-Poole, Stanley	1530, 1533	Lee, M.	1750
Lange, Rudolf	1660	Lefort, Albert	1386
Langdon, William B.	0049	Leiter, Hermann	0095
Lanier, L.	0132	Lemoine, Laurent	0583
Lanman, Charles	1524	Lemosof, M.P.	0099
Lannelongue, O.M.	0353	Lengyel, Emil	0864
Larrouy, Maurice	0389	Leonard, A.B.	1973
Larsen, Kay	0845	Leroy-Beaulieu, Pierre	0440, 0964, 0975
Lasker, Bruno	0149, 1078	Leslie, Frank	2101
Lasker, Edward	1843	Lesourd, Paul	1893
Latourette, Kenneth Scott	0813, 0854, 1122, 1241, 1940	Lesseps, Jean Baptiste Barthelemy	0406
Lattimore, Owen	0585, 0586, 0587, 1073, 1080, 1091, 1166	Levis, M. de	1716
		Levy, Roger	1041, 1051, 1186
		Levy, Sylvain	1864
Laufer, Berthold	1989	Lew, T.T.	0172
Launay, Adrien	1568, 1569,	Lewis, Karl	2121

Leyritz, A.	2041	Lowell, Percival	0239, 1641, 1872
Li, Chi	0858	Lowrie, Walter Macon	1594
Li, Hung Chang	1531, 1532,	Lucy, Armand	1380
	1536, 1537,	Lukoff, Fred	1688
	1540, 1615	Lum, Bertha	0515
Li, Kolu	1356	Lundquist, Ernst	0615
Li, Ung Bing	0837	Lütke	0345
Lim, Professor	1978	Lyall, L.A.	0177
Lindley, Augustus F.	0555	Lyde, Lionel W.	0144
Lindner, Friedrich Ludwig	0122	Lynch, George	1404
Lindsay, Captain A.B.	1454, 1474, 1479	Lyttelton, Edith	0509
Lindsay, H.H.	0548	MacArtney, Lord	0335, 0539,
Lindt, A.R.	0591		0540, 0541, 0542
Ling, Pyau	1123	McCarthy, E.T.	2080
Linthicum, Richard	1406	McCarthy, Michael J.F.	1224
Little, Archibald	0977, 1610	McCaul, Ethel	1400
Lloyd, Arthur	1432, 1609	McClintock, Samuel	0139
Loch, Henry Brougham	0552	McCormick, Frederick	1119
Lockhart, J.H. Stewart	1832	McCully, Elizabeth A.	1558
Lome, Enrique Dupuy de	0202	McCune, George M.	0266
London, Jack	1721	McCune, Shannon	0232, 2043
Long, John D.	0294	MacDonald, A.J.	1004
Longford, Joseph H.	0221, 0797,	MacKenzie, Frederick Arthur	0368, 0717,
	0879, 0888,		1339, 1340,
	0891, 0924, 1232		1350, 1417, 1646
Longrais, F. Jouoan de	0494	McKenzie, W.J.	1558
Loon, Hendrik Willem van	0776	McLaren, Walter Wallace	1235
Lorenz, D.E.	0269	MacLeod, John	0413, 0414,
Lostalot-Bachoue, M.E. de	0760		0416, 0417, 0418
Loti, Pierre	0481, 1723,	M'Leod, N.	1953
	1724, 1725,	McMenamin, Daniel	1574
	1777, 1779	MacMurray, John V.A.	1129
Low, Lt. Charles R.	1508	MacNair, Harley Farnsworth	2008

MacNair, Henry Farnsworth	1027, 1054, 1092	Mason, W.B.	0302
McPolin	1579, 1926	Maspero, George	0174, 0799
Madsen, Juel	2115	Matania, Fortunio	1443
Maffei, Giovanni Pietro O.S.J.	0780, 0781, 0784	Materi, Irma Tenant	1639
Mahon, Patrice	1455	Matignon, J.J.	0448, 1469
Makeev, Nicholas	0193	Matsui, General Iwane	1264
Malone, Lt. Colonel l'Estrange	0187, 0188	Matsuoka, Koji	2100
Mallory, Walter H.	0948	Matsuzawa, Tatsuo	0260
Mandel, William	0194	Matthews, Basil	1082
Mandelslo, Johann Albrecht	0404	Matumoto, Julius Kumpei	1388
Mannix, William Francis	1540	Mauer, J.P.	0656
Mannsegg, Jg. Sch.	1904	Maufroid, A.	0471
Manson, Marsden	0933	Maunder, Samuel	1522
Mantandon, George	1290	Mauny, P.J. Reviers de, Rev.	1151
Mar, Walter del	0350, 0351	Maurer, Herryman	1158
Marchand, Rene	1421	Maurras, Charles	1778
Marchant, F.P.	1451	Mavor, James	0861
Mardrus, J.C.	1694	Mavor, William	0335
Marinan, Gerard	1628	Maxwell, James L.	1975
Markino, Yoshio	0720	Maxwell, William	1458
Marriott, John A.R.	0772, 0863	May, Henry John	1153
Marques-Riviere, Jean	1151	Mazeliere, Marquis M. de la	0890, 0898
Marsay, Comte de	0449	Medhurst, W.H.	0154
Marshall, T.W.M.	1928	Mee, Arthur	0047
Marstrand-Mechlenburg, K.	1473	Meiklejohn, J.M.D.	0112
Martin, Felix	0205	Melchisedec, Thevenot	0534
Martin, L.	0468	Mendelssohn, Peter de	1315
Martin, R. Montgomery	0156	Mendez-Pinto, Ferdinand	0405, 0507, 0778, 0878
Martin, William Alexander Parsons	0165, 1109, 1847	Mendoza, Juan Gonzalez de, O.S.A.	0817, 0819
Martini, Martini O.S.J.	0054, 0329, 0818, 0820, 1898	Menpes, Mortimer	0714

Meppen, K.N. van	0827	Moose, J. Robert	2005
Merlier, A.	2041	Morat, George Soulie de	1804
Metin, Albert	0976	Morery, Louis	0756
Metz, Charles William	1986	Morga, Antonio de	0428
Metzger, Berta	1709	Morgan, Richard Cope	0355
Meyer, L.C.	0270, 0271, 0272	Morgenstern, Laure	1797
Meyl, Hugo	1793	Morgenthau, Henry	1022
Mikami, Y.	1974	Mori, R.	2040
Milet-Mureau, M.L.A.	0407, 0408	Moriya, Sakau	1357
Millard, Thomas F.	0981, 0988, 0990, 1005, 1019	Morley, Felix	1022
		Morris, Charles	1430
Miller, Frederick S.	1765, 1768	Morris, John	1215, 1216, 1385, 1635
Miller, J. Martin	1101, 1398		
Miller, Lilian May	1707	Morris, Richard	1507
Miller, Oliver Beaupre	1706	Morse, Edward S.	0621, 1823
Miln, Louise Jordan	0248, 0252	Morse, Hosea Ballou	1027, 1111, 1128
Minch'ien Tuk Zung Tyan	0035	Morton-Cameron, W.H.	0225
Milton, G.E.	0361	Moshemii, Laurenti	1902
Mitchell, Kate	1063	Mott, John F.	1973
Mitchell, Kate L.	2079	Moubach, O.	1856
Mitchell, Mairin	0865	Moule, Arthur Evans	0170
Mitford, E. Bruce	0222	Moule, G.H.	1848
Mockford, Julian	0777	Moulton, Harold G.	2048
Moisel, M.	0062	Mousset, Msr.	1579
Moji, Sobei	1044	Mowrer, E.A.	0938
Monaghan, Rev. Patrick	0739, 1578, 1629, 1630, 1979	Muller, Hendrik P.N.	0469
		Münsterberg, O.	1802
Moncharville, M.	0393	Munzinger, Carl	0218
Monnier, Marcel	0442	Murchie, Guy Jr.	0387
Monroe, Paul	0045, 1138	Murdoch, James	0891
Montgomery, Helen Barrett	0220, 1937	Murray, A.M.	0931
Montgomery, Henry H.	1932	Murray, D.L.	1591
Moore, Harriet L.	1084	Mutel, G.	1567, 1924

Nachod, Oskar	0005, 0894	Nourse, Mary A.	0902
Nakamura, Koya	1549	Novikoff, Olga	1534
Nansen, Fridtjof	0603	Nyberg, Ragnar	0285
Negrier, de	1449	Nym Wales	1551
Neill, Stephen	0526	O'Connor	0695
Neligan	2017	O'Conroy, Taid	1268, 1328
Nelson, M. Frederick	0264	O'Hara, Valentina	0193
Nelson, T.	0241	Oakley, Jane H.	1419
Nettancourt-Vaubecourt, Jean de	0452	Ogawa, Gotaro	1515
New, Ilhan	1756	Ogilby, John	0535
Newman, Barclay Moon	1316	Ogilvy, John	0289
Neziere, Joseph de la	0286	Oh, Seung Kun	1680
Nielsen, Aage Krarup	0528	Oinuma, Kazuo	2047
Niessel, Capitaine Brevete	1447	Okada, T.	1974
Nieuhof, Jan	0533, 0534, 0535, 0536	Okakura, Kakuzo	1219, 1849
		Okubo, Toshitake	0230
Niox, Lieutenant Colonel/General	0130, 1452	Okuma, Count	1467
Nisbet, Mrs. Anabel M.	1617	Olearius, A.	0404
Nishimura, Shinji	0886, 2071	Oliphant, Laurence	0550
Nitobe, Inazo	1214, 1260	Olichon, Armand	1892
Nobb, W. Arthur	1956	Oliva, Joanne Paulo O.S.J.	1899
Noble, W. Arthur	1746	Oliver, Robert T.	1360, 1371
Noble, M.W.	1572	Ono, Giichi	1249, 1517
Noerregaard, B.W.	1463	Oppert, Ernst	0638, 0639
Nohara, Komakichi	1284	Orchard, Dorothy Johnson	2074
Norman, Henry	0192, 0957, 0985	Orchard, John E.	2074
Northcliffe, Alfred Viscount	0370	Orlandino, Nicolao O.S.J.	1897
Northrop, F.S.C.	1650	Ortman, Blanche Sellers	0364
Northrop, Henry Davenport	0200, 1105	Osborne, Sidney	1246
Norton, Henry Kittredge	1203	Ossendowski, Ferdinand	1204, 1205
Norton, W.J.	2096	Ozaki, Madame Yukio	1722
Notestein, Frank W.	1981	Pai, Edward W.	1686

Pai, Ping Ch'i	1691, 1692	Peck, Ellen M.H.	0463
Paik, L. George	1970	Peffer, Nathaniel	1143, 1170, 1619
Palafox, Juan de	0821	Pelcovits, Nathan A.	1171
Palen, Lewis Stanton	1204	Pelle, Clement	0290
Palmblad, Vilhelm Fredrik	0105	Pellier, A.	1106
Palmer, Aaron H.	2085	Penfield, Frederic Courtland	0456
Palmer, Albert W.	1378	Penlington, John N.	1187
Palmer, Frederick	0499, 1399	Pennant, Thomas	0121
Palmer, Samuel	0014	Penrose, E.	2078
Pan, Chao-Ying	1165	Perigny, Maurice de	0721
Pange, Jean du	0665, 0666	Perouse, Jean François	
Papinot, E.	0080	Galoup de la	0406, 0407,
Paquier, P.	1922		0408, 0409,
Pares, Bernard	0862		0431, 0492,
Park, K.D.	1687		0502, 0504, 0531
Park, No-Young	0809	Perrinjaquet	1343
Parker, E.H.	0171, 1127, 1513	Perry, Jean	1738, 1739, 1740
Parkes, Sir Harry	1530, 1533	Perry, M.C., Commodore	0608, 0880, 0903
Parlette, Ralph	0378	Petersen, Josef	1593
Parmelee, Maurice	2009	Peterson, Maurice	0952
Parne, Ralph D.	1540	Pfizmaier, A.	0905
Parry, Albert	0010	Pflug, Henrich Ovesen	0100
Pasfield Oliver, S.	0451	Phillips, Grace Darling	0731
Passek, W.	2091	Piacentini, Abbe Arthur	1554
Paton, Frank H.L.	0732	Picard (Picart), Jean	
Paton, William	1048	Frederic Bernard	1856, 1857
Patric, John	0525, 1314	Pickering, Ernest H.	1282
Patrick, David	0077	Pierce, Franklin	1188
Paul, Cedar	1261	Pike, H.	1750
Paul, Eden	1261	Pike, Kenneth L.	1664
Pauley, Edwin W.	1363	Pimentel, Mariano Lopez	1903
Pauthier, M.G.	0826	Pimondan, Commandant de	0441
Payne, Robert	1170	Pinkerton, John	0103

Piolet, O.S.J.	1890	Rasmussen, O.D.	1038
Plan de Carpine, John	0560	Rattenbury, Harold B.	0178
Po Ch̆-I	1529	Ray, Jean	0231, 1190
Pogio, M.A.	0246	Raynaud, Jean	1058
Politovsky, Eugene S.	1456	Rea, George Bronson	1177, 1194
Pollard, Edward B.	2004	Recoully, Raymond	1425
Polo, Marco	0395	Reclus, Elisee	0109, 0131, 0167
Ponder, Capt. S.E.G.	0513	Redesdale, Lord	0616, 1616, 1655
Pooley, A.M.	1236, 1535	Redman, H. Vere	1044
Porter, Robert P.	1234, 1239, 2046	Reed, Edward J.	0872
Postel, Raoul	0128	Reese, J. Holroyd	0376
Pott, F.L. Hawks	1099, 1120	Regis, Jean Baptiste, O.S.J.	0331
Pott, John J.	1160	Reid, Gilbert	1943
Powell, E. Alexander	1012	Reidemeister, L.	1793
Pratt, James Bisset	1871	Rein, J.J.	0198, 0199
Pratt, John T.	1135	Reinsch, Paul S.	1355
Price, Willard	0233, 0235,	Reischauer, August Karl	1869
	0633, 1298,	Renard, Robert	1205
	1302, 1318, 1319	Renouvin, Pierre	1085
Prostoi, Michel	1089	Retord, Pierre-Andre	1552
Pumpelly, Raphael	0346	Reventlow, E. Graf zu	1441
Purchas, Samuel	0341	Rey, Maria del	0530
Pyun, Yong T'ae	1368, 1711	Rhee, Syngman	1308, 1354
Quantin, J.	2105	Ri, Chai Uk	1769
Quinlan, Thomas	0694, 0738, 1580	Ricci, Matteo O.S.J.	0151, 1896
Quinn, Vernon	0150	Richard, L.	0168
Rackham, Bernard	1824	Richardson, Teresa Eden	1429
Rajchman, Marthe	0938, 1069	Richter, Julius	1933
Ramming, M.	0053	Richthofen, Ferdinand von	0564, 0956
Ramstedt, G.J.	1684, 1689	Richthofen, Wilhelm von	1393
Ransome, J. Stafford	1217	Ridel, M.	1554, 1602
Raquez, A.	2107	Ridder, P.H.A.	1465

Ridger, A. Loton	0360	Russell, Bertrand	1130
Ritter, Gustav A.	0722	Russell, Lindsay	1237
Rockhill, William Woodville	0560, 1335	Rutgers, H.C.	0482
Rodgers, John	1382	Ruud, Ingolf	0750
Roget, Peter Mark	1663	Rye, Reginald Arthur	0004
Rohde, Hans	1018	Sacchini, Francesco	1897
Rojestvensky, Admiral	1456, 1480, 1483	Sadler, A.L.	0927, 1528, 1845
Rollin, M.	0785, 0825	Sage, A. le	0056
Rolt-Wheeler, Francis	1726	Saint-Ives, G.	1104
Rommel, Daisy	0475	Saito, Hiroshi	1275
Ronaldshay, Earl of	0460, 0467, 1542	Saito, Hisho	0881, 0882
Roosevelt, Kermit	2116	Sakurai, Tadayoshi	1467
Roosevelt, Nicholas	1024	Salaman, Malcolm	1817
Roseberry, Lord	1592	Salangar, F.	1491
Rosebury, Earl of	0217	Salmon, Th.	0782, 0783
Rosny, J.H.	1736	Samson, Camille	0914
Rosny, Leon de	0237, 0907, 0908, 1855	Samson, Gerald	1065, 1081
		Sansom, George B.	0843, 0853,
Ross, Colin	0523, 2122		0895, 0899,
Ross, I. Clunies	1042, 2067		0903, 0904, 1657
Ross, John	0912, 1094	Sands, William Franklin	1026
Rossetti, Carlo	0250	Satow, Sir Ernest	1544
Roth, J.	0746	Saunby, John B. (Rev.)	0201
Roth, Lucius O.S.B.	1683	Saunders, Kenneth	1648, 1649,
Rougemont, Francisco de, O.S.J.	0822		1853, 1867
Rouski Invalid	1446	Savage-Landor, A. Henry	0249, 0371
Roux, Hugues le	1240	Sazanami, Iwaya	1229
Rowe, David Nelson	1164	Schalek, Alice	0627
Roxey, Percy M.	2065	Schall, Johann Adam, O.S.J.	1899, 1904
Rubruck, William	0560	Schanz, Moritz	0349
Ruddick, Lilian S.	0267	Scharschmidt, Clemens	0234
Rufus, W.C.	0754	Scherer, James A.B.	0186, 1271, 1299
Ruschenberger	0345	Scherzer, F.	1735

Schiff, Jacob H.	0617	Sewell, William G.	0570
Schjöth, Fr.	1842	Shaw, Edward R.	0710
Schlechter, R.	1988	Shepherd, Charles R.	1297
Schley, Winfried Scott	1548	Shepherd, K.M.	1656
Schnee, Heinrich	0589	Sherill, Charles H.	1007
Schoenmeyr, Alfredo	1462	Sherwood, Martyn	0400
Schoop, Hermann	1258	Sherwood, Robert E.	0946
Schroeder, Seaton	1383	Shigemi, Shiukichi	1718
Schumpeter, E.B.	2078	Shinjo, S.	1974
Schurhammer, Georg	1875	Shirai, M.	1974
Schwabe, J.J.	0333	Shirasaki, Kyoichi	2039
Schwalbach, Luiz	1035	Shoemaker, James	2054
Schweinitz-Brunner, Edmund de	1969	Shoemaker, Michael Myers	0446
		Sickler-Williams, Rose	1823
Scidmore, Eliza Ruhamah	0273, 0435, 0445, 1464, 1605	Siebold, Philipp Franz von	0195, 0203, 0229, 0702
		Sieburg, Friedrich	0634
Scidmore, George H.	1973	Sieroszewski, Waclaw	0672
Scott, J.W. Robertson	0227	Sievers, Wilhelm	0136
Seaman, Louis Livingston	1433, 1450	Simon, Theodor E.	1793
Sedgwick, F.R.	1408, 1475	Singer, Caroline	1619
Segalen, Victor	1694	Sion, Jules	0143
Seitz, Don C.	0618	Sitwell, Osbert	0527
Sekino, Tadashi	0926	Sladen, Douglas	1521
Selkirch, Alexander	1717	Sleman, J.B.	1973
Sellin, Thorsten	0944	Smedley, Agnes	1159
Semenoff, Captain Vladimir	1454, 1480, 1483	Smith, Arthur H.	0707, 1944
		Smith, C.A. Middleton	1126
Semler, Johannes Salomon	0788	Smith, F.E.	1436
Serruys, Jenny	1849	Smith, Frank Herron	1352
Seu, Ring-Hai	1758, 1764	Smith, F. Porter	0072
Seversky, Alexander P. de	1520	Smith, Guy Harold	0232

Smith, Robert Aura	1064	Stewart, Alexander	0108
Smith, Wilfred	2072	Stidger, William L.	0365
Snow, Edgar	1068	Stimson, Henry L.	1046
Sokolski, George W.	1034	St. John, H.C.	0611
Soothill, W.E.	0840, 1139	Stoddart, Anna M.	1585
Sorge, Wolfgang	0593	Story, Douglas	0458, 1397
Sowerby, Arthur de C.	0582	Straight, Willard	1589, 1590
Soyeshima, Michimasa	1020	Strang, Herbert	1416, 1487, 1489
Spaits, Alexander	1457		
Speiser, Werner	1801	Stratemeyer, Edward	1407
Spencer, Cornelia	0180	Street, Julian	0624
Spencer, Selden P.	1353	Strong, Anna Louise	1369
Spencer, Sidney	2118	Suetonius	0762, 0771
Spiers, E. Louis	1449	Sunderland, Jabez T.	1237
Spillmann, Joseph O.S.B.	0434, 1749	Sunoo, Harold W.	1685
Sprengel, Kurt	0606	Suyematsu, Baron	1225, 1226, 1775
Sprengel, M.G.	0336		
Sprigade, P.	0062	Swinehart, Lois H.	1754, 1971
Spring Rice, Sir Cecil	1543	Swinton, E.S., Major	1474, 1479
Staden, Hermann von	0033	Sykes, Percy	0773
Stamp, L. Dudley	0146, 0148	Taburno, J.	1418
Stanford, Edward	0059	Tadamesa, Miduno	1994
Stanley, Henry A.	0428	Taeuber, Irene B.	1981
Starr, Frederick	1866	Taft, Henry W.	1263
Staunton, George	0540, 0541	Takeuchi, Tatsuji	1279
Stead, Alfred	0208, 0210, 0211, 0217	Tamsen, David	1695
		Tanaka, Giichi	1255, 1303, 1311
Stead, W.T.	1534		
Stefansson, Vilhjelmur	0377	Tappan, Eva March	0798
Steiger, G.N.	0805	Tayler, Constance J.D.	2006
Stein, Christian Gottfried Daniel	0104	Taylor, Bayard	0609
Stein, Guenther	2113	Taylor, Charles M.	1702
Stettinius, Edward P.	0949	Taylor, George E.	1069

Taylor, Howard	1561	Tomimas, Shutaro	1125
Taylor, Hudson	1561	Tompkins, Pauline	1090
Tcheng Kui-i	1198	Toree, Olof	0538
Temple, Richard	0970	Toucy	1510
Terada, T.	1974	Toulouse, Jean	1728
Terauchi, Viscount Masatake	0255	Tournafond, Paul	0242
Terry, T. Philip	0303, 0310	Towitsch, A.G.	0698
Tessan, François de	0185, 0228	Townsend, George H.	0761
Tettau, Eberhard Freiherr von	1470	Toyotomi Hideyoshi	1526
Tewksbury, Donald G.	1372	Toynbee, Arnold J.	0385
Thalasso, Adolphe	0718	Trautz, F.N.	0229, 0282, 0283
Thevenot, Melchidsedec	0534		
Thiess, Frank	1491, 1492, 1493	Treat, Payson J.	0806, 1039, 1248, 1265
Thomas, James A.	2095	Trollope, Constance	1573
Thomas, Lowell	0517	Trollope, Mark Napier	0247, 1573, 1963
Thomson, John Stuart	0169, 1118	Tronson, J.M.	0426
Thompson, R. Wardlaw	1608	Trousset, Jules	2103
Thompson, Warren S.	1087	Tsurumi, Yusuke	1028, 1254
Thunberg, Karl Peter	0335, 0605, 0606, 0607	Turley, Robert T.	0577, 0578
		Tyler, Sydney	1435
Tiessen, E.	0564	Ular, Alexandre	1108
Tietjens, Eunice	0626	Underwood, Horace Grant	1565, 1670, 1675, 1711, 1862, 1954, 1957, 1958
Tilmann, Klemens	1914		
Tiltman, H. Hessell	1191		
Timkovski, George	0420, 0421		
Tisdale, Alice	0581, 0680	Underwood, Horace H.	0006
Tizac, H. d'Ardenne de	0584	Underwood, Lilias H.	1565, 1606, 1745, 2003
Togo, Admiral Marquis Heikachiro	1549, 1550	Unger, Frederic William	1430
Tokugawa Ieyasu	1528	Urquhart, E.J.	0683
Tomaselli, Cesco	1278	Ursyn-Pruszynski, St. Ritter von	0246

Utley, Freda	1291, 1293, 1326, 2094		1773, 2007
		Walcott, Frederica A.	0477
Vaccari, Oreste	1665	Waldschmidt, Ernst	0815
Valdes, Manuel Antonio	1903	Waley, Arthur	1529
Valentin, F.	0431	Walsh, James A.	0479, 1566
Vaneix, M.	1291	Walters, W.T.	1821
Varat, Charles	0642, 0644, 0647	Walton, Joseph	0966
		Walworth, Arthur	0903
Vaudon, Chanoine Jean	1925	Wang, Ching-Chun	1307
Vautier, Claire	0641, 0699, 0700	Wang, Whitewall	1358
Vaya, Count Vay de .. et de Luskod	0455, 0459	Wannata, Onoto	1719
		Warner, L.O.	0247
Veitch, James Herbert	0436	Weale, B.L. Putnam (Simpson, Bertram Lenox)	0978, 0983, 0986, 1002, 1015, 1124, 1173
Venables, E.K.	1281		
Verbiest, Pere, O.S.J.	0329		
Verkuyl, Johannes	1883		
Vernadsky, George	0939	Weber, Norbert O.S.B.	0678, 0684, 0688, 1570, 1757
Viaud, Samuel	0481		
Victoria, Queen	1541		
Viegas, Artur	0770	Webster, Hutton	0802
Vigneron, Lucien	0437	Wegener, G.	0668
Villiers, Frederic	1423, 1587	Weitzel, A.W.T.	0126
Vinacke, Harold M.	0807, 0811	Wells, Carveth	0521
Vincent, Benjamin	0075	Wells, H.G.	0768
Viollis, Andree	1267	Wells, Linton	0377
Virtue, G.	0067	Wells, Sumner	0942
Vladimir	0190, 1391	Weston, Walter	2118
Vosberg-Rekow, Max	0034	Wheeler, G.C.	1804
Vosgien	0066	Wheeler, Post	1322
Wade-Koone, Edward	1680	Wheeler, W.W.	0359
Wagner, Ellasue Carter	1748, 1751, 1753, 1761,	Wheeler, William H.	0626
		Whigham, H.J.	0137

Whillbley, Charles	0762	Russian PM 1903-1906	1485
White, Trumbull	1388, 1642	Woermann, Karl	1788
Whittle, James	0081	Wolf, Eugen	0562
Whyte, Frederick	1033, 1136, 1309, 1996, 2117	Wolferstan, Bertram O.S.J.	1908
		Wollant, Gregoire de	0214
		Wood, James	0041
Widler, Elly	1131	Woodhead, H.G.W.	0588, 2012
Wijnaendts, H.	1465	Woodsmall, Ruth Frances	2010
Wildes, Harry E.	1272	Wright, Herbert	1045
Wilhelm, Richard	0842	Wright, Quincy	1279
Wilkes, Paget	1614	Wright, Stanley F.	1583
Wilkinson, W.H.	1332	Yakhontoff, Victor A.	1283
William, Botting Homesley	1982	Yamada, Nakaba	0885
Williams, Edward Thomas	1147	Yamasaki, N.	1974
Williams, Frederick W.	0831	Yamatoya, M.	0057
Williams, Graeme	0115	Yang, Lien-Sheng	0856
Williams, Henry Smith	0769	Yano, Tsuneta	2039
Williams, S. Wells	0166, 0831	Yi, Tai Tjo	1512
Williamson, Alexander	0553	Yohannan, Abraham	0567
Williamson, H.R.	0852, 1950	Yong, Thaddee Ann Yuen	1192
Willis, Geo. R.	1734	Young, A. Morgan	1256, 1257, 1294
Willoughby, Westel W.	0934, 1043		
Wils, David	1326	Young, C. Walter	1179, 1182, 1183, 1184
Wilson, E.H.	1990		
Wilson, H.W.	1402, 1514	Young, Eugene J.	0936
Wilson, Woodrow	1242	Young, Frederick	0432
Wingate, Col. A.W.S.	0571	Young, John Russell	0200, 0347
Winnington, Alan	1375	Yui, John	1980
Wirt, Gerrare	0599	Zabel, Rudolf	0673
Wirth, A.	0880	Zacke, Alvar	0285
Wiseman, Cardinal	1556	Zenzinoff, B. de	1336
Witte, Comte Serge,		Zimmermann, E.A.W.	0124

Zischka, Anton	1274, 1280	Zwemer, Samuel M.	0138
Zuber, M.H.	1381		

Bibliography of Western Language Publications on Korea

INDEX OF PERIODICALS

Note : In case no catalogue number is given, the magazine is not listed as such in the catalogue, but individual articles appearing in it are listed instead.

The index does not claim to be complete; a number of periodicals of whom the collection has only a single issue concerning Korea have been omitted.

Americana Annual	0951	ENG 1403
Annales de la Propagation de Foi	1884	FRE 16
Annals of the Propagation of the Faith	1885	ENG 513
The Annual Register. A Review of Public Events at Home	0928	ENG 1291
Annual Report of Reforms and Progress in Chosen		ENG 747
Asia. The American Mgazine on the Orient	0023	ENG 106
The Asiatic Journal and Monthly Register for British and	0024	ENG 1458
Asien. Organ der Deutsch-Asiatischen Gesellschaft	0034	GER 149
Britannica Book of the Year	0940	ENG 1351
Bulletin de la Societe de Geographie Commerciale de Paris	0091	FRE 256
Chamber's Journal of Popular Literature, Science and the Arts	0015	ENG 159
China Year Book	2012	ENG 1257
Chinese Repository	0025	ENG 126
The Chinese Social and Political Science Review	0035	ENG 1393
Compte Rendu des Seances de la Societe de Geographie	0092	FRE 257
Le Correspondent	0019	FRE 56
The Cornhill Magazine	0018	ENG 1290
Diplomatic and Consular Reports on Trade and Finance : Corea		ENG 1329
Du. Schweizerische Monatsschrift		GER 44
The Far East	0026	ENG 900
Fortune	0021	ENG 965
Geist des Ostens	0033	GER 152
The Geographic Journal	0094	ENG 865
The Graphic	0011	ENG 796
Harvard Journal of Asiatic Studies	0036	ENG 11677
Hansei Zasshi	0027	ENG 324

Myongji-LG Korean Studies Library

Illustrated London News	0012	ENG 795
Illustreret Tidskrift før de Nyeste Reisebeskrivelser	0340	DEN 3
Illustriertes Jahrbuch der Weltreisen	0328	GER 132
L'Illustration	0013	FRE 288
Japan Christian Yearbook	1881	ENG 305
Japan-Manchukuo Yearbook	1172	ENG 369
The Japan Times Year Book	1210	ENG 282
The Japan Year Book	1208	ENG 366
Japon et Extreme Orient	0029	FRE 205
Journal Asiatique	0030	FRE 189
Journal des Voyages et des Aventures de Terre et de Mer		FRE 68
Journal of the North China Branch of the Royal Asiatic	0032	ENG 704
Die Katholischen Missionen	1886	GER 138
Korean Repository	0037	ENG 792
Korean Review	0038	ENG 793
Manchuria Year Book		ENG 359
Memento Geographique	0099	FRE 276
Mitteilungen der Geographischen Gesellschaft in Wien	0095	GER 186
National Geographic	0093	ENG 625
Ost-Asien	0031	GER 45
Over Sea and Land	0022	ENG 1385
The People's Magazine	0016	ENG 179
Petermanns Geographische Mitteilungen	0096	GER 24
Proceedings of the Royal Geographic Society and Monthly	0097	ENG 506
Quarterly Returns of Trade for the Ports of Jenchuan, Fusan	2027	ENG 662
Royal Geographic Society, Supplementary Papers	0098	ENG 1118
Story of Our Time	0943	ENG 1436
Le Tour du Monde		FRE 67
Transactions of the Asiatic Society of Japan	0028	ENG 693
Transactions of the Korean Branch of the Royal Asiatic	0039	ENG 794
A Travers le Monde		FRE 72
Voice of Korea	0040	ENG 1327
The Weekly	0017	ENG 1094
Who's Who	1521	ENG 1312

About the Compiliers

SUNGHWA CHEONG is Professor of History at Myongji University in South Korea. He has published books on Western images on Korea.

ALEXANDER GANSE is Professor of World and European History at Korean Minjok Leadership Academy in South Korea. He studied history at Ruhr University in Germany.